DEMOCRATIC THEORIES AND THE CONSTITUTION

Suny Series in
Political Theory: Contemporary Issues
John G. Gunnell, Editor

Martin Edelman _____

DEMOCRATIC THEORIES AND THE CONSTITUTION _____

State University of New York Press   *Albany*

PUBLISHED BY
STATE UNIVERSITY OF NEW YORK PRESS, ALBANY
©1984 STATE UNIVERSITY OF NEW YORK

FOR INFORMATION, ADDRESS STATE UNIVERSITY OF NEW YORK
PRESS, STATE UNIVERSITY PLAZA, ALBANY, N.Y., 12246

Library of Congress Cataloging in Publication Data
Edelman, Martin.
    Democratic theories and the Constitution.
    (SUNY series in political theory. Contemporary issues)
    1. United States—Constitutional law—Interpretation and construction.   2. Democracy.
3. Political science—United States.   I. Title. II. Series.
KF4550.E36   1984   342.73   83-18143
ISBN 0-87395-872-1   347.302
ISBN 0-87395-873-X (pbk.)

10   9   8   7   6   5   4   3   2   1

To Miriam

בָּרוּךְ אַתָּה יְיָ, אֱלֹהֵינוּ מֶלֶךְ הָעוֹלָם, אֲשֶׁר
בָּרָא שָׂשׂוֹן וְשִׂמְחָה, חָתָן וְכַלָּה, גִּילָה
רִנָּה דִיצָה וְחֶדְוָה, אַהֲבָה וְאַחֲוָה וְשָׁלוֹם
וְרֵעוּת.

Blessed art Thou, O Lord our God, King of the universe, who created joy and gladness, bridegroom and bride, mirth and exultation, pleasure and delight, love, brotherhood, peace and fellowship.

CONTENTS

PREFACE

    This book argues that Justice Holmes' famous dictum, "General Principles do not decide concrete cases," is misleading as applied to constitutional law. Significant clauses of the Constitution are not self-defining. The Justices must fall back upon extra-constitutional ideas, especially their conceptions of democracy, when interpreting that document. Yet the Justices have never reached agreement about the meaning of democracy. Hence different constitutional interpretations are most frequently based upon different theories of democracy. Justice Holmes is undoubtedly correct that "Constitutions are intended to preserve practical and substantial rights, not to maintain theories," but almost two hundred years of experience with the Constitution of the United States teaches us that the Great Charter has served that function only by being interpreted and re-interpreted in light of changing social theories.

    The choice among "general principles" has significant ramifications for American society. Constitutional law does matter. The Constitution, as intended, helps shape the force and direction of our country. This book attempts to clarify the elements involved in that important part of constitutional interpretation which is based upon different conceptions of democracy. A wider appreciation of alternate ways of interpreting the Constitution is surely appropriate; all contemporary American theories of democracy talk about the importance of public participation. This book was written in the belief that at least that aspect of democratic theory is still relevant. If my belief is not misplaced, then any additional knowledge about a process shaping our lives can only enhance the quality of public participation.

In order to reach a wider audience, I have deliberately kept specialized terminology—both legal and social scientific—to a minimum. I trust my professional colleagues will not therefore find the book lacking in merit. I was unable, however, to omit one scholarly feature—the use of abundant footnotes. As any reader of scholarly journals knows, the practice is endemic. Whether it stems from the nature of the material or from a pernicious effect of academic training is difficult to tell. I hope the general reader will compensate for this vice of mine by simply making a determined mental effort to remove those little numbers. For those who share my vice, the text provides ample opportunity for them to indulge themselves.

I have struggled with the material in this book for more years than I wish to admit on paper. One unfortunate consequence of that fact is that I am literally unable to recall, and therefore thank, all the individuals who gave me assistance during that process. Some people stand out. It was a particular group of faculty at the University of California, Berkeley, who first set me on this course: Thomas Barnes, John Schaar, Sheldon Wolin, Joseph Tussman, and, most especially, my mentors in constitutional law the late Charles Aikin and the late Jacobus tenBroek. My peers among the Berkeley graduate students sustained my efforts by their constant friendly, yet focused, criticism: Mason Druckman, John Gunnell, Paul Kress, Frank Marini, Gene Poschman, Matt Stolz, Kirk Thompson. Along the way, the comments of Professor Leo Snowiss proved most helpful, and Malcolm Sherman provided support at a most critical moment. I have a particular intellectual debt to John Brigham and Paul Kress for their careful reading of the completed manuscript. John Gunnell, the editor of this series, merits separate mention. He has helped see me through the entire process from its intellectual conception to its finished product by offering his usual insightful comments and his constant human support. Like the rest of his colleagues and peers, I am fully aware of the extraordinary role he plays in my academic life. And I am grateful for it.

In its early stages, the technical production of the manuscript was in the capable hands of the GSPA typing pool: Maxine Morman, Suzanne Hagen and Addie Napolitano—and Ann Wright, then Secretary of the Department of Political Science at SUNY-Albany. At a later stage, the financial support of David Andersen, Dean of the Graduate School of Public Affairs, SUNY-Albany and the dedication and skill at the word processor of Judy Kane were of vital assistance. At the last stage, my editorial tasks were assisted by three helpful graduate students—Karen Sotherland, Julio Vidal and Esther Fine. Luana Noto patiently typed and retyped the corrections. Thanks are also due to Hannah Applebaum for careful, thoughtful preparation of the index. I am particularly grateful to Nancy Sharlet, my editor at SUNY-Press, and her staff, for the care they took with the manuscript.

Most of all, I wish to express my love and gratitude to my severest critic and greatest booster. She stayed the course and paid the price. That is why this book could only be dedicated to my wife, Miriam.

Martin Edelman

Albany, NY

INTRODUCTION ————————————

The United States is a democracy. That is the label the American people unhesitatingly bestow upon their governmental system. Walk down any street, in any part of the land, and ask the people to define the nature of our government. Sample the pulse of the people. Use the method of the Ancient Mariner or the more refined techniques of George Gallup, Louis Harris, and the social scientists. Almost invariably you get the same answer: America is a democracy. Here and there you might receive a different reply from a John Bircher or a Communist or a believer in some equally marginal doctrine. But statistically these deviations are too insignificant to affect the conclusion. That the United States is a democracy is an integral part of the American consensus.[1]

Yet the degree of consensus on the nature of our government should not be exaggerated. There is considerable disagreement about what democracy means and implies.[2] Even if we put aside the views of the general public—because many theorists claim that a logical, consistent, and viable understanding of such abstract ideas as democracy is too much to expect from the mass of people—a universally accepted American definition of the word still eludes us. While most American social scientists have reached agreement on what *they* mean by democracy, a respectable number of their fellow intellectuals hold contrary notions.[3] Variety, not unanimity, characterizes American discussions of the nature of democracy.

This study will be concerned with variations of the three democratic paradigms most prevalent in America today. Though the "natural rights," "contract," and "competition" paradigms are similar in many ways, the differences between them are significant. Moreover, because a paradigm is a general framework for social and political analysis,[4] the theories based on each paradigm can also differ on important matters. Stressing different ideas, each democratic theory leads to a different constellation of concepts for evaluating important political questions. Since no one has ever devised a litmus test for separating constitutional from political issues in the United States, each democratic theory leads to a different interpretation of the Constitution, a different constitutional theory.

It is not surprising, therefore, that the same differences in political theory are found among the Justices of the United States Supreme Court. They are frequently called upon to resolve issues by interpreting the Constitution. This task is not, and cannot be, mechanical; the significant clauses of the document are not self-defining. Each Justice must fall back upon extraconstitutional ideas to aid his interpretation. Sooner or later the more theoretically inclined Justices evolve a consistent theory to support their interpretations. Although these constitutional theories are not always articulated, in the modern period they have invariably been democratic. The Justices, like other American thinkers, share the basic consensus about the value of democracy. It is equally obvious, however, that the Justices have not reached agreement on the meaning of democracy. Time and again disagreements over the landmark decisions have centered around different theories of democracy. Each Justice has defended his interpretations not only on the basis of the constitutional text and holdings in prior cases but also, and significantly, in terms of his idea of democracy.

For a political scientist, this close relationship between democratic theories and constitutional interpretations is a golden opportunity. We can best see the political implications of judicial theories when we view them as expressions of widely held theories of democracy. This type of analysis greatly enhances our understanding of recent controversies on the Court. Similarly, an examination of the constitutional ramifications of political theories yields a better understanding of them, because we can see the relative merits of "natural rights," "contract," and "competition" theories in the situational contexts provided by Supreme Court cases.

The analysis of contemporary democratic theories and the Constitution must be delayed, however, until Part II. The historical material in Part I is necessary so that we can more fully understand the points at issue. The historical material is admittedly selective rather than exhaustive, though I do not believe it is therefore inaccurate. It is designed to help us understand a peculiarly American phenomenon: all the basic concerns about the nature of our polity—distribution of power, the limits on power—are discussed within the boundaries of democratic theory. Those boundaries are admittedly wide, but they nonetheless narrow the range of discussion.[5] The historical material also explains the absence of any single, authoritative American theory of democracy.

The last point is most important. Too often proponents of one or another theory of democracy defend their position on the comforting, though erroneous, assumption that it represents *the* American political theory. When we discover, as we shall, that neither the Constitution nor the development of American political thought can serve as an authoritative basis for any one theory of democracy, we shall learn to discount such claims. Americans mean many different things by the word *democracy*, and unless we take the time and make the effort to clarify what *we* mean by it, we conceal rather than explicate our major premises. That is not the way to reason together.

One of the arguments of this study is that an adequate theory of American constitutionalism must give sufficient weight to the appeal to reason inherent in our basic charter. The primary purpose of the famous constitutional checks and balances was to curb the irrational tendencies of man so that reason might flourish. Earlier generations used the processes created by the Constitution to fashion a dominant paradigm for their era. The constitutional mechanisms insured that private interests could not be ignored. And those processes gave leadership elements the space and the time to combine those interests in a new way. Once a new conception of the public good emerged in the statutes, it was sooner or later legitimated by the Supreme Court. As such, the new conception became part of the supreme law of the land, and created a new constitutional order. That constitutional order functioned as written constitutions were intended by the Framers: it transcended the realm of ordinary politics and gave it shape until a new order emerged.

We appear to be in the throes of yet another transition. This book argues that we too shall have to utilize our reason to fashion a new conception of the public interest sufficient unto our day. If we are ever to reason together we must come to grips with the values inherent in each of our differing conceptions of democracy. The latter parts of this study aim at clarifying those latent values in each of the democratic theories currently influencing judicial interpretations of the Constitution. Each theory is examined in terms of three concepts deemed central to any democratic theory: citizenship, political participation, and political freedom. I have written with the assumption that when values themselves are at the heart of a controversy, the most fruitful way to clarify the issues is by examining the consequences of each value position.

I have taken different approaches in each part of the book. My method in the historical part is that used in intellectual history and traditional political theory. In reconstructing the distinctive ideational patterns of each theory, I have turned to the writings of those individuals generally thought to be the leading exponents of that position. When discussing the political theory of the Framers of the Constitution, for example, I focus on the authors of *The Federalist Papers*, particularly James Madison who has long been called the Father of our Constitution. At no point do I attempt to describe all variations of the theory under discussion. Those wishing to find a justification for the imputation of paternity to Madison must turn elsewhere. In a study primarily concerned with the contemporary period, the cost of any other strategy—in terms of the price of the book and the reader's patience—would simply be too high.

The reader should also be aware of another limitation inherent in the methodology employed in the historical part. In focusing on some of the major thinkers in American history, I have attempted to discuss their theories in terms of their assumptions, their beliefs, their ideas. In discussing Jefferson's political theory, for example, I have sought to explicate his conception of democracy, not mine. Things which posed no great problem for Jefferson, such as the exclusion of women from the franchise, are not discussed. In our day, no democratic theorist could support such an exclusion. Again for reasons of economy, I do not stop to remind the reader of the obvious: that for people like Jefferson, the functional body politic did not include women and slaves. In the context of *his* time Jefferson was a democrat. If *we* want to use his ideas we must make certain changes. That change is precisely what has occurred to Jeffersonian concepts throughout later periods in American history and is what I seek to demonstrate by using historical material.

The historical material is included solely to provide sufficient background for understanding the richness and diversity of important American theories of democracy which preceded World War II. That war is used as the beginning of the contemporary period. I have attempted to present the material in as straightforward a manner as possible. I did not want to "stack the deck" in favor of any particular contemporary theory, only to account for the variety of theories and their roughly equal constitutional and historical legitimacy.

In the analytic parts of the book, I employ the methods of both intellectual history and social science. The focus is the period from the end of World War II until the early 1970s. A decade permits ample time for reflection. Moreover, no new *theoretical* pattern has yet emerged in Supreme Court opinions or in American social thought. The analysis proceeds in three steps: first, a discussion of each contemporary democratic theory; second, an exposition of the distinctive constitutional theory related to that political theory; and finally, a critique of both the constitutional and political theories. In the first two steps, I use the methods associated with intellectual history, and the cautionary notes above are equally applicable here. In the third step, the analysis borrows heavily from the social sciences. I seek to test each theory by reference to how well it pragmatically deals with the particular problems of citizenship, participation, and political freedom.

Focusing on these concepts necessarily means other concepts are played down. For example, if Court opinions dealing with reapportionment are examined for what they have to say about political participation, judicial ideas about federalism may not be given their proper importance. This distortion becomes a tolerable cost only because of the advantage we gain in our understanding of contemporary American democratic theories.

While this method is common for evaluating the works of political theorists and social scientists, it does pose problems when applied to the Supreme Court. Court cases are not exercises in the application of political theory to political problems, nor are they disinterested studies of political phenomena. The Supreme Court is an agency of government which seeks solutions to pressing problems. Consequently, there is much in the Supreme Court's processes which can best be explained by treating the Court as simply another decision-making agency, subject to the same kinds of pressures as the President and Congress. As with those agencies of government, there is much in the Court's institutional processes which fall below the level of observable acts. Obviously, the ideas of the more reflective Justices are not the only factors in determining Supreme Court decisions.[6]

Because ideas do play an important part in Supreme Court decisions, neither can they be ignored. The ideas in those opinions may be technical legal concepts or the simple common sense of the matter; the ideas may be supported by the use of precedent, by an appeal to conscience, or by any number of other types of arguments. The objective is always the same. The Supreme Court is seeking support for its decisions by trying to convince us that they are the "right" decisions. Consequently, legal discussions, criticism, and controversies always revolve around the ideas expressed in the opinions. Those opinions show that the Justices are affected by the demand for theoretical clarity, consistency, and soundness. Some Justices internalize this demand more than others, some are better equipped to meet the challenge, but none can ignore it.[7] Whatever other factors are considered in evaluating the Supreme Court, the ideas expressed in the opinions cannot be overlooked.

If judicial ideas are examined, a most fruitful way of conducting that analysis is by putting those ideas into the framework of democratic theory. This study is designed to show why that is a useful, indeed the most useful, way for examining judicial ideas about citizenship, political participation, and political freedom.

I

HISTORICAL
BACKGROUND

One

THE REPUBLICAN CONSTITUTION

From the perspective of the history of Western political theory the ideas shared by the American leadership of 1787–1788 are much more striking than those which divided them.[1] Those Americans believed that individuals possessing natural rights of life, liberty, and property entered into a compact to protect those rights. Whatever the origins of *society*—there was some disagreement about whether to attribute it to a conscious arrangement or to gregarious human nature—*government*, all agreed, was created by a contract among individuals. Authority originated in the freely given consent of the governed and representation maintained the continuity of consent. A written constitution, granting power and authority to government and designating the ends for which they were to be used, was the tangible and logical manifestation of such thought. Within this paradigm men disagreed about its particular components and about the proper emphasis to be placed on each element, but it can truly be said that the intellectual horizons of the founding generation were bounded by the ideas of John Locke and the eighteenth-century Whigs.[2]

If American political thought in the eighteenth century is a series of variations on a Whig theme, the differing motifs are nonetheless very enlightening. The Americans of 1787–1788 had to decide which elements to stress and which to keep in a minor key. The same broad concepts could be used to support and justify a variety of positions. The Anti-Federalists urged rejection of the Constitution in the name of democracy; the Federalists urged its ratification in the name of sound republicanism.[3] Both conformed to the basic Whig paradigm. Thus at the beginning of our nation, as in our time, consensus on fundamental concepts narrowed the range of political discussion and action but did not preclude significant disagreement. For our present concerns, the intellectual history surrounding the adoption and ratification of the Constitution has an added significance. Each of the three contemporary democratic paradigms has strong roots in the Constitution itself, yet that document cannot provide an authoritative basis for any particular theory current today.

The Constitution, taken alone, cannot provide us with a single theory of democracy because it was the product of republican, not democratic, theory. Throughout most of the colonial period there was no controversy over the meaning of the term *democracy*.[4] Later, during the Revolutionary period, *democracy* and *republic* were sometimes used synonymously.[5] Yet most of the active participants in the debate surrounding the ratification of the Constitution perceived a difference.[6] For these men, democracy meant political equality, majoritarianism, and public participation in the governmental decision-making process.[7] The physical distances involved made direct public participation in colonywide government impossible, so most colonial American spokesmen had engrafted the concept of representation onto the original theory of direct or pure democracy. The basic thrust remained: "To approach rule by the people as nearly as possible, democrats espoused governments in which the people predominated and operated all functions."[8]

It is important to note the centrality of one conception of representation to this theory of democracy. Representation was a device to mirror the interests of the people. The proper function of the representative was not to make decisions according to his own best judgments but to reflect the interests of his constituents. He was to act as a majority of his constituents would have acted had they been present. Only the identity of interest of the representative and his constituents made democratic or popular government possible. At the time of the Revolution, American democratic theory explicitly rejected any conception of virtual representation; rather, democratic theory entailed a conception of actual representation.[9]

The idea of democracy outlined above formed the basis of the Anti-Federalists' articulated objections to the Constitution. They opposed the Constitution on the grounds that there was "no substantial representation of the people provided for in a government in which the most essential powers, even as to the internal police of the country, [was] proposed to be lodged."[10] The Anti-Federalists would have opposed the Constitution even if it had established a majoritarian form of democracy. They were not simply majoritarian democrats. These "men of little faith"[11] saw democracy only as a necessary condition for good government, not a sufficient one. A majoritarian national government would still need to have its power and authority circumscribed to a much greater extent than in the Constitution. Such restrictions were necessary to protect the parochial social, economic, and political interests for which the Anti-Federalists spoke. Still, it is important to note that this opposition was articulated in terms of a widely held democratic theory. The prior acceptance of that theory by large numbers of Americans was bound to make them skeptical of the Constitution. Their democratic ideas meant they could not fully trust any government they thought was not truly representative of all the interests of the people and which did not operate on the principle of majoritarianism.

The men who drafted the Constitution, on the other hand, deliberately rejected the prevailing idea of democracy. They believed, as Elbridge Gerry so succinctly put it at the beginning of the Convention, that "the evils we experience flow from the excess of democracy."[12] The Framers viewed their task as constructing a system which would, as Alexander Hamilton wrote, "tend to the amelioration of popular systems of civil government."[13] For this purpose they framed a constitution put forward and defended in terms of republican political theory.

The basic task, according to Madison, was to construct a just government—a government so structured that it would serve the interests of all the people without oppressing any of them. Dependence on the people was only the most important institutional device to secure just government; it could not be *the* purpose of government because a majority could also tyrannize. A republic, Madison believed, should be government by the "cool and deliberate sense of the community."[14]

The Framers sought to protect the commonwealth by giving each substantial segment of the community the means to protect its interests within the government. This safeguarding was done by a system of checks and balances, and by a heavy reliance on federalism, which multiplied the variety of interests as it extended the sphere of government.[15] Proper structuring would prevent any faction, be it a minority or a majority, from using government for its own advantage.

The republican theory embedded in the Constitution differed from the prevailing theory of democracy chiefly with respect to the value of majoritarianism. Yet, both republican and democrat adhered to the Lockean notion of popular sovereignty. "The *will of the people* certainly ought to be the law," remarked John Jay, "but the only question was, How was this will to be expressed?"[16] For the Anti-Federalists, majoritarianism was the logical answer to this question; popular sovereignty implied, nay commanded, democratic government. The Framers, on the other hand, did not identify popular sovereignty with the will of the majority; rather, the will of the people was identified with something they believed more permanent and more significant—the public interest. The Constitution they drafted was designed to allow that more basic and more inclusive interest to emerge. In rejecting majoritarianism based upon popular sovereignty, then, the Framers did not reject the idea that the ultimate, sovereign authority resides in the people;[17] rather, they gave the concept a different meaning than did the proponents of democracy.

Their attitude toward majoritarianism also indicates the Framers did not share the democrats' unswerving faith in the idea that a representative should mirror exactly the interests, opinions, and feelings of his constituents. Madison's objection to this concept, like his rejection of majoritarianism, was based on his fear of faction. A true representative, he argued, should act not as a mere messenger boy for popular sentiment no matter how prejudiced or unjust; he should filter out popular passions, and thus bring the interests of his constituents into accord with the true interests of the country. If such men were elected, the public decision—as pronounced by the representatives of all the people—would be more consonant with the public good than if pronounced by the people themselves convened for that purpose.[18] One of the advantages of the Constitution, Madison argued, was that the larger electoral districts made the election of proper representatives possible. But he was not at all sanguine about this system being a sufficient safeguard against faction—the representative was just as likely to transmit popular passions into the national councils as he was to filter them out. Passion was the enemy of clear reasoning; passion made it impossible for men to arrive at reasonable, mutually satisfactory policy agreements. Representation alone, therefore, was not sufficient to guarantee a republic. Madison placed his primary reliance on the workings of federalism and the separation of powers. "He was," said Madison, "an advocate for the policy of refining popular appointments by successive filtrations."[19]

This concern does not mean, though, that either Madison or the Convention ever attempted to curb faction by destroying the representation of actual interests. Their concern lay in filtering out the emotions attached to interest. Madison, in urging a Senate whose members would be proportional to numbers, argued in terms of the representation of interests. He told the Convention that the real security of the people, in the small states as well as the large, lay in the diversity of interests.[20] In rejecting this proposal, the Convention did not reject his conception of representation, but merely asserted that a Senate giving each state an equal vote was a better means of protecting the various, diverse interests of the people. And once the Great Compromise was accepted, only Luther Martin opposed the idea of a popularly elected House of Representatives. The rest of the delegates were agreed that the interests of the people were to be represented directly in Congress. The Framers, like their opponents in 1787–1788, believed in the idea of actual representation; but, unlike the Anti-Federalists, they placed a negative value on popular feelings and emotions. Representation of interests, however, was an essential feature of the Constitution.

Though the Framers and the Anti-Federalists interpreted the concepts of popular sovereignty and representation differently, there was no significant difference in their approach to another basic idea. In 1787–1788 Americans shared a belief in a state of nature and its Lockean corollary—that men entered into civil society to protect and promote some fundamental rights they had enjoyed in a state of nature. Probably this consensus resulted from the failure of either side to be very specific about what they meant by natural rights. No one bothered to spell out the substantive content attributed to individual natural rights, and few men even bothered to enumerate the rights they deemed natural. Perhaps no one felt the need to do so because all shared the same ideas. Be that as it may, there is no doubt about the American consensus on the *idea* of natural rights when the Constitution was drafted and ratified.[21]

Both the Framers and their opponents also believed in the contract theory of government. During the Constitutional Convention, before the problem of equal state representation was resolved, some delegates argued that the Articles could not be superseded. A contract could only be broken by the mutual consent of the contracting parties, in this case the states. Other delegates, including Madison and Wilson, argued that government was the product of an agreement among the people—the source of all authority—and that the people could form a new government by ratifying a new compact.[22] Once the Convention decided to give each state an equal voice in the Senate, however, only one delegate continued to press this theoretical point.[23]

The same difficulty in combining the concepts of a state of nature, popular sovereignty, and the social contract reappeared in the state ratifying conventions. All agreed that government was formed by an agreement among the people, but some of the Constitution's supporters now argued it was not really an original compact. When the North Carolina Convention ground to a halt on this question of whether the Constitution was a contract, Goudy— a man with no special claim to fame—arose and gave his understanding of the matter: "I wonder that these gentlemen, learned in the law, should quibble upon words. I care not whether it be called a compact, agreement, covenant, bargain or what. Its intent is a concession of power, on the part of the people, to their rulers."[24]

This statement did not end the discussion of this point at the North Carolina Convention because partisans on both sides were intent upon marshalling support for their positions by using contract theory. Since the intent here, however, is more modest—merely to demonstrate that Americans in

1787–1788 agreed with Locke and the Whigs that governments were created by some sort of agreement among the people—we do not have to make such fine distinctions and Mr. Goudy can have the last word on this point.

The political activists of 1778–1788 also shared the idea that a constitution was a written superior law against which all acts of government were to be measured. In fact, the idea of a written constitution as the embodiment of fundamental law tied together all the other elements: social contract, popular sovereignty, representative government, and natural rights. If all authority was ultimately derived from the people, that idea was best expressed through the "medium of [a] constitutional compact, which binds them together in one body."[25] If popular sovereignty was vested in the people, then a written constitution was the proper vehicle for making the intention of the people manifest; it represented the superior will of the people.[26] If democrats and republicans both insisted that government must actually represent the will of the people (though they held different conceptions of representation), then a written constitution was the most desirable means for delegating authority to their agents in government.[27] Finally, the written delegations of power in the Constitution, and the specific limitations on that authority, served as a protection for the natural rights of the people.[28] In short, the idea of a written constitution as something distinct from and superior to the government, the idea of the Constitution as fundamental law, encompassed all the major political ideas of the period.

A constitution as fundamental law was to be the measure of legitimacy for all governmental acts. It was expected, however, to do more. A written constitution was expected to perform an architectonic function; it was to shape and direct the government and thereby the entire polity. To quote James Wilson: "By the invigorating and overruling energy of a constitution, the force and direction of the government are preserved and regulated; and its movements are rendered uniform, strong, and safe."[29]

Thus, there is no single, authoritative American theory of democracy embedded in our Constitution because the men who drafted it were creating a republic, not a democracy. The ultimate purpose was not democractic government—which at that time meant representative majoritarianism—but a government so structured that it would invariably promote the public interest. Ideas such as the natural rights of man, the social contract, and the representation of interests—drawn from the eighteenth-century Whig heritage common to all Americans—were used in creating a constitutional republic. The same basic concepts, some of them given different meanings, are also part of the contemporaneous American theory of democracy. If the United States lacks a single authoritative theory of democracy, it suffers from no scarcity of ideas from which to form such a theory. Most importantly, lacking an authoritative definition of democracy embedded in the Constitution of

1787–1788, different theoretical models of democracy can be used to interpret our fundamental law with equal constitutional justification.

Two

THE CONSTITUTION CONSTRUED AND DEMOCRATIC THEORIES VINDICATED

If the Constitution does not provide an authoritative theory of democracy, neither do American intellectual or political history. As democracy became the predominant political theory, Americans utilized the same fundamental concepts as the founding fathers. Alone or in combination, the ideas of natural rights, contract, and representation formed the bases for varying democratic theories. Variety, not unanimity, has characterized American discussions of democracy. The very abundance of democratic theories neutralizes whatever authority historical experience provides.

From the beginning, Americans interpreted the Constitution in light of their own political theories. By 1800 this inclination was true even of the democrats who had opposed the document drafted by the 1787 Philadelphia Convention. In part, their acceptance of the Constitution was necessitated by the very theory the Anti-Federalists had used to oppose its adoption. In a very short time, the overwhelming majority of white male Americans had clearly given their consent to the new governmental system.[1] Since the electorate clearly favored the new system, the Anti-Federalists, with their belief in majority rule and the duty of the representative to obey the wishes of his constituents, now had no theoretically consistent choice but to support the Constitution. Although they vigorously opposed many Federalist policies and the constitutional interpretations used to justify those policies, the democrats of 1787–1788 had ceased opposing the Constitution itself by the time the first democratic administration took office in 1801.[2]

In part, too, the democrats' decision to interpret their theories into the Constitution rather than drafting a new document was the result of that first democratic administration. Thomas Jefferson was neither a Federalist nor an Anti-Federalist.[3] The political party he led to victory in 1800 may have included most of the former Anti-Federalists, but Jefferson had always believed democracy could flourish under the Constitution. He did not advocate retaining the Constitution because he was adverse to constitution making. Jefferson always defended the people's right to draft new charters when they deemed it necessary.[4] He simply believed that change was unnecessary: democracy as he understood it was compatible with Madison's Constitution.

This same belief in democracy differentiated Jefferson from the men at the Philadelphia Convention. In propounding a democratic theory different from that of the Anti-Federalists but compatible with the Constitution, Jefferson solidified public acceptance of that document. Henceforth there could be no question that American democrats would seek to accommodate their theories to the Constitution by interpretation or, at most, by amendment.

Unlike the Anti-Federalists, Jefferson approved of the great mass of what was new in the Constitution, including the consolidation of government, the separation of powers, and the different manner of electing each house of Congress.[5] Jefferson's commitment to the separation of powers, his refusal to endorse a simple representative majoritarian theory of democracy, did not mean he was an advocate of republican theory. He shared the democrats' conviction that the will of the majority should always be translated into government by a majority of the people's *representatives*. Yet, since his early political experience in Virginia, Jefferson opposed a simple representative majoritarian theory of democracy. Elected representatives, too, might tyrannize.[6] Unlike the adherents of republican theory, he did not fear the sentiments, feelings, or emotions of the people; he viewed the separation of powers as a device to check their *agents*. Jefferson was a democrat, not a republican: the cornerstone of his political theory was that the will of the people should always prevail.[7]

Nor should Jefferson's use of the word "republican" blur the differences between his political theory and that of the Framers. To Jefferson a republic meant a "government by its citizens in mass, acting directly and personally according to the rules established by the majority; and that every other government is more or less republican in proportion as it has in its composition more or less of this ingredient of direct action of its citizens."[8] To men like Madison, however, a republic emphatically did *not* mean government by the mass of citizens; to them, a republic meant, as it had to Polybius, Cicero, Machiavelli, and Harrington, a government so constructed that the interests of one class or group would be balanced by the other interests in society. What Jefferson called a republic, colonial Americans had previously labelled a democracy. His fixed belief that the rule of the people was the best form of government for conducting the *res publica* led Jefferson to call his theory republican. This label does not, however, alter the fact that he was advocating a theory of politics quite different from that of Madison and the other members of the Philadelphia Convention.[9]

Instead of limiting popular control of the government or refining public sentiment by a system of progressive filtrations, Jefferson was always seeking to expand public participation in governmental decision-making. He had the same notion of representation as the Anti-Federalists—the right of the people to instruct their representatives and the agents' duty to obey.[10] Not only would more participation produce the best government but such a system would also be the most free. The secret of freedom lay in: "making [each man] the depository of the powers respecting himself, so far as he is competent to them, and delegating only what is beyond his competence by a synthetical process, to higher orders or functionaries, so as to trust fewer and fewer powers in proportion as the trustees become more and more oligarchical."[11]

Jefferson's concept of structuring public participation led to a restricted view of the power of the federal government, confining it largely to matters of national defense and foreign relations. Representation could make the federal government the agent of the people, separation of powers could keep the agents in line, but the people could never really participate in its decision-making processes. Far better, Jefferson reasoned, to handle most matters at the state and local levels. He read this theory of democracy into the Constitution. The Jeffersonian "strict" construction of the federal government's powers was based on Jefferson's theory of democracy.

The Justices on the Supreme Court at this time, however, shared neither Jefferson's theory of the Constitution nor his political theory. Under the leadership of Chief Justice John Marshall (and Marshall dominated the Court during his tenure as no other man has ever done)[12] they sought to interpret the Constitution according to the theory, objectives and purposes of the men who drafted it.[13]

Marshall's political theory contained no notion that the Constitution was designed to facilitate majority rule. On the contrary, he assumed that a just society imposed certain restraints on the numerical majority and that the Constitution made this theory the law of the land. He accepted Madison's view of representation and the separation of powers, and the ideas of Hamilton about national supremacy, judicial review, and the special need to protect the natural right of property in a representative republic. In short, the political theory behind Marshall's interpretation of the Constitution was much closer to the republicanism of the Framers than to the democratic theory of Jefferson.

Nowhere is this difference more evident than in their attitudes toward issues of federalism. Jefferson saw the growth of state power vis-à-vis national power as an extension of democracy. John Marshall believed the very purpose of the Constitution would be destroyed by the Jeffersonian interpretation. In his view, the republic was not destined to perish by the overwhelming power of the national government, but by the resisting, counteracting, centrifugal pull of the states.[14] To Jefferson, centralization worked against the democratic purpose of the Constitution; to Marshall, the Constitution was adopted to avoid a continuation of the near anarchy under the Articles of Confederation.

In these circumstances, the tension between Jefferson's and Marshall's construction of the Constitution inevitably led to an acrimonious debate about which institution should be the final interpreter of the document.[15] Behind this disagreement, however, was a shared concept of the function of a written constitution. A constitution was to keep the government within the limits set by society. The key elements of American political thought, republican and democrat alike—the natural rights of man, the social compact, and the right to representation—were embodied in the Constitution of the United States. This made the Constitution a "higher law," a law which transcended the realm of ordinary politics because it enunciated the means and ends of government.

The American leadership also believed the higher law was meant to be binding on governmental decisions. This belief was a truly novel American innovation. The belief in the existence of a fundamental higher law had long been a part of Western political thought. The idea that constitutions are created by the people was an easy deduction from contract theory. What, in the final analysis, gave substance to the Constitution was neither its fundamentality nor its origin in an act of the people, but, rather, the Americans' insistence that the Constitution was law and had to be enforced.[16]

During the next major period of American history, primary emphasis must be placed on the American agreement about the importance of private property. This agreement helped mitigate political conflict, gave Jacksonian democracy an individualistic cast, and led to the creation of still another American theory of democracy.

The Jacksonians shared Jefferson's faith in the mass of the people.[17] They, therefore, continued the Jeffersonian movement to extend the franchise by removing the property and tax qualifications for voting by white male Americans. In addition, several states introduced the secret ballot to insulate the individual's electoral choice from economic and social reprisals.[18] Like the Anti-Federalists and Jefferson, the Jacksonians believed the people's agents were to obey the wishes of the voters. President Jackson said as much in his first State of the Union message: "the first principal of our system [is] *that the majority is to govern* . . . in . . . all . . . matters of public concern; policy requires that as few impediments as possible should exist to the free operation of the public will."[19] Like their democratic predecessors, the Jacksonians thought representation was a device for implementing the popular will.

In the states, this notion of representation led the Democrats to adopt policies similar to those of the Anti-Federalists. By creating more elective offices and having more frequent elections, Jacksonian politicians came close to implementing the representative majoritarian theory of government favored by Patrick Henry. At the national level, this concept of representation led to a new method of nominating presidential candidates. The national conventions were designed to extend the power of the electoral majority. Both the new nominating procedure and the idea of representation behind it gave credence to Andrew Jackson's claim that the President was the Tribune of the People.

Still, at the national level, the Jacksonians sought to accomplish their goals by interpolating their democratic theory into the Constitution. Following Jefferson's example they worked within the existing system. This method meant there was no extended effort to dispense with the electoral college, and a president less popular than Old Hickory might still be elected by less than a popular majority. Nor was there an attempt to have United States Senators elected by the populace. Similarly, Jackson was probably second to none in his dislike of the Marshall Court, but he made no frontal assault on its independence from the electoral majority and their representatives in Congress and at the White House. Jackson followed Jefferson's tactic of using the political branches to neutralize the Court's doctrines as much as possible.

In short, the Democratic Party was the repository of all American democratic ideas developed to that time, and our federal system enabled the Jacksonians to combine them in a new way. Because it did not change the content of any significant democratic concept, Jacksonian democracy was a movement which applied old doctrines in new areas rather than one which generated a new theory of democracy.

Nowhere is this fact better illustrated than in the Democratic Party's attitude toward the relationship between government and private property. Jacksonian economic policy was based squarely on Jefferson's concept of equal opportunity—each man had the same natural right to earn a living. The Democrats sought to apply this concept by a vigorous policy of laissez-faire. This economic policy gave the Jacksonian movement its crusading and dynamic quality.[20] Although the national economic policies especially favored by the banking and commerical interests were scuttled, it is important to remember that the Jacksonian Democrats did not break down the *protections* given private property. There was in Jacksonian economic policy neither animus toward private property nor desire to regulate its use. The goal was to extend the enjoyment of property to more Americans.[21]

Under the leadership of Roger B. Taney, the same policy was enunciated and followed by a new Supreme Court majority. By strictly construing state corporation charters, for example, the Court limited the vested rights an individual could acquire through them. The Jacksonian Chief Justice did not want to stifle the *private* development of new methods and new means of communication and commerce.[22] The community's interests were to be furthered by eliminating barriers to private competition. The Democrats on the Supreme Court, like their political and judicial counterparts throughout the country, sought to diffuse entrepreneurial opportunities. The public interest meant an extension of the individual right of economic opportunity.

The Whig politicians opposing Jackson came to understand that there was no cause for alarm. The less restrictive franchise requirements and the addition of more Western states had broadened the American electorate. Only the rhetoric of democracy could now win elections. The Whigs realized that successful electoral politics required a change in language, the modification of one aspect of conservative political theory, not a major shift in policies. As Jefferson called his democratic theory republican, the Whigs now spoke as professed democrats. Except for the Southern slavocracy, American political figures were using the two words—democracy and republic—interchangeably.

One interesting consequence of this synonymous use was that after Joseph Story[23] left the Supreme Court in 1845, the Justices found it extremely difficult to give a definitive meaning to the constitutional provision guaranteeing each state a republican form of government. The newer Justices had not been exposed to an avowedly republican political theory untinged by the issue of slavery because the country's major political leaders used democracy and republic interchangeably. John Marshall and Joseph Story had known that the Constitution meant to protect republican government even from the inroads of democracy. By 1848, when the Court had its first opportunity to expound the meaning of the Guaranty Clause, the Justices could no longer distinguish a democracy from a republic.[24]

More than just a terminological change was involved, however. The Whigs had made a discovery of truly monumental proportions: in the United States, professed democrats were willing to accept a democratic theory which explicitly placed limits on the majority. The American majority could be relied upon because every man believed he had an equal opportunity to amass wealth. The majority would even support laws and constitutional interpretations which benefited the wealthy minority so long as each man thought that he, too, might one day share that privileged position. A new American theory of democracy was thus born.

The novelty of the Whig theory of democracy was the explicit limits it placed on the electoral majority. Like the Anti-Federalists, Jefferson, and the Jacksonians, the Whig politicians were willing to base their political theory directly on the feelings and sentiments of the people. As with all the other American theories up to this time, the Whig theory of democracy was based on a version of man's natural rights. But where the other democratic theories had implicitly assumed the people would respect their own rights, the Whigs made the limitations on the majority explicit.

The protection of property was central to the Whig theory of politics. The party carried forward the republican concept of a natural right to property. Since the American Union, according to the Whigs, had been framed to protect this sacred natural right, among others, equal opportunity could never even imply substantial restrictions on the ownership and use of property. Governmental agents were justified in following the demands of the people they represented only insofar as these claims did not interfere with any of man's natural rights, including the important right to property.

By casting this conception of property into a democratic political theory, the Whigs emphasized the limits on majority rule which had only been implicit in other American theories of democracy. The Whigs had a natural rights theory of democracy which stressed the limitations on the popular majority. Yet the Whig politicians were confident that in America the people could be convinced of the value of limiting their own power and thus would refrain from making unjustified claims. The Whig politicans, therefore, did not talk about the need for an external agency (like the courts) limiting the electoral majority in order to protect individual rights.

Without changing its inclinations, the party of Webster and Clay began preaching the American democratic creed: the people should rule. In 1829 Daniel Webster had argued for judicial intervention:

> If at this period there is not a general restraint on legislatures, in favor of private rights, there is an end to private property. Though there may be no prohibition in the Constitution, the legislature is restrained from acts subverting the great principles of republican liberty and of the social compact.[25]

By 1842, he had come to feel that external judicial intervention was not necessary:

> America has furnished to Europe proof of the fact, that popular institutions, founded on equality and the principle of representation, are capable of maintaining governments, able to secure the rights of person, property, and reputation.[26]

As 1840 demonstrated, the American environment made it possible for the Whigs to come to office without abandoning their policy of aiding entrepreneurs. By encouraging each American to believe he had an equal chance of success—a belief sustained by the American economic situation—the Whigs created a democratic theory which placed great emphasis on the self-imposed limits to majority rule.[27]

The shared belief in the equal opportunity of each white man to amass a fortune made it possible to accept not only the popular majoritarianism of Jefferson and Jackson, but also a democratic theory advocating only a limited majority rule, especially where those limitations involved the rights of private property. "Property is the fruit of labor—property is desirable—is a positive good in the world. That some should be rich," said Abraham Lincoln, "shows that others may become rich, and hence is just encouragement to industry and enterprize. Let not him who is houseless pull down the house of another; but let him labor diligently and build one for himself, thus by example assuring that his own shall be safe from violence when built."[28] Lincoln, the former Whig, supported policies aiding the business community. But his belief in equal opportunities for all Americans enabled him to reconcile his economic policies with his faith in "government of the people, by the people, and for the people."

To be sure, some of Lincoln's contemporaries did not espouse democratic theories. During the period leading up to the Civil War, the white Southern leadership had formulated a nondemocratic theory of politics and read it into the Constitution; but the overtly nondemocratic aspects of this theory collapsed with the Confederacy.[29] Then, like the rest of America, the white Southerners advanced their programs in terms of democratic values. By the end of the Civil War, the New World's abundance and space, an environment which made unregulated economic activity acceptable to all major groups, had facilitated the total acceptance of democratic theory.

In the mid-nineteenth century, of course, the ruling populace did not include all people. By that time white male suffrage was a fact of American life. The inclusion of blacks, women, and Indians awaited later generations. On a comparative world scale, however, the United States was the most democratic nation.[30]

During this era men also began to endow the Constitution with the trappings of divine origins. It became "the greatest document ever struck off at a moment by the hand of man," the symbol of liberty and popular sovereignty. While men continued to quarrel about its meaning, the Constitution itself was regarded as the almost sacred source of ultimate authority. The Jeffersonian period marked the political acceptance of the Constitution; the pre–Civil War period, its deification.[31] As Walton Hamilton has remarked about the broad phrases of the Constitution:

As the Bible wanted exegesis, the Constitution demanded exposition
. . . it became the great storehouse of verbal conflict, and rival truths
were derived by the same inexorable logic from the same infallible
source. The Civil War was waged for a Union it had created; the object of secession was to secure rights guaranteed by the Constitution.[32]

In the period leading up to the Civil War, men challenged each other's constitutional doctrines and even the binding authority of what they considered
faulty constitutional interpretation, but no one questioned the need for relatively fixed fundamental rules when governing a nation. The debate was
about the content of the rules, not the importance of having a constitution
to limit and define governmental policies.

Three

CONSTITUTIONAL EXEGESIS OLD AND NEW

In the aftermath of the Civil War, the conditions which had supported an agreement about the great value of substantially unregulated private property began to disintegrate. The war had encouraged rapid industrial growth and technological innovations which began to change the infrastructure of American society radically. The decentralized economy of the prewar era gave way to an integrated national economy. Fewer and bigger corporations now made decisions and pursued policies affecting an ever greater percentage of the population. Industrialization created a large urban labor force with interests distinct from both agricultural and business groups. In time, labor became a significant political factor. Agriculture was losing its central place in the American economy. The economic and social loci of power were shifting.

The full impact of these changes on American political thought would not be felt for a long time. The process which eventually shattered the American consensus on natural rights, and which altered ideas about representation and the social contract had begun. All this upheaval, however, was in the future. In the years immediately following the Civil War, Americans felt no need to go beyond traditional concepts when they thought about politics.

During the first two decades after the Civil War, for example, a majority of the Supreme Court gave a new content to the concept of the public interest. The rhetoric of the Taney Court had been rich in references to a superior community interest limiting the uses of private property, but the issues then had not involved extensive governmental interference with private economic activity. The decisions of the Taney Court, therefore, had only implemented the laissez-faire economic policies of Jacksonian legislatures. Now the Court began upholding state legislation involving considerable regulation of economic activities. In declaring such laws constitutional, the Court majority talked about the public interest in much the same way as the Taney Court, but for the concept's application, they developed a new doctrine about the relation between private property and governmental regulation.[1] The same words in a different age were used to develop new policies.

Thus, what Justice Story had feared when he opposed Jacksonian democracy had come to pass. Under the impact of a depression, the popular majority in several states had decided to regulate and restrict the minority's property rights. And the Supreme Court, interpreting the Constitution in the light of existing democratic theories—none of which posited an *external* restraint on the electoral majority—had done what Story had dreaded when he railed against democracy. The Court had failed "to stay the arm of legislative, executive or popular oppression."[2]

Nonetheless, the business and commercial groups had to look to the courts, especially the Supreme Court for protection. When even their profits could be limited by the legislatures, men of substance plainly could not trust their property to the popular majority. They now believed that Story, not Webster, had been right about the dangers of democracy. But they also recognized, with Webster, the political futility of challenging that creed: in post–Civil War America, all policies had to be put forth in the name of democracy.

The conservative groups solved this dilemma by building upon the natural rights theory of democracy first advanced by the Whigs. That theory had stressed the limits imposed on the polity by the natural rights men sought to preserve by entering into the social contract. Unlike the original expression of this theory, the courts were now seen as the agencies designed to protect these natural rights, especially the natural right of every man to acquire, use, and enjoy his property. In an earlier period, this type of external limitation on the power of the electoral majority would have been advanced as a nondemocratic, republican theory of government. Now, in the name of democracy, the courts were called upon to limit the will of the popular majority. By emphasizing an external institutional restraint on the electoral majority and its elected representatives, a new American theory of democracy was created.

The task confronting the business community and its legal representatives was to convince the judges, particularly a majority of the Supreme Court Justices, of the validity of this new theory. Their effort was made considerably easier by the publication of a major new treatise on American public law. In the preface to his *Constitutional Limitations*, first published in 1869, Thomas M. Cooley frankly stated that:

> he will not attempt to deny—what will probably be sufficiently appar-
> ent—that he has written in full sympathy with the restraints which
> the caution of the fathers has imposed upon the exercise of the powers
> of government . . . and he has also endeavored to point out that there
> are on all sides definite limitations which circumscribe the legislative
> authority independent of specific restrictions which the people impose
> by their state constitutions.[3]

Cooley "intended to build up a comprehensive and well organized system, which had hither to been lacking," Benjamin Twiss has remarked, "by which those limitations which he and others felt were inherent in the American constitution could be implemented in cases where there was a contest between private rights and governmental power."[4]

Cooley was articulating a new theory of democracy. Story had been an avowed opponent of democracy; Cooley professed the democratic faith. The difference involved more than a change in political rhetoric, more than the fact that by 1868 no one bothered to distinguish the word republic from the word democracy. Justice Story saw popular attacks on property rights as an indication that the balanced, mixed institutions created by the Constitution were under siege from the increasingly "popular cast" of the American polity and that only the courts could reinforce the original foundations. With the single and important exception of slavery, Story opposed any substantive changes in the American governing institutions put in place by the Framers. Judge Cooley, on the other hand, never opposed the increasingly popular cast of American institutions. Cooley wanted to exclude certain individual rights from the "jurisdiction" of the institutions directly accountable to the electorate. Cooley had indeed incorporated Story's ideas about the courts' need to protect entrepreneurial property, but within a theory which otherwise endorsed popular control of government. By such incorporation Judge Cooley wound up legitimating the popular cast of our nonjudicial institutions which had so troubled Justice Story.

In the years immediately after the publication of *Constitutional Limita-tions*, only a minority of the Court could be mustered behind Cooley's inter-pretation of the Constitution. Only a minority of the Justices espoused a democratic theory stressing the Court's role as protector of man's natural rights. The leading spokesman for this minority was undoubtedly Justice Stephen J. Field. In the American democracy, Field maintained, every man was entitled to enjoy the rights enunciated in the Declaration of Independ-ence. American governments were instituted to protect life, liberty, and the pursuit of happiness, not to interfere with them. Because the equal right of all men to acquire, use, and enjoy property was an essential condition for the pursuit of happiness, that right was a first principle of democratic government. It was precisely to "secure to every individual the essential conditions for the pursuit of happiness" that the Fourteenth Amendment was added to the Constitution.[5]

When the Court upheld legislative regulations on business activities, Justice Field dissented because the decision was "subversive of the rights of private property." "All that is beneficial from property arises from its use and the fruits of its use," he asserted. "If the constitutional guarantee extends no further than to prevent a deprivation of title and possession," it is meaningless. Field thought that under the Constitution, the power of the states over the property of individuals was well defined. The Justice's definition of the scope of state regulatory power was the same as Cooley's: with certain well-recognized exceptions, "the doctrine that each must so use his own as not to injure his neighbor . . . is the rule by which every member of society must possess and enjoy property."[6]

Justice Field was not unaware that "the inequalities in the condition of men were becoming more marked and disturbing," and that the "enormous aggregations of wealth possessed by some corporations" was causing uneasiness lest this power "should become dominating in the legislature of the country and thus encroach upon the rights or crush out the business of individuals of small means." Because, however, he believed the prosperity and progress of America depended upon the security of property, that is, its protection from all but minimal regulations of its use, Field insisted that the "imperative duty of the Court" in the face of this popular unrest was "to enforce with a firm hand" the "limitations upon legislative power arising from the nature of the Constitution and its specific restraints in favor of private rights."[7] In short, Justice Field's theory of the Constitution held that the business of government was not to regulate private economic activity or to set bounds for its domain, but that the business of the Court was to implement this theory.

By the mideighties, Field's views on the relationship between private property and governmental regulation began to emerge as the majority position, and by 1897 Field's triumph was complete. A new Court majority began to stress a constitutional theory aimed at freeing private property from substantive governmental regulation. In the United States, the economic order was to be independent of governmental control.

At the end of the nineteenth century, those wishing to defend the policy of substantially unregulated private economic activity could buttress their theory of democracy with the latest " findings" of science. Popular Darwinian slogans, "the survival of the fittest" and "the struggle for existence," reinforced the laissez-faire arguments of the business community and its professional allies.[8]

A public address by Justice David J. Brewer most clearly indicated how Social Darwinism was combined with natural rights theory.[9] When he talked about the division of wealth in society, gone was the emphasis his uncle, Justice Field, had placed upon the natural right of each individual to own, use, and enjoy property. The new age of industrial and financial combinations had diminished the equal opportunity to enjoy this right. In such changed circumstances, Justice Brewer defended unregulated private economic activity by an "unvarying law of society." Great wealth did not now demonstrate what each man could achieve given equal opportunity in America, but, instead, it illustrated the iron law of Social Darwinism—survival of the fittest. Because a majority of the Court agreed with Justice Brewer that the "paternal theory of government is . . . odious," and that the "utmost possible liberty to the individual and the fullest possible protection to him and his property is both the limitation and duty of government,"[10] the Supreme Court began interpreting the Fourteenth Amendment as if it had enacted into law Mr. Herbert Spencer's *Social Statics*.[11]

When Justice Brewer began to talk about the primary purpose of government, however, he fell back into traditional natural rights terminology. In the United States, where all political theory had become democratic, no theory could defend an unequal division of wealth on the basis of a fairly rigid class structure. To square his Social Darwinistic elitism with democratic theory, Justice Brewer stressed the equal protection which government must evenhandedly apply in the defense of the naturally inevitable unequal division of wealth. Only a policy of total government noninterference in economic matters, a policy which did not distinguish between rich and poor, would be in accord with both the "scientific" natural law of survial and the democratic imperative of treating men as equals. The political theory of those defending private economic activity from substantive government regulation had been modified by Social Darwinism. The emphasis had shifted from equal *opportunity* to equal *protection*.

The Justices only occasionally felt called upon to stress this new theoretical underpinning in their opinions; rather, their political objectives were usually pursued in terms of Justice Field's more traditional theory. Not only did Field's dissents show how natural rights theory could be used to protect private economic activity, but his concepts had the great advantage of being basic to all previous American political theories and of having been used in prior opinions of the Court. Primary reliance on traditional concepts of individual rights made it easier for Justices like Brewer and Peckham to gain the support of men, like the first Justice John Marshall Harlan, who did not share their Social Darwinism. Greater use could be made of the dicta in past cases, no small advantage for a court of law. Despite the advent of Social Darwinism and the important role it played in *confirming* a conservative interpretation of the Constitution, the greater part of the Court's opinions at the turn of the century could have been written by Justice Field. Constitutional decisions continued to stress individual natural rights.

The Court's limitation of a state's ability to regulate economic activity began in 1886 when it unanimously accepted that the word *person* in the Fourteenth Amendment applied to corporations as well as to natural persons.[12] Then, in 1890, the Court majority said that the *Justices* could determine the reasonableness of economic regulations under the Due Process Clause. As the three dissenters noted, the Court's opinion overruled the *Granger Rate Cases* "in which the governing principle was that the regulation and settlement of fares . . . is a legislative prerogative and not a judicial one."[13] The doctrine of judicially determined reasonableness was read into both Due Process Clauses. The Justices could now strike down state and federal regulatory laws they deemed confiscatory, or otherwise arbitrary or capricious.

The Court, however, did more than read the concept of substantive reasonableness into the Due Process Clauses. It also expanded the clauses to include the concept of "liberty of contract" which had been advanced by Cooley. Once they had created this new constitutional right, the Justices could say that under due process, "If this right be struck down or arbitrarily interfered with, there is a substantial impairment of liberty."[14]

As the Justices applied the liberty of contract concept, it soon became clear that the Court, not the legislatures, would determine which regulations were necessary for the health, safety, and morals of the workers.[15] The Court majority believed there was a basic right to make contracts, and that any abridgment of this right was invalid until government could justify its action to the Justices' satisfaction.

To further limit federal regulation of business activity, the Court also developed the doctrine that there was a distinct activity known as interstate commerce. Marshall had not only held that Congress had plenary power over commerce among the states, but he had also defined the reach of that power to include any activity whose extent and effect was not limited to one state.[16] In 1895 the Court held that Congress could not destroy the Sugar Trust under the Sherman Antitrust Act because manufacturing was not itself an activity in interstate commerce.[17] Similarly, a Federal Railroad Liability Act was limited only to those employees actually engaged on railways crossing state lines,[18] and labor management relations such as unionization were also outside the corpus of activity known as interstate commerce.[19] This new conception of interstate commerce, however, did not prevent the Court majority from striking down state regulatory statutes it deemed as interfering with interstate commerce, even when Congress was silent.[20]

These doctrines and others, applying to both the federal and state governments, were connected by a political theory whose basic tenet was that private economic activity (or as the Court would put it, the right to own, use, and enjoy the fruits of property) should be free from all but the most obviously necessary governmental regulation.[21] Behind this political theory, and behind the constitutional interpretations based on that theory, there remained the same notion of the function of the Constitution. This idea had not changed since the Revolution. The Justices who upheld the Granger rate regulations shared it—they had insisted the Constitution was designed to impose on the nation certain vague features inherent in the nature of free government. These men may not have precisely defined the pattern the Constitution was to impose, but they never doubted a Constitution was designed to impose some pattern. When the Court came to accept Cooley's and Field's political and constitutional theory, the contours of that pattern became more definite—fewer options were available to the elected political leadership when they sought to deal with the changing socioeconomic conditions. The Justices believed, in the words of Cooley, that:

> A constitution is not to be made to mean one thing at one time and another at some subsequent time when the circumstances may have so changed as perhaps to make a different rule in the case seem desirable. A principle share of the benefit expected from written constitutions would be lost if the rules they established were so flexible as to bend to circumstances or be modified by public opinion.[22]

While the statement serves as an injunction to judges to stand firm, its basic premise is that a written constitution serves to create a certain pattern and to mold the nation in that image. This purpose, this architectonic function of a written constitution, Cooley is arguing, could not be achieved if the rules were constantly changing.

At the turn of the century, then, a majority of the Justices had accepted the natural rights theory of democracy which emphasized the Court's role in protecting those rights. The same basic concepts, including liberty of contract and interstate commerce as a concrete activity, continued to be used by a later group of Justices until the Court was reconstituted during Franklin D. Roosevelt's second term. This is not to say that for forty years a Court majority consistently used these ideas in striking down all state and federal regulations of economic activity, because such statutes were sustained at times.[23] The political theory underlying this interpretation of the Constitution, however, remained the same, the major social group espousing the theory—the business and financial community—remained the same, and the constitutional doctrines, no matter how often distinguished, were never replaced in certain judicial minds. The ideas expressed by Cooley and Field, which were later buttressed by Social Darwinism, were the same ideas used to strike down social and economic legislation during the Great Depression.

When, in the closing decades of the nineteenth century, a Supreme Court majority first began writing the ideas of Cooley and Field into American constitutional law, that doctrine had some beneficial consequences. By preventing governmental interference with the private accumulation of capital, the Supreme Court hastened the industrialization of the American economy. Under the protective umbrella of the new legal doctrine, private entrepreneurs helped make the United States a major world economic power.

As Supreme Court Justices continued to use a natural rights theory of democracy to develop positive protections for substantially unregulated private economic activity, their constitutional theory became more logically formal.[24] In deducing constitutional limitations from the fundamental rights of property and contract, these Justices were using a theory which ignored the changes that had reshaped the socioeconomic infrastructure of America. Giant corporations are obviously not the same as the individual self-sufficient farms of Jefferson's day, yet a Supreme Court majority often talked as if they were. "By calling a business property," Justice Holmes once noted in dissent, "you make it seem like land, and lead up to the conclusion that a statute cannot substantially cut down the advantages of ownership existing before the statute was passed."[25] Based upon logical deductions from natural rights theory, the Court's decisions too often emphasized a type of property which no longer corresponded to the dominant economic factors.

For most Americans, of course, the real problem was not the constitutional theory of the Court majority, but the substantive results produced by using that theory. The long line of Supreme Court decisions stressing private property proved uniformly favorable to business and financial interests and equally detrimental to almost everyone else. A vigorous reform movement developed in order to bring private economic activity under some form of regulation in the public interest. As a matter of course, these demands were expressed in terms of democratic values and theory.

The first, the habitual, the instinctive—one is tempted to say the natural—theoretical response was the reformulation of traditional concepts. Once again American political and constitutional theories were to be placed at the service of the popular majority by rearranging the emphasis on individual natural rights. Justice Field had argued business activity should not be regulated because such activity derived from each man's natural right to use and enjoy his property. The reformers argued that, in an industrial society, policies based upon Field's theory were depriving the majority of Americans of the equal opportunity for economic success. The reformers' goal was the restoration of every American's Jeffersonian right for equal opportunity in the pursuit of happiness. That reestablishment could not be done by an exact governmental impartiality to all groups. Only governmental intervention could remove the feeling of frustrated opportunity held by large numbers of Americans.

The need to restore equal opportunity was the dominant passion of the Populist movement in the last two decades of the nineteenth century. This movement sought an alliance of the producers against the nonproducers.[26] Unfortunately for the Populists, the agrarian origins of their movement prevented them from gaining sufficient support in the industrial areas to become a dominant force on the national level. Populism made no direct impact on constitutional doctrines. Lacking support from the industrialized sectors of the economy, Populist thought often appeared quixotic: a restatement of Jefferson's faith in the small, independent farmer seemed ill suited for the age of industry. But the underlying Populist belief that the "powers of government—in other words, of the people—should be expanded . . . as rapidly and as far as the good sense of an intelligent people and the teachings of experience shall justify, to the end that oppression, injustice and poverty shall eventually cease in the land,"[27] carried over to the Progressive movement in the first decade of the twentieth century.

To give each American an equal opportunity for economic success, the Progressives also adopted many of the Populists' specific proposals. Those dealing with the workings of political institutions included the direct elections of United States Senators, the initiative, and the referendum. As most Supreme Court decisions continued to favor industry, various proposals for reversing the Court without resorting to the amendment process were also put forward by the Progressives. In the area of economic policy, many Populist proposals for subjecting private economic activity to a larger public interest were also continued by the Progressives. This fact is not surprising, since the Progressive movement followed hard on the heels of Populism and its basic goal was the same—to make individual opportunity a reality in industrial America.[28]

The Progressives, however, had a different view of the American public. Where the Populists had divided society into producers and nonproducers and saw conflict only between these two groups, the Progressives saw conflict everywhere. The America of Progressive thought was a pluralistic society of many groups—farmers, laborers, merchants, clerks, capitalists, immigrants, and Yankees—all striving for their own interests. When the Populists talked about "the people" they meant the producing mass; when the Progressives talked about "the people," they meant the various groups in society. The chief theoretical problem for Progressive thought was uniting these competing groups behind a common, public interest. The public interest was, of course, usually stated as giving each man the equal opportunity to run the race and fight the fight of life.[29]

The political theory of the Progressives was another response to industrialism within the framework of natural rights theory. While emphasis was placed on the need for collective action through the government, the purpose of that action was individual opportunity. The Progressives believed, moreover, that opportunity was not a simple matter in a complex industrial nation. The plurality of groups would create a variety of goals for Americans, and these differing pursuits of happiness would generate different and often competing claims on government. The Progressives met this problem by using another traditional concept—representation of interests. The elected representatives were not simply committed to obeying the commands of their constituents; they were also primarily responsible for reconciling the varying demands made on government. The use of technical experts would help assure the success of this reconciliation, but it was not meant to shift the basic responsibility from the elected leaders.[30] The attainment of the Jeffersonian goal of equal opportunity was to be achieved by relying upon a Federalist means—the representation of interests. Progressive political theory begins and ends within the traditional American paradigm.

The most prominent Progressive to reach the Supreme Court was Louis D. Brandeis. He brought to the study of law not only a superb legal mind, but also a sure grasp of statistics, accounting, economics, and related social sciences. He was the Progressive expert par excellence.

As a charter member of the New Freedom school of Progressivism—he had helped Wilson prepare that manifesto—Brandeis sought the accommodation of Jeffersonian ideas and industrialization by limiting the size and power of trusts and monopolies. He summarized this idea in his famous phrase, "the curse of bigness." According to Brandeis, modern corporations were so big that they were economically inefficient; they had outgrown the capacity of individual man. This same lack of human control over industrial forces created a great social danger. The ultimate curse of bigness was the power over the entire nation which large corporations were exerting without responsibility and beyond human control. Industrial organizations were shaping, not serving, the ends of man.

In Brandeis's well-thought-out political theory, breaking up the trusts would reduce organizations to human dimensions. The workers could participate in decision making because they could understand what was involved. Owners would have to assume responsibility because they could see the consequences of their action and inaction. Planned competition would abolish cutthroat practices, mitigate the impact of any one decision, and demand greater efficiency all around. The smaller units would, according to Brandeis, act as efficiency checks on one another and permit social and economic groups to keep businesses responsible. This divestiture, in turn, would obviate the need for governmental control of a person's life, an equally obnoxious alternative to Brandeis.[31]

Brandeis brought this political theory to the Supreme Court. In part, his judicial method stemmed from his political theory, in part, from his legal experiences. As a Progressive, Brandeis believed that the elected leadership—informed by expert knowledge, he hoped—should be the primary agents in adapting society to the new circumstances. Such action was the function of political leadership in a democracy, according to the Progressives. In matters of social and economic policy, therefore, Brandeis always insisted that "when the validity of a statute is questioned, the burden of proof, so to speak, is upon those who assail it."[32]

Justice Brandeis, however, agreed with his more conservative brethren that the Constitution was designed to impose certain restrictions upon elected representatives. He, too, insisted that the Court's function as interpreter of the Constitution was to impose some pattern on society. He, too, thought that Justices should prevent action that was "so clearly arbitrary or capricious that legislators, acting reasonably, could not have believed it necessary for the public welfare."[33] Because Brandeis believed that political leaders should be allowed to experiment with ways of adapting the traditional American values to existing economic and social conditions, however, he warned his colleagues of the Court that "we should be ever on our guard lest we erect our prejudices into legal principles."[34]

In heeding this warning his legal experiences as a lawyer and his mastery of facts entered the picture. To avoid writing his prejudices into law in a case properly before the Court, Justice Brandeis continued to use the technique he had demonstrated in his famous brief on behalf of an Oregon statue establishing a ten-hour day for women laundry workers. Whether a piece of legislation was reasonable was not primarily a matter of logic, but of factual circumstances.[35]

This technique proved effective for combating the prevailing theory on the Court. During his entire period as a Justice, Brandeis had to deal with the constitutional theory first expressed by Cooley and Field. For all but his last two years that theory was, more often than not, being applied by the majority of his colleagues. The majority insisted they would sustain any reasonable regulation, but they continued to write opinions showing how, in formal logic, most of these were unnecessary interferences with natural rights and, hence, unreasonable. Justice Brandeis wrote one opinion after another showing how the facts and the conclusions of recognized experts could support legislation interfering with private economic activity as reasonable exercises of power. Since even on those rare occasions when he wrote the opinion for the Court in these cases he had to contend with arguments and precedents based upon a natural rights theory of democracy which emphasized the Court as the guardian of the private economy's autonomy, Justice Brandeis's opinions abounded with references to committee reports, legislative debates, and expert studies. In the process of championing the right of the people's elected leaders to regulate private economic activity for the greater public interest, Brandeis helped create a new judicial method and style.

Given the importance of social and economic experimentation in Brandeis's democratic theory and given the necessity of First Amendment freedoms if individuals were to propose new methods for meeting new problems,[36] Brandeis also believed that the "right of free speech, the right to teach, and the right of assembly are . . . fundamental rights."[37] It is important to note that freedoms fundamental to Brandeis's political theory were accorded a higher priority in his constitutional theory. These rights, however, were not absolute, nor were they spoken of in absolute terms. They were fundamental for the functioning of a democracy, and therefore judicial scrutiny in cases involving these liberties must be exacting.

Just as Brandeis always maintained that the Constitution permitted political experiments for providing economic opportunity in an industrial age, so, too, he insisted that the Constitution mandated the protection of man's individuality from governmental interference.[38] Brandeis believed that both these types of rights—one requiring governmental action, the other requiring protection from government—could best be achieved by following the democratic political theory of the New Freedom school of Progressivism. He conceded, however, that reasonable men might pursue other economic and social policies, and he believed that in a democracy the nonelective branch of government should not prevent experimentation unless it conflicted with the basic pattern of democratic society. That pattern was imposed by the Constitution, according to Brandeis, and while it encouraged reasoned experimentation in economic and social matters, it greatly discouraged interference with man's individuality. Brandeis used his position on the Supreme Court to interpret the Constitution in the light of this political theory and to advocate his particular solutions to the problems confronting the United States. He wanted to make the United States a country where each person enjoyed, to the maximum extent possible, the equal opportunity to pursue happiness in his own way.

Although the democratic theory of the Progressive movement derived from America's political heritage, Progressives no longer spoke of the natural rights of man. A natural right suggests something absolute, an activity or possession totally beyond governmental or societal control. While the natural rights of others justifies certain minimum public interferences with a man's natural rights, the basic premise of freedom from government control serves to keep regulations to a minimum. The Progressives, however, envisioned regulations which were so extensive, so basic to the economic workings of society, that it no longer made sense for them to talk about the natural right of property. Americans were to have a right to equal opportunity, according to the Progressives, but that right was to come from governmental action, not as a gift of beneficent Nature or Nature's God. Their pluralism meant that the Progressives could not talk about natural rights other than the right of property either: they realized that in America all claims were justified in terms of individual rights and that the job of political leaders was to reconcile these conflicting claims. In such an intellectual universe, some values could be more important than others, but none could be absolute. In earlier periods, when Americans spoke of a fundamental right they meant a *sacred* natural right; for the Progressives, a fundamental right meant a basic value, something essentially desirable in American democracy.

There is, of course, a much greater emphasis on inviolability when something is conceived of as a natural right than when it is thought of as a basic value. This shift in thinking can be illustrated by comparing the ideas of Justices Field and Brandeis. Field believed that government had no authority to abridge man's natural rights, rights to which every man was entitled by virtue of being a man. Field, therefore, did not hesitate to declare statutes unconstitutional if he thought they violated a fundamental (natural) right— the legislatures simply had no power to enter a forbidden area except in a few clearly defined circumstances. Brandeis believed that the same rights were essential for man's individuality and that a democracy must have, above all else, man. Brandeis, therefore, always took great pains to demonstrate the important societal function of individual rights in an American democracy; yet, because he believed that political leaders had to reconcile conflicting values, Brandeis was much more hesitant about declaring statutes unconstitutional. When ruling against statutes, he preferred to show that, in the particular circumstances in which the law was applied, there was little or no justification for violating a fundamental right (a socially important value). This argument implied that under different circumstances such actions could be deemed constitutional. Field always implied that, apart from the few common law exceptions, he had difficulty even imagining conditions which could justify an infringement of a natural right. The difference in the conception of rights has significant consequences.

It would not do, however, to exaggerate the difference. The basic purpose of society for Brandeis, as for Field, was to be derived from and set in an individualistic framework. If the Progressives no longer conceived of individual rights as being absolute, they did assume that those norms were fixed. The Progressives did not challenge the validity of traditional American political ideas.

As democracy became the predominant political theory, the same concepts used by the Framers became the bases for differing American conceptions of democracy. The representative majoritarianism of the Anti-Federalists and the popular majoritarianism of Jefferson and the Populists stressed the right to equal opportunity inherent in man's natural equality. The Whigs emphasized the limits that the majority should place on itself and its agents in order to protect the natural right to property. The Cooley-Field theory stressed the Court's role as protector of man's natural rights, especially his right to property. The Progressives maintained that no right was natural, but, in order to obtain the fundamental value of equal opportunity, they used the concept of representation of interests. Each of these democratic theories was derived from and set within the traditional paradigm. In each, the Constitution was seen as the necessary and essential means for imposing a particular conception of democracy upon the nation.

Thus, even within the original paradigm, American history supplies no single authoritative theory of democracy. The men who drafted the Constitution were creating a republic, not a democracy, and the very variety of democratic theories in our history destroys whatever authority a uniformly accepted theory might have provided. Lacking an authoritative definition, different theoretical models of democracy can be used to interpret the Constitution with equal justification. Today's theories, like those of the past, must be evaluated in terms of their consequences, not their sources.

Four

THE CHALLENGE
TO TRADITION

Not all Americans, however, responded to industrialism by formulating democratic theories within the natural rights paradigm. Instead, they began to set the problems of society in an entirely different framework. These intellectuals viewed themselves as men of science, and the social science they helped to create eventually culminated in a new paradigm for democracy. Not only did the new social science challenge, question, and seek to go beyond traditional concepts, it even ushered in a new attitude toward the Constitution. For the first time in American history, influential social theorists began doubting the efficacy of written constitutions.

New theories of social and legal science reflected the growing impact of the idea of science. The American founders of pragmatic philosophy and social science all cut their intellectual eyeteeth on Darwin. Ironically, men like John Dewey and Oliver Wendell Holmes, Jr., were encouraged to do so by the vogue of Social Darwinism. Going beyond Herbert Spencer and Charles Sumner, some of the more inquisitive Americans began reading *The Origin of Species* itself.[1]

Much to their surprise, they found Darwin's work propounding a thesis at odds with Social Darwinism. Darwin maintained there was no clear, unidirected pattern of evolution—a term he did not even use in the first edition—which would enable men to predict a successful adaptation to the environment. Only after a new variety had survived could its superiority be explained. Darwinian evolution was a continual process of adaptation to the environment, not a fixed, known law proceeding inexorably in a single direction as Spencer and Sumner claimed. Social Darwinism, with its natural rights overtones and its belief that humanity progressed from societies based upon fixed social groups (status) to societies based upon individual choice (contract) according to a law of nature, was a social theory based on Lamarck and not on Darwin. To an emerging group of American thinkers, Darwin's work was a call for a social theory built upon experimentation, upon the need for adapting the human species to its changed environment through new social policies. In America, Social Darwinism was used to buttress a defense of the right of property; Darwinian social science was used to supersede the categories of natural rights theory itself.

Not only were the new breed of theorists convinced of the need for experimentation, they also began using an organic conception of society. John Locke and the radical Whigs had viewed society as the product of an agreement among individual men; society and government were created to serve the needs and interests of individuals. American theorists, whatever their differences, had worked within that individualistic paradigm. Now, at the end of the nineteenth century, some Americans began viewing society as a social organism, akin to the biological organisms in Darwin's work, with interests and purposes distinct from the individual members of society. Continental theory in the nineteenth century—conservative and radical alike—assumed that the body politic comprised persons sharing common habits and customs, bound together by affective ties as well as those of mutual self-interest. Auguste Comte, Karl Marx, Emile Durkheim, Max Weber, and George Simmel, the founders of social science, wrote in this tradition. Society, for them, had an independent existence; it was not called into being at the command of man. From a Lockean perspective, restrictions on individuals emerged from the interests and the rights of other individuals (usually of the majority); "society" was just a convenient word for expressing this idea—it had no independent existence. To the organic theorists, restrictions could also emerge from the needs of a distinct entity known as society.[2]

It was from the perspective of the organic nature of human society that Dewey and Holmes criticized the prevailing natural rights theory of democracy which emphasized the sanctity of private economic arrangements. If at times it was difficult to distinguish their criticism from that of the Progressives, it is because they used the same techniques and often advocated the same reforms; but the theoretical bases for criticism were distinct. A Progressive like Brandeis used the techniques and findings of social science to retain and revitalize natural rights concepts. Dewey insisted that a clear understanding of the problems confronting this nation could not be achieved within the traditional American paradigm. He always maintained that the first intellectual task in any program of modernization was abandoning the idea of fixed norms. The patrician Holmes was no social engineer—he remained skeptically aloof from the search for programmatic solutions for society's ills. But using a Darwinian conception of society, Holmes became a leader in the attack on Field's political theory in particular and natural rights theory in general. Progressive theory stayed within the original American paradigm; the theories enunciated by Holmes and Dewey posed a direct challenge to it.

In the thought of John Dewey the rejection of fixed, absolute norms was bound up with his revolt against all types of philosophical formalism. His philosophical method, instrumentalism, was designed as a substitute for the quest for certainty, for fixed values, which Dewey believed was the fundamental weakness of the Western philosophical tradition. His pragmatic theory emphasized adjustment, the problem-solving process, and the intelligent study of consequences—in short, the application of the scientific method to human affairs. For Dewey, the basic weakness of the quest for certainty was its incompatibility with the scientific method.[3]

The scientific method provided Dewey with more than the means of investigating social problems. It was also the *source* of all values.[4] Rather than starting from any fixed values, Dewey's instrumentalism asserted that values were created by careful, intelligent examination of the context of a problem requiring action, and of the likely consequences of different actions. Instrumentalism was never meant as a philosophical gloss for expediency: "The fact that something is desired only raises the *question* of its desirability; it does not settle it."[5] Despite the difficulty of forming a judgment about values within a situation, Dewey insisted that it must be done. Instrumentalism would help man make moral as well as intelligent decisions.

The same process was also the basis of Dewey's conception of freedom— the absence of external restraints distinguishing a free man from a slave was only part of real, effective freedom. To be truly free, a man must consciously set his own goals and possess the skills and resources to achieve them. Otherwise, he will be in bondage to other men, his environment, or his own instinctual appetites.[6] Real freedom, for Dewey, required the effective utilization of the instrumental method.

With social values, constructive social policies, and effective freedom all involved in the same process, it is no wonder that Dewey placed immense emphasis on education. The proper education would teach a person how to use the scientific method in all aspects of his life. It would teach him the skills, deliberation, and power of intelligent self-control necessary for confronting his own and his society's problems. It would prepare a person for the exercise of effective freedom. Above all, education would enable man to choose wisely: to create values in a contextual situation.

Dewey insisted that society, as a distinct entity, did not exist; rather, there are a series of independent, though often overlapping, associations called publics. A public "consists of all those who are affected by the indirect consequences of transactions to such an extent that it is deemed necessary to have those consequences systematically cared for."[7] A public is a natural, spontaneous human organism, growing out of the interactions of human beings. New circumstances inevitably force the evolution of established publics or generate new ones. Over time, men created various institutions of government to care for those consequences which affect the entire polity. Men did not, according to Dewey, create human associations, publics, or society by contract; they gradually developed institutions to meet changing needs.[8]

Constitutions, therefore, have no great value for Dewey. In fact, constitutions are more of a hindrance than a help.[9] Nor could this mistake be rectified, as the Progressives proposed, by constantly adjusting the principles to changing conditions. The updating of principles still presumed the existence of a single standard, still sought to impose a uniform pattern on society. The Progressives' method discouraged the only technique Dewey would recognize for meeting an evolving society's problems: the use of intelligence to judge consequences.

What all Americans until this time had seen as the great virtues of written constitutions, Dewey saw as a near fatal weakness. For the first time in American history, a major thinker questioned not only the desirability of molding society in accordance with certain interpretations of natural rights theory, but the desirability of having any fixed norms at all. Dewey's "revolt against formalism" in American philosophy[10] led him to challenge the architectonic function of a written constitution. There was no need for permanent formal institutions with fixed goals in an ever-evolving society of intelligent men.

If there was for Dewey no a priori rule for a good state at all times and in all circumstances, then the only conceivable fixed value could be a political version of the instrumental method itself. That was the great virtue, according to Dewey, of democratic government. First, he defined a political democracy as a "mode of government, a specified practice in selecting officials and regulating their conduct as officials."[11] Then, having defined democratic government without any fixed moral values, Dewey was in a position to assert that the scope of governmental power must be critically and experimentally determined.

Governing was the function of the elected leadership. The function of the electorate was to keep the leadership responsible by selecting those men who produced what the majority considered to be the best policies. In Dewey's theory, therefore, the leadership had one responsibility even more important than defining the tasks of government and formulating policies. They must supply the people with the *reasons* for their policies. The people, by matching their knowledge of "where the shoe pinches" with the reasons advanced for supporting a particular policy, could evaluate the leaders. The ends of government would be determined by the same political processes which, in a democracy, would hold governmental officials responsible.[12]

This complete reliance on the political process had other advantages. Dewey's conception of democracy gave every man a say over his own destiny. Each adult would count for one and only one in making decisions and the decision of the majority would be binding. There was no standing, permanent electoral majority—it came into existence at a particular time, around certain issues, and had to be re-formed at each election. Not only did pluralism dispel the fear of tyranny of the majority, it also made the democratic political process open and receptive. The different publics were formed into a majority by antecedent debate and modification of their views. Even minorities were given the satisfaction of having been consulted, of having had a chance to be influential, and of knowing that the next time they might form part of the majority. Finally, since Dewey assumed a majority was mobilized around specific proposals for resolving concrete problems, he was obviously equating democracy with instrumentalism. In the end, democracy and instrumentalism were one and the same thing to Dewey.

Morton White has suggested there are two John Deweys, one opposed to any fixed, permanent ends for society, and the other wanting to get on with the task of building a liberal society.[13] The two viewpoints are not irreconcilable. If the real John Dewey were to stand up he would be an engineer rather than an architect or theoretical scientist. His faith in the values embedded in American theories of natural rights was similar to that of the Progressives, yet, unlike these liberals, Dewey thought the only test of an idea was its effect in a concrete situation. For an engineer, the test of an idea is not its abstract beauty but its practical utility in application. So, too, with Dewey's social engineering. His democratic creed can almost be summarized by a set of methodological injunctions: be bold in imagination, be careful in the examination of a problem, and be intelligent in your evaluations of plans for action. Dewey had faith that by reasoning together Americans could create the "great community." His instrumentalism was designed to help us achieve that goal.

No one has ever accused Oliver Wendell Holmes, Jr., of wanting to be a social engineer. When he said, "I have no belief in panaceas,"[14] Holmes was expressing an attitude shared by Dewey; but, when Holmes considered proposals for reform, his pessimism immediately set him apart from the social engineers. Not only did he doubt the possibility of making America into a New Jerusalem, he also thought there was little likelihood of making significant improvements in the lot of the average man.

Holmes's resistance to the idea of social engineering, his rejection of the optimistic belief in progress shared by Lockean and Darwinian reformers, was based on his acceptance of Malthus. The lot of most men could not be "affected appreciably by any tinkering with the institution of property"[15] because "every social improvement [was] immediately absorbed by an increase in the population."[16] The only hope lay in either a systematic policy of birth control or in eugenics, "by taking in hand life and trying to build a race."[17] Until Western civilization evolved to a point where it would be ready for such proposals—and Holmes saw no likely prospect of it happening—the course of human society would continue to be determined by a struggle for life. Perhaps it would be more accurate to say the struggle to avoid death, for Holmes believed that "every society rests upon the death of men."[18] Man was by nature a predatory animal and the rules of society were based on the will of the dominant segment.[19] To the objection that this view of society meant treating man as a thing, an object, Holmes replied, "If a man lives in society, he is liable to find himself so treated."[20] Holmes was willing to acknowledge that the "sacredness of human life" could be a valid municipal ideal, but he obviously held no such ideal himself. For Holmes, society was not founded on contract and agreement but on force, struggle, and, ultimately, death.

Although he completely accepted the notion of the struggle to avoid death, Holmes did not accept the Social Darwinist's corollary that government could not interfere with this process. The belief that all life was a struggle for survival, when coupled with the idea that society and the State were founded on force and not on principles, led Holmes to the conclusion that various groups in society would seek to use governmental power for advancing their own interests. The businessmen who turned to the courts for "justice" and for the protection of their "natural right" of property were seeking to advance their own interests as much as the farmers and workers demanding substantive changes in the economic system. Because he conceived the State as without moral purposes, Holmes could see no a priori reason for favoring one claim over another.

There was, thus, only one way to approach the traditional American idea of natural rights—with a corrosive skepticism. Like Dewey, Holmes maintained that the whole search for moral and ethical absolutes was marked by men equating certitude with certainty.[21] For Holmes, an individual's rights depended solely upon the expectation that society would enforce those rights. Man's rights were predicated on force, not Nature or Nature's God. "I don't talk much about rights," he wrote Laski, "as I see no meaning in the rights of man except what the crowd will fight for."[22] To him, that did not seem to be the "same thing as the assertion of a preexisting right. A dog will fight for his bone."[23] With a characteristically pithy Darwinian analogy, Holmes abruptly dismissed natural rights theory.

Holmes would not study law in terms of ethical values; he studied it by the science of law. That science was not primarily an enterprise of formal logic; rather, it aimed at laying bare the "often inarticulate and unconscious judgment" "as to the relative worth of competing legislative grounds," which was at "the very root and nerve of the whole proceeding."[24] The legal scholar, according to Holmes, must keep his eye on the main target: the social goals men seek through law.

By focusing on the function of law, of the aims men sought through law, Holmes emphasized that judges could not avoid influencing the direction of social policy when they resolved legal conflicts. He sought to have the courts consciously take their law-making function into consideration as they went about their tasks. Holmes did not want judges to become social engineers, to use their positions for improving society according to *their own* lights; rather, he was asking the judges to put their legal science at the command of the dominant will of society.

By no stretch of the imagination, then, can the legal theory of Oliver Wendell Holmes be called democratic. Its central concepts were that all laws embody certain values and that the dominant interests in society make the law. Holmes attached no special value to majority rule, to representation of competing interests, to contract theory, to the natural rights of man, or even to such vague ideas as the dignity of man. These concepts had been used by Americans as central to their democratic theories, yet they are either absent from the legal theory of Holmes or they are subjected to scathing criticism and discarded as arbitrary value preferences. Not that Holmes's theory was antidemocratic; democracy was simply an irrelevant concept in his theory of law. In the hard, carefully polished Holmesian style there was no room for irrelevancies. Holmes was indeed a rare American, not least because he seemed neutral about or indifferent to democracy.

The deep and lasting impact Holmes undoubtedly made on American ideas about the relationship between democracy and the Constitution is attributable solely to his long tenure on the Supreme Courts of Massachusetts and the United States. His legal theory told him that law reflected the will of the dominant group in any society and that judges should seek to interpret and expound the law according to its basic purpose. Because Holmes identified the dominant group in America as the popular majority,[25] his Court opinions have a decidedly democratic tone. Ironically, a man who was basically neutral as to the value of democracy had a major influence on democratic thought because he became a member of the agency charged with interpreting a republican constitution for an avowedly democratic nation. The accident of position turned the patrician Yankee into a "democratic" theorist.

Not surprisingly, for Justice Holmes the ultimate justification of the Constitution was death. The validity of the Constitution as the constituent act of the nation stemmed from the fact that it had survived because men were willing to die for it. The meaning of the Constitution, then, "must be considered in the light of our whole experience,"[26] and not solely in terms of the Framers' intent. Valid constitutional principles emerged as part of the document in the course of history. Brandeis applied Jeffersonian principles to new conditions; Holmes sought for principles in the process of change itself.

Because in Holmesian theory change was a product of social conflict and the Constitution was to be interpreted in the light of change, the Constitution had to be neutral as to the outcome of the social struggle. Thus, the Justice's famous statement that: "a constitution is not intended to embody a particular economic theory, whether of paternalism and the organic relation of the citizen to the State or of *laissez faire*. It is made for people of fundamentally different views . . . [27] Any other idea would be interpreting the Constitution in a way that would prevent change.

To avoid this interference, said Justice Holmes, the Court must give real meaning to its oft repeated sentiments about the presumptive validity of legislative acts. Since the days of John Marshall, the Court had been pro-claiming that all challenged acts were presumed valid until that presumption was conclusively shown to be false. The Court should now actually operate on that basis. According to Holmes, the doctrine of presumptive validity of governmental acts necessitated the application of judicial self-restraint. The purpose of this judicial self-restraint was to facilitate "the natural outcome of dominant opinion."[28]

In cases involving claims of the deprivation of some economic right protected by the Due Process Clauses, Justice Holmes's approach differed from that of Justice Brandeis as well as from Justice Field. Field construed due process as requiring the protection of private property from all but minimal governmental regulation. While Brandeis and Holmes both urged judicial tolerance of economic and social legislation, they arrived at that conclusion via separate and distinct theories. Justice Brandeis held that when laws were challenged under the Due Process Clauses the government must show a relationship between the means chosen and an authorized power. He always gave the government the benefit of the doubt in these matters. Brandeis would not substitute his notion of the wisest policy for that of the elected officials; but, he demanded reasoned explanation for the officials' decisions. By requiring a demonstration of reasonableness, Brandeis sought to force the government to conceive, develop, and implement policies in accordance with the traditional Lockean values of the American nation. An economic or social policy which could not reasonably be justified in terms of those values was, for Brandeis, an arbitrary exercise of power and hence a violation of due process. Justice Holmes was satisfied that due process had been accorded when the government showed it had the constitutional power to act and that it had not violated some historically well-understood provision of the Constitution.[29]

As a result, on economic and social issues, substantive due process came close to being an empty concept for Holmes. A governmental assertion of power usually sufficed; he rarely urged a detailed investigation into the lines the government drew. Unlike Brandeis, there simply was no need for a Justice with Holmes's legal theory to engage in a careful scrutiny of the circumstances. Despite his attacks on the overly formal, abstract, and logical method used by Justice Field's successors, Holmes used the very same methods—only his categories and premises were different.[30]

Beyond all doubt, Holmes's most famous opinions involve the First Amendment right of free speech. It is difficult to overestimate the impact of those opinions on subsequent American political and constitutional thinking. His *Schenck*[31] opinion supplied the first Supreme Court gloss of the meaning of this right; he made the "clear and present danger" test part of our language and thought. Because varying conceptions of free speech are at the core of all contemporary American theories of democracy, all subsequent theorists have had to come to grips with Holmes's concept of free speech, if only to reject it as inadequate.

The arguments about the meaning, scope, and viability of the "clear and present danger" test are endless, but the sources of the concept in Holmes's thought seem clear enough. First, free speech was an explicitly enumerated right and, as such, part and parcel of the historic Constitution. Second, only a concern for protecting speech would insure that the Constitution was not interpreted to prevent change. Holmes viewed speech in terms of its social function. Ideas were a means by which people asserted their interests and helped bring about the policies they desired. If the Constitution was not to prohibit change it must protect the free exchange of social and political ideas.

This belief in change, in experimentation based upon imperfect knowledge, was then read into the Constitution. In fact, according to Holmes, it is *the* theory of the Constitution. Because free speech is an essential element in the social processes leading to change—it helps to mobilize dominant opinion and, over time, to change that opinion—we must be eternally vigilant against attempts to stifle free speech.[32]

Just what restrictions on free speech Holmes had in mind when he framed the "clear and present danger" test[33] is far from clear. Was the test meant to be a general criterion for constitutionally permitted speech? Or was it limited to those cases where restrictions were justified in terms of national survival? In general, Holmes's opinions do not demonstrate any great concern for extending the opportunity to engage in constitutionally protected speech.[34] His opinions in the Debs[35] and Frokwerk[36] cases, decided the same time as Schenk, and posing the same question, do not use the clear and present danger language at all.

For Holmes, the test was probably never more than a shorthand phrase, his way of saying that a liberty as fundamentally important as free speech should be restricted only for the most important and pressing reasons.[37] So he never bothered to refine the phrase "clear and present danger" to make it a more precise legal test, and his use (or nonuse) of it in subsequent cases only made it more ambiguous.[38]

Be that as it may, there is no doubt that Justice Holmes placed a great value on the free exchange of ideas.[39] Some civil libertarians have complained that the "clear and present danger" test is ambiguous, vague, and therefore useless. Others have said that it does not offer sufficient protection for "the thought we hate." But they, as well as those who still swear by Holmes, must acknowledge their debt to the Justice, for Holmes's opinions dealing with free speech played a significant part—perhaps even a decisive one, given his enormous prestige and authority in later years—in putting the First Amendment's Free Speech Clause squarely on the American liberal agenda. Holmes's "clear and present danger" test was not a major intellectual breakthrough, nor did it solve many problems. Holmes's First Amendment opinions, however, do express the Western liberal tradition's skeptical attitude toward claims of infallibility and absolute truth.

Thus, the Boston Brahmin, whose legal theory contained not a single inherently democratic premise, became the ideal type Justice for those democrats rejecting Lockean values as a priori limitations on the American political process. Doubtful as to the ultimate benefits to be derived from the political struggle, he made doubt itself a virtue: "To have doubted one's own first principles in the mark of a civilized man."[40] The patrician, dispassionate Holmes, with his terse style and memorable epigrams could not fail to be the very archetype of a Justice for those Americans wanting to free their democracy from the fixed values of natural rights theory.

During the first three decades of this century, then, many Americans no longer conceived of the main task of political theory as bringing politics into correspondence with natural rights theory. This attitudinal change, of course, was part of a major trend in political thought throughout the Western world. As Max Weber noted, at this time natural law was deemed to "have lost all capacity to provide the fundamental bases of a legal system."[41]

During the same period, however, the decisions of the Supreme Court which had done so much to discredit natural rights theory in the eyes of Dewey and Holmes also served to conceal the full extent of change. The reformers engaged in the political struggle focused attention on the Court's role in American politics, a role most Justices continued to see primarily as an institutionalized protection of man's right of property. Dissenting from most of these decisions, Brandeis amassed data to show that the laws were plainly constitutional and Holmes used his skepticism to show they were not, at any rate, plainly unconstitutional. In the heat of the struggle, few bothered to distinguish the theory of Holmes from that of Brandeis; liberals were united by the fixed conservative reaction to social experimentation. There was no need to be concerned about John Locke when struggling with Justice Sutherland.

When the Great Depression came, the Court at first seemed willing to require a more tolerant attitude of social and economic legislation.[42] The decisions, however, had been close—Justice Roberts and Chief Justice Hughes joining the trio of Justices (Brandeis, Stone, and Cardozo) who consistently supported social welfare programs. The four other Justices—Sutherland, McReynolds, Van Devanter, and Butler—continued to maintain that an emergency did not justify infringing on the right to own, use, and enjoy property.

In 1935, "the New Deal was revealed in all its terrifying dimensions to the conservatives of the nation."[43] Justice Roberts and usually Chief Justice Hughes joined the Old Guard in striking down major New Deal programs using Commerce Clause doctrines enunciated by the Court at the turn of the century.[44] State laws were not immune either—under the liberty of contract doctrine a New York minimum wage statute was found unconstitutional.[45] The Court majority was acting to protect the private economy from substantial regulation.

Unwilling and unable to function within the pattern the Supreme Court was imposing upon the nation, the liberals mounted a massive attack on the Court. The gravity of the emergency had produced an unprecedented demand for remedial legislation. When the Court threatened the whole reform effort, some attacked the Supreme Court for even having the power of judicial review, not merely for using that power foolishly. They had come to agree with Dewey, at least temporarily, that democracy was defined solely by the processes of finding electoral and legislative majorities within the system. Others attacked the interpretations of the Court majority, citing the powerful dissents of Brandeis, Stone, and Cardozo. These critics felt that the Court majority's faulty reading of the Constitution was frustrating attempts to insure equal opportunity. The Court was attacked as never before.

President Franklin D. Roosevelt, fresh from his landslide election in 1936, introduced his Court "reform" plan and brought the crisis to a climax. Before Congress acted, a Court majority indicated that they were now prepared to accept legislation previously held unconstitutional. The Court upheld, five to four, a state minimum wage law, explicitly overruling the liberty of contract doctrine.[46] Two weeks later, the same majority—Chief Justice

Hughes and Justices Brandeis, Stone, Cardozo, and Roberts—upheld the Wagner Labor Relations Act, rejecting the narrow interpretation of interstate commerce.[47] Later that term, the same majority upheld the Social Security Act, even though it imposed a tax for purposes Congress could not then reach via the commerce power.[48] The revolution in American constitutional law had begun. When it was completed in the early 1940s, the entire economic part of the Cooley-Field theory of the Constitution—the very heart of that theory—had been rejected.[49]

Soon the recalcitrant Justices left the Court, encouraged by a more generous pension system and a sustained sense of futility. The four Old Guard "villains" in the liberal scenario had rendered the reformers a significant service: their adamancy had united all reform elements and helped conceal the extent of change in the thinking of some reformers. As Justices Butler, Van Devanter, Sutherland, and McReynolds were replaced by Franklin D. Roosevelt appointees, most of the issues which had been shaping American constitutional theory passed from the scene.

The new Justices were united in their toleration of social and economic experimentation. The Court would still play a role—insured by federalism—and the Brandeis approach to due process permitted it. The Court's economic role, however, would be minor. Economic and social policy could vary pretty much at the will of the electoral majority and their elected leadership so long as it did not interfere with a constitutional right.

This qualification, in turn, meant that the Court's role in defining the pattern of governmental policy would be determined by the Justices' theory of the nature of those rights and their view of the Court's function in a democracy. Though the issues had changed and, with them, certain theories of democracy, the 1937 revolution in constitutional law had not changed one basic fact of American politics: the Supreme Court still existed as an institution and its powers remained intact. The use of that power, in the future as in the past, would be determined in large part by the democratic theory of each Justice.

II

CONTEMPORARY THEORIES OF DEMOCRACY: THE COMPETITIVE THEORIES

Five

THE COMPETITIVE PARADIGM FOR DEMOCRACY

The challenge to the natural rights paradigm which began with men like Dewey and Holmes was carried still further by social scientists. From the beginning of this century they have been investigating the American political system. As the years went by and the amount and precision of their information increased, social scientists saw that certain concepts did not conform to the data. Since those concepts had been derived from traditional notions of democracy, the social scientists began to question the democratic theories propounded by distinguished American thinkers of the past. In the two decades after World War II their questioning led them to reject the traditional paradigm itself.

In its place, contemporary American social scientists accepted a new definition of democracy as their basic paradigm. The new notion was stated in a nutshell in a definition by Joseph A. Schumpeter: "the democratic method is that institutional arrangement for arriving at political decisions in which individuals acquire the power to decide by means of a competitive struggle for the people's vote."[1] By accepting this definition the social scientists consciously rejected the historical American paradigm. The rule of the people had been a core concept of past democratic theories. The Anti-Federalists, the Jeffersonians, the Jacksonians, the Whigs, the Republicans, the Populists, and the Progressives had all maintained that in a democracy governmental policy must flow from the wishes of the people. Despite the authority vested in the traditional paradigm by its association with great names in American history, the social scientists opted for a new definition of democracy.

THE WEAKNESS OF THE TRADITIONAL PARADIGM[2]

No matter which way they looked at the functioning political system in the United States, social scientists could not use government by the popular majority as a core concept in their democratic theory. The people, or even the popular majority, could not be said to rule through a shared conception of the public good which could be translated into public policy by their agents. In twentieth-century America there was no interest sufficiently cohesive and inclusive to guide public policy on a wide range of issues. Whatever may have been the case in an agrarian society of freeholders, social scientists writing after World War II knew that industrialization had led to a complex social structure with diverse interests. The diversity of economic functions and the multiplicity of ethnic and religious groups shattered the idea of a unified public. The concentration of decision making in large organizations in both the public and private sectors further belied the reality of government by public opinion. To post–World War II social scientists, pluralism and organization, not a unified public, were the dominant realities of the American polity.[3]

Nor could the social scientists argue that democracy meant a system of government in which the people instruct their agents on specific issues through the electoral process. Instead of treating the majority as united by a common conception of the public interest, the public could be viewed as composed of atomistic individuals, each with his own private interests. If democracy is conceived in this way, each individual calculates his own interests, and when the sum of private interests results in a numerical majority public policy is determined. Democracy, according to this theory, would be the institutionalization of the Benthamite calculus—the greatest good for the greatest number based on each individual's calculation of his own interest.[4]

Here again a plausible theory of democracy yielded to the evidence. To act on an issue a person must first be aware of its existence and then have an opinion. The American electorate, however, was not aware to the extent required to set policy in a direct way. Based on survey data, as V.O. Key put it, "substantial percentages of the population were shown to remain happily unaware even of issues that commanded the attention of Congress for weeks, provided screaming banners for newspapers, and occupied the time of frenetic newscasters."[5] Major decisions of our government could not possibly be made at the direct command of the American popular majority.

Social scientists' examination of political parties was yet another reason for concluding that the people do not, in any meaningful way, determine policy. Both the Democratic and Republican parties are multifactional coalitions. They undoubtedly perform many functions, but they rarely offer clear policy choices to the electorate. Lacking sustained and distinct party platforms, the major American parties cannot serve as vehicles through which the people register their opinions about governmental policy. At times, the parties do indeed offer the public a choice rather than an echo, but that choice has plainly not been the case for long periods in American history. It was not the case, for example, during the first two decades after World War II when most American social scientists rejected the heretofore traditional paradigm.

Moreover, the survey data generated by the social scientists indicated that most Americans did not make their electoral choice primarily on the basis of ideology. The studies showed the people had almost no conception of the actual policy stands of our political parties.[6] Indeed, at times more people voted for the party *they themselves* perceived as being further away from their own ideological preferences.[7] The people did not always act in an ideologically consistent manner.[8] Social scientists, therefore, could not accept a theory based upon the idea that the voters controlled the course of future policy by consciously choosing between conflicting views of the public interest.

Thus, in the period after World War II, no matter which way they looked at the functioning political system of the United States, social scientists believed they could not use the concept of government by the popular majority as part of a viable scientific theory of democracy. They could not treat their own findings as anomalies; there were too many and they all pointed in the same direction.

American intellectuals also felt a need to reassess their ideas about democracy in light of the new world situation. There was increased social pressure—encouraged and fostered by government leaders[9]—for developing a democratic theory to counter first the Fascist and then the Communist challenges to "our way of life." In the "struggle for men's minds," a political theory which had ceased to explain the workings of existing democracies could be labeled propaganda and would be counterproductive. The world situation had increased the pressure on American intellectuals to reassess their ideas about democracy. The American social scientists never doubted that the United States was, in fact, an example of a functioning democracy; that belief was just too ingrained, too fundamental, to be cast aside. When some European social scientists—Mosca and Pareto, for example—had found that the people did not, and probably could not, govern, they had denounced democracy as a sham and a fraud, as just one more myth to delude the common man. When American social scientists came to the same conclusions about the United States, they did not reject the first article in their society's political creed. Instead of renouncing democracy, they opted for a new paradigm.

If the new paradigm could not use the role of the popular majority as a central concept, neither would the social scientists use other concepts of Lockean theory. In the past, when Americans wished to oppose or limit the idea of popular majoritarianism, they had invariably constructed a political theory around the individual natural rights of men. Field and Cooley, for example, had espoused a political and legal theory of democracy stressing man's right to property. American social scientists, however, did not take this route. They were part of the tradition which had developed in opposition to the idea that society was governed by immutable natural laws or unidirectional, inevitable laws of evolution. They had participated in (or observed at first hand) the struggle against the decisions of the conservative Justices on the Supreme Court, decisions based on the theory of Field and Cooley. Those decisions only confirmed the social scientists' belief that any theory based on fixed transcendental values was inherently unscientific. Because the Court majority had refused to demonstrate the worth of maintaining man's immutable rights in terms of social costs, they had made the entire higher law tradition seem subjective and arbitrary. In the eyes of American social scientists, natural rights theory was a discredited doctrine. They were the intellectual heirs of Dewey and Holmes.

A new social science paradigm for democracy, then, had to satisfy two negative conditions. It must avoid concepts like popular majoritarianism and it could not use concepts whose validity depended upon some transcendental value system. These constraints were operative when the social scientists came to reassess their ideas about democracy.

THE VIRTUES OF THE COMPETITIVE PARADIGM

The reassessment of democratic theory ultimately led to a new paradigm. Dissatisfied with the explanatory power of the traditional paradigm, social scientists were receptive to new ideas. Schumpeter shared the dissatisfaction; because of it he defined democracy in terms of the competitive struggle for power.[10] When his claim that his new definition could account for the empirical data was substantiated, his fellow social scientists were impressed. As the new conception also proved to be a fruitful source for continued investigation of American democracy, they were convinced.[11] Because of its ability to resolve the existing crisis and its success in guiding future research, Schumpeter's definition became the basic social science paradigm for democracy.

Does the pluralistic nature of American society prevent the emergence of a unified public opinion about the common good? No matter. The competitive paradigm is not dependent upon the existence of a shared conception of the public interest; pluralism is easily accommodated within the competitive struggle for power. In such a system governors must always operate with the fear that the opposition might seize upon an issue to catapult themselves into office. The politicians have few reliable gauges of what their constituents are thinking, and more important, how deeply the public feels about issues. In the face of this uncertainty, prudence requires politicians to pay attention to the demands of groups claiming support among their constituents.[12] If "access" to governmental officials is the first requisite for the political success of an organized group, its ultimate success depends upon the self-interest of the politicians. The political activity of organized groups does not explain all of American politics, but whatever part of that process can be explained in terms of group activity can be accounted for within the Schumpeter paradigm.

Do the American people lack the information they need for accurate perceptions of the issues and for wise decision making? The competitive paradigm assumes that people are incapable of governing. In Schumpeter's definition the political function of the electorate is to produce a government, not to govern. One of the things the social scientists liked most about the new paradigm was that it assigns functions in the political process which seem to match capabilities: the people select the government and the government rules.

Thus the competitive paradigm explicitly acknowledges the importance of leadership. Not only do the political leaders decide issues by framing government policies, but, because the general public is politically uninformed and inarticulate, the leadership raises most issues in the first place. The strongly felt demands of the electorate do occasionally set the political agenda. Those demands, however, only become politically important when politicians decide they can be exploited in the interests of obtaining or retaining office. According to the competitive paradigm, issues enter the political arena as part of the politicians' struggle for office.

Do parts of the electorate cast their votes on the basis of their commitment to a particular ideology? Surely. But now, the very existence of those long-standing party loyalties can be explained more rationally. Faced with the need for distinguishing themselves from one another in order to win elections, the leadership of each party seeks a distinctive ideological image. In turn, organized groups mobilize support for the party which favors their special interest. Over time, a circular reinforcement pattern sets in: the organized groups ally themselves with the party most receptive to their demands and each party supports the groups which help it at the polls.[13] By emphasizing certain elements in the party platform, the party's programs help create its public image. The electorate's ideological image is related to acts of the competing leaderships.

Given each party's need to develop its own distinctive image in a competitive election system, why has the ideological cleavage in American politics remained so slight? The major reason, of course, is that politics has so little relevance for so many people that ideology cannot be the primary basis of their electoral choice. Why did this situation, so markedly different than the European democratic experience, develop in the United States? The answer to this question can also be approached within the confines of the competitive paradigm. Again, the starting point is that ideology is a product of the party leaders. Their primary purpose is winning elections, not expounding ideas. Although the standing alliances between parties and groups at any given time is beneficial to the then dominant party, the same cannot be said for the minority party. To break out of its position, the opposition party offers programs to attract groups away from the majority coalition. Often, this means the minority party must support many of the same proposals as the majority. What prevents the parties from being completely identical is both the need to retain a distinct public image and the fact that it is devilishly hard to add new groups without alienating some of the old. In a two-party competitive election system there is likely to be issue consensus as well as issue cleavage among the party leaders. This complex situation is bound to be confusing to the voters; even the more attentive are likely to develop only the vaguest images of our parties.

The competitive paradigm for democracy, then, can account for marked ideological differences among the party elites, for issue consensus among those elites, and even for the total absence of the seemingly relevant issues from the political arena. This explanation appears to be a classic example of explaining nothing by explaining everything. Actually, it shows that the competitive paradigm is not dependent upon political issues at all; on this point it is entirely neutral. A country may be a democracy, according to this paradigm, regardless of the extent of political discussion in that country, provided that discussion is not systematically precluded. A country's parties may be ideologically distinct or Tweedledee or Tweedledum, they may offer the people a choice or an echo, and the governmental system may still be a democracy. According to the competitive paradigm, issues enter democratic politics when advantageous to one or another group of political leaders; issue conflict is not demanded by democracy itself. The essential condition for democracy is only the "free competition for the free vote."[14]

Consequently, the competitive paradigm is not affected by the findings about electoral behavior. In this idea of democracy, it does not matter if Republican followers have occasionally supported the domestic policies of the Democratic leadership. What is important is that the voters were offered a choice at election time between opposing candidates freely competing for office. That many people vote for candidates on the basis of considerations other than issues, is, according to Schumpeter's definition, no reason to question the existence of a democratic political system. For the social scientist, the low issue orientation of most voters is a fact to be explained,[15] or a situation to be remedied to make the United States a *more perfect* democracy;[16] but, within the competitive paradigm, it and similar facts cannot be used to question the existence of democracy. Democracy's existence is determined by the presence of a system of free competitive elections.

Ironically, by their reliance upon the competitive paradigm the social scientists found themselves presenting a very institutional view of the democratic political process. The revolt against the formalism of the traditional paradigm was conducted with the behavioral techniques of social science. To explain the behavioral data, however, the new men of science accepted an equally formal, legalistic definition of democracy: a system of free competitive elections.

The new formulation also gave indication of being a fruitful source of new investigations. By accepting the importance of leadership, a key element in the competitive paradigm, the social scientists accepted the necessity of giving the government the means to govern. The debate about the merits of positive government ended. The detailed discussion of the method by which elected leaders can control the administrative apparatus began.[17]

Similarly, the competitive paradigm seemed successful in matching fact with theory. A striking example was its explanation for the cyclical pattern of one party's dominance for an extended period. Critical election theory centers on the competing party leaderships. When a major calamity occurs, if the party in power handles it effectively no change occurs. If, in the eyes of the public, those in power fail, a major realignment of the parties does not automatically take place. Only if a new leadership group convinces the public it is handling the problem effectively does that happen. Thus, the responsibility for the cyclical pattern of party dominance is with those who, according to the competitive paradigm, really govern in a democracy—the leadership elements.[18]

The final virtue which strongly recommended the competitive paradigm to social scientists was the intimate relationship it developed between democracy and individual freedom. The felt need to explicate the advantages of democracy had added to the dissatisfaction with the old paradigm. Schumpeter's definition could not only explain how a democratic political system like the United States "really" operates, it could also emphasize the importance of individual freedom in a democracy. To contemporary social scientists confronted with the spectre of modern totalitarianism, nothing was more important than individual freedom.

Schumpeter had defined democracy as the "free competition for the free vote." If political leaders are to compete for public support they need the freedom to communicate with the public. Because everyone is *formally* free to compete for political leadership by campaigning for office, the system requires a significant amount of free speech for individual citizens.[19] Similarly, if the decision of the electorate is to be meaningful, the people cannot be coerced. An electoral decision made by individuals operating under fear of reprisals would make a mockery out of a system in which "the reins of government should be handed to those who command more support than do any of the competing individuals or teams."[20]

Further, as Schumpeter clearly saw, his definition enabled social scientists to make a clear distinction between democracy and other forms of government—in a democracy the rulers are periodically selected by free elections. Once this litmus-like test was applied and the world's governments were categorized as democratic or nondemocratic, the social scientists could defend the former in terms of personal freedom.[20]

The connection between democracy and freedom, like other ideas in Schumpeter's definition, was subsequently articulated in greater detail by other social scientists. The more it was developed, the more satisfied the social scientists became with the competitive paradigm. Faced with societal pressure to explain the virtue of democracy in the battle for men's minds, American social scientists placed ever greater stress on the advantages a democracy extends to its citizens in terms of individual freedom.[22] Except for rhetorical flourishes about the Western tradition, democracy's virtues were not expounded by using notions developed from the traditional natural rights paradigm. This defense of democracy was not based upon faith in transcendental values; it relied only on the close logical and functional necessity for personal liberty in a system built around free competition for the free vote. Such an argument had obvious advantages in a period dominated by scientifically inspired skepticism and value relativism. Using the competitive paradigm, social scientists could and did make the existence of civil rights the key virtue of democracy.

Schumpeter's definition of democracy did more than offer the social scientists a possible solution to the problems provoked by the traditional paradigm's inability to account for the empirical data. It also provided a fruitful source for new investigations and new explanations, and it had the great positive advantage of enabling social scientists to extol the virtues of democracy as a system which protects individual liberty.

Little wonder, then, that the competitive paradigm pervaded the social science literature of the post–World War II generation. Social scientists concerned about democratic theory invariably subscribed to some version of that paradigm. Two political sociologists, Robert M. MacIver and Seymour Martin Lipset, argued that the public, or at least the electoral majority, retained some influence over the major trends of policy primarily through the com-

tin Lipset, argued that the public, or at least the electoral majority, retained some influence over the major trends of policy primarily through the competitive electoral process.[23] Three eminent political scientists, V. O. Key, Robert A. Dahl, and David Truman, maintained we must not overlook such "linkages" between rulers and ruled as groups and associations.[24] But, of course, the three political scientists agreed that the existence of free competitive elections was the necessary precondition for insuring that political leaders will be responsive to the wishes of the ordinary citizen. Even those social scientists doubting the efficacy of popular influence on public policy under the existing system—E. E. Schattschneider, for example—maintained that "democracy is a political system in which the people have a choice among the alternatives created by competing political organizations and leaders."[25] When the competitive paradigm was not explicitly stated, the social scientists assumed it.[26] It became commonplace in political science I textbooks.[27] After World War II, social scientists viewed democracy as the free competition for the free vote. Schumpeter's definition became the social science paradigm for democracy.

Six

REALIST THEORY

The competitive paradigm has become widely accepted and has been used in several ways by its American proponents. Designed to account for empirical data about the democratic political process, it has been used in differing prescriptive political theories. This chapter is devoted to an analysis of one such theory—the realist theory of democracy.

The distinctive feature of realist theory is its justification, in practice and by implication, of existing American political processes. This feature has some noteworthy consequences. The competitive paradigm gained adherents because it could spell out the close logical connection between democracy and the liberties most Americans believe essential for human dignity. Realist theory has often been used to justify governmental restrictions of basic individual freedoms. In this democratic theory, the Constitution is no longer seen as a uniform and universally recognized supreme law designed to mold society in a particular image. Instead it is seen primarily as outlining the peculiarly American way of carrying out the competitive struggle for power. To the adherents of realist theory, the Constitution has frequently lacked any other substantive content and is therefore unable to restrict or limit the policies of agencies directly associated with the competitive electoral process.

REALIST THEORY AND THE COMPETITIVE PARADIGM

The place to begin is with the transformation of Schumpeter's descriptive definition into this prescriptive political theory. To Schumpeter, the competitive paradigm was most explicitly not a defense of democratic politics. He saw democracy as a method for arriving at political decisions. It was not an end in itself, no more than any other method could be. If a man valued democracy, it was because in his circumstances that method was producing results he favored. Schumpeter formulated his definition of democracy solely to explain a method of governing.[1]

To serve as a defense of democracy, however, a theory that would also justify the results produced by the democratic method was needed. Those proponents of the competitive paradigm most concerned about defending democracy from the Fascist and especially the Communist challenges have used it in a way explicitly rejected by Schumpeter—as a defense of democracy as the ultimate good.

The first step was to resurrect the permanent relevance of issues to the competitive struggle for power. The second was to change Schumpeter's *logical connection* between democracy and freedom into an established *result* of the democratic political process. Democracy could then be seen as the method best designed to give the people what they wanted while simultaneously preserving their freedom.

The Realist Social Scientists

Although Schumpeter's formulation could account for the empirical data of American politics, its acceptance also involved certain costs. Not the least of these was the loss of one of democracy's great, historic attractions: the idea that democracy means self-government. In Schumpeter's definition, the people's function is limited to selecting the government.

Schumpeter's separation of issues and democracy has been least palatable to those American thinkers intent upon using the competitive paradigm as a defense of democracy. "In this respect," wrote Robert Dahl, "the otherwise excellent analysis of democracy in Joseph A. Schumpeter, *Capitalism, Socialism and Democracy* . . . seems to me somewhat defective."[2] Only if the people *necessarily* have some impact on governmental policy, only if popular ideas were somehow related to at least some major decisions could American social scientists use the competitive paradigm in a prescriptive theory of democracy.

In arguing that citizens do, to some extent, influence policy in a systematic way, the Realist is able to maintain that democracy still means self-government. True, it is no longer the self-government of the New England town meeting, but it is a means by which people in a large society can have some say about major policy decisions. How does a democratic citizen participate in policy making in realist theory? How, in other words, is it still possible for a Realist to say that people are self-governing?

The answer depends upon the theorist. To Robert M. MacIver and Seymour Martin Lipset, a citizen participates in government policy making by selecting those rulers he believes will advance his own interests, particularly his economic interest.[3] Because political parties enable the people to influence the basic societal decisions affecting their lives, Lipset can say that "democracy is not only or even primarily a means through which different groups can attain their ends or seek the good society; it is the good society itself in operation."[4]

The self-governing process as described by Professors Dahl* and Key is more complex. For these political scientists there is no direct, immediate link, as with MacIver and Lipset, between elections and policy. According to Professor Dahl, "In no large nation state can elections tell us much about the preferences of majorities and minorities beyond the bare fact that among those who went to the polls a majority, plurality, or minority indicated their first choices for some particular candidate or group of candidates."[6]

Aware that this position seemed to drive the notion of self-government from a free competitive election system, Professor Key, in his last work, attempted to salvage that idea. Scrupulous scholar that he was, however, Key did not think the empirical date permitted him to go as far as MacIver and Lipset. All he could say was that national elections "reflect the electorate in its great, and perhaps principal role as an appraiser of past events, past performances and past actions. It judges retrospectively; it commands prospectively only insofar as it expresses either approval or disapproval of that which has happened."[7]

This argument hardly reasserts the idea of self-government. Because the citizen is stripped of his ability to select his ruler on the basis of his appraisal of party ideologies, Key effectively denied the citizen's ability to make rational *prospective* decisions through our election system. In turn, this view of the

---

*Professor Dahl later rethought this issue and came to the conclusion that meaningful popular influence on the policies of a large nation state is probably impossible on a systematic basis. Since I am more interested in the content of each political theory than in its advocates, and because Professor Dahl invariably illuminates what he discusses, I have used his earlier writings to clarify realist theory. The reader should note, however, that the works cited in this chapter may no longer represent Dahl's thought.[5]

citizen's ability means that the minority party "must appear to be a common scold rather than a bold exponent of innovation."[8] Self-government is thereby reduced to saying yea or nay the next time the actual governors of society come up for reelection. At most, according to Key, that decision will be made on an appraisal of past actions. During the crises which confront any society from time to time, at turning points in a country's history, the people are capable of giving only the vaguest of all prospective mandates: do something, quickly!

In the realist theory of Dahl and Key, elections may be a crucially important *prerequisite* for popular influence on policy making, but they are not the principal vehicle for exerting that influence.[9] It is the pluralistic nature of American society which enables the citizen to have some influence on public policy.[10] Each party is constantly seeking to put together an electoral majority (or plurality) for the next election. Their success depends upon aggregating a winning combination from among the diverse groups in our society. To Key, the politicians' necessary responsiveness to group demands means that a parallelism develops between the policy stands of a party's leadership and its supporters.[11] To Dahl, the necessary responsiveness to group demands means that the "making of governmental decisions . . . is the steady appeasement of relatively small groups." Through the politicians' need to build and rebuild electoral alliances, "minorities rule."[12] The office seeker's self-interest forces him to be concerned about the claims of the diverse groups in his constituency and enables the people to exert some influence on policy. The citizen has some say over how he is governed not as a voter but as a member of various interest groups. Because of American pluralism it would be unwise to underestimate the extent to which voters may exert *indirect* influence on the decisions of leaders by means of elections.[13]

Thus MacIver, Lipset, Dahl, and Key all accepted the competitive paradigm embodied in Schumpeter's definition: democracy is the method by which certain people acquire the power to make political decisions by means of a competitive struggle for the people's vote. These social scientists also insisted, however, that this system is the only known method by which a large number of people can help determine the policies shaping their lives. In the hands of the realist social scientists the competitive paradigm thereby became more than the descriptive model it was for Schumpeter. They were not saying merely that this is how certain political systems operate; they were saying that this is how political systems should operate if they are to be reasonably good governments. The model was reified; an "is" became an "ought." Enter the realist theory of democracy.

The Realist Theory of Sidney Hook

The realist version of the competitive paradigm also appears in the writings of a leading American philosopher, Sidney Hook, the self-proclaimed chief disciple of John Dewey.[14] The key to understanding Hook's theory of democracy is in comprehending what he means by the method of democracy. His definition of democracy is, for an American, very conventional: "A democratic society is one where the government rests upon the freely given consent of the governed."[15] Hook, however, immediately restates this paraphrase of the Declaration of Independence exclusively in terms of the electoral system. Periodically, the governing group in a democratic society submits its policies to the governed for approval or disapproval. A country whose rulers are chosen by the uncoerced decision of the majority is a democracy.[16] Hook's definition of democracy is exactly the same as the realist social scientists.

By defining democracy exclusively by electoral procedures, Hook can answer the question of whether a government is democratic. It is simply a matter of empirical verification[17] This advantage is exactly one of the great virtues Schumpeter claimed for the competitive paradigm and is the way the paradigm has been used by the realist social scientists.[18] Professor Hook, however, does not regard the competitive paradigm solely as a descriptive account of democratic political systems. Instead, taking it as an accurate description of how democracy works, Hook treats it as an hypothesis and evaluates its consequences.[19] His analysis leads to the conclusion that democracy is the best available system of government.

Professor Hook believes that one immediate and crucially important consequence of democracy is the preservation of individual freedom. Without freedom of speech, press, and assembly, without protection from government pressure insured by procedural safeguards such as fair trial, there could be no political opposition. Without political opposition the electorate cannot be said to have freely given their consent to their present rulers. Political freedom, therefore, is the minimum necessary condition of a democracy, and insofar as a democracy doesn't treat all citizens equally in this respect it is imperfect. Democracy, according to Hook, is the one system in which equal political freedom of all its members is a necessary requirement.[20]

About this logical and necessary requirement of democracy Schumpeter and Hook are in complete agreement. Professor Hook, however, makes one additional point: democracies do, in fact, respect the freedom of their citizens. Thus Hook is able to say that in the actual world democratic government is better than any other form of government.[21]

Another significant consequence which develops from the institutionalized free competitive struggle for power is a cluster of values Professor Hook calls ethical democracy. In a democracy, he maintains, political equality creates a moral imperative for treating individuals of unequal talents and endowments as persons equally entitled to relevant consideration and care.[22]

Just as important for Hook is the fact that when democracy institutionalizes the consent of the governed on the question of who shall be their rulers, it simultaneously institutionalizes the conditions most likely to create reasonable policies. For an instrumentalist, reasonable policies are those which most people support as satisfactory ways of solving their personal and community problems. The political participation, as a matter of right, of people with differing views makes each man aware of the needs of others and thereby enlarges everyone's perspective. Because a properly functioning democracy formulates policy by the methods of public discussion, criticism, argument, and rejoinder, its decisions are more likely to be reasonable.[23]

Not only is this institutionalization of the scientific method more likely to produce reasonable policies, but the instrumental method is the real basis for consensus, solidarity, and loyalty. A political system built upon a particular normative theory containing substantive values is bound to alienate those holding rival theories, Hook argues: "For what could be clearer than the perception that it is notoriously much more difficult to win agreement for a set of metaphysical or theological premises than for a pattern of institutional behavior which because it is neutral to any kind of transcendental notions can let them all flourish?"[24] The application of the instrumentalist method of meeting problems enables a democracy to bridge rifts which divide men, to extend the community of shared values. The democratic community is the result of the successful application of the method of democracy—instrumentalism.

Hook's evaluation of the consequences of democracy produces an entirely favorable judgment. Of course Hook is not claiming that these norms are guaranteed by democracy, for the freely given consent of the governed does not guarantee just or wise decisions. Hook does argue that democracy is the necessary though not sufficient condition for the continuation of Anglo-American liberties and values.[25] He also claims that the actual operations of Western democracies have produced consequences favorable to their citizenry. While philosophically rejecting the notion that democracy can be an absolute value, his examination of the consequences from existing democratic systems leads to the conclusion that democracy is the best form of government: "When democracy is taken strictly as a form of political government, its superiority over other forms of government can be established to the extent that it achieves more security, freedom, and cooperative diversity than any of its alternatives."[26] Professor Hook sees everything that the institutionalization of freely given consent can make, and, behold, it is very good.

When Hook makes the connection between certain rights and democracy he introduces a problem never explicitly confronted by Dewey. Following Dewey, he holds that values emerge in a problem context; he cannot argue that any values are fixed, i.e. that they are *always* relevant in the sense of producing desirable consequences in all situations. Hook maintains, however, that certain values—strategic political freedoms, he calls them—are fundamental to the workings of a democracy. The central theoretical problem to be confronted when establishing a government is, therefore, "who is to determine which rights are fundamental, and which are to receive precedence when rights conflict as they often do."[27] Hook must supply an answer which satisfies the twin requirements of his democratic theory: it must unite instrumentalism and certain Anglo-American rights.

In essence, he combines these factors by building upon the pluralism inherent in Dewey's theory. Dewey maintained there was no standing majority and that the very process of forming a majority from among divergent social groups was more likely to produce reasonable policies than any other system. Hook agrees. Then he is always careful to spell out the conditions for insuring that the majority is not coerced—the lessons of the majorities produced by modern totalitarian regimes have not been lost on Hook. Because strategic freedoms are the essential conditions for meaningful choice at the polls, he believes that the process of finding an electoral majority in a democracy involves a respect for those political rights. The democratic process of periodically electing the leadership group, Hook asserts, is the best guarantee of the rights of man, as well as of reasonable policies. Like Lincoln, Hook regards the only real alternatives to the democratic process of governing by the consent of the electoral majority as anarchy or despotism.[28]

What, then, of the Supreme Court of the United States, a nonelected group of nine individuals with life tenure and considerable power to make policy? Judicial review, Hook maintains, makes the Court supreme, not coordinate with the other organs of government. Nor does Professor Hook believe the Court can reasonably be cast as a liberty-loving institution. Its past record of long indifference to segregation and its usual practice of sustaining congressional laws when challenged on First Amendment grounds should be enough, he feels, to convince even the most ardent supporter of judicial review that the Court is not significantly superior to Congress and the President as a protector of the country's liberties. Further, Hook always asks us to remember how the pre-1937 Court used its powers for protecting what the judicial majority (but not the popular majority) thought was the most precious of all liberties—economic freedom.[29] According to Hook, the "power [of judicial review] is patently incompatible with the assumptions of a democratic, self-governing community";[30] it was recognized as such by the founding generation,[31] and thus poses a threat to the people's liberties.

Hook proposes two methods for excising this important undemocratic feature from our governmental system. One would be a rule requiring judicial unanimity before a congressional or presidential (though not a state) decree is declared unconstitutional. "That this rule would have a restricting influence on the power of the Court is obviously true, but it mitigates the galling possibility that where constitutional issues of life and death are at stake, the vote of one man would be decisive against the deliberative processes of representative government."[32] There would be an additional benefit. By giving Congress and the President the almost exclusive responsibility for determining the constitutionality of an act, Hook believes the elected leaders would be more conscientious about their constitutional obligations. The elected leaders would not be as able to pass the buck to the Supreme Court; the Court would no longer be considered the sole repository of constitutional wisdom.[33]

Hook would go even further in the event that his proposed unanimity rule did not prevent serious conflict between Congress and the Court. He would then favor an amendment giving Congress the power to override a unanimous Court by a two-thirds vote of the entire membership of each chamber. A unanimous judicial decision that an act was unconstitutional would not be the end of discussion; it would signal the beginning of a great national debate. This debate would make for better decisions in the long run because:

> The democratic decision is much more likely to be a right decision when it is an informed decision. An informed decision, hammered out in the give and take of public debate, would be closer to the second thoughts and reflective will of the people—whose conscience the Court would like to be—than the closed discussions of the Court's . . . briefing sessions.[34]

These drastic alterations in our current political system are proposed in the name of reform, in the name of perfecting our existing democracy by making it still more democratic. Democracy, for Hook, means that the free consent of the governed is expressed in the electoral process and in the decisions of the representatives selected by that process. Within Hook's realist theory, authority is derived solely from the electoral processes. Public officials who are not periodically elected have no independent source of authority. That objection is the core of Hook's attack upon the Supreme Court: the Justices are currently exercising power without authority. His reforms are intended to unite power and authority in the only way consistent with this theory of democracy. The authoritative allocation of values must be made solely through the free electoral processes of representative government.

THE REALIST THEORY OF JUSTICES FRANKFURTER AND HARLAN

The constitutional interpretations of Justices Felix Frankfurter and John Marshall Harlan were rooted in the realist theory of democracy. This commonality does not mean the Justices invariably reached the same conclusion in any given case;[35] they simply shared a basic theoretical conception of the nature of American democracy that profoundly influenced their opinions. Although neither Justice ever endorsed the radical formal restraints on the Supreme Court's power proposed by Professor Hook, their attitudes of how the Court should use its existing power can best be understood in the context of realist theory. Like Hook, Frankfurter and Harlan defined American democracy in terms of the free electoral processes of representative government.

While still a professor at the Harvard Law School, Frankfurter wrote that "the very notion of democracy implies the right of the public to decide" major policies "on its own choice."[36] For this assertion about the meaning of democracy he gave the same reasons that later appeared in scores of his judicial opinions. As the Justice put it in 1949, the people must have ultimate say regarding large policy decisions because: "[M]atters of policy . . . are by definition matters which demand the resolution of conflicts of values, and the elements of conflicting values are largely imponderable. Assessment of their competing worth involves differences of feeling; it is also an exercise of prophecy."[37]

Justices Frankfurter and Harlan recognized that the people are in no position to make the actual accommodations of conflicting values. That being the case, they believed it was obvious that "the proper forum for mediating a clash of feelings and rendering a prophetic judgment is the body chosen for those purposes by the people."[38] As Justice Harlan once put it, "legislators can represent their electors *only* by speaking for their interests—economic, social, political . . . ."[39] The elected agents of the people are authorized to decide policy because they were elected to make those decisions, selected on the basis of how they would make those decisions, and are directly responsible to the people for making those decisions.[40]

Holding the same theory of democracy as Professor Hook, Frankfurter and Harlan had similar misgivings about the political power of the Supreme Court. Like Hook, Justice Frankfurter always supported this notion by pointing out that the Justices were appointed for life and that the secrecy of their deliberations removed them from the pressures generated by conflicting groups in the electorate. Having defined democracy in terms of realist theory, Justice Frankfurter could not help but see the Supreme Court as "inherently oligarchic."[41]

Like Professor Hook, both Justices continually warned of the danger to American democracy inherent in the Court's active use of its power of judicial review. Above and beyond the possibility of judicial decisions running counter to prevailing opinions, thereby temporarily frustrating democratic decisions, lay the long-term impact of judicial policy making. According to Frankfurter:

> Our constant preoccupation with the constitutionality of legislation rather than its wisdom tends to the preoccupation of the American mind with a false value. The tendency of focusing attention on constitutionality is to make constitutionality synonymous with wisdom, to regard law as all right if it is constitutional.[42]

According to Harlan:

> The vitality of our political system, on which in the last analysis all else depends, is weakened by reliance on the judiciary for political reform; in time a complacent body politic may result.[43]

A democracy cannot rely on the courts to save it from its own unwisdom. Democracy must rely on the firm commitment of the people to democratic values. The people must learn to protect their freedom and interests by a diligent and alert vigilance over their elected representatives. Invalidation of law by a court "debilitates popular democratic government."[44]

Unlike Professor Hook, however, neither Justice urged that the Supreme Court abandon its power of judicial review. History had legitimatized that power. The "right to pass on the validity of legislation is now too much a part of our constitutional system to be brought into question."[45] For Frankfurter and Harlan to use their positions on the Supreme Court to implement the changes suggested by Hook would have involved the Justices in the very value-selecting process they would reserve for the people and their elected representatives.

Although Justices Frankfurter and Harlan accepted the *existence* of judicial review, it is of the utmost importance to recognize that their understanding of how the Court should *use* the power was based on its nondemocratic nature. The judges were not to attempt the accommodation of diverse groups in the community. "If the function of this Court," said Justice Frankfurter, "is to be essentially no different from that of a legislature, if the considerations governing constitutional construction are to be substantially those that underlie legislation, then indeed judges should not have life tenure and they should be made directly responsible to the electorate."[46] To maintain both the constitutional independence of the federal judiciary and democracy, "it is vital" that in "the day-to-day working of our democracy . . . the power of the non-democratic organ of our Government be exercised with rigorous self-restraint."[47]

Judicial self-restraint is the shorthand phrase that people like Frankfurter and Harlan use to indicate their belief that the power of judicial review must be exercised with the constant awareness that it is a power whose authority is not directly rooted in their conception of democracy. To be sure, judicial self-restraint is, as Hook claims, logically unsatisfactory,[48] but as Frankfurter's favorite authority, Justice Holmes would say, history is not always logical. As Hook has recognized, the argument for judicial self-restraint is based on the same democratic theory he shares. Unwilling to challenge the existence of judicial review, Justices Frankfurter and Harlan used judicial self-restraint as a method of taming the great power John Marshall won for the Court, and of bringing that power into accord with the realist theory of democracy. The argument of judicial self-restraint by the post-1937 Court is inextricably bound up with that particular theory of democracy. When men like Justices Harlan and Frankfurter use the language of self-restraint they are giving voice to one aspect of a larger political theory, they are talking about the role the Court should play in a democracy which functions according to the realist theory.

AN ANALYSIS OF REALIST THEORY

The relative merits of realist theory, like other contemporary American democratic theories, may be evaluated through the concepts of citizenship, political participation, and political freedom. Supreme Court opinions will be used to clarify the meaning of those broad concepts. We shall then be in a better position for evaluating the relative merits of the realist theory of democracy and of Supreme Court opinions which reflect that theory.

Citizenship

Defining the status of the citizen—one's rights, privileges, and obligations as a member of a political community—has never been an easy task in either political theory or law. The complexity involved in the various relationships among citizens and between a citizen and the state makes definition difficult. It is especially difficult in this country where many of the most valued protections of the Constitution are accorded all natural persons, citizen or alien.[49] Nonetheless, Congress' power to exclude aliens is limited only by the requirements of administrative due process;[50] the resident alien may be deprived of his rights under the Constitution by exclusion from the United States.[51] The relationship between an American citizen and his country is seemingly subject to different considerations.

Two different elements are involved in contemporary American discussions—one is primarily a legal notion, the other stems from political theory.[52] The legal notion, derived from English common law, does not emphasize the distinction between *subject* and *citizen*. The crucial distinction is between *citizen* and *alien*. According to English common law, subjects owed allegiance to the Crown and were reciprocally entitled to the Crown's protection; at a later date, the terms *citizen* and *subject* were used interchangeably. Early American legal authorities continued this idea: "'Subject' and 'citizen' are, in a degree, convertible terms as applied to natives" said Chancellor James Kent in his *Commentaries*, "and though the term 'citizen' seems to be appropriate to republican freemen, yet we are, equally with the inhabitants of all other countries, 'subjects,' for we are equally bound by allegiance and subjection to the government and law of the land."[53] The Anglo-American legal concept of citizenship stresses the connection between the individual's allegiance and the government's protection.

In the Western political tradition, however, many theorists treat the allegiance-protection relationship as only a minimum condition of citizenship. Beginning with Aristotle, these theorists have made a sharp and important distinction between citizen and subject. Citizens are seen as active participants in the political community; subjects—a category which at various times has included such groups as slaves, serfs, aliens, children, and women—are essentially passive objects of the political community. The right of political participation, in the theoretical tradition, elevates the status of citizen above that of mere subject.[54]

A citizen is thereby a person worthy of respect as a full, participating member of society. As a participant, a citizen counts for something in the polity's decision-making process. As a member, the citizen has certain obligations to his fellow citizens. The right to participate and the obligations to one's fellow members fosters a feeling of community. Citizenship as an overlapping network of rights, obligations, and affective bonds also promotes the sense of belonging indispensable to a person's self-identity and psychic individuality. In short, some political theorists use the distinction between citizen and subject, with its great emphasis on the value of citizenship, to say something about the quality of membership in a political community.[55]

In one sense, of course, Chancellor Kent is correct. In terms of formal rights and privileges, American democracy has destroyed the formal distinction between citizen and subject, at least as to native born persons. With the passage of the 1965 Voting Rights Act, blacks and other racial and ethnic minorities at long last obtained a meaningful opportunity to participate in political processes in all parts of the country. With the ratification of the Nineteenth Amendment (1920), the right of citizens to vote could no longer be denied or abridged on account of sex. Under the Twenty-fourth Amendment (1964), a citizen's right to vote could no longer be denied or abridged for the failure to pay a poll or other tax. The Twenty-sixth Amendment (1971) extended the right to vote to all citizens, otherwise qualified, of at least eighteen years of age. The democratization of the electorate which began in the early nineteenth century was completed.

With no significant legal barriers to universal suffrage by adult citizens of the United States,[56] it is perfectly understandable why social scientists, political philosophers, and judges adhering to the realist theory of democracy have not used the distinction between citizen and subject. Essentially all adult American citizens are eligible to vote; they can participate if they so choose. Making the two terms synonymous, therefore, is not in itself significant. What is important is that in all areas of life except one, all versions of realist theory treat the citizen as essentially passive. Merging the categories of political theory into Anglo-American legal categories has not made citizens out of subjects. On the contrary, in this theory citizens are all reduced to the status such theorists as Rousseau reserved for subjects. Except for the act of voting—an exception the Realists regard as making a world of difference, but which is still just one activity—their theory treats citizens as the passive objects of political power.

This idea becomes evident when the issue of expatriation is discussed by judges subscribing to realist theory. An expatriated American with no other nationality loses his membership not only in our political society but in any organized political society. Until and unless he acquires a new citizenship he is a man without a country. An expatriated American living abroad cannot seek protection from the United States government; he is at the mercy of the state wherein he resides. An expatriated American who continues to live in the United States is legally an alien in the country of his birth; the protections he is accorded under our laws are those given to all aliens. Like other aliens here, he is subject to deportation; unlike other resident aliens in the United States, no other country has any obligation to protect him. However one views the status of citizenship, an expatriated American who has no other nationality is in the least-favored category. An expatriated American with no other nationality is legally an alien and politically a subject.

The involuntary expatriation of American citizens[57] involves a judicial construction of the first sentence of the Fourteenth Amendment (1869): "All persons born or naturalized in the United States, and subject to the jurisdiction thereof, are citizens of the United States and the State wherein they reside." This sentence resolved some matters relating to American citizenship and helped settle several more. It settled the long-standing controversy over whether national citizenship was dependent upon prior citizenship in a state. With the ratification of the Fourteenth Amendment, national citizenship was in no way dependent upon state citizenship; the latter could be obtained by any United States citizen merely by the fact of residence. That fact made national citizenship primary.[58]

Primary national citizenship was, by the Amendment's own terms, obtained either by birth in this country or through congressionally authorized naturalization procedures. The first route was plainly intended to reverse the Court's argument in *Dred Scott v. Sandford* (1857)[59] that a black person could not be an Americian citizen. From the first, the Supreme Court so read the Citizenship Clause.[60] In *United States v. Wong Kim Ark* (1898),[61] the Court went on to give a basically literal reading to the clause. Almost any person—even the child born of Chinese alien parents who could not themselves become citizens—became a citizen of the United States by being born in this country. The only exceptions—because they were not fully subject to American jurisdiction—were children born of diplomatic representatives, children of alien enemies held in hostile occupation,[62] and the children of Indians subject to tribal laws.[63] American Indians were eventually nationalized, as a group, by congressional law in 1924.[64]

It was not clear what, if any, meaning the Citizenship Clause had for questions relating to the loss of American citizenship. The literal wording did not address that issue. Plainly, our whole history and tradition permitted a person to voluntarily surrender American citizenship, so that point has never been contested; but could a person's citizenship be taken away against his wishes? If so, are there any constitutional limits on the congressional power to expatriate?

Until the decision in *Afroyim v. Rusk* (1967),[65] Congress and the Supreme Court maintained that the Citizenship Clause neither denies nor provides Congress any power to expatriate; its *only* purpose was to declare the classes of individuals to whom the status of citizenship initially attaches.[66] In *Afroyim*, Justice Black's opinion for the five man majority held that Congress is without any power, express or implied, to expatriate a citizen without his consent.

Justice Harlan objected to that decision in an opinion fully consistent with all other opinions on this matter by judges who hold the realist theory of democracy. He argued that "nothing in the history, purposes or language" of the Citizenship Clause of the Fourteenth Amendment "suggests that it forbids Congress in all circumstances to withdraw the citizenship of an unwilling citizen."[67] That clause refers only to the attainment of citizenship; it neither provides for nor denies Congress any power of expatriation. Absent any specific language, citizenship, once obtained, is only protected from arbitrary actions by the Due Process Clause. Congress may, therefore, deprive a person of his citizenship if a rational nexus exists between that deprivation and a specifically granted congressional power. Nexus is demonstrated when it can be shown that Congress could reasonably have thought there was a relationship between expatriation and a program which Congress has the authority to promote.

In *Perez v. Brownell* (1958)[68] and in *Afroyim*, Justice Frankfurter for the Court and Justice Harlan for the minority respectively argued that Congress could attach the loss of United States citizenship to voting in a foreign election. Congress could reasonably find that voting in a foreign election was an act fraught with the danger of embroiling our government in international dispute or of embarrassing it in the conduct of foreign affairs.[69] In *Trop v. Dulles* (1958),[70] Justice Frankfurter, in a dissenting opinion joined by Justices Burton, Clark, and Harlan, argued that Congress could withdraw a person's citizenship for wartime desertion. There was a rational connection, he maintained, between the two acts. "Congress may reasonably have believed the morale and fighting efficiency of our troops would be impaired if our soldiers know that their fellows who had abandoned them in their time of greatest need were to remain in the communion of our citizens."[71]

The opinions of Justices Frankfurter and Harlan in these expatriation cases indicate that they conceived of citizenship solely in terms of Anglo-American legal doctrine. In his *Trop* dissent, Justice Frankfurter wrote: "Possession by an American citizen of the rights and privileges that constitute citizenship imposes correlative obligations."[72] The deserter had not met his end of the mutual obligations. Wartime desertion could reasonably be taken as evidence of the lack of allegiance to the United States, and the lack of allegiance eliminated the basis for recognizing a person's citizenship.

In the expatriation cases, the Justices adhering to the realist theory of democracy never saw citizenship as involving anything more than the reciprocal obligations of allegiance and protection. This observation is not surprising. Making a sharp distinction between the rulers and the ruled, the theory assigns to the leadership the activist role of suggesting, debating, influencing, and formulating policy. Except for the act of voting, except for the act of selecting their temporary rulers, the citizenry are cast in a role which in no way differs from that of subjects in a nondemocratic state: the people are governed. Even in exercising their one governmental function, even when selecting their rulers, the people are seen in an essentially passive manner. Like consumers in the marketplace, the voters select from among the choices *made available to them.*

With the realist theory of democracy to inform them, it is little wonder that Justices Frankfurter and Harlan viewed citizenship solely in terms of the legal concepts of allegiance and protection. As judges, they were trained to use legal conceptions and their theory of democracy offered no enlarging conception of citizenship. Justices Frankfurter and Harlan, therefore, never even entered into a discussion of the theoretical nature of American citizenship.

By way of contrast, the late Professor Alexander Bickel came to the same conclusion as the two Justices about Congress' authority to expatriate; but, he defended his position by arguing that we are fortunate that "the concept of citizenship plays only the most minimal role in the American constitutional scheme."[73] Bickel maintained that it is easier to think of someone as a non-citizen than to decide he is a nonperson; therefore, it is easier to take away an individual's rights when we rely upon an abstract, metaphysical category like citizenship—we simply declare that person an alien.[74] Professor Bickel was almost certainly wrong; other contemporary American theories of democracy, discussed in subsequent chapters, use the concept of citizenship as a way of significantly protecting individual rights. Professor Bickel, however, was willing to discuss the theoretical dimension of American citizenship. To Justices Frankfurter and Harlan it was merely a legal status.

Further, realist theory offers a positive encouragement to think that only the Due Process Clause of the Fifth Amendment is involved in the constitutional issue raised by expatriation statutes. The great advantage of the theory's distinction between rulers and ruled is that it seems to recognize existing competencies. The poorly informed people are unable to make policy; policy making becomes the function of the better-informed leadership elements. The primary responsibility of the elected rulers is to govern according to their own estimates of public needs; they were chosen for that purpose by the free competition for the free vote. The Justices of the Supreme Court, in this theory, are not to interfere with policy decisions unless the action is explicitly prohibited by the Constitution or unless no rational nexus can be found between the government's policy and its enumerated powers. Not being directly selected by and responsible to the democratic mechanism the Justices are authorized to overrule the elected leadership only in the unusual conditions just mentioned.

Because there is no specific prohibition against expatriation, the constitutional problem raised by the statutes was resolved by an examination of due process reasonableness; yet, these Justices did not make an independent examination. They upheld any statute which a rational and fair man could find a reasonable way to carry out a congressional power. Congressmen must be presumed reasonable—they are chosen by the process which defines democracy in the realist theory. To challenge congressional rationality is to challenge the rationality of democracy itself. Since those rational men always place reasons for supporting a bill into the Congressional Record, every law is presumptively a way in which a rational and fair man could carry out a congressional power.

Thus, as Justice Whittaker complained in his *Perez* dissent, Frankfurter deprived a man of American citizenship for voting in a foreign election without demonstrating that the foreign government viewed it as an act fraught with the possibility of embroiling the United States in an international dispute.[75] Congress thought there was a reasonable possibility, and that was enough for Frankfurter and the other Justices who held with the realist theory of democracy. When those Justices considered the constitutional problem raised by expatriation, it was "the institutional logic rather than the impact on individuals that [was] decisive."[76]

The "institutional logic" led Justices Frankfurter and Harlan to argue that deprivation of citizenship was not really a punishment. Not only was expatriation not a "cruel and unusual punishment" within the historically defined meaning of the Eighth Amendment, it was "not a 'punishment' in any valid constitutional sense."[77] Because Congress was promoting such legitimate nonpenal ends as an intelligent foreign policy and protecting our war effort, there was "no warrant for this Court's labelling the disability imposed by [congressional statute] as a punishment."[78]

The argument makes a great deal of sense when it is remembered that these Justices conceived of citizenship only in terms of the mutual obligations of allegiance and protection. Not having conceived of citizenship in terms of political participation in *some* society, there was no need to discuss the loss of citizenship in those terms. As Hannah Arendt noted, jurists are used to thinking in terms of specific punishments, which deprive individuals of certain specific rights. The deprivation of citizenship, which involves not the deprivation of certain rights within a given community but the loss of any community willing to guarantee any rights whatsoever, seems too abstract to be considered a punishment.[79] Not being informed by a political theory which uses the concept of citizenship to emphasize the importance of political participation (or the importance of actively belonging to a society in order to assert one's claims to human rights and dignity), the Justices holding the realist theory treated the loss of citizenship as less than many specific punishments of criminal law. A *citizen* and a *subject* are not very different after all in the realist theory of democracy.

Political Participation

The Realists, however, would not agree with this assessment, for according to their theory, an American citizen does participate politically in the only way the average man can in a large modern democracy—periodically he helps select his rulers. This one activity becomes, in their minds, the means of giving the citizen some voice in the use of governmental power. In fact, Professor Lipset identifies the "citizenship issue" with the "ways in which different societies handle the 'entry into politics' crisis—the decision as to when new social groups shall obtain access to the political process."[80] If in realist theory a democratic citizen is distinguished from a subject, it is because his participation in the electoral process enables him to influence governmental policy.

As we have seen, Lipset and MacIver argue that voting is the principal means of public participation in the policy-making process. The social science data, however, do not indicate that the American people govern by choosing between party ideologies presented to them at election time. In terms of policy making (as opposed to simply selecting rulers through the competitive election system), the people are even more passive than the MacIver-Lipset market analogy suggests. Sometimes party support may be based primarily on policy agreement between party leadership and the people who voted for those leaders. At other times, however, this correlation clearly is not the case. If the people only occasionally select their rulers on the basis of issues and policy, the Lipset-MacIver argument cannot demonstrate popular self-government, unless, of course, self-government is reduced to sporadic demands for a shift in the "broad march of policy," and the electorate's influence on government policy is not meant to be a continuously functioning part of these Realists' democratic system. If popular political participation is to be a regular, systematic feature of democracy, then this part of Lipset's and MacIver's work need not be considered further: for a realist theory it is not a very realistic description of the political process in the United States.

Professors Key and Dahl argued that public participation in the policy-making process comes about through the activities of the pluralistic groups in American society. This contention is predicated on two other arguments: first, that the leaders of those groups represent the interest of their members in the political arena; and second, that all relevant interests in society can make themselves heard in this way at some crucial stage in the process of reaching a decision. Each of these subsidiary points, however, is open to considerable doubt.

The pluralism of Key and Dahl revolves around the politics of a relatively small group of activists. They do not expect most people to be actively involved in internal group affairs.[81] Within this pluralistic explanation of how the American public exercises some influence on governmental policy, we again confront the fact that most people are politically inactive. How can the political participation of this small group of activists account for popular influence on government policy?

The realist theorist cannot argue that the leaders democratically represent the views of the members. Their realist theory of democracy requires free, competitive elections for selecting leaders, but it is no longer to be doubted that the leaders of important groups are selected by a process better described as co-optation than as election. Where private groups do use elections, competition is the exception not the rule.[82] Professors Dahl and Key (and Hook) would not call a country democratic if it selected its president as the American

Medical Association, the Teamsters' Union or General Motors select theirs. The realist theorists, therefore, do not say that the leaders of private associations represent their members' views in the same way as politicians are held to represent their constituents.

Faced with this dilemma, all they can do, as Key admits, is conjecture along the following lines: those members identified with an organization are most likely to adopt the organization's policy lines (the greater the identification the greater the likelihood of policy agreement).[83] The leadership elements, the activists, thus *may* speak for the interest of their more apathetic followers in the organization, and for people in the same "objective" circumstances.

Further, apart from "such objective circumstances and from acceptance of announced policy lines, subcultures within the population doubtless carry and maintain characteristic outlooks significant for opinion upon public policy."[84] Existing ethnic and religious groups thus *may* reflect the views of the nonaffiliated or marginally affiliated, or, alternately, *may be taken* to so represent the entire subculture if no other groups exist in a society which permits group organization.

Admittedly, this statement is a reasonable conjecture. We are not certain in what ways, if any, the leaders of private associations reflect the views of their members, let alone those of nonmembers similarly situated. I would feel a lot more comfortable with this line of reasoning, however, if it could be shown that groups and leaders *do* spring up whenever existing organizations fail to reflect the views of major segments of the population. Then it would be easier to agree with Key and Dahl that existing leaders of the diverse groups in our society do reflect all major segments of opinion and that through their activities they help the people influence policy.

In fact, many of the people in what Michael Harrington once called *The Other America*[85] are not represented by any organized group. No one speaks for the rural poor or the migrant worker. Their marginal condition may reflect their inability to organize, but it does not inspire confidence that all those entitled to participate are considered in the decision-making process.

Are all major segments of opinion reflected by groups which have *access* to the decision-making process? Few, if any, national systems offer more opportunity. The American political system provides groups with innumerable places of access for registering their claims. Nor is the system very much more selective about the means a group can use to exert influence at those access points. An almost endless variety of resources—time, money, jobs, contracts, numbers, etc—have all proven their effectiveness. Manifestations of influence on governmental decisions in the United States can only be explained by taking into account the availability of a great variety of access points and types of resources.

Professors Dahl and Key build upon this fact. They make frequent references to the numerous points of access in our governmental structure and the variety of resources which can be used to influence government.[86] This point is necessary but not sufficient. For their argument Dahl and Key must also insist that resources in our society are dispersed and not cumulative, and that therefore widespread opportunity exists for influencing policy.

Professor Dahl insists that our system of highly dispersed resources is not to be confused with one of equality of resources and influence, rather, we have a system of dispersed inequalities.[87] Although influence resources are unequally dispersed, the inequalities are *noncumulative*. Individuals (or groups) with ready access to one resource often cannot muster other kinds of resources. Different kinds of resources are decisive at different times and in different decision areas; therefore, Dahl does contend that the wide spread of resources means the fragmentation of power and influence. "Virtually no one, and certainly no group of more than a few individuals, is entirely lacking in some influence resources."[88] In context, clearly Dahl is saying that virtually no American lacks the opportunity to influence policy.

This argument is highly questionable. For certain Americans the inequality of resources is cumulative. For unemployed miners of West Virginia and Kentucky, migratory farmworkers, and lower-income blacks, the inequalities of education, skills, money, and status all feed on one another and prevent the people in *The Other America* from exploiting the few resources they do have. The conditions of the poor in the United States can best be understood by recognizing the *cumulative inequalities* imposed by poverty. Even by Dahl's own standard, there are sizeable groups of people lacking the opportunity to have any say on policies affecting their lives. In our present system they lack influence resources of all kinds.[89]

Even for those who do have some opportunity to influence policy, the extent of that influence is sometimes so minimal as to create alienation from the political system. Although recognizing that dispersion of influence does not eliminate inequalities in influence, Dahl does not deal with the cumulative impact of political failure on the systemic level.[90]

Nonvoting is a characteristic response of those whose needs and interests are *not* being met by alternate avenues of activity.[91] Professor Dahl, however, contended that the primary reason for the nonparticipation of *homo civicus* is his ability to attain his goals through nonpolitical channels. Dahl converted political apathy into a middle-class response to the abundance of opportunities offered by American society.[92] Actually, it is more generally the response of the lowest classes, of those frustrated by both the socioeconomic system and the political system.[93]

Professors Dahl and Key were unwilling to abandon two ideas: America is a democracy and democracy means self-government. They argued, therefore, that if the people do not participate in the policy-making process, at least the existing political process enables them to influence government policy systematically through the activities of pluralistic groups. America is a democracy because in its "normal" political system "there is a high probability that an active and legitimate group in the population can make itself heard effectively at some crucial stage in the process of decision."[94]

Individual political participation thereby became the attribute of a small group of activists. The success of the democratic system, of self-government, was now to depend upon the actions of this relatively small number of people. "The masses do not corrupt themselves," V. O. Key concluded, "if they are corrupt, they have been corrupted." In the democracy of realist theory, "the critical element for the health of a democratic order consists in the beliefs, standards, and competence of those who constitute the influentials, the opinion-leaders, the political activists in the order . . . If a democracy tends toward indecision, decay, and disaster, the responsibility rests here, not in the mass of the people."[95]

The realist theory of Dahl and Key retained the notion of political participation only for "the influentials," while claiming that their activity enabled the masses to influence public policy. That claim was supported by the conjecture that the leaders of organized groups represent the views of their members. The claim was also supported by the hypothesis that the leaders of existing groups speak for all major segments of our population. The conjecture is uncertain; the hypothesis is untrue. It is very disconcerting to find our foremost realist political scientists making arguments that ignore reality, but then, so did the realist sociologists Lipset and MacIver. The realist social scientists are therefore in a most embarrassing position. Only by giving the political system attributes it does not possess are they able to talk about self-government. Could it be that our hard-nosed Realists still have a bit of the old myth maker in them? The evidence suggests that they do. While upset about certain features of American democracy, these social scientists have created a myth about self-government which justifies the system as a whole.

When dealing with social scientists, the prescriptive implications of realist theory are clues to their value biases. Examining the prescriptive implications serves as a cautionary hedge against a too-ready acceptance of the conclusions of realist social scientists. When dealing with policy makers, the prescriptive implications of realist theory are important clues (among others) as to why they came to a particular decision. Nowhere is this more true than in examining the opinions of Supreme Court Justices on legislative apportionment.

As Justice Frankfurter aptly noted, what the Court was asked to do in the apportionment cases was nothing else than "to choose among competing bases of representation—ultimately, really, among competing theories of political philosophy—in order to establish an appropriate frame of government . . . for all the States of the Union."[96] Since equal protection of the laws has never been interpreted as requiring complete egalitarianism but only an equality of persons standing in the same relation to whatever governmental action is challenged, the judges first must define the nature of that relation. With apportionment, that process means the judges must discuss the theoretical basis of representation.

Of course, Justices Frankfurter and Harlan claimed to be avoiding that discussion. They held that the Supreme Court should refuse to hear the apportionment cases under the "political question" doctrine—the peculiarly "political" nature of the issue was unsuitable for judicial determination.[97] When the reasons they give for holding apportionment to be a "political question" are examined, however, it becomes apparent that their reasoning derives from their own theory of democracy—the realist theory.

Justices Frankfurter and Harlan maintained there were three factors behind their reasoning that the apportionment cases should be dismissed under the "political question" doctrine: the nature of the problem, the difficulty of devising constitutional standards, and the problem of devising relief.[98] The second factor was decisive for the two Justices. Frankfurter and Harlan did not say that the nature of the apportionment problem—involving the structure and organization of state political institutions—was automatically exempted from the application of constitutional norms. They only said that there were excellent reasons why this should be so in the absence of an explicit and clear constitutional imperative.[99]

If clear guidelines were available to the judges, the third factor—the problem of devising judicial relief—would hardly be significant. Clear constitutional standards not only tell the Court how to decide a case but also suggest remedies. Besides, when the Justices think the constitutional standard is clear, the difficulty of devising appropriate relief does not prevent them from reaching a decision: witness the *School Desegregation Cases*.[101] Nor did Frankfurter and Harlan hold otherwise. Their argument was that in the absence of satisfactory criteria for deciding the issue, the Court has no firm basis for choosing among modes of relief. Lacking satisfactory criteria for judgment, the Court would be more than likely to compound the damage when fashioning relief.[101] The key factor, then, in the Frankfurter-Harlan political question argument was their firm belief that the judges lack constitutional standards to deal with apportionment.

The difficulty in devising satisfactory constitutional guidelines for handling this problem relates both to the nature of the apportionment issue and its history in this country. As for the historical part of this argument, Justice Frankfurter, in his powerful dissent in *Baker v. Carr* (1962) found that representation based upon relatively equal population districts had not been the universally accepted standard in either England or the United States. Frankfurter found that Anglo-American political history had created no universally accepted standard which the Court could read into the vagueness of the Equal Protection Clause for the purpose of deciding these cases.[102]

Justice Harlan's dissent in *Reynolds v. Sims* (1964) argued that "the Equal Protection Clause was never intended to inhibit the States in choosing any democratic method they pleased for the apportionment of their legislatures."[103] He did not, like Frankfurter in *Baker*, look primarily at the extra-constitutional practice in England and the United States. He was looking at the intent of the Equal Protection Clause in regard to apportionment and he used other factors to illuminate that intent. Harlan's constitutional history leads to the same conclusion as Frankfurter's political history: there is no basis for the Court to decide the question of state legislative apportionment.

Justices Frankfurter and Harlan made strong historical arguments. For a variety of reasons, however, their history cannot resolve the issue conclusively; at most, it provides strong auxiliary support for their major contention. Justice Frankfurter's political history suffers from the need to make a case. The history of Anglo-American apportionment practices is not a single piece; it is a complex pattern. Some scholars, therefore, agree with Frankfurter that representation based upon relatively equal population districts was not the historically accepted principle in either the British or the American democracies.[104] Other scholars argue that, during the course of the nineteenth century, the democratic impulse made that principle dominant in both theory and practice. These scholars maintain that representation based upon relatively equal population districts had evolved into a clear enough standard of political equality to warrant inclusion in the Equal Protection Clause.[105]

My own assessment is that there is more support for Frankfurter's position. The point to remember, however, is that the historical data are not so unambiguous as to automatically lead to Justice Frankfurter's conclusion that no suitable standard exists. Even using Frankfurter's method of deriving standards from historical practice, a person with a different political theory could come to a different conclusion without grossly distorting history. If Justice Frankfurter chose to read history the way he did, it was more than likely because of his basic political theory.

Justice Harlan's argument about intent raises different problems, problems of constitutional construction. To support his contention that the Equal Protection Clause was not intended to require apportionment of both houses of a state legislature on a relatively equal population basis, Justice Harlan referred to the language of the amendment, congressional debates, and state, congressional, and federal judicial practices up to the 1962 *Baker* decision.[106] Each of these points is well taken, but they are controlling only if constitutional interpretation is limited by the Framers' intent. After all, many of the same points could have been made with equal force against the 1954 *School Desegregation* decision, yet Justice Harlan has never questioned the validity of that decision. In fact, he explicitly concurred with it.[107] Justice Harlan rarely placed sole reliance on intent when interpreting the Constitution, and especially the Fourteenth Amendment.[108] He did so in the apportionment cases only to buttress a more basic argument.

For Frankfurter and Harlan, then, history was *not* the primary reason behind their belief in the Court's inability to frame constitutional standards for dealing with apportionment. The heart of their objection lay elsewhere: their political theory caused them to view the problems of apportionment as wholly within the competence of elected officials. Starting with a realist theory of democracy these Justices saw apportionment as an improper function for the judiciary.

The Court should refrain from deciding apportionment questions because they involve factors that do not "lend themselves to evaluations of a nature that are the staple of judicial determinations or for which judges are equipped to adjudicate by legal training or experience or native wit."[109] Any apportionment plan would involve the judge in choosing from among different theories of representation and any choice was bound to benefit certain interests at the expense of others. As we have already seen, at the center of the realist theory of Justices Frankfurter and Harlan was the belief that this choice is the proper job of officials elected precisely to do this and who are directly responsible to the electoral process. "Courts are unable to decide when it is that an apportionment originally valid becomes void because the factors entering into such a decision are basically matters appropriate only for legislative judgment."[110] That reason was also why, Frankfurter maintained, the Court had correctly refused to decide the issues arising under the clause guaranteeing each state a republican form of government.[111] In those cases, as in the apportionment cases, the real issue was the political power of competing interests.[112]

To avoid deciding issues directly involving the political influence of groups in society, the Court has refused to handle questions dealing with the structure and organization of state government. This refusal was the most excellent of reasons behind the soundest of traditions. It should be continued in the apportionment cases. "[T]here is not under our Constitution a judicial remedy for every political mischief, for every undesirable exercise of legislative power."[113] The weighing of competing interests is a political issue to be made by those held responsible by the political process.

Clearly, neither the Supreme Court's decision to decide the apportionment issue nor its formula for resolving that issue was inevitable. It is too late in the day for anyone to maintain, as in the Blackstone-Field-Sutherland tradition, that the Court only discovers law; and no one so holds. Were, however, Justices Frankfurter and Harlan correct in their assertion that the cost of the Court's intervention was too high? Not if one examines the consequences of the Frankfurter-Harlan alternative. By advocating total abstention, these judicial proponents of realist theory placed themselves in an incongruous position. Their political theory prevented them from using the power of the Court to change legislative malapportionment; yet, malapportionment made a mockery of the representative process which lies at the heart of realist theory.

First, there should be no question that these Justices were arguing for total judical abstention in this matter. That abstention was the plain intent of Justice Frankfurter's political question doctrine—the matter was simply nonjusticiable. Justice Harlan's dissent in *Baker* (which Frankfurter joined) seems to discuss the apportionment issues on its merits. He concluded, however, that the allegations of malapportionment, even if true, "do not, parsed down, or as a whole, show an infringement by Tennessee of any rights assured by the Fourteenth Amendment."[114] The Equal Protection Clause, Harlan insisted, "does not demand of state enactments either mathematical identity or rigid equality . . . All that is prohibited is invidious discrimination bearing *no rational relation* to any permissible policy of the State."[115]

Note how Justice Harlan immediately converted an equal protection question into one of due process reasonableness—governmental action will be sustained as constitutional so long as there is some rational basis for that action. This argument is, in itself, a logical result of judges applying the realist theory of democracy. It is the way the notion of judicial self-restraint, which stems from that theory, is applied to particular problems. It permits the widest possible leeway for government to act without formally abandoning the practice of judicial review.

In regard to the apportionment issue, Harlan was plainly carrying out a ritual. Since in his view any apportionment scheme was obviously a rational calculation by the politicians to promote their own and their constituents' interests, no state apportionment scheme could ever be declared unconstitutional by Harlan. His attempts to find a rational state policy in the Tennessee apportionment involved in *Baker*[116] were highly imaginative and totally unconvincing. As Justice Clark caustically noted in criticizing Harlan's "fanciful" conclusions: "If present representation has a policy at all, it is to maintain the *status quo* of invidious discrimination at any cost."[117]

Except for what he regarded as the almost perverse activism of his brethren, Justice Harlan would not have bothered to go through his labored analysis. To him, the main thing was that the courts are unable to decide this type of issue; the factors involved are matters appropriate only for politically responsible officials. Apportionment is not meet for judicial action. In short,

Justice Harlan began and ended his opinion in total agreement with Justice Frankfurter that "Courts ought not to enter this political thicket."[118]

Second, the obvious consequence of total judicial abstention would have been continued state legislative malapportionment. Both Frankfurter and Harlan conceded that some states were badly malapportioned, but they insisted relief must come through the political process: "Appeal must be to an informed, civically militant electorate."[119] State legislators may not have appreciated the sentiments behind Justice Frankfurter's plea that "relief must come through an aroused popular conscience that sears the conscience of the people's representatives,"[120] but they would certainly have appreciated a Court majority behind the Frankfurter-Harlan position. In this instance, there could be no appeal from Philip drunk to Philip sober. Neither the politicians in office nor the groups which benefitted from the existing state legislative apportionments were about to vote against their own political interests. Before 1962 the state governments were not reapportioning themselves periodically; many had not even reapportioned to take account of such long-term trends as urbanization.[121] An appeal to the political process to cure this particular vice was an exercise in pure futility.

Why such an exercise would enhance the Court's authority, as Justices Frankfurter and Harlan claimed,[122] is clear only to those who view judicial effacement as always being in the interests of democracy. One does not have to agree with the Court's standard for reapportioning state legislatures to hold that some judicial relief was warranted—witness Justices Clark and Stewart.[123] In his concurring opinion in *Baker*, Justice Clark replied to Justice Frankfurter's contention about the Court's authority by saying:

> It is well for this Court to practice self-restraint and discipline in constitutional adjudication, but never in its history have those principles received sanction where the national rights of so many have been so clearly infringed for so long. National respect for the courts is more enhanced through the forthright enforcement of those rights rather than by rendering them nugatory through the interposition of subterfuges.[124]

American history since 1962 has given Clark much the better of this argument, at least with respect to the apportionment issue.

Last, and most important, the consequences of judicial abstention in this matter are impossible to equate with the basic premise of realist theory. Realist theories can define democracy exclusively in terms of the political process because all groups in society are presumed to have the equal opportunity of access to that process. Only given that equality of access can realist theorists *begin* to make an argument about self-government and democracy. Only given that equality of access does the notion of judicial self-restraint make sense: the judges are not to interfere with the elected policy maker's weighing of competing interests because those officials are chosen to represent, and are responsible to, the divergent groups in society. In a grossly malapportioned legislature, however, certain groups will not be represented at all, and others will be given influence out of all proportion to their strength in society. The conditions for the kind of self-government envisioned by realist theory were simply not present. There certainly may be differences of opinion about whether some state legislatures were in fact malapportioned, but a legislature as grossly malapportioned as Tennessee's was in 1962 could represent only the entrenched minority.

Since all avenues except appeal to the federal courts were closed, what sense did it make to appeal to self-government through the electoral process? Justices Frankfurter and Harlan knew that the actual access accorded different groups was so grossly unfair in many states as to prevent some interests from being effectively heard at *any* stage in the political process; yet, since the apportionment had resulted from the competitive struggle for power in Tennessee, their realist theory told them it was the result of democratic politics and should be cured only by that process. In the name of self-government, Justices Harlan and Frankfurter urged judicial self-restraint in a situation where it would result in the continued denial of self-government to a majority of a state's population.

Realist theory, then, prevented Justices Frankfurter and Harlan from coming to grips with the actuality of American politics. Because realist theory defines democracy exclusively in terms of the political process, they saw judicial review as an undemocratic power. To Justices Frankfurter and Harlan, self-restraint therefore became the essence of the judicial function. But when the political process itself is partly functioning on an undemocratic basis— by every standard including that of realist theory—the argument on behalf of judicial self-restraint loses much of its viability.

The problem of political participation raised by the apportionment cases also poses serious questions for the realist theory of Professor Hook. It shows this instrumentalist's political theory to be something less than pragmatic. The consequences of judicial abstention would have been continued minority rule in certain sectors of American politics. As we have seen, Hook grounds his democratic theory on the opportunity afforded the people to select their rulers through the electoral process and on the system of majority rule within that process. He thus could not help but view the situation in such states as Tennessee (pre-1962) as a deplorable departure from democracy: in those states the governing group could not be changed at the discretion of the electoral majority. He also insists that the determination about whether a system is democratic or not must be made through evaluating the entire system. By that measure, Hook calls the United States a democracy: generally, the procedures for public participation and majority rule do exist.

How does Hook propose to change undemocratic apportionments within the democratic process? Certainly not through the Supreme Court—he views that agency as inherently oligarchic and undemocratic. The only democratic way to change an undemocratic feature is through the process designed to institutionalize the competitive struggle for power. He must, therefore, join Justices Frankfurter and Harlan in urging the people in the states with grossly malapportioned legislatures to live with that condition until they are able to change it through the political process. The faith of a consistent realist democrat is that a change is only worthwhile if done through the give and take of the competitive struggle for power, and that changes can indeed be accomplished in the long run.

This faith has important implications. Because of his faith in the virtues obtained from an exclusive reliance on the electoral process, a Realist like Hook is willing to allow the political system in a country he deems democratic virtually to define its own social universe. Once a country has been declared a democracy by Professor Hook, all future policies should be determined by the competitive struggle for power. Not only are the winners of that competitive struggle to determine the substantive content of social and economic policy, they are also to determine the extent to which groups in society participate in the electoral process itself. The extension of effective political participation as well as the rates of taxation are to be left to the judgment of those individuals politically responsible to the electoral process. The people and interests who have already won in the existing political game are to be given the exclusive power to decide whether to change the game by enlarging its scope.

Since the nature and extent of the political universe is a critical factor in determining who is elected and what policy will be pursued, this definition of democracy benefits groups already within the system. Realist theory contains a bias in favor of the status quo. The extent of that bias is determined by the extent of a Realist's unquestioned faith in democracy as defined exclusively by the competitive struggle for power.

Political Freedom

An examination of various aspects of political participation is not the sole indication that realist theorists are willing to allow the political system great discretion in defining the nature of democracy. The same conclusion emerges from an analysis of their treatment of political freedom. In Schumpeter's competitive paradigm, political freedom is an indispensable prerequisite for the free competition for the free vote. In realist theory political freedom takes on an even greater significance. Realists have difficulty, as we have seen, demonstrating popular self-government within democracies, but they can point to the existence of political freedom. The fact that citizens in democracies are enjoying widespread political rights is the single most important factor in their defense of democracy. Our primary concern here is with how the realist theorists define that concept.

What distinguishes the Realists from other democratic theorists is their willingness to let politically elected officials define the substantive content of our constitutional rights. The Realists maintain they are merely accurately describing the situation. Politically elected officials, responding to the pressures of the activist leaders of groups within their constituencies, do, in fact, define political freedom. That lesson is taught by American history.[125] But the Realists also believe that the elected leadership should define the substantive content of political rights in a democracy.[126] Political freedom is just one more policy. Not the Constitution but the decisions of our elected representatives do and should determine the meaning of political freedom within our political system.

This conclusion is why realist social scientists believe democracy is compatible with widespread popular misunderstanding about the norms of democracy, even the norms which Realists believe are essential for maintaining the free competitive election process. Earlier political theorists had believed that a massive consensus behind the norms of democracy was necessary. We now know that such a consensus exists only in support of vague, abstract generalities. Almost all Americans agree that the fundamental norms of democracy, as defined by realist theory—free speech, for example—are important values and should be enjoyed as a matter of right by all Americans. Nonetheless, many Americans see no contradiction in professing a belief in these norms in the abstract and denying them to certain groups in practice. In the functioning American political system, a majority of voters frequently hold views which go against the political freedom necessary for the maintenance of a free, competitive electoral process.[127]

However fatal these findings may be to the democratic theories of earlier generations, they do not overturn the realist theory of democracy. If political freedom is a policy like other policies, what matters to a realist social scientist is not the belief of the masses but the beliefs and activities of the leadership elements. Lack of popular consensus about the applicability of normative rules is not ordinarily of much importance because the public does not make policy. Maintaining the system, including the practices of political freedom, is a function of activists and, most especially, politicians. Ordinarily, what these individuals decide is decisive.[128]

For the Realists, the clearest example is the fate which befell the American Communist Party after World War II. Treating the Communist Party as the internal enemy, Congress used its investigating committees to dramatize the danger posed by the Communists and passed laws that had the cumulative impact of outlawing the Communist Party.[129] As Dahl notes, the Communist Party ceased to be regarded as a legitimate group; the preponderant portion of the leadership elements had decided to curtail the political freedom of the Communists.[130]

While Professor Dahl's characterization is undoubtedly a correct description of the factual situation, its true importance lies elsewhere. It has profound implications for the Realist's view of the function of the Constitution. Because the realist social scientists see great protections for political liberty in the pluralistic social order governing itself through the electoral process, they do not regard such constitutional provisions as the First Amendment as being of much importance. To Dahl, the evidence seems "overwhelming" that in the various democracies of the contemporary world, "the extent to which minorities are bedeviled by means of government action is dependent almost entirely upon non-constitutional factors; indeed, if constitutional factors are not entirely irrelevant, their signficance is trivial as compared with the non-constitutional."[131] Within realist theory, the Constitution is not seen as a uniform body of law to shape society by guiding and restricting governmental policy. "Constitutional rules are mainly significant because they help to determine what particular groups are to be given advantages or handicaps in the political struggle."[132]

Once again the prescriptive implications of realist democratic theory become clearer when examining the opinions of Justices sharing that theory. The line of cases under the First Amendment which deal with the American Communist Party has the advantages of the clear example: it will show how the Justices adhering to the realist theory of democracy would permit elected officials to define a basic political liberty, free speech. To avoid the disadvantage of the clear example—the distortion caused by the special features which make it stand out—we shall also examine the First Amendment cases involving another minority group—American blacks. The reasoning of Justices Frankfurter and Harlan remains constant.

Dennis v. United States (1951)[133] involved the conviction of the eleven top leaders of the American Communist Party under the Smith Act. According to Justice Frankfurter, "The Smith Act and this conviction under it no doubt restrict the exercise of free speech and assembly."[134] The Court had to decide whether this restriction was unconstitutional under the First Amendment.

To Justice Frankfurter, that the Smith Act plainly restricted speech and assembly was only the beginning, not the end, of judicial analysis. He rejected the idea that the categorical constitutional command—"Congress shall make no law . . . abridging the freedom of speech"—compels a judicial decision against the government. To read the First Amendment in a literal way would produce harmful consequences: "Absolute rules would inevitably lead to absolute exceptions, and such exceptions would eventually erode the rules."[135]

He also would not resolve the conflict posed by the Smith Act's restriction of speech and the language of the First Amendment by relying upon the Holmes-Brandeis "clear and present danger" test. The plurality opinion by Chief Justice Vinson claimed to be deciding the case under the authority of that doctrine. Actually, Vinson accepted and applied Judge Learned Hand's reformulation: "In each case [courts] must ask whether the gravity of the 'evil' discounted by its improbability, justifies such invasion of free speech as is necessary to avoid the danger."[136] Such verbal fakery—claiming to be retaining the old test while actually changing it—was not for Frankfurter. As he noted, "clear" and "present" obviously does not mean an "entertainable 'probability.'"[137]

Unable to join the Vinson opinion, Frankfurter wrote a remarkable concurring opinion putting forth his judicial approach to First Amendment cases—the balancing test:

> The demands of free speech in a democratic society as well as the interest in national security are better served by candid and informed weighing of the competing interests, within the confines of the judicial process, than by announcing dogmas too flexible for the non-Euclidian problems to be solved.[138]

The Frankfurter-Harlan balancing test proceeds on the assumption that claims based upon First Amendment rights are best discussed as an interest. Not every American thinker would have so stated the problem. Madison, for one, would have treated the *right* to free speech as something distinct from an *interest*. Using natural rights concepts, Madison believed that the right to free speech was entitled to the protection of the law in any just society and was not subject to infringment. On the other hand, an interest referred to precisely those claims by groups and individuals which he believed were the essence of politics. Madison's Constitution was designed to protect *rights* by bringing about an accommodation of *interests* through the governmental system. Not that Madison, faced with the type of problem posed by the Communist Party, would have automatically opposed such legislation as the Smith Act, since as Frankfurter noted, Madison also believed that "[s]ecurity against foreign danger is one of the primitive objects of civil society."[139] Madison, however, and the nineteenth century Justices who accepted the traditional American paradigm would never have treated the right of free speech as the equivalent of an interest.

That equivalence is basic to the Frankfurter-Harlan balancing test. The notion that all legal claims can be treated as interests stems from the Realists' conception of how certain values come to be written into statutes and constitutions. The legislative and constitution-making processes involve the accommodation of conflicting interests. The values embodied in those legal documents—legally protected rights and interests—are the end products of the politics of interest accommodation. Justice Frankfurter did not make a distinction between rights and interests because he saw the former emerging from the latter.

In *Dennis* Justice Frankfurter used the words *rights* and *interests* interchangeably. At the outset he talked about the issue in terms of the conflict between the Communists' right to advocate certain ideas and the Government's right to protect national security. His next sentence referred to the issue as a "conflict of interests." Since he concluded this paragraph by talking about "conflicting claims," clearly he treated claims of a legal right as equivalent to the claims of a legally recognized interest.[140] After elaborating upon the nature of each of the two conflicting rights or interests (he continued to use the words interchangeably) he formulated, in the excerpt above, the balancing test in terms of competing interests. Finally, these competing interests were, in turn, seen as emerging from "competing political, economic and social pressures."[141]

Describing the problem in terms of competing interests (by treating rights as equivalent to interests) permitted Frankfurter to say that the weighing of the two interests involved in *Dennis* is best left to the elected representatives. "Primary responsibility for adjusting the interests which compete in the situation before us of necessity belong to Congress." Why? Because "[c]ourts are not designed to be a good reflex of a democratic society." The Supreme Court is "to set aside the judgment of those whose duty it is to legislate only if there is no reasonable basis for it."[142] Justice Frankfurter bowed to the legislative decision in part because his legal theory regarded all claims as interests.

The failure to make a distinction between rights and interests does not, of course, mean that Frankfurter was compelled to resolve *Dennis* and similar cases the way he did. Treating rights as interests only facilitated that outcome. A judge could use the concepts of rights and interests interchangeably and still insist that *he* must rank competing interests on some theoretical scale; but, to create priorities requires imposing a set of value judgments on the situation, a task which in Frankfurter's democratic theory must be done by the electorally responsible agencies.

In the last analysis, then, it was the democratic theory of Justice Frankfurter which compelled him to defer to the wishes of the elected representatives when their will has been made known. Justice Frankfurter developed the balancing test to keep the Court from becoming a superlegislature. Because judicial adherents of realist theory see the reconciliation of competing interests as the function of the elected representatives in a democratic society, they are unwilling to have the Court set aside the legislative judgment unless there is no reasonable basis for it.

The most immediate consequence of this effort to keep the Supreme Court's power within the confines of realist theory is to convert First Amendment cases like *Dennis* into issues of due process reasonableness. In fact, Justice Frankfurter used examples from the area of economic due process to buttress his argument in *Dennis*.[143]

> Free speech cases are not an exception to the principle that we are not legislators, that direct policy-making is not our province. How best to reconcile competing interests is the business of the legislatures, and the balance they strike is a judgment not to be displaced by ours, but to be respected unless outside the pale of fair judgment.[144]

The elected political leaders will thus decide substantive questions about the extent of political freedom in American democracy. In the framework of realist theory it was perfectly understandable for Frankfurter to begin the last paragraph of his *Dennis* opinion by saying: "Civil liberties draw at best only limited strength from legal guarantees."[145] The remainder of the paragraph clearly agrees with Dahl and the realist social scientists that the real protection for freedom is to be found in the values of the people as they are reflected in the political process. This reliance has to be the real protection for freedom to Justices Frankfurter and Harlan because their approach to the First Amendment makes the decisions of political leaders the decisive factor.

With this viewpoint, sustaining the constitutionality of the Smith Act, even though it restricts free speech, came easily. "Congress has determined that the danger created by advocacy of overthrow justifies the ensuing restriction on freedom of speech."[146] Since the determination was made after due deliberation, and on the basis of ample evidence of the type outlined above, Justice Frankfurter could not say the Smith Act was unreasonable. If it was not unreasonable, it was constitutional. Not the categorical command of the Constitution but the judgment of the political leaders was to mark the limits of political freedom for the Communists.

Justice Harlan's majority opinion in *Barenblatt v. United States* (1959)[147] noted that the Court had previously decided that the First Amendment does limit congressional investigations, and that in some circumstances it protects an individual from being compelled to disclose his associational relationships. That protection, as Frankfurter said, is just the beginning, not the end, of judicial analysis for the Justices adhering to the realist theory of democracy. "Where First Amendment rights are asserted to bar governmental interrogation, resolution of the issue always involves a balancing by the courts of the competing private and public interests at stake in the particular circumstances shown."[148] Here, the Supreme Court had to decide whether an inquiry by a subcommittee of the House Committee on Un-American Activities into Barenblatt's past or present membership in the Communist Party violated the First Amendment.

In analyzing their assessment of the relative merits of the competing interests it must be remembered that Frankfurter and Harlan always do their balancing "within the confines of the judicial process"—i.e. the Justices will sustain any reasonable government act related to a consitutionally permissible end. Justice Harlan maintained that the interest of Congress in forcing Barenblatt to testify related to a valid legislative purpose.

There was no need for Harlan to elaborate the competing interests in *Barenblatt* and the Justice does not do so. Congress has power to legislate in the field of Communist activites; to aid that legislation Congress has the related right of conducting investigations. The subcommittee had decided it needed to know about Barenblatt's associational activities as a graduate student at the University of Michigan; the Court could not say that request was unreasonable. With the "right of self-preservation, the *ultimate* value of any society,"[149] thrown on the side of the House Committee on Un-American Activities, "the balance between the individual and the governmental interests here at stake must be struck in favor of the latter, and that therefore the provisions of the First Amendment have not been offended."[150]

In the wide-ranging realm of Congressional investigations the Frankfurter-Harlan balance test permits elected governmental officials to define the extent of a person's free speech. In so doing, Harlan explicitly rejected the judiciary's ability to evaluate the motives behind the exercise of investigatory power. If the political leaders abuse their power by investigating purely for the sake of exposure, the remedy lies in the hands of the elected officials, responsible to the people through the process of free competitive elections.[151]

In *Communist Party v. Subversive Activities Control Board* (1961),[152] Justice Frankfurter held that the registration provisions of the Subversive Activities Control Act of 1950,[153] as applied to the Communist Party did not constitute a restraint of freedom of expression and association in violation of the First Amendment. Although "compulsory disclosure of the names of an organization's members may in certain instances infringe constitutionally protected rights of association," to "state that individual liberties may be affected is to establish the condition for, not arrive at the conclusion of, constitutional decision." A balance must be struck: "Against the impediments which particular governmental regulation causes to entire freedom of individual action, there must be weighed the value to the public of the ends which the regulation may achieve."[154]

While "a governmental regulation which requires registration as a condition upon the exercise of speech may in some circumstances affront the guarantee of free speech," it is still necessary for the restriction and the right to be "weighed in the constitutional balance."[155] Here, whatever restriction of free speech may take place was warranted because the Court could not say it was unreasonable for Congress to require the registration of an organization the board had found, on sufficient evidence, to be under foreign domination and dedicated to advancing the objectives of the world Communist movement.[156]

"Little remains to be said concerning the claim that the statute infringes First Amendment freedoms," wrote Justice Harlan that same day in *Scales v. United States* (1961).[157] The statute involved in this case was the membership clause of the Smith act,[158] but the statement indicates the results of the Frankfurter-Harlan balancing test as applied to all legislation dealing with the First Amendment rights of American Communists. On the basis of previous decisions, Harlan, writing for the same five-man majority as in the *Subversive Activities Control Board* case, could summarily dismiss the First Amendment claims posed by the membership clause. By this time, the case against the Communist Party had been so well established in Court opinions that Justice Harlan, a leading proponent of the balancing doctrine, did not even bother to go through the steps of weighing the competing interests involved in this particular situation. The balance, whatever the circumstances, would inevitably be tipped in the government's favor by its claim that the ultimate value of any society was involved. The Court could not say the government's act was not reasonably related to that purpose, and, therefore, it would uphold the membership clause of the Smith Act. Why prolong the inevitable by going through all the steps required by the balance test to justify a known conclusion? It was sufficient to rest upon prior decisions.[159]

Little remains to be said also about the authority given legislative bodies to investigate the activities of Communists and suspected Communists under the Frankfurter-Harlan balancing test. "As the *Barenblatt* opinion makes clear, it is the nature of the Communist activity involved, whether the momentary conduct is legitimate or illegitimate politically, that established the Government's overbalancing interest."[160] Whenever a congressional committee can show it has reason to believe a person can shed some light on Communist activity, his First Amendment rights do not protect him from the committee's questioning.[161] Under this line of reasoning, the same is true of state legislative investigatory bodies.[162] The Communist Party had been found to be a threat to national security by Congress. Legislative bodies, therefore, had an overbalancing need to find out about Communist activity so that they might consider ways of dealing with the problem.

Once the assumption that the Communist Party, by its very nature, poses a threat to our national security is accepted by judges adhering to the realist theory, almost any laws the elected officials pass to curb the party become reasonable. The same assumption makes legislative investigation of any activity of almost any person believed to have knowledge of Communist activity reasonable. When a government action is reasonable, in the due process sense of that word, the Frankfurter-Harlan balancing test will sustain it as constitutional.

The due process reasonableness proviso does require the Court to put some limits on government action. A clear violation of a fairly definite constitutional provision cannot be sustained.[163] Criminal proceedings against a person charged with violating the laws regarding Communist activity must withstand judicial scrutiny. There must be enough proof to warrant a finding of guilt.[164] The evidence must be presented at an individual's own trial.[165] When the courts are used to penalize contempt of Congress citations the same strict judicial standards apply.[166] In short, statutes used to punish Communists are to be treated like other penal laws—they are to be strictly construed.[167]

Administrative actions, also, must meet rudimentary standards of fairness such as notice and hearing, even when the ostensible purpose is national security.[168] Even when the stated reason for a government action is national security, there still must be some connection between the means and the end. If Communist activity is seen as the threat, it will not do for the government to restrict all political unorthodoxy in the name of national security: the shadowy possibility of dangerous action by small, dissident, non-Communist groups is too remote. Laws aimed at Communist activity are reasonable only if they stifle that activity, not all political dissent.[169]

Despite all these restrictions, whose importance is not to be deprecated, the fact remains that Justices Harlan and Frankfurter were most reluctant to hold that the First Amendment imposes *substantive* restrictions upon the power of the politically elected representatives to deal with domestic Communists. The consequence, as we have seen, is that the political leaders define the political freedom of American Communists and, to a somewhat lesser extent, of "suspected" Communists.

These cases are just illustrative of the general approach Justices Frankfurter and Harlan took toward the problems of political freedom in American democracy. When other problems arose, they were similarly willing to let the elected leadership resolve them in any manner consistent with the tenets of due process outlined above. On the entire range of issues they were willing to allow the people directly responsible to the electoral process to define the substantive content of political freedom.[170]

For example, Justices Frankfurter and Harlan responded to the questions of political freedom posed by the Negro American's drive for equal citizenship in the same way they handled the Communist Party cases. The most relevant cases begin with *NAACP v. Alabama* (1958).[171] In the wake of the NAACP's successful suits to desegregate public schools and other facilities, Alabama, like other Southern states, organized a program of "massive resistance." Part of that program was a direct effort to drive the NAACP out of the South, thereby preventing further legal challenges to "the Southern way of life." The issue before the Court in this case was whether Alabama could compel the NAACP to reveal its membership lists to the state's attorney general. The result which would ensue from such a disclosure was obvious to all. Once the names of the NAACP's members were known, Alabama would not need further political or legal action to crush the organization—it could leave that task to the not so tender mercies of private groups.

Justice Harlan wrote the opinion for the unanimous Court, a noteworthy opinion on several counts. He squarely held for the first time what many prior opinions had suggested: there is a constitutionally protected freedom of association under the First Amemdment.[172] Further, the NAACP as an organization was recognized as having judicial standing to assert claims on behalf of its members, a departure from the general rule that parties are only able to assert constitutional rights personal to themselves. Harlan recognized that to require individual members to assert a right of associational privacy "would result in the nullification of the right at the very moment of its assertion."[173]

Obviously, just from his treatment of these two factors Justice Harlan's approach does not make him insensitive to claims of political freedom. He knew in this case that the "inviolability of privacy in group association may in many circumstances be indispensable to preservation of freedom of association, particularly where a group espouses dissident beliefs."[174] Far from being unconcerned about the need for political freedom, both Harlan and Frankfurter always explicitly stated their belief in its importance. The interesting thing was how they treated this important complex of rights—on what basis they defended political freedoms against other claims, and on what basis they were willing to subordinate those important political freedoms.

In this case, when Harlan came to the merits, he constructed his balance of competing interests in this way:

> whether Alabama has demonstrated an interest in obtaining the disclosures it seeks from [the NAACP] which is *sufficient* to justify the deterrent effect which we have concluded these disclosures may well have on the free exercise by [the NAACP's] members of the constitutionally protected right of association.[175]

Given this wording, our interest centers on what Harlan was willing to accept as a *sufficient* justification. The sole justification Alabama offered for its needs for the membership list was to determine whether the organization was conducting interstate business in violation of the state's foreign corporation registration statute. Harlan was unable to fathom how the disclosure of names of the NAACP's rank and file membership could further that state interest. Although Harlan cited a Frankfurter opinion for the proposition that if political rights are to be infringed the "subordinating interests of the state must be compelling,"[176] he actually found that in this case there was no relationship at all between the disclosure demanded and the Alabama law cited to justify the infringement of political rights; rather, in this case the state failed to show any legally cognizable basis for its claim. Lacking a showing of *any* relationship between the stated purpose and the chosen means enabled Harlan to defend freedom of association by relying on a basic tenet of due process.

Six years later, when the same legal action was before the Supreme Court for the fourth time, Justice Harlan again wrote the opinion for a unanimous Court.[178] He again based his opinion on Alabama's inability to show any reason for barring the NAACP from operating within the state. Alabama's claim of independent state procedural grounds for finding against the NAACP were dismissed because it was "crystal clear" to the Court "that the rule invoked by [Alabama] cannot reasonably be deemed applicable to this case."[179] Further, "the consideration of asserted constitutional rights may not be thwarted by simple recitation that there has not been observance of a procedural rule with which there has been compliance, in both substance and form, in every real sense."[180] The substantive issues were similarly settled on the basis of due process: the asserted grounds for excluding the NAACP furnished no foundation for that action.[181]

Harlan's opinion bristles with anger at Alabama's all too obvious attempt to drive the NAACP out of the state because the organization opposed continued segregation. He was even more upset by the Alabama Supreme Court's complicity in these tactics, conduct he felt was unbecoming of a court. In this type of case, the Frankfurter-Harlan approach is at its best. Because it makes due process reasonableness the key factor, it clearly exposes the lack of any legally cognizable claim in Alabama's harassment of the NAACP. It is a fine opinion. Still, it is important to note that Harlan defended the NAACP's First Amendment right of association by using due process arguments.

Justices Frankfurter and Harlan, therefore, had no difficulty joining the opinion of the Court in *Bates v. Little Rock* (1960).[182] Once again the issue was the NAACP's refusal to supply Southern officials with its membership list. Once again the Court found no relevant correlation between the stated need (here, the enforcement of the city's occupational license tax) and the compulsory disclosure of the names of the people in the organization. Although Justice Potter Stewart's opinion contained references to Supreme Court opinions requiring the state to show a "cogent" interest, or a "subordinating interest which is compelling" in these type of cases, he actually held that Little Rock's action bore no reasonable relationship to the governmental purpose asserted as its justification.[183] This reliance on due process led Frankfurter and Harlan to join Stewart's opinion.[184]

What if the statute satisfied the requirements of due process? Would Harlan and Frankfurter take that as sufficient justification to limit political freedom? Apparently they would. In *Shelton v. Tucker* (1960)[185] the issue was whether Arkansas could compel every teacher in a state supported school or college, as a condition of employment, to list all organizations to which he has belonged or regularly contributed money within the preceding five years. The history of this statute leaves little doubt that it was designed to expose members and supporters of the NAACP and other civil rights organizations. Justice Stewart's opinion for the five-man majority held that the statute was unconstitutional because in its "unlimited and indiscriminate sweep. . . . the statute's comprehensive interference with associational freedom goes far beyond what might be justified in the exercise of the State's legitimate inquiry into fitness and competency of its teachers."[186]

Writing for the four dissenters, Justice Frankfurter stated he was personally opposed to these "crude intrusions" into the private lives of Arkansas teachers. "But in maintaining the distinction between private views and constitutional restrictions, I am constrained to find that it does not exceed the permissible range of State action limited by the Fourteenth Amendment."[187] As was his wont, the Justice did not even mention the First Amendment as the applicable restriction here, only the Fourteenth. This viewpoint was because he saw his balance of competing interests solely in terms of the Due Process Clause: "The issue remains whether, in light of the particular kind of restriction upon individual liberty which a regulation entails, it is *reasonable* for a legislature to choose that form of regulation rather than others less restrictive."[188]

He did not find the state statute unreasonable. The state may want to know if a person has overcommitted his time to demanding and distracting organizational activities. The type of activities, plus the people who meet him while he is engaging in those activities, may help the authorities evaluate the teacher's general competence, ability, honesty, etc. All these things considered, Frankfurter was "unable to say, on the face of this statute, that Arkansas could not reasonably find that the information which the statute requires—and which may not be otherwise acquired than by asking the questions it asks—is germane to [the] selection" of teachers.[189]

Justice Harlan also wrote an opinion for the four dissenters. He began by saying that where official action claimed to invade the rights of free speech and association, "the controlling inquiry is whether such action is justifiable on the basis of a superior governmental interest to which such individual rights must yield."[190] This language certainly sounds different than a balance test framed solely in terms of due process reasonableness. It says *superior* governmental interests are required to overweigh those important political rights. Seemingly, a showing of reasonableness would not be sufficient. In the very next sentence, however, Justice Harlan made it clear that a showing of reasonableness will be sufficient to sustain the statute in his opinion; for Harlan viewed this law as establishing an investigatory procedure. On the authority of *Barenblatt* he said that investigations require the Court to ascertain two things: "First, whether the investigation *relates* to a legislative purpose; second, whether judged in the light of that purpose the questioned action has *substantial relevance* thereto."[191] "Superior governmental interest" has been very quickly reduced to due process reasonableness.

In answering those two questions Justice Harlan made his total reliance on due process even more evident. The end, he said, is legitimate: the state has the right to choose its teachers on the basis of fitness. The means relate to that end: "information about a teacher's association may be *useful* to school authorities in determining the moral, professional and social qualifications of the teacher."[192] The prior Court decisions dealing with a state's right to find out about Communist Party affiliation support the contention that a state may inquire into associations to aid a legitimate state interest. Given the type of information which a state may find useful in evaluating "moral, professional and social qualifications," Harlan could see no way of limiting the inquiry beforehand. When a state could show a reasonable relationship between its professed purpose and the disclosure of a person's associational activities, there was no basis for denying the state's claim even though it infringed the constitutional right of association.

While the opinions of Frankfurter and Harlan made a showing of reasonableness a sufficient test in this case, they were not willing to say that it was always going to be sufficient. Here, they argued, the Court is confronted only with the validity of the statute on its face. Both insist that if the statute is biased in its application—"by unwarranted publicizing of required associational disclosures,"[193] or "to further a scheme of terminating the employment of teachers solely because of their membership in unpopular organizations"[194]—the Court should strike that application down. Both asserted there would be time enough for the Court to act then.

By that time, however, the very damage to the right of association which Harlan noted in the 1958 *NAACP v. Alabama* case would have been done. Disclosure of a teacher's support of organizations seeking to end segregation and discrimination would have meant reprisals by the white community if not by the school authorities. Reprisals would occur for the same reason Harlan thought unconscionable in 1958—to cripple the drive for equal citizenship. If the damage was done by community pressure and not by state officials, it is difficult to imagine what redress the Court could supply after the fact. Because in *Shelton* the state could claim a relationship between its method of attack (disclosure of associational membership) and one of its legitimate purposes (hiring qualified teachers) which Justices Harlan and Frankfurter thought not unreasonable, they were "constrained" by their own standard from protecting political freedom.

That same judicial standard is evident in *NAACP v. Button* (1963).[195] Virginia, as part of its legislative program of massive resistance, had revised its barratry laws to prevent the NAACP from instigating suits to challenge racial segregation. The Supreme Court opinion by Justice William J. Brennan, Jr., held that the legal activities of the NAACP, its affiliates, and its legal staff are modes of expression and association protected by the First Amendment. The NAACP, the Court reasoned, used litigation as a "means for achieving the lawful objectives of equality of treatment by all government . . . It is thus a form of *political expression*. Groups which find themselves unable to achieve their objective through the ballot frequently turn to the courts." [196]

Justice Harlan, in dissent, saw the issue differently, partly because he did not believe that the bringing of law suits could be categorized simply as a First Amendment right. Although recognizing that "litigation is often the desirable and orderly way of resolving disputes of broad public significance, and of obtaining vindication of fundamental rights,"[197] he also maintained that "litigation, whether or not associated with the attempt to vindicate constitutional rights is *conduct*; it is speech plus."[198] As conduct, "the state may impose *reasonable* regulation limiting the permissible form of litigation and the manner of legal representations within its borders."[199]

Justice Harlan then asked "whether the particular regulation of conduct concerning litigation has a *reasonable relation* to the furtherance of a proper state interest."[200] Virginia's interest was very clear to him: maintaining the high professional standards of its legal practitioners. The statute had a reasonable relation to that interest: it prevented any interference in the uniquely personal relationship between an individual and his lawyer. Virginia, Harlan argued, was seeking to prevent organizations from exploiting individuals. The barratry statute was therefore reasonably related to a valid state purpose.

Since the conduct regulated by the Virginia law did involve some aspects of constitutionally protected speech, Justice Harlan also felt called upon to examine "whether that interest *outweighs* any foreseeable harm to protected freedoms."[201] When he came to that balance in his opinion, however, the weighing was decided in terms of sufficient relation. The state had a substantial interest in the calibre of its bar. The methods of obtaining litigants prohibited by the statute "are not conducive to encouraging the kind of attorney-client relationship which the State may reasonably demand."[202] The statute was therefore constitutional. It measured up to the requirements of due process.

Finally, in *Gibson v. Florida Legislative Investigation Committee* (1963)[203] the Supreme Court was confronted with a state challenge to the associational privacy of the NAACP based on its power to investigate Communist activity. The opinion for the Court by Justice Arthur J. Goldberg, the man who replaced Frankfurter on the Supreme bench, did not actually reach the question of whether the state had demonstrated "an immediate, substantial and subordinating" interest. It held the committee had failed to establish the necessary nexus between the questions it asked and subversive activity by the NAACP. Justice Goldberg's opinion protected the NAACP's associational privacy on due process grounds.[204]

Justice Harlan, writing a dissent joined by Justices Clark, Stewart, and White, thought that Goldberg had badly misread Court precedents. His principal objection was that "until today, I had never supposed that any of our decisions relating to state or federal power to investigate in the field of Communist subversion could possibly be taken as suggesting any difference in the degree of governmental investigatory interest as between Communist infiltration *of* organizations and Communist activity *by* organizations."[205]

The Court's reliance on this unfounded distinction, said Harlan, led it to misapply the due process test of substantial relationship. The committee had heard testimony that some fourteen persons who were, or had been, Communists or members of Communist fronts or "affiliated organizations," had attended meetings of the NAACP and/or were members of that branch. This preliminary information was "sufficient to satisfy under any reasonable test the requirement of nexus." To hold otherwise would be to require "an investigating agency to prove in advance the very things it is trying to find out."[206] Because the state had established a reasonable relationship, had met the due process requirement of nexus, Justice Harlan thought the NAACP official was required to answer the questions on pain of a contempt citation.

Justice Harlan was entirely correct when he said that Justice Goldberg had misconstrued the Court's prior decisions about investigations of alleged Communist activity. Those cases did not make a distinction between investigations of the Communist Party or its members, and investigations of Communist activity within concededly nonsubversive organizations like the NAACP. Despite a valiant effort, Goldberg was unable to make a plausible distinction between *Gibson* and *Uphaus v. Wyman* (1959)[207] which involved alleged Communist activity at the World Fellowship camp in New Hampshire. Nor was the testimony about alleged Communist activity before the Florida Legislative Committee any less substantial than the testimony before the New Hampshire

committee in *Uphaus*. If precedent was to be a controlling factor in determining both the range of governmental investigations of alleged Communist
activity and of the government's showing of nexus, Harlan clearly had the
better argument.

The consequences of Harlan's argument are also quite clear. Whenever
a "witness" before a governmental investigating committee asserts that an
organization or some of its members are Communist, the nexus has been
established which will permit an infringement of an important political freedom, the right of associational privacy. During the heyday of the civil rights
movement in the South, finding such a witness was not difficult. One of the
stock-in-trade ideas of many groups was that any individual, private organization, or governmental agency (not excluding the United States Supreme
Court) promoting the end of racial discrimination was, by definition, Communist. In several Southern states that idea had become official state policy.
Under the authority of Louisiana's Subversive Activities and Communist Control Law and its Communist Propaganda Control Law, the offices of the
Southern Conference Educational Fund (a civil rights group) were raided,
its records seized, and its officers prosecuted.[208] Justice Harlan's criteria would
have paved the way for the Southern states, under the guise of fighting
Communism, to destroy the very political freedom which Harlan had found
to be protected by the First Amendment.

Once again Justice Harlan was constrained by his realist theory from
deciding against the government. The theory told him that in a democracy
the nonelected Court should interfere with the decisions of the elected policy
makers only when they were patently unreasonable. As in previous cases, he
knew that investigations sometimes infringe First Amendment rights, but he
also insisted the Court should consider the government's interest in obtaining
information. When he came to weighing the government's interest against
the individual's, Justice Harlan, in this case as in all others, read the resultant
balance through his realist theory. As long as the government could meet the
test of due process reasonableness, Harlan and Frankfurter would sustain its
claim.

Weighing competing interests in cases involving the "strategic freedoms"
covered by the First Amendment is not, of course, unique to Justices Frankfurter and Harlan. What is distinctive was their consistent use of due process
as the test for resolving the conflict. This use means that the "balance" in all
these cases was deliberately and consciously tipped in favor of the government,
as is only proper in realist theory. The democratic theory of Frankfurter and
Harlan gave elected leaders great latitude in defining political freedom in the
United States.

It must be emphasized that the latitude which the two Justices would
give to the elected leaders is *not* restricted to defining the meaning of political

freedom in marginal cases. It extends as well to the cases at the very core. Whether the overt activities of the Communist Party are within the context of democratic political freedom is considered by many to be a debatable issue. The Communist Party cases may therefore be considered marginal cases. The political activities of the NAACP examined here do not raise that kind of issue. They are, under any theory, squarely within the ambit of democratic political freedom, yet Justices Frankfurter and Harlan applied the same standards to both sets of cases. When the issue raised was whether a particular activity should be considered a political freedom *and* when they knew the case did indeed involve the exercise of a political freedom, reasonable governmental actions were sustained. Both the extent and the core content of political freedom are to be determined by the reasonable actions of the individuals directly responsible to the democratic electoral processes.

The Frankfurter-Harlan balancing method has been defended by Professor Hook and others as a necessity created by the highly ambiguous language of the First Amendment, an ambiguity unclarified by American history. Largely because of the absence of self-defining standards, the Justices resorted openly to balancing in cases involving political freedoms protected by the First Amendment.[209] Since the Amendment does not embody a fixed corpus of legal standards, so the argument runs, the Justices must inevitably decide cases by weighing political interests. Far better that they should do so openly: "We have had too many opinions that hid the inevitable weighing process by pretending that decisions spring full-blown from the Constitution—a document written generations ago by men who had not the slightest conception of the world in which *we* live."[210]

This defense of the inevitability of balancing based on the ambiguity of the First Amendment's language is too sweeping. It confuses the inevitable problems in defining the *scope* of a vague constitutional provision—the problems of the margin—with the problems of its central meaning. After all, "Constitution writing is not a practicable undertaking if inexplicitness is to be treated as a total failure to say anything."[211] Other vague provisions of the Constitution have been given some clear central meaning, although the extent of applicability is often far from clear. For example, in dealing with racial issues, the Equal Protection Clause now is read as barring state actions which discriminate against racial minorities, even though we are a long way from having an adequate definition of the extent of state action.[212]

The First Amendment's absolute prohibition does not necessarily require an intelligent person to use the Frankfurter-Harlan balancing approach. An intelligent, rational individual might choose to believe that once a central meaning is defined, and despite borderline cases, there is a range of political freedom covered by the First Amendment's clauses which cannot be outweighed by other claims. Even in our rapidly changing society, there are some political rights always relevant in a democracy—e.g. the right of a group like the NAACP to advocate a new governmental policy or to oppose an existing one. Once such core meanings of various political freedoms were recognized, there would be no necessity of balancing them away for the sake of competing interests.

If Justices Frankfurter and Harlan did not treat rights as equivalent to interests, it would have been much more difficult to say that the primary responsibility invariably rests with the elected representatives. When the two claims are distinct, it is immediately necessary to view conflicting legal claims in terms of three separate categories: conflicts between one constitutional right and another;[213] conflicts between two legally recognized interests;[214] and conflicts between claims based upon a constitutionally protected right and a legally recognized interest.[215]

With such a legal theory, only cases in the second category—conflicts between two interests—should be the primary responsibility of legislative judgment. Perhaps the legislature's primary responsibility should also extend to cases in the first category because there is no a priori best way of resolving a conflict between two rights. Resolving a conflict between two rights, however, could also be seen as primarily a judicial function in which the Court interprets the Constitution to create a consistent pattern of imposed limitations on granted powers. In any event, with a legal theory which took rights seriously,[216] those cases falling into the third category would find the Court enforcing constitutional rights against political forces. Justices Frankfurter and Harlan were able to deny the Supreme Court's primary responsibility in all three of these areas because they saw no distinction between rights and interests.

As treated by Frankfurter and Harlan, moreover, the political freedoms protected by the First Amendment are not affirmatively definable. They are defined only in relation to the weight of the interests arrayed against them. Freedom is inversely proportional to the weight accorded those interests. Granted the difficulty in defining core meanings, and granted also that no definition could remove the problem of cases at the margin, a judicially created core would still give at least a minimum content to our political freedoms which would be absolutely protected by judicial enforcement of the Constitution. That is not an advantage to be dismissed lightly.[217]

If Hook et al. still object because grave emergencies might make it necessary to subordinate even the most basic right in a democracy—the right to have a functioning opposition (as in Great Britain during both World Wars)—that still does not necessarily lead to the Frankfurter-Harlan balancing position. An intelligent, rational person might choose to believe that given the firm negative of the First Amendment, and given the admitted importance of political freedoms in a democracy, those freedoms are not to be overborne unless the government makes a detailed, specific showing of the compelling need to subordinate a particular freedom in that particular emergency situation. Unlike the position advocated by Justices Frankfurter and Harlan, this "preference" position would at least require that the Court give more than lip service when weighing "strategic political freedoms" in the balance.[218]

The defenders of the Frankfurter-Harlan position have not been content with resting their case on the asserted inevitability of balancing. They have also maintained that it has positive virtues. One of these virtues is most clearly stated by Professor Wallace Mendelson:

> Open balancing compels a judge to take full responsibility for his decisions, and promises a particularized, rational account of how he arrives at them—more particularized and more rational at least than the familiar parade of hallowed abstractions, elastic absolutes, and selective history. Moreover, this approach should make it more difficult for judges to rest on their predispositions without ever subjecting them to the test of reason.[219]

To the extent that the Frankfurter-Harlan approach does produce an informed and candid weighing of the particular factors which the judges inevitably use in deciding cases, it is a net gain. Without reliance upon rationally stated argument, judicial opinions would be undistinguishable from arbitrary fiat, the very antithesis of the "rule of law" on which Western man has staked so much. Insofar as the Frankfurter and Harlan approach is more likely to force the Justices into a rational explanation of the reasons behind their decisions, it is surely a considerable mark in its favor.

Even assuming *arguendo* that this approach is more likely to lead a judge into giving a more "particularized, rational account of how he arrives at his decisions," that does not automatically eliminate the taint of arbitrariness from his opinions. In fact, it is likely to have exactly the opposite effect. The more particularized the decisions become, the more difficult it is to see the general "neutral-principles"—"the standards which transcend the case at hand."[220] When decisions are limited to resolving only the particular case at hand in light of the particular facts involved, decisions tend to take on an ad hoc quality. In that memorable phrase of Justice Roberts, such decisions are like "a restricted railroad ticket, good for this day and train only."[221]

There is basis for this criticism. In *Watkins v. United States* (1957)[222] Frankfurter and Harlan joined in overturning a conviction for contempt of Congress arising from an investigation of the House Committee on Un-American Activities Committee. Harlan actually signed Chief Justice Warren's opinion for the Court. Frankfurter, unwilling to join the majority's wide-ranging attack on the committee's authority, rules, and procedures, wrote a separate opinion. He relied solely on the narrow grounds the Court actually used to decide the case—the committee had failed to explain to Watkins how the questions asked were pertinent to the subject matter under investigation.[223]

Two years later, Justice Harlan, in an opinion which Frankfurter signed, made an all-out effort to distinguish the facts in *Barenblatt*[224] from those in *Watkins*, but to no avail. Commentators have not been convinced by Harlan's explanation that the factual situations were so different that Barenblatt should have been convicted for relying upon the same grounds which led to Watkin's acquittal. Instead, the commentators have regarded *Barenblatt* as a retreat from the more libertarian decision of 1957, in the face of congressional and other attacks on the Courts.[225]

Much the same ad hoc quality can be found in the Frankfurter-Harlan approach in the Smith Act cases. *Yates v. United States* (1957)[226] involved the convictions of fourteen middle-level Communists under the conspiracy clauses of the act. *Dennis* had sustained the conviction of the eleven top leaders of the Communist Party under the very same sections. The *Yates* opinion was written by Justice Harlan and it reversed the convictions. He maintained the jury had not been instructed about the government's need to prove that these Communists presently advocated the forcible overthrow of the government, not as abstract doctrine, but by the use of language reasonably and ordinarily calculated to incite persons to action, immediately or in the future. Justice Harlan claimed that the distinction between advocacy of abstract doctrine and advocacy of action was basic to *Dennis*;[227] but, as Justice Clark in dissent maintained, no such distinction clearly emerges in the opinions sustaining the convictions in *Dennis*.[228] The government, which had relied upon the same type of evidence in *Yates* as it had used in *Dennis*, did not think it had sufficient evidence to meet the new rule and let the indictments drop.

Professors Alexander Bickel and Robert McCloskey have defended these First Amendment decisions involving Communists as examples of judicial political wisdom.[229] They argue that the Court should rarely declare a congressional action against Communists as unconstitutional under the First Amendment. That decision would bring a head-on collision with Congress, a risk the Court should not take on the Communist issue where the masses are bound to ignore sophisticated distinctions and think only in terms of for or against the Communists. Thus *Dennis, Subversive Activities Control Board* and *Scales* are all politically wise decisions. When the Court is convinced that anti-Communist fever is high, it should be most reluctant to challenge actions against Communists, as in *Barenblatt*. When the Justices think the country is less concerned, the Court should zealously guard political freedom, but it should perform that role by basing its decisions on narrow, technical, legal principles, as in *Yates, Noto*, and Frankfurter's concurrence in *Watkins*. By acting in this politically sophisticated way, the Court can best protect itself and occasionally take effective action on behalf of political freedom.

This defense, of course, directly counters that of Professors Hook and Mendelson. Instead of appreciating their candid and informed weighing of the relevant factors, the Justices were being applauded for their reliance on technical, legal requirements which protect individuals by *obscuring* the basic underlying issues. The opinions do seem best explained in terms of political prudence. Prudence is a virtue that politicians ignore at their own peril. It is not, however, a virtue calculated to instill faith in an impartial court acting on the basis of legal principles. The line between prudence and expediency often defied as astute a political cartographer as Niccolo Machiavelli; to less gifted mortals that distinction is more likely to depend on such mundane factors as whose ox is being gored. Without a rule which can be impartially applied, there are bound to be grave doubts about whether the Frankfurter-Harlan balancing approach can assure or even promote impartiality.

If, on the other hand, the Justices try to avoid ad hoc decisions by relying upon precedent, they are bound to play down the importance of the particular facts of the particular case at hand. If they rely upon precedent they are back to the very reliance on general principles from which balancing was supposed to extricate them. The reliance upon precedent accounts for a strange quality in the Court's opinion in *Scales*, a case which involved a conflict between a First Amendment political freedom and a government interest. The Court said it was weighing the competing interests of the particular case at hand, but it based the opinion squarely upon the *Barenblatt* precedent. The Court didn't even bother going through the motions of balancing, although it used the language of the Frankfurter-Harlan balancing approach. It must have been small comfort to Scales that the Court actually made a detailed examination of the particular circumstances involved in Barenblatt's conviction (if only to distinguish his case from *Watkins*); Scales did not receive the benefits of individualization which were supposed to accrue to the use of the Frankfurter-Harlan balancing approach.

To talk in terms of individual benefits, though, would be missing the basic defense of the Frankfurter-Harlan position on the First Amendment. Once again, it is the systemic logic rather than the impact on individuals which is decisive. The single most important virtue claimed for the Frankfurter-Harlan balancing position is its compatibility with realist theory. The reduction of the First Amendment's absolute language to due process reasonableness is calculated to leave the sovereign prerogative of choice to the people and the men electorally responsible to them. The extent of political freedom in a country is also a matter of policy. "And," says Professor Hook, "responsibility for policy rests with the elected representatives who may be refused our confidence at election time, and not with judges who are beyond reach. As far as policy goes, a judge's vote counts for one and no more than one, and is cast like every other citizen's vote."[230] The Frankfurter-Harlan position is a device to insure the least possible interference with policy choices, given the existence of judicial review. In the end, the defense of this position is a defense of the realist theory of democracy.

CONCLUSIONS

The defense of the Frankfurter-Harlan position reveals four weighty objections to realist theory. First, by making the political-electoral process the ultimate determinant of all policies, realist theory cannot prevent the constriction of democracy even as defined by that theory. "The consent upon which free government rests," wrote Justice Frankfurter, "is the consent that comes from sharing in the process of making and unmaking laws."[231] What if the people who operate that process, the political leaders, restrict a group's access to the making and unmaking of laws? In realist theory that action would be regarded as a valid policy if there was some reasonable basis for it. When democracy is seen as an institutionalized method for reconciling the competing interests of diverse groups, a reasonable basis is not all that difficult to find. In fact, in this framework when the authorized people—the elected officials—make policy choices, it is very difficult to say their choices were unreasonable; the policy reflects their considered judgment on how best to reconcile competing interests. Almost any policy which can be related to a governmental purpose will therefore be deemed reasonable, even if it restricts access to the political process itself.

The evidence for this conclusion can be found in the way all three concepts discussed here are used in realist theory. The expatriated American is denied the most basic right in realist theory—the right to participate through the electoral process in the making and unmaking of laws—yet, the Realists would permit the government to deny a person citizenship if that is a reasonable means of pursuing some valid objective. The structuring of the electoral process is often decisive in determining which laws shall be made or unmade, which group interests will be advanced or retarded; yet, realist theory would leave all questions of adequate representation to the discretion of those individuals and groups already in control of the political system. Realist theory insists that certain strategic freedoms are essential to the free competition for the free vote; yet, Realists would permit elected officials to curtail those very same rights if they could reasonably deem that curtailment to be the necessary cost of promoting some other interest. These types of actions, actions which cut to the very bone of this theory, are treated like all other policies and their ultimate determination is to be made through the political-electoral process.

Realist theory defines democracy exclusively in terms of the political-electoral process: democracy is the free competition for the free vote. It also uses that process as its standard of validation: all actions which emerge from the political-electoral process are valid as long as there is a reasonable basis for them. Realist theory, therefore, regards as valid actions which are at odds with its own definition of democracy. This consequence is, to say the least, paradoxical.

Second, realist theory all but destroys the utility of a written constitution. As we have seen, the realist social scientists believe "that constitutional rules are not crucial, independent factors maintaining democracy; rather, the rules themselves seem to be functions of underlying non-constitutional factors." The "constitutional rules are not significant as guarantors either of government by majority or of liberty from majority tyranny."[232] Realist theory also leads Professor Hook and Justices Frankfurter and Harlan to see all authority in a democracy as flowing from the free, competitive, electoral process.

When in certain circumstances a tension or conflict is created between what the elected rulers deem necessary and what the Constitution may have orginally intended to be protected from government, Realists cannot interpret the Constitution as authorizing a particular way for resolving such conflicts. Obviously, the Constitution does not look forward to a consistent plan of democratic government: the Framers were not democrats. As democrats, the Realists maintain, we must interpret the document in light of democratic theory—the struggle for political power through the free competition for the free vote. We must also recognize that it is always necessary for our elected leaders, in each circumstance, to weigh competing interests. The elected rulers must rule; they cannot avoid hard decisions by hiding behind the Constitution.

In realist theory, the Constitution contains procedures for selecting temporary rulers of the American democracy and procedures those rulers must follow in office. It contains little else. The Constitution no longer contains substantive norms to make the United States the good society. If the good society is to be created here, it must emerge through "the processes of intelligence as they develop from the matrix of freely given consent."[233] Contrary to Justice Frankfurter, it is the realist theorists who are treating the Constitution as an "outworn parchment,"[234] for in the areas of citizenship, political participation, and political freedom—three critical concepts in any democratic theory—they would reduce the Constitution to due process reasonableness. Little remains of the Constitution save an admonition to the elected officials, an admonition which says: be reasonable.[235] In realist theory the Constitution has ceased to be an independent source of authority.

Third, this view of the Constitution reduces the role the Supreme Court would play in our democracy. This reduction, of course, is quite deliberate. Since their theory sees democracy exclusively in terms of the political-electoral process, Realists are bound to view the Court as inherently nondemocratic and oligarchic. They therefore consciously seek to curtail the power of this vestigial remnant of our nondemocratic past either by an adamant insistence on a rigorous judicial self-restraint or by the abolition of the power of judicial review as we know it.

One could properly charge the Realists who advocate a rigorous judicial self-denial with theoretical inconsistency. The advocates of judicial self-restraint, such as Justices Frankfurter and Harlan, admit this inconsistency; they defend judicial self-restraint on the basis of historical tradition. Self-restraint, however, is itself inconsistent with the original view of the function of a written constitution. It is inconsistent with the practices of the men who developed and used judicial review, thereby making the Supreme Court an important factor in our history. It is inconsistent with the American people's historical support for the Court, *with* the power of judicial review, and their reluctance to change the institution—most notably during the great confrontation in 1937 between Franklin D. Roosevelt and the Supreme Court. Self-restraint is also inconsistent with the function the Court has historically played in legitimizing political decisions, and in making the American nation aware of the great value of traditional Anglo-American political norms.[236] Those are the very norms which Frankfurter, Harlan, and Hook believe are the most valuable assets of our civilization.

No one could properly charge Professor Hook with inconsistency on the subject of judicial review. It was the philosopher's need for internal consistency which led him to abandon an earlier defense of judicial self-denial for a more institutionalized check on the Court's power.[237] Only this type of restructuring of our institutions could prevent some misguided judges from imposing their value choices on us, from governing us like modern day Platonic Guardians. Inconsistency, then, cannot be made the major criticism of realist theory.

The objection is more fundamental. The Realists claim that the greatest value of democracy is its preservation and promotion of human dignity. They believe that praiseworthy goal is to be achieved by giving due recognition to norms like those embedded in our Constitution. But how are those norms going to remain influential factors in American life? By what means do the Realists think the traditions of freedom and individual dignity are going to survive?

According to the Realists, survival of these traditions certainly cannot be done through the courts; yet given its structure and tradition, the Supreme Court has almost the sole institutionalized opportunity for using those norms as the basis for arriving at decisions. Like all Americans, the Realists know that "principles are largely instrumental as they are employed in politics, instrumental in relation to results that a controlling sentiment demands at any given time."[238] This instrumentalism all but destroys other opportunities for principled action in the American political system. The great principled actions of United States Senators can be captured in one slender volume called *Profiles in Courage*. Their theory, however, leads the Realists to insist that the one agency having the institutionalized *possibility* of treating norms and principles in a different way must either conform to the instrumentalism of the political process or face destruction. If realist theory is to be criticized for its attitude toward judicial review, it is for its failure to take advantage of existing institutions in order to promote the larger ends it seeks—a free, tolerant, libertarian society.

Alas, if we exclude magic and mystical faith in the Anglo-American tradition we are unlikely to find a satisfactory substitute mechanism in realist theory for creating a "persistent, positive translation of the liberating faith into the feelings and thoughts and actions of men and women."[239] The Realists insist only on giving the existing political-electoral process greater leeway; it is their instrument for preserving and increasing political freedom and the other values necessary for human dignity. Consequently, "the only things [Realists] can be fanatical about are the processes of democratic consensus."[240] Because we have seen that those same processes can be used in realist theory to limit the range of permissible political activity and to reduce the possibility of all groups having effective access to the political process, we are not likely to find a total reliance on those processes very satisfactory. We may be fanatical about the political-electoral process, but since it can and has been used for actions deleterious to the ultimate values of democracy, even as defined by the Realists, we can hardly restrict our passion to that one mechanism.

Indeed, it is difficult to see how the structure of ideas in realist theory advanced the values the Realists claim for democracy. Although the theory insists that political freedom and other values related to human dignity are necessary for the free competition for the free vote, it does very little to give those values a cherished place in political practices.

Perhaps we can arrive at a clearer understanding of this deficiency if we once again turn to a realist objection to judicial review. In addition to all the reasons mentioned above, the Realists maintain that the Court cannot be relied upon because the "judges howsoever they may consciously seek to discipline themselves against it, are too apt to be moved by the deep undercurrents of public feelings."[241] This statement, from the pen of Felix Frankfurter, who tried as hard as any other Justice in United States history to discipline himself against relying upon his personal prejudices, is very revealing. It indicates that the Realists cannot rely upon the Court to translate constitutional norms into principled actions because they doubt the very possibility of principled action. The history of the Supreme Court's role in American life shows them that the Justices have frequently failed to act differently than politicians; it proves to the Realists the utter futility of expecting the Justices to behave otherwise. In this situation, there is no advantage in having a nonresponsive agency make policy decisions in a democracy.

At heart, the Realists are unable to believe in any kind of action other than that motivated by self-interest. The most they would concede on this count is that the number of people genuinely motivated by principle are far too few to be used as the basis of a political theory. This disbelief in principled action is not only reflected in their distrust of judicial review, but, more importantly, it is built into the very language of realist theory.

As we have seen, Realists refuse to make a distinction between different types of claims—principles and rights are regarded as another type of interest. Principles and rights are not invested with any great moral or ethical content. They are given a recognized place in realist theory—especially as they relate to the competitive electoral process—and one can make a legitimate claim for their protection on that basis. Nonetheless, rights and principles are not accorded a distinctive place in realist theory. Like all other claims they must be treated as means designed to advance group interests.

Realist theory offers no encouragement for the individual to think in terms other than his own interests. When individual rights—even the political freedoms necessary for the free competition for the free vote—conflict with a deeply felt interest, realist theory gives no presumptive validity to the claims of individual rights. Instead, such claims are treated as an interest, and the conflict of interests is to be resolved according to an intelligent assessment of their relative merits in the particular situation. When each person makes a decision as to what he thinks best, therefore, he is likely to do so in a way which advances and protects his own self-interest.

To escape this bind, the Realists become fanatical about the virtues of the political system. For them, the free competitive political process elevates private self-interest to a concern for the public well-being by requiring an accommodation of conflicting private interests. Within the system, the same sort of calculation as at the level of the private individual must be made. Realists believe that in a situation where claims of political freedom conflict with other important interests, the political leaders, like individual citizens, are bound to resolve the conflict as they think best.

In such a situation, as we have seen in the discussions of political participation and political freedom, the political leadership's reliance upon their own self-interest can have disastrous consequences for those groups having little political muscle. Realist theory, however, is in no position to demand a different kind of behavior by political leaders. Its whole system of democracy is built upon the competitive self-interest of politicians.

To be sure, there is a great deal of language in all realist writings about the functional importance of political freedoms and other such values in a democracy. On the basis of their own findings, the realist social scientists believe that political freedom in American democracy is sustained by the leadership stratum in American society, and that, in turn, this leadership consensus about the meaning of the democratic creed is consistent with the general public's vague, inarticulate belief. As long as stability remains the predominant condition of American politics, as long as basic cleavages do not divide important groups in our society, the average individual's lack of meaningful comprehension about the importance of political freedom for all citizens is not likely to threaten the existing pattern. No important leadership element would see any benefit in challenging the existing system because it would fall on the deaf ears of the contented masses. In such a situation, Professor Dahl[242] and other Realists are undoubtedly correct when they point to the function a widespread belief in democracy plays in limiting the types of appeals made by political leaders and, thereby, in maintaining the free competition for the free vote.

The low level of comprehension among the mass of people about the operational necessity of political freedom in a democracy does mean, however, that in times of unrest the people can be led into supporting, in the name of democracy, actions which threaten its viability. Since the general populace's understanding of the values of the democratic creed is so vague, it is not very difficult for unscrupulous leadership elements to deceive the people by cloaking their appeals in democratic rhetoric. Dahl concedes this possibility,[243] but he still insists that Americans' widely held beliefs in democratic values places a "critical limit" on the way American leaders may operate.

A decade before Dahl wrote the particular book just cited, another prominent social scientist, David Truman, also pegged his belief in the continuance of democracy on a broad, popular consensus concerning the rules of the game.[244] The force of events later caused Truman to have serious doubts about the viability of this loose and ambiguous popular consensus as a sufficient support for democracy.[245]

When one recalls how the madness of McCarthyism ended, there is little reason to reject Professor Truman's sober second judgment. McCarthyism ended only when the Korean truce had so reduced the salience of Communism as a political issue that a majority of United States Senators could believe it was not against their own self-interest to censure their colleague from Wisconsin. Before this political trend was evident in American politics, precious few senators had acted in a manner that could lead to their inclusion in a later, enlarged edition of *Profiles in Courage* (and that small group did not include the distinguished author of the book).[246] In addition to McCarthyism, the appeal of racism has frequently been successful despite its "pretty evident" inconsistency with the values of the democratic creed.

In short, Professor Dahl's insistence that Americans' widely held beliefs in democratic values operate as a "critical limit" on the substantive policies of American politics is like a priestly incantation of a widely held myth: the myth is effective only so long as no deeply felt interest compels people to challenge it, but when the challenge is made no magical forces rally to support the myth. In primitive society, as in democracy, the norms will be sustained only so long as people are willing to defend them. Unfortunately, realist theory does not provide important enough reasons for most people to forego what they perceive as their self-interest on behalf of the rules of the game.

More often than not the Realists' words about the importance of political freedom to the democratic political process serves no operational function other than incantation. Like their approach to problems of political participation, Realists always urge action in the realm of political freedom which would enhance democracy, but they sustain all "reasonable" actions whether they advance that process or not. The Realists' practice makes their talk about the importance of political freedom sound like mere exhortation to do the right thing. The failure to insist upon the *practice* of democratic values and habits is a strange omission in a democratic theory which places an almost exclusive reliance on the political-electoral mechanism.

People learn, as John Dewey insisted, by seeing and doing as well as listening. Too often Realists rely upon sermons about the values of democracy as their chief weapon against attacks on those values. Their practices do not always seem to be based on a full awareness of the consequences actually working against a "persistent, positive translation of the liberating faith into the feelings and thoughts and actions of men and women." The Realists' inaction against attacks on the "liberating faith" can only emphasize their theory's reliance on self-interest. The frail support which realist theory gives to public values, then, even the greatest of all values in this theory—the free, competitive electoral process—proves to be no support at all.

The fourth and weightiest objection to realist theory is its failure as an educational theory of democracy. It has no way of inculcating the values necessary for the free competition for the free vote into the feelings, thoughts, and actions of men and women.

OPTIMALIST THEORY _____

Realist theory is not the only prescriptive variety of the competitive paradigm. A significant minority of American democratic thinkers have repeatedly disagreed with realist theory while accepting the basic tenets of Schumpeter's definition. They too believe democracy should be defined as the free competition for the free vote and that the United States can therefore be described as a democracy. Like the Realists, they have made the competitive paradigm the basis of a prescriptive political theory and have used that theory when interpreting the Constitution. In short, this group of political thinkers have much in common with the Realists.

Unlike the Realists, they have not made their peace with the existing political process. Rather, they insist upon the need for restructuring the existing political institutions in order to make the American polity *more* democratic. In their eyes, the United States is a democracy whose institutions prevent us from enjoying the full benefits of democratic government. They want to create structures which would make those additional benefits possible. These individuals are Optimalists: their prescriptive theory seeks to optimize the advantages they see flowing from a more nearly perfect system of free competition for the free vote.

Using optimalist theory for interpreting the Constitution does not make that document into a uniform and universally recognized body of law designed to mold society in a particular image. Such an assumption would run contrary to the basic premises of the competitive paradigm, shared by Realists and Optimalists. This paradigm requires that both schools of thought see the Constitution primarily as an outline for the peculiarly American way of selecting our governors, not as a binding set of norms designed to impose a consistent pattern on society. Because they always seek to extend democracy, the Optimalists are in a position to rank-order certain values: those claims which would enhance the free competition for the free vote are given a higher status. Unlike the Realists, the Optimalists can prescribe theoretical priorities when values conflict. As Americans, they naturally seek to use the Constitution for imposing their priorities on our society. Although the Optimalists are in no position to maintain that the Constitution is a blueprint for creating the good society, they can argue that the Constitution required that certain priorities generally be recognized when inevitable value choices are made.

OPTIMALIST THEORY AND THE COMPETITIVE PARADIGM

Optimalist Political Scientists

For many years an important group of political scientists has been arguing that the United States will never have an effective democracy until our major political parties are realigned. The idea of two cohesive national parties organized around differing policies dates, in America, from at least the time of Woodrow Wilson's *Congressional Government* (1870). In 1950, the Committee on Political Parties of the American Political Science Association, led by its chairman, E. E. Schattschneider, brought forth its now famous report, *Toward a More Responsible Two-Party System*. Since the publication of that report, the idea of party realignment has been discussed by those persons concerned with the proper organization and functions of political parties in American democracy.

The basic model of the party realignment advocates was summarized by Professor Austin Ranney:

There must exist at least two (and preferably only two) unified, disciplined political parties. Each has a conception of what the people want and a program of various measures designed to satisfy those wants. In a pre-election campaign each attempts to convince a majority of the people that its program will best do what the people want done. In the election, each voter votes for a particular candidate in his district, primarily because that candidate is a member of the party which the voter wants to take power, and only secondarily because he prefers the individual qualities of one candidate to those of the other. The party which secures a majority of the government has the entire responsibility for what the government does. . . . [A]t the next election the people decide whether, on the whole, they approve of the general direction that the party in power has been taking—in short whether their wants have been satisfied. If the answer is yes, they return that party to power; if the answer is no, they replace it with the opposition party.[1]

The proposals for party realignment are always advanced in order to make our government *more* responsive, *more* democratic. Never for a moment do the political scientists urging those changes doubt that the United States is, in fact, a democracy. Professor Schattschneider, for example, defines democracy as "a political system in which the people have a choice among the alternatives created by competing political organizations and leaders."[2] By accepting Schumpeter's definition of democracy, Schattschneider is in no position to maintain that the United States is not a democracy, for even without realigning our party system Americans have a choice between competing political organizations and leaders. All that advocates of party realignment such as Professor Schattschneider can argue, therefore, is that if we adopt their proposals we shall have a more perfect democracy.

Not only does this group accept Schumpeter's definition of democracy, they also agree with his divisions of functions: the people periodically select their rulers and the rulers govern. Optimalist political scientists believe that "in a modern, thickly populated society like the United States, democracy should be conceived of as popular *control* over government, and not as popular *participation* in the day-to-day activities of government."[3]

Realists and Optimalists, then, are as one in accepting the competitive paradigm. They part company only when it comes to deriving prescriptive doctrines from Schumpeter's definition. What divides the realist social scientists from their professional brethren advocating party realignment is the issue of popular control under the existing system. The Realists, as we have seen, believe that the existing party-governmental system, while far from perfect, does provide for effective popular influence on governmental policies. The party realignment group believes that our multifactional two-party system does not enable the people to control their governors effectively, and that therefore the people cannot effectively influence governmental policy.

As the political system now operates, the only place where popular control exists is in each constituency. Presumably, the representative can be held responsible by that portion of the electorate, but the party realignment advocates refuse to accept this presumption. They argue it is impossible to hold a man responsible for things beyond his control and that, they claim, is exactly the condition created by the existing system:

> [P]ower in Congress is so fragmented and the whole legislative proc-
> ess so complex and confusing that the bewildered voter usually has
> great difficulty in deciding whether his representative should be
> blamed or rewarded—since he seems to have so little effect on what
> Congress has done or has not done.[4]

According to the party realignment advocates, then, our multifactional party system, in conjunction with the fragmentation of power within our governmental system, frustrates even the notion of the individual representative's responsibility to his constituency on national policy issues.

Their most important criticism, however, is that under the existing system the government as a whole cannot be held accountable. "In such a system there is no government as a whole, no individual or set of individuals possessing control of the government and capable of being effectively blamed or rewarded for what it does."[5]

Because advocates of party realignment see politics in terms of issues, and because they see popular influence on governmental policy as flowing from electoral behavior, the advantages of certain changes become obvious. Create at least two unified, disciplined, ideologically coherent parties. Each party would then be, in the words of Edmund Burke, "a body of men united for promoting by their joint endeavors, the national interest upon some particular principle in which they are all agreed." Then "encourage" the candidates for office to run on their party's position. This arrangement would presumably offer the electorate a choice, not an echo. As a result, the people would be in a position to hold the politicians accountable for their party's policies, facilitating popular control over governmental policies.

In addition, optimalist social scientists argue that realigned parties would improve the operation of our governmental system. As it now operates, they claim, there is a tendency toward presidential dictatorship. In the absence of an effective party program, and in the void created by the absence of organized party support in Congress, the President is forced to create a broad political program on his own. Then he goes out and builds the necessary support for that program through his personal effort, using his political party as only one of the tools at his disposal. Congress may block the program, but it is in no position to substitute one of its own. Under the existing system, the people look exclusively to the President for leadership, a tendency conducive to personal government.[6]

To optimalist political scientists, realigned parties are the most feasible solution to the problem created by the growth of presidential authority.

Changing the organization of national parties—in Congress and at the presidential nominating conventions—would restore a balance of power relationship between Congress and the President. In the words of Professor Schattschneider: "Only when the national parties are strong enough to dominate Congress will that body discover and exploit public issues so effectively that the presidency will cease to be the sole rallying point of the great public interests of the country."[7] Disciplined parties would control the tendency toward personal government and overcome the constitutional barrier created by the separation of powers. In this sense, neither the President nor Congress would be rallying points. The parties are to be the primary mobilizers of the people.[8]

Congress would be important as a forum for the opposition party, and serve as "a rallying point for the great public interests of the country." While the minority party would not have the power to block the governing party's program, it would have ample opportunity to "act as the critic of the party in power, developing and presenting policy alternatives which are necessary for true choice in reaching public decisions."[9]

In their attitude toward separation of powers, the Optimalists reveal a strong bias against the Madisonian system of internal governmental checks on governmental power. Their basic belief is that "political responsibility is more flexible, comprehensive, and powerful than the system of legal responsibility set up in the separation of powers."[10] In this bias against the efficacy of internal governmental restraints these social scientists have much in common with their realist brethren. Both groups see the government as being regulated by the democratic political process. In fact, Optimalists have an additional reason to mistrust Madison's Constitution. In their more candid moments they admit that a realigned party system is not entirely compatible with the existing constitutional system, that the Constitution has been a barrier to the establishment of government along party lines.[11]

As sophisticated observers of the American polity, the Optimalists realize that proposing wholesale changes in the Constitution is not a practicable way of achieving more unified, disciplined, ideological parties. To a nation which views the Constitution as almost sacred writ, slight adjustments are acceptable; proposals for changing such major matters as the separation of powers are acts of futility. The party realignment advocates, therefore, generally take the position that the Constitution is flexible enough to accommodate their proposals: "The roles of the President and Congress are defined in the Constitution in terms which leave both free to cooperate and to rely on the concept of party responsibility."[12]

A reformist impulse forces the advocates of party realignment to have an ambiguous attitude toward the governmental structure created by the Constitution. On the one hand, their proposals arise out of a dissatisfaction with the existing system and reflect a bias against it. On the other hand, their desire to succeed prevents the party realignment advocates from making an all-out, frontal assault on the system. By no stretch of the imagination can the advocates of party realignment be called radicals or revolutionaries. They are part of the Anglo-American tradition of liberal reform and have the basic attitudes and instincts of reformers. They want to change the system without destroying it. Because of their desire to succeed as reformers, optimalist political scientists have adopted the approach used by all American democrats since Jefferson: they read their democratic theory into the Constitution.

The Optimalists' goal is nothing less than the reform of the entire American political process. Their claim is that American democracy would be improved if the major parties were realigned into two unified, ideologically coherent parties with differing conceptions of the public interest. A competitive party system so organized would enlarge popular influence on governmental policy; a party system so organized would optimize democracy.

The Optimalist Theory of Thomas L. Thorson

The optimalists' attitude toward the Constitution and the governmental system it helped create can also be discussed in terms of majoritarianism. All proposals for reforming the party system are suggestions for implementing popular majoritarianism by means of majority rule within the government. Of course, the Constitution was not designed to facilitate government by either a popular or an elected majority. Linking the concept of majoritarianism with the competitive paradigm meant that optimalist political scientists were bound to be uncomfortable with certain aspects of the existing American political system. That linkage also meant that Optimalists would have to confront the perennial issue of American democratic thought—the possible tyranny by the majority.

In *The Logic of Democracy*,[13] Thomas Thorson explores the issue of majority rule and minority rights. He concludes that democracy demands the limits upon the majority necessary for maintaining the process of finding the majority. As we have seen, this conclusion in itself is not a novel one for an American political theorist. Our interest is in the logic of democracy as developed by Professor Thorson; it is the logic behind the optimalist theory of democracy. His book will be examined here not so much for its conclusions about majority rule and minority rights, but for what it tells us about optimalist theory.

Thorson maintains that a rational justification for democracy cannot be deduced from any grand theory of the universe or of the nature of men. Such a theory will not persuade a doubter. Thorson is also unwilling to go the route of a Realist like Professor Hook. He will not treat democracy as an instrumental hypothesis whose sole justification lies in the results produced by the system. To operate without certain *fixed* values is to leave the choice of values to the personal preferences of the majority, the political representatives, or the experts. Treating democracy as a hypothesis is little more than value relativism in disguise.

Thorson approaches the problem of justifying an ultimate political commitment by a lengthy discussion of scientists' justification of their ultimate—the scientific method. This approach is particularly appropriate because the modern problem of justifying a political order stems from the acceptance of science as the model for all reasoning.

People engaging in a purposeful activity like science, he argues, are by that fact committed to the goals of the enterprise. "The aim of science is to find out the way the world is."[14] Acceptance of this goal is the context in which scientists operate. For scientists, then, the ultimate question becomes, "What method will best enable us to discover the truth about the way the world operates?" Thorson insists that the answer for fallible men must be the recommendation of Charles Sanders Peirce: "Do not block the way of inquiry."[15] Peirce's recommendation, because it is the most rational in the context of scientific inquiry, becomes a *binding* recommendation; it is the ultimate justification for the scientific method.

Turning back to his basic concern, Professor Thorson believes he is now in a position to find a rational justification for democracy. He will find the binding recommendation—i.e. the most rational recommendation—for the context created by political life. Again, man's fallibility is the most important factor:

> Just because the rightness of a political decision *cannot* be proved—because its consequences, short-or long-range, cannot be predicted with certitude nor its ultimate ethical supremacy demonstrated—are we obligated to construct a decision-making procedure that will leave the way open for new ideas and social change.[16]

Because all men are fallible, we have no way of knowing beforehand that some men will be wise on all issues and others stupid on all issues. We must therefore establish a decision-making process open to all, but which is *capable of deciding*. Like Hook, Thorson quotes Lincoln to show that only a government founded on majority rule is compatible with those requirements. The majoritarian principle, when coupled with the free competition for the free vote, provides the only system of government in accord with Thorson's recommendation. Thorson has provided his binding recommendation for democracy.

Thorson stated his justification for democracy in absolutist terms: "If truth is desirable in public policy, then for reasons already indicated we are *never* justified in blocking the way of inquiry."[17] Thorson, however, has no intention of creating an absolute. He knows that a changed context might necessitate a different recommendation. This intention becomes evident when he turns to the question of majority rule and minority rights. Gone is the absolutist language. Instead, his recommendation is based on a pragmatic assessment of the situation: "The choice between giving majorities free rein or constitutionally checking them can be sensibly made only by assessing the relative costs of the alternatives."[18]

In making that assessment, Thorson rejects the notion that democracy is incompatible with formal institutional limitations on the power of popular majorities or their elected representatives. That argument cannot apply to the very process which legitimizes the majority's authority to make those choices.[19] If democracy is justified because it keeps the road to social change open, Thorson argues, decisions which block that road cannot be called democratic. It matters not whether those decisions are made by a majority or a minority. "Fallibilism prescribes no . . . simple numerical rule but a general directive on leaving the way open for a change in social goals."[20]

Thorson also recognizes that the political context he used in formulating his recommendation does not completely describe the context of actual political societies. He realizes that his argument cannot, therefore, establish an immutable universal value. When dealing with the problem of majority rule and minority rights in an actual society like the United States, Thorson cannot talk about *absolute rights*; he can only recommend a priority of *interests*. He does this in the language of the optimalist theory of democracy:

> The categorical of fallibilism demands that the way be kept open for a change in goals . . . [It] implies the *maximization* of political equality, popular sovereignty, minority political rights, and majority rule.[21]

Of course, as a result of this last argument Professor Thorson can no longer logically argue that he has made any binding recommendation at all; for when he admits that the context of actual political life is not adequately described in his model, he pulls the logic of that argument out from under himself. By his own criterion of justification, a recommendation is only binding when it is the most rational proposal in a given context. Change the context and you may have to change the recommendation. At the very least, you cannot assume that the same proposal will be the most rational in the new context; you must show that it is through logical argument. When the context changes in the course of Professor Thorson's argument—from the ideal context of his model to the context of the real world—he does not change his recommendation, he only softens it. At the end of his book, because the context has changed, he cannot recommend that blocking social change is never justified. He can only suggest that the opportunities, interests, and values required for the free competition for the free vote be maximized. His binding recommendation has become a preference for optimizing political freedom.

The Preferred Freedoms Doctrine

I do not mean to minimize Professor Thorson's contribution. A justification for optimizing political freedom can still be of great importance. It provides, for example, a justification for the existence of judicial review, since democracy is no longer equated solely with majority rule. Thorson's logic of democracy also supplies a guide for the exercise of that power. Given his theory, "it is quite consistent for judges empowered with judicial review to be self-restrained in the face of majority preferences on general social policy *and* to be aggressive in the use of their power when free expression, suffrage, or the right to run for public office is in question."[22]

When Supreme Court Justices have advocated the same guidelines, they have talked in terms of the preferred freedoms doctrine. Systematic judicial discussion of that position began with a footnote in an otherwise unimportant 1938 opinion by Harlan Fiske Stone.[23] The famous footnote 4 discusses three types of cases: (1) a governmental action which appears to violate a specific constitutional prohibition, such as those in the Bill of Rights; (2) a governmental action which appears to restrict the political processes ordinarily available for changing political decisions; and (3) an apparently prejudicial governmental action which is aimed at discrete and insular minorities who cannot rely upon the ordinary political processes for protection. In these areas, Justice Stone suggested, it may be wise for the Court to suspend the usual presumption in favor of governmental acts in order to further political freedom.

In the years immediately after World War II, the preferred freedoms doctrine suffused several important Court opinions,[24] but the doctrine's status was always tenuous because the supporting majority rarely consisted of more than five Justices.[25] Several Justices, led by Frankfurter, never accepted the doctrine.[26] With a change in Court personnel and the advent of the Cold War, the preferred freedoms doctrine no longer influenced Supreme Court decisions. *Dennis v. United States* (1951) seemed to spell its demise.[27]

In the calmer times of the early 1960s, when the pressures, passions, and fears about the dangers posed by domestic Communists had subsided, Supreme Court decisions once again reflected the preferred position doctrine.[28] The language of the earlier period reappeared.[29] Opinions again referred to the special nature of certain rights, but few opinions squarely invoked the preferred freedoms doctrine itself as the explicit justification for the Justices' position.[30]

The judicial reluctance to explicitly invoke the preferred freedoms doctrine is largely the result of the doctrine's ambiguity. Which rights are deemed so essential to our democracy as to be accorded a preferred position? It is far from clear. There has never been an exhaustive and exclusive list of the preferred freedoms, although certain rights such as free speech are always included. More important, what does it mean to place a right in a preferred position? It clearly does not mean that such a right can be treated as an absolute bar to governmental action; rather, "acceptance of the preferred concept implies a balancing of the preferred freedom at issue against any other interest which stands in counterbalance."[31]

How does one go about making this reasonable accommodation? What is put on the balance when weighing a preferred freedom against another interest? When should the right prevail? Under what circumstances can government legitimately restrict even a preferred freedom? Since the factors involved are bound to differ from one situation to another, from case to case, no clear, unambiguous standard has emerged. The doctrine cannot "provide a set of objective standards to guide decision-making. Even those who accept the doctrine may differ fundamentally about important kinds of decisions it requires."[32]

As Professor Robert B. McKay has stated, "the preferred position concept does no more than state a mood."[33] But that mood has important consequences when felt by judges, for, despite the vagueness of the concept, it can still order priorities in several significant areas. What matters in determining the importance of any given claim, is its perceived relationship to the workings of a democractic political system. This relationship is why free speech is always stressed when the preference doctrine is used. Like Professor Thorson, the judges using that doctrine see a necessary connection between speech and the free competition for the free vote. Intelligent decision by the electorate requires the maximum feasible discussion of policies and candidates.

Similarly, the preference position is used to stress the importance of access to and participation in the political process via the ballot box. Like the optimalist social scientists, the judges using the preference doctrine believe that democracy can flourish only by assuring a meaningful exercise of the franchise. They have insisted upon the need for judicially protecting those rights essential to the free competition for the free vote. "The Court thus becomes the ultimate guardian against abuses that would poison the primary check on government—the ballot box."[34]

Since everybody's rights are not in equal jeopardy, the preferred freedoms doctrine "suggests a special role for the Court as protector of minorities and of unpopular groups peculiarly helpless at the polls in the face of discriminatory or repressive assault."[35] Only with such judicial activity can all citizens enjoy the benefits of living in a democracy. Only by judicially protecting certain basic rights can a democratic society benefit from each individual's contribution. Only then can the democracy of the competitive paradigm be optimized.

As used by the Court, the preferred freedoms doctrine has certain tactical advantages. Because it stresses the obvious importance of certain basic rights, the doctrine can serve as the rallying point for a judicial compromise favoring an individual's claims against government. Its ambiguity facilitates compromise for it commits no Justice to any position other than recognizing that in a particular case the particular right asserted by the individual is more important than the opposing governmental interest. In other cases, a Justice can always distinguish the circumstances. With its stress on the great importance of individual rights, the doctrine is often the lowest common denominator for a majority wishing to uphold certain claims by individuals.[36]

Because of the way the preferred freedoms doctrine tends to be used in the current period, we are not going to be able to identify any particular Justice as consistently adhering to the preference doctrine and the optimalist theory on which it is based. Our concern, however, is not with labelling various Justices, but with examining the implications of various theories. Different Justices have used the preferred freedoms doctrine in enough cases for us to examine the impact it would have in our polity if consistently applied.

AN ANALYSIS OF OPTIMALIST THEORY

Citizenship

Writing for the majority in *Schneider v. Rusk* (1964),[37] Justice Douglas said:

> Views of the Justices have varied when it comes to the problem of expatriation. There is one view that the power of Congress to take away citizenship for the activities of the citizen is non-existent absent expatriation by the voluntary renunciation of nationality and allegiance. . . . That view has not yet commanded a majority of the entire Court. Hence we are faced with the issue presented and decided in *Perez v. Brownell* . . . i.e., whether the present Act violates due process.[38]

Since he ultimately resolved that issue on the basis of the preferred freedoms doctrine, this statement clearly shows that the doctrine was used by Justices like Douglas only because their own views could not command a majority. It was used in *Schneider* and other expatriation cases[39] as a vehicle for compromise among the Justices supporting an individual's claim to retain his citizenship. In *Afroyim v. Rusk* (1967)[40] a majority of the Court did subscribe to the proposition that expatriation can only follow from a voluntary renunciation of nationality and allegiance. Once that happened, further reliance upon the preferred freedoms doctrine was precluded.

Justice Douglas's statement reveals the similarity between the preferred freedoms doctrine and realist theory. Both are based upon the due process notion of reasonable relationship. For the realist Justices, once that relationship is established, the issue is resolved in favor of the government. For the Justices using the preferred freedoms doctrine, finding a reasonable relationship is only the first step. They also seek to optimize the right of citizenship as they judicially weigh the competing claims.

When Justices have used the preferred freedoms doctrine, citizenship is called "a most precious right."[41] It assumes that high position only in comparison with the legal status of an alien, especially a stateless person.[42] The citizen-alien dichotomy also defines the nature of the sanction. Because of the possibility of creating a stateless person, non-voluntary expatriation is penal in character, not merely regulatory.[43] The possibility of statelessness creates the "manifest severity of this sanction."[44] The high value of citizenship derives from the possible consequences of alienation, the possible severity of those consequences gives the involuntary imposition of alienation its penal characteristics.

Because the Justices using the preferred freedoms doctrine rely upon the legal conception of citizenship, they view denationalization in terms of the reciprocal obligations of protection and obedience.[45] They are, therefore, in no position to assert that Congress may never impose the punishment of expatriation;[46] but they can "look closely" to see "whether Congress's imposition of expatriation as a penal device is justified in reason."[47] Given the nature of the right, a mere reasonable relationship is not sufficient. Legislation "so profoundly destructive of individual rights must keep within the limits of palpable reason and rest upon some modicum of discoverable necessity."[48]

Looking closely at the attempt to expatriate Perez simply for voting in the 1946 Mexican election, Justice Whittaker could see no reasonable basis for saying the act was "fraught with danger of embroiling our Government in an international dispute or of embarrassing it in the conduct of foreign affairs."[49] Mexico did not and would not object to Perez's action; its laws explicitly permitted him to vote. Whittaker could, therefore, discover no modicum of necessity for imposing the severe sanction of expatriation on Perez.

Scrutinizing the situation in *Trop v. Dulles* (1958),[50] Justice Brennan admitted that "Congress' belief that expatriation of the deserter might further the war effort may find some—though necessarily slender—support in reason."[51] An act so destructive of an individual right, however, needed a more substantial justification, and Brennan could find none. Expatriation obviously did not rehabilitate the deserter, nor was it likely to act as a deterrent. A man undeterred by such penalities as long imprisonment or death was most unlikely to be swayed from his course by the prospect of expatriation.[52] As he said in a later case, Justice Brennan did not believe "that expatriation was to be found in Congress' arsenal of common sanctions, available for no higher purpose than to curb undesirable conduct, to exact retribution for it and to stigmatize it."[53] In *Trop*, Justice Brennan concluded that "any substantial achievement, by this device, of Congress' *legitimate* purposes under the war power seems fairly remote . . . [The] requisite rational relation between [the] statute and the war power does not appear."[54]

In *Kennedy v. Mendoza-Martinez* (1963),[55] Justice Goldberg's opinion for the Court held that Congress could not expatriate a citizen for draft evasion without affording the procedural safeguards guaranteed by the Fifth and Sixth Amendments.[56] Congress plainly intended to use the deprivation of citizenship as a punitive sanction. Because citizenship was "a most precious right," at the very least it could not be taken away without due process of law. "Any lesser holding would ignore the constitutional mandate upon which our essential liberties depend."[57]

The *Schneider* case involved a law expatriating a naturalized American citizen for residing in the individual's native land for more than three continuous years. All nations with large immigrant populations confront the problem of naturalized citizens voluntarily returning to their native lands to reside. They rarely renounce their naturalized citizenship, yet they functionally resume their lives as citizens of their native country. As Justice Clark's dissent notes, Congress, therefore, had reason to believe that prolonged residence in one's former homeland showed much less than unswerving allegiance to the United States. Moreover, those naturalized American citizens sometimes sought the intervention of the United States on their behalf. For more than a hundred years, the government had wrestled with this potential source of international friction. The provision of the 1952 Immigration and Nationality Act was aimed only at those citizens whose presence in their native homelands could embroil the United States in conflict with such countries. Justice Clark could not fathom how such a narrowly drawn statute could be deemed unreasonable.[58]

Using the preferred freedoms doctrine, Justice Douglas's opinion for the Court refused to accept the "assumption that naturalized citizens as a class are less reliable and bear less allegiance to this country than do the native born."[59] Without this assumption, they could find no overriding public necessity justifying the act. Living abroad, by itself, could not then be viewed either as a lack of allegiance or as a voluntary renunciation of United States citizenship—it might be compelled by family, business, or other reasons. Absent any overriding public necessity and given the importance of the right involved, the majority found this section of the act unconstitutional.

Like their realist colleagues, the Justices using the optimalist theory decide expatriation questions by an examination of the government's claim, not by defining the nature of the individual's right of citizenship. "[W]here Congress has determined that considerations of the highest national importance indicate a course of action for which an adequate substitute might rationally appear lacking," Justice Brennan could not say that expatriation "lies beyond Congress' power to choose."[60]

Justice Brennan found himself in an awkward situation because his method of analysis, derived from optimalist theory, led him to focus on the sufficiency of the government's claim. On the same day that he justified as constitutional the expatriation of Perez who had committed no crime by voting in a Mexican political election, he found unconstitutional a statute expatriating Trop for the very serious crime of desertion during wartime. He wrote an extensive opinion explaining why he found the requisite rational relationship between the particular expatriation statute and Congress's powers present in the former situation and not in the latter. For our purposes, his opinion demonstrates that as important as citizenship is in optimalist theory, it can, at times, still be overridden by the government's assertion of a more important claim.

Neither optimalist theory in general nor the preferred freedoms doctrine in particular provides anything like a clear standard for determining the importance of the government's claim. The theory and the doctrine call citizenship a fundamental right. To "look closely" at a government action which infringes the fundamental right of citizenship might be an adequate standard when there has been a total absence of procedural due process (as in *Mendoza-Martinez*) or where the Court can see no rational relationship at all. Where procedural due process has been accorded and a rational relationship does exist, optimalist theory provides precious little help to the judge. He is thrown back on his own evaluation of the competing claims. So it was that in *Perez* Justices Whittaker and Brennan, using the same standard, could come to opposite conclusions. So, too, Justice Brennan found himself in the awkward position described above.

Perhaps the Justices using the optimalist theory could avoid this predicament by starting with an analysis of the right claimed by the citizen.

After all, the loss of citizenship may be as severe a loss for the individual facing expatriation for one act as for another. An investigation of the full dimensions of citizenship—not just a citizen's legal status as compared with an alien's—might better indicate the situations justifying expatriation.

The Justices using optimalist theory are unable to make such an analysis. Not being informed by a political theory which uses the concept of citizenship to emphasize the importance of actively belonging to a society, they can see only the traditional legal distinction between citizen and alien. Their theory enables them to see that a citizen has important prerogatives not possessed by an alien; it does not focus on a citizen's relation to his society. The Justices using optimalist theory, thus, have a difficult time defining the basis of an individual's claim, as a citizen, against his own government. They can only protect a right they believe is important by carefully scrutinizing government actions affecting it.

Political Participation

If optimalist theorists were to make any use of the distinction between citizen and subject, their acceptance of the competitive paradigm would limit it to one activity. Within the competitive paradigm only a citizen's participation in the electoral process distinguishes him from a passive subject. E. E. Schattschneider, for example, recognized the importance of changing the passive response of consent into the active response of support based upon participation. The only type of political participation he talked about, however, was voting.[61]

Similarly, James MacGregor Burns approvingly quotes Tocqueville about the importance of "interesting men in the welfare of their country [through participation] in the Government," but Professor Burns identifies Tocqueville's "civic zeal" with the activity of voting.[62] In short, political participation in optimalist theory is equated with voting behavior.

The Optimalists believe that in a properly structured political system, this one activity would be sufficient for Americans "to regain control of their national politics and to define and assert their national purpose."[63] This contention is supported by a critique of the existing system. "If the people seem complacent or inert," Burns writes, "the cause may lie less in them than in a political system that evades and confuses the real issues rather than sharpening and resolving them."[64] Uninterested by many of the alternatives presented to them by our present party system and unable to see how they can effect policy in that system, the people are bound to be passive and apathetic.

Schattschneider believed that a satisfactory rate of political participation—increasingly higher voter turnouts—would develop if we restructured our political parties. In their competition for a national majority, the parties would be more likely to seek ways of expanding the participating political community because "it is easier to bring a new voter into the system than it is to induce an old partisan to change sides."[65]

The historical data indicate that voter turnout declined when the two major national parties became less clearly distinguishable. In 1840, eighty percent of the estimated electorate voted for a presidential candidate. In 1860, the figure is estimated at eighty-one percent. After the Civil War, turnout ranged from a low of seventy-five percent in 1872 to a high of eighty-six percent in 1876. By 1896, it had fallen to seventy-nine percent, but that level has never been reached in the twentieth century despite the progressive relaxation of registration requirements. After falling to forty-nine percent in the 1920s, turnout increased in the New Deal era; it was approximately sixty-two percent in 1940. In 1960, slightly under sixty-three percent of the voting age population cast ballots in the very competitive Kennedy-Nixon election. Turnout in presidential elections declined seven percent between 1960 and 1972. More recently, despite close elections in 1976 and 1980, the decline of voter turnout has continued; it is estimated that only 52.4 percent of the eligible electorate cast ballots in 1980. The decision whether to vote or not hinges on many things besides the ideological differences between the two major parties, so the decline in turnout does not prove the Optimalists' contention. Nonetheless, the parallel is striking.[66]

Professor Burns also believes that our high rates of nonvoting indicate the basic flaw of our political system. He sees an additional benefit from a realignment of our political parties. Burns stresses the educative implications of voting.[67] Of course, if realigned parties would make voting more meaningful for today's habitual nonvoter, a restructured political system would have the same effect on many of today's voters. Those who now vote primarily from force of habit or in response to the "fatuous get-out-the-vote movement conducted through the mass media at election time,"[68] would have a new incentive to vote. They would be in a position to control the government.

In no way can optimalist theory be understood as suggesting that the mass of people would be actively engaged in governing themselves. At best the bulk of the American electorate would be composed of intelligent consumers of competing political programs. Having equated political participation with voting and voting with selecting the most desirable available political program, the Optimalists are in no position to argue that democracy means that each person will have a share in the governmental decision-making process. They have removed all the active overtones surrounding the word participation. The entire argument for party realignment is predicated upon the electorate functioning as essentially passive consumers of the political goods offered to them.

The passive role of the citizen can be seen in another way. The argument depends upon political ideology serving both as the basis for party programs and for voter motivation, yet the Optimalists would make changes only at the level of party organization. To make sense of their argument, therefore, one must assume that restructuring the parties on an ideological basis would impose on the public a similar frame of reference. Given the nature of the realigned parties, the public could only choose its representatives on the single dimension of party programs and principles. The Optimalists view party realignment as constructive social engineering. It might also be viewed as forced feeding. Either way, the electorate is a passive object. Little wonder then that Schattschneider and Burns talk about popular control over government rather then popular participation in government.

How effective is popular control likely to be even if our parties were realigned? That, of course, depends upon the kinds of choices the rival political leaders offer the people. Even during the period when there was a considerable similarity in Democratic and Republican programs (1952–1976) scholars detected ideological differences between the leadership elements of the two parties.[69] The core of the Optimalist argument is best understood as an organizational rationalization of that situation. If the internal party structures were organized around policies and principles already present in the leadership elements, the differences between our parties would no longer be too confused and ill defined to be readily understood by the electorate.

The model for this suggested change is, of course, the British political system. According to Schattschneider, "The [American] political system *has never assigned to the elective process a role as overwhelmingly important as that played by British elections.*"[70] Systematic electoral studies in Britain, however, seriously undermine this type of statement, for they indicate the British political system does not invariably conform to the Optimalists' model.

The Conservative and Labor parties are indeed examples of highly structured, mass political parties.[71] The ideological beliefs of the party activists add considerably to the internal coherency of each party;[72] but, this cohesiveness has not meant that the party leaders have always made their primary appeal for votes on policy issues. In the 1960s and 1970s, both parties' advertising campaigns played down ideology and program; the emphasis was on personalities and vague slogans. The British election campaigns became increasingly "Americanized."[73]

For almost two decades, then, the most that can be said is that the British political culture enabled the voter to understand that the "Conservative and Labor parties continue to espouse somewhat different conceptions of human nature, society, and the state."[74] Of course, much the same thing can be said of the American voter's understanding of the differences between Republicans and Democrats during the same period. If the British experience is as important as the Optimalists claim, the electorate's chances of being presented with ideologically distinct alternatives will depend, as in the past, on whether the party leaders believe it will help win elections.

That theory, then, contains no persuasive reason for realigning our party system. The Optimalists may be dissatisfied with the existing situation, but they are unwilling to question the social science notion of democracy embedded in the competitive paradigm. As a result, their prescription for increasing popular influence on governmental policy is a mechanical reorganization of our political institutions. They do not examine or suggest the possibility of changing people's attitudes towards and expectations of a democratic polity. In the future, as in the past, democracy will mean the free competition for the free vote. As long as that fact remains true, a realigned party system is at best a dubious, though well intentioned, prescription for increasing political participation in a mass democracy.

Once again, an examination of the prescriptive implications of a social science theory provides valuable insights for understanding judicial opinion derived from that theory. In the reapportionment cases, the opinions of Justices Clark and Stewart indicate their reliance upon the preferred freedoms doctrine, the judicial variant of optimalist theory. Viewed in this light, it is not surprising that the opinions of Clark and Stewart had much in common with those of their realist brethren. They, too, saw democracy as a system in which legislators represent people with "identifiable needs and interests."[75] Elected officials arrive at public policy by a process of compromise and accommodation.[76] This process required, in the words of Justice Stewart, that "population factors must often to some degree be subordinated in devising a legislative apportionment plan which is to achieve the important goal of assuring a fair, effective and balanced representation of the regional, social and economic interests within a State."[77] Like Justices Frankfurter and Harlan, Stewart and Clark thus viewed the Court's equal population standard as unduly doctrinaire and restrictive.[78] This correspondence in judicial viewpoints arose from the common source of both optimalist and realist theories of democracy: the competitive paradigm.

It is not surprising to find that the differences between Justices Clark and Stewart, on the one hand, and Frankfurter and Harlan, on the other, paralleled the disagreements between optimalist and realist social scientists. Unlike Key and Dahl, Schattschneider and Burns believed that the very notion of democracy requires institutional changes to increase popular political participation. Unlike Justices Frankfurter and Harlan, Stewart and Clark believed malapportioned legislatures required judicial intervention, for the "legislative strait jacket"[79] created by malapportionment denied effective political participation to large numbers of our citizens. Although they all believed that enlarging the opportunities for political participation is a desirable objective, they differed as to whether democratic theory *requires* structural alterations in a country like the United States. To repeat, that difference is at the heart of the debate between Realists and Optimalists.

Justices Stewart and Clark thus recognized the need for a standard which would prevent the "systematic frustration of the will of a majority of the electorate of the State."[80] Neither man specified why "any plan which could be shown systematically to prevent ultimate effective majority rule would be invalid under accepted Equal Protection standards."[81] As Frankfurter and Harlan noted, majority rule was not specified in the Constitution. The reason, however, seems clear enough. Justices Clark and Stewart accepted the idea that the United States had become a democracy and that majority rule must be considered the keystone of a democratic political system. Limiting the effectiveness of popular political participation would transform the system's basic institution—the electoral process—into a meaningless ritual. Preventing that possibility—protecting and nourishing the democratic political process itself—is the basic rationale of the preferred freedoms doctrine. Malapportionment justified judicial intervention.

Justices Stewart and Clark proposed a two-part standard for evaluating a state's apportionment scheme. In the long run, a state must permit the popular majority to have the ultimate say upon this policy matter as on all others. In the short run, they would require that "in the light of the State's own characteristics and needs, the plan must be a rational one."[82] Justice Clark suggested that the applicable criterion for the first part of this standard was whether a state provided the popular majority with "practical opportunities for exerting their political weight at the polls."[83] Opportunity could be built into the method of adopting an apportionment plan. For example, a plan could be approved by a popular referendum[84] or adopted by a popularly elected convention.[85] Opportunity could also be provided by other parts of a state's constitution such as referendum and initiative provisions.[86] Justice Clark, at least, would also view a state as having satisfied this part of the standard if one house of a bicameral legislature was apportioned on an equal population basis. Presumably, he believed that in the give and take of the legislative process, control of one chamber gave the popular majority all the leverage needed to implement an ultimately effective majority rule.[87]

As for the second part of this standard, both Justices used the traditional equal protection formulation for nonracial matters. A state policy will be upheld even if in practice it results in some inequality. It will be struck down as irrational and capricious only if its categories are wholly irrelevant to the achievement of the state's objective. The use of this test is therefore dependent upon what the Justices consider to be the objective of the state's policy. Only in light of that factor can the Justices determine whether a law is rational—

i.e. reasonably calculated to achieve its objective—or merely capricious and arbitrary.

As just noted, Justices Stewart and Clark maintained that in the short run an apportionment should be designed to achieve the effective and balanced representation of all substantial interests within a state. Failure to seek the attainment of that objective was treated as prima facie evidence of lack of rationality; the apportionment plan would than reflect "no policy but simply arbitrary and capricious inaction."[88] Justice Clark therefore denounced the Tennessee apportionment plan under consideration in *Baker*, a plan designed to perpetuate the status quo, as "a crazy quilt without rational basis."[89] So long as a state's apportionment plan, in light of that state's characteristics, was reasonably calculated to achieve effective and balanced representation of all substantial interests, however, it satisfied this part of the Clark-Stewart standard.

The double-barrelled standard suggested by Justices Stewart and Clark raises several problems. First, there is the vagueness inherent in any guideline defined in terms of reasonable or rational. How is one to know beforehand what the Supreme Court will accept as a reasonable attempt at an effective and balanced representation of all substantial interests? Each of the key words—"effective," "balanced," "substantial"—lacks precision. Since each state has unique characteristics, separate problems are posed. The decision in one case can have only limited utility for guiding actions in other states; unless, of course, one is willing to accept as reasonable virtually any apportionment plan for which some rationale could be found and which is not patently absurd on its face. That acceptance, of course, would call into question the utility of judicial intervention in the first place. To insure the meaningfulness of judicial review of apportionment plans, the Stewart-Clark standard may well have required the Court to supervise the apportionment plans in all fifty states.

Justices Stewart and Clark used a reasonableness test as part of their apportionment standard to increase the options available to the states. As with the preferred freedoms doctrine itself, this part of their standard sought to reconcile judicial intervention with a conception of democracy based upon a competitive election system. The judges are to intervene only when it is necessary to protect and enlarge access to the political process. The people selected through that process are to be given the widest possible latitude in making policy. The detailed scrutiny required by this reasonableness doctrine, however, might prove even a greater limitation on the elected leaders than a more rigid standard.

A vague standard, it must be remembered, not only permits a variety of responses by the elected leadership, but also gives the judges wide discretion. A rigid constitutional standard may often seem doctrinaire, but it reduces the danger of a political decision being second-guessed by the Supreme Court. The "understanding respect for the unique values"[90] of our political system sought by Justices Clark and Stewart might perhaps be better served by a standard whose clarity limits the need for continuous Supreme Court review. Such, at least, is suggested by our experience with judicial review of criminal procedures under due process.[91] It might also apply in other areas, including apportionment.

Perhaps this problem is why Justice Clark suggested that if one house of a bicameral legislature is fairly apportioned by population, then there should be some latitude permitted in the method of apportioning the other house. The equal population standard would insure that all substantial interests were represented so that Justice Clark could be considerably less rigorous in his scrutiny of the rest of the plan. Without abdicating judicial responsibility, he could avoid the danger of turning the Court into a supreme boundary commission.

The vagueness inherent in any reasonableness test is, therefore, hardly an insuperable objection to the Clark-Stewart standard. Because it allows for considerable play at the joints, a reasonableness test may be ideally designed for judicial supervision of the multiple intricacies of any apportionment plan. Too much judicial intervention in an essentially legislative process—if one were concerned about that factor—could be avoided by Justice Clark's suggestion.

His suggestion does raise a more serious problem for the overall Clark-Stewart approach to apportionment: how to reconcile the two parts of their standard. An equal population base for one chamber may enhance the popular majority's position in the give and take of legislative politics. It is hardly calculated to make the minority interests in the other chamber more willing to suspend their operative veto. Rather than an ultimately effective majority rule, a more probable result would be the frustration of the majority by minority power in the house not apportioned on a population basis.

Justice Stewart was not consistently able to reconcile both parts of his own standard. In *WMCA v. Lomenzo* (1964),[92] he would have upheld New York's 1961 reapportionment of the state legislature. Depending upon the method used, it was possible to calculate that a majority of the state's population was represented by a majority in both houses of the legislature. The plan, by allocating greater representation to the smaller counties while placing limitations on the allocations to the larger counties, was clearly designed to reduce the power of urban areas, especially metropolitan New York. As a result, there were wide disparities between the population sizes of various districts.

Although he conceded that the urban population was proportionately underrepresented, Justice Stewart maintained that New York's plan provided for effective majority representation and control of the state legislature. Admittedly, what is meant by effective control is far from clear, and Justice Stewart's calculations may be as good as any other. Nonetheless, he still had to explain why an urban majority should have to labor under the handicap of being proportionately underrepresented when they sought to enact their will into law. Stewart explained this by arguing that the apportionment plan was a reasonable way to counterbalance the concentrated power of New York City. Since the overall plan had a reasonable objective, the population disparities between districts which resulted from rationally pursuing that objective could hardly be deemed unreasonable.[93]

That reasonable objective was to be accomplished, however, at the *expense* of the concentrated population centers. There is nothing in the idea of an "effective and balanced representation" which necessarily requires that some substantial interests should have more than their proportional representation in the legislature. Stewart's acceptance of such a plan becomes even more puzzling in light of the second part of his apportionment standard. For however reasonable its objective, the New York plan made the attainment of an ultimately effective majority rule more difficult, if not impossible, when the popular majority happened to be concentrated in one area. By what reasoning should one particular type of popular majority be impeded from exercising effective political power?

No doubt this objection is why Justices Stewart and Clark felt more comfortable with the 1962 state apportionment plan involved in *Lucas v. Colorado General Assembly* (1964).[94] It had been "adopted by a popular referendum in which not only a 2–1 majority of all voters in Colorado but a majority in each county, including those urban counties allegedly discriminated against, voted for the . . . plan in preference to an alternative proposal providing for equal representation per capita in both legislative houses."[95] If there was any discriminatory representation of the popular majority they had chosen to be so treated, and, under the initiative provisions of the Colorado constitution, the majority could later reverse their decision. "Therefore, there can be no question of frustration of the basic principle of majority rule,"[96] Justice Stewart concluded.

The Colorado apportionment, if not New York's, enabled Justices Stewart and Clark to reconcile both parts of their standard. It was a conscious attempt by the elected leadership to accommodate all substantial interests. Nor could there be any question about an ultimately effective majority rule. Even if the apportionment of the upper house of the Colorado legislature might frustrate the urban majority—and Justice Stewart doubted that it would[97]—the popular majority had itself chosen to protect the minority's interests by giving the latter disproportionate political power. The ready availability of the referendum and initiative, moreover, gave the popular majority a mechanism to effect its will at a later time. The prior use and future availability of those mechanisms in Colorado gave the Clark-Stewart approach a consistency it did not have in the New York case. The tension between the two parts of the standard was resolved in a way seemingly designed to win the approval of any democrat—by the popular majority itself.

The Colorado case demonstrates the possiblity of simultaneously providing for effective and balanced representation of all *substantial* interests and an ultimately effective majority rule. It does not demonstrate that the Clark-Stewart standard provides adequate avenues of political access for *all* interests. The balance, after all, is to be struck among the interests already represented. Interests which, for one reason or another, have not previously been effective politically are likely to find their disadvantaged position perpetuated. The Clark-Stewart standard might force a different accommodation upon existing political forces; it does not require a recognition of different political interests.

The apportionment of the Colorado Senate recognized that existing divisions centered around the state's four distinct geographical regions. The plan sought to work out a balanced representation for *those* interests, not others. This reapportionment meant there was likely to be a built-in structural bias against interests which had been ignored in the past. That traditional *regional* interests had worked out a mutually satisfactory accommodation does not mean that the interests of *racial* minorities, for example, were also satisfied. Similarly, newly emerging political interests which cut across the old political division would face the same built-in obstacles to effective political participation.

The requirement of an ultimately effective majority rule is not an adequate safeguard against the built-in advantage for the status quo. In Colorado, majority rule in apportionment matters operates through the initiative and the referendum. To be placed on the ballot, an initiated measure requires the signatures of 8 percent of those who voted for the secretary of state in the last election. Even granting that a group which feels itself inadequately represented could initiate a vote for a new reapportionment plan, its future representation would still be decided by the majority. The popular majority of their representatives determine which interests are to be directly represented by the political process.

By assuming the constitutional significance of existing political forces, the Clark-Stewart standard lends support to the status quo. This objection is one of the reasons some senators opposed the constitutional amendments based upon the Stewart-Clark standard.[98] Behind the usual hyperbole and inflated rhetoric of political debate, there was a sensitivity to the political power of minority groups, especially blacks. By way of contrast to the Clark-Stewart standard, the Supreme Court's equal population standard places all interests on the same formal plane simply by ignoring their constitutional relevance. Focusing on people *may* make it more difficult to ignore interests not currently represented.[99] It will surely require periodic reapportionment, with the attendant possibilities of reassessing the relevant political forces. These were the hopes expressed by such liberals as Senator Robert Kennedy when they defeated the proposed amendments.[100] The Court's equal population standard still permits ample opportunity for political bargaining so that existing political forces would continue to dominate the apportionment process. Within bounds, this domination is as it should be; for, if the goal is that "groups, and coalitions of groups, including the majority coalition itself, are to be heard" in the governing process "in rough proportion to their popular strength,"[101] there is no justification for penalizing existing groups. Neither is it necessary to buttress their political strength by giving their predominant position a constitutional sanction.

The failure of Justices Clark and Stewart to confront these implications arose from the contradictory impulses of optimalist theory. The theory expresses a desire to extend and enlarge political participation. It also recognizes that a political system built upon the free competition for the free vote requires political leaders to formulate policy by reconciling competing interests. A tension is thereby created between ends and means. A more perfect democracy is to emerge out of a pluralistic consensus of existing forces.

Justices Clark and Stewart recognized that malapportioned legislatures blocked effective political participation. The preferred freedoms doctrine supplied them with a justification for judicial intervention. It did not supply them with a vision which challenged the conception of democracy embedded in the competitive paradigm. As a result, their prescription for increasing popular influence in government could rectify the obvious imbalances among organized groups already functioning within our political system. Because the doctrine gives wide latitude to the elected representative, however, there is no built-in requirement for enlarging the effective political universe. There is nothing in the doctrine which explains how and why the existing system will develop a dynamic which may work against the interests benefitting from the system. Like the optimalist social scientists, Justices Clark and Stewart failed to explain why a more perfect democracy would emerge out of a pluralistic consensus of existing forces—except, of course, that as men of good will they hoped for the best.

Political Freedom

Since no radically different view of the American political system—of citizenship in our society or participation in our political processes—is offered by optimalist theory, at best it can only suggest making incremental improvements. There is, therefore, a certain unsatisfying quality to the theory.

The prescribed remedies are not commensurate with the maladies underlying the Optimalists' call to action. In the area of political freedom, however, marginal increments appear to be all that is required for improving the benefits of the American democratic system. With significant political freedom already present in American society, questions of political freedom seem ready made for this theory. Inevitably, the ultimate justification for optimalist theory comes to rest upon its tender, loving concern for the values of political freedom.

Even when dealing with these questions, the social scientists, the political theorists, and the judges relying upon optimalist theory have been unable to resolve the underlying tension of their position in a convincing manner. Their dilemma arises from their commitment to both the political process and individual freedom. When the two sets of values collide, optimalist theory prescribes a preferential treatment for individual political rights. Pragmatically, this preference has benefitted our democracy. Nonetheless, the failure to develop an entirely convincing rationale for this preference entails costs we must also examine.

Let us turn first to the social scientists. Professor Martin Shapiro has attempted a justification for the preferred freedoms doctrine which relies neither on political theory nor on constitutional interpretation. Instead, he offers us reasons of political wisdom. An examination of the social science literature about how our system operates convinces him that sound policy requires judicial protection of libertarian values.[102]

In "the real political world," the world as described and analyzed by the social scientists, it makes little sense to talk about American politics in terms of majority rule or even democracy. These are only simplistic labels. "[W]hat really emerges from an examination of Congress and the Presidency is not a simple picture of democratic, majoritarian bodies, voicing popular will and responsible to it, but an elaborate political structure in which groups seek advantage through maneuvering among the various power centers. The results are not necessarily the enunciation of the will of the majority of the American people, but often of compromises among competing interest groups."[103]

Professor Shapiro extends this type of social science analysis to cover the Supreme Court. He finds that "the Court, like all agencies of the central government, inevitably exerts more influence on some issues than on others, depending on the nature of the problem, the political alignment of other groups, the amount of popular support it can command, and so on."[104] Generally, the Court has been most effective when it has acted on behalf of widely held but politically unfocused norms. Usually those claims are advanced by minority groups not adequately represented in the elected bodies.[105]

This analysis of the role and relative power of the Supreme Court in our national government supplies the basis of Professor Shapiro's recommendation. The Court would "make its maximum contribution to the governing process" by devoting "its major energies to those groups which have little other access to government."[106] Their political weakness means they are the very groups most likely to appeal to general social values for protecting their interests. By consciously acting on behalf of marginal groups, the Supreme Court could help make a practical reality out of the widely held norms of our society.

Professor Shapiro's analysis of the American political system has led him to prescribe a course of action for the Supreme Court which parallels Justice Stone's famous footnote. Shapiro has given us a social science justification for the preferred freedoms doctrine. There are troubling aspects to this defense of the optimalist position however. Professor Shapiro's descriptive attempt roughly to equate the elected branches and the Court, in which the Court is simply one more non-majoritarian actor in the political process, is open to question.[107]

Even assuming he is correct, the important question is whether Shapiro has recommended a politically wise course. As Shapiro himself pointed out, much of the Court's power depends upon the Justices' ability to convince the public that their decisions are constitutionally legitimate.[108] If the Supreme Court consistently supports certain groups, however, it risks being labelled a political partisan. A judicial practice of constantly supporting the claims of the underrepresented will hardly endear the Court to the groups adequately represented through the competitive electoral process. Sooner or later, the groups within the system will question the supposed neutrality of the Court. To question its neutrality is to undermine the very foundation of a court of law, for the primary values of "the rule of law"—justice, fairness, reasonableness—all entail the neutral application of agreed upon standards in which sometimes the dominant groups will also prevail. By recommending that the Court "play favorites," Professor Shapiro jeopardizes its political power to pursue that very goal.

In Shapiro's argument, neither can the Justices use the Constitution to defend their decisions. They can claim no special authority for deciding issues involving political freedom. The Court is just another agency, with its own special constituency, participating in the on-going political process. Shapiro, unlike the Realists, does not view elected officials as the only decision makers authorized by the democratic process. Neither does he see the Court possessed of any unique source of authority. In Shapiro's argument, the Justices, in making a decision, are simply pitting their own assessment of competing interests against the judgments of other officials.

How are the Justices to defend their decisions when they are challenged about the prudential wisdom of favoring political freedom of marginal groups? Shapiro sometimes suggests the need for the Court to cloak its decisions under the guise of principle.[109] Since he believes our widely held norms are ambiguous,[110] however, he also knows the Court's opponents will play the same game on behalf of curtailing political freedom. As in all political contests, the outcome will depend on the position, popular support, and ultimately the power of the opposing forces. This contest is why Professor Shapiro maintains that the Justices are likely to prevail in their preference for freedom only when the issues are not important enough to rouse much concern. When political freedom is most in jeopardy, when the rights of a dissident minority face the sustained opposition of the groups within the system, Shapiro does not think the preference for freedom can be sustained.[111]

Professor Shapiro has provided a nice rationale for judicial activism on behalf of political freedom. The judges should enter the political fray on behalf of their particular constituents, the marginal groups advancing values the Justices profess to hold dear. It is the only practical way to make a reality out of their expressed value commitments. The Justices, however, should not be deluded into believing they will always prevail. Win some, lose some, that is the nature of the political game. Shapiro's argument will no doubt provide comfort for the Justices, professors, and others not directly affected by any given decision. Those individuals whose political rights are immediately at stake, however, are not likely to be so comforted by Shapiro's political wisdom. Understandably, they are likely to continue searching for an argument which offers the possibility of protecting their rights in hard times as well as good.

Thomas L. Thorson attempted to supply that sort of foundation by arguing that man's fallibility required a political system which did not block the road to change. In the context of his ideal model of political life, Professor Thorson sought to draw a binding political recommendation comparable to Charles S. Peirce's prescription for the scientific pursuit of truth. Peirce had little difficulty showing why truth should be the central value of science— no other value would do as much to promote the discovery of the laws of the universe. In the context of the search for truth, Peirce's fallibilism is eminently sensible. Arguing by analogy to Peirce, Thorson posits truth as the.central concern for political actors; but, he never explains why the makers of public policy are to be concerned about finding the truth.

Politics, Professor Thorson later recognized, is a goal-oriented activity; it is not like games where the purpose is primarily in the playing. In politics, the conflict of interests appears inevitable;[112] that inevitability was certainly recognized by the Framers.[113] That being the case, why should the rational men establishing the political rules make them neutral? It is surely more rational for them to set up rules which favor their own interests and values. The republicans who framed the Constitution were not neutral as to major-itarian democracy. They were opposed to it and their political rules reflected that animus. If, according to Professor Thorson, political decisions involve the authoritative allocation of values, a rational man should be concerned about protecting and promoting his values and interests. Using a political model which ignores the stuff and substance of politics cannot provide a rational justification for any political system, including democracy. In short, even in the realm of his ideal political context, Professor Thorson has not provided a binding justification for his concept of democracy.

This shortcoming means that when he shifts his discussion to the real political world, his justification for maximizing political freedom lacks a firm foundation. Professor Thorson recognizes that the need for national security must sometimes be weighed against the values (interests) required for maintaining the democratic political process. Nonetheless, he contends that the balance should be weighted in favor of political freedom because a sound political order must be built around rules which do not block the way to change. Unless we accept Thorson's prior argument, we are unlikely to be convinced about the wisdom of supporting political freedom even at the risk of jeopardizing our national security. Unless the reader instinctively shares Thorson's value priorities, his recommendations will seem less than binding even as a preference.

The Justices on the Supreme Court have been no more successful than the social scientists and political theorists in developing a completely satisfactory justification for the preference doctrine. Again, as in the previous chapter, this assessment can best be seen by two lines of cases clearly posing problems of political freedom—the Communist Party cases and those arising from the civil rights movement.

To Justices Black and Douglas, the freedom to advocate political ideas was the essential issue in *Dennis v. United States* (1951).[114] They maintained that the Smith Act and the convictions of the eleven top leaders of the Communist Party under that act violated the First Amendment. In support of that position, each Justice wrote a dissent explaining why speech, at least as to public mtters,[115] "occupied an exalted position" in our constitutional scheme.[116]

Their arguments, of course, did not fail to point to the First Amendment's absolute prohibition against any law abridging the freedom of speech. In 1951, however, neither Justice believed the Amendment could be given a literal interpretation. What they did insist upon was that the Amendment's emphatic language must be interpreted to mean something more than a mere admonition to be reasonable. In the words of Justice Douglas, "The command of the First Amendment is so clear that we should not allow Congress to call a halt to free speech except in the extreme case of peril from speech itself."[117]

Nonetheless, neither Justice placed his primary emphasis on textual analysis or on the intent of the Framers; rather, their opinions stressed the functional necessity of protecting political speech in a democracy. Without full and free discussion, they contended, intelligent judgment is impossible and necessary changes in the status quo are unlikely to be made;[118] therefore, "[f]ree speech—the glory of our system of government—should not be sacrificed on anything less than plain and objective proof of danger that the evil advocated is imminent.[119]

The government had produced no such proof at the trial, they claimed. All it had introduced were texts and other printed materials used by the Communist Party. To Justices Douglas and Black, such evidence meant that these convictions could not be sustained. That the Smith Act called for these kinds of indictments conclusively demonstrated the act itself was an unconstitutional abridgment of free speech. With the benefit of hindsight, there is not the slightest doubt that Dennis and the other leaders of the Communist Party posed no grave, substantial, or immediate threat to our internal security. It is difficult to believe that even in 1951 the official, overt Communist spokesmen were anything other than as described by Justice Douglas—"miserable merchants of unwanted ideas."[120] In terms of handling the immediate issues, optimalist theory and the preference doctrine would have provided a satisfactory basis for a Supreme Court decision in the *Dennis* case.

In *Communist Party v. Subversive Activities Control Board* (1961)[121] the Supreme Court upheld the Internal Security Act's registration provisions, and the Control Board's order to the Communist Party to comply with those provisions. Only Justice Douglas applied a First Amendment preference test. As in *Dennis*, he insisted that the "Bill of Rights was designed to give the fullest play to the exchange and dissemination of ideas that touch the politics, culture and other aspects of our life."[122] Unlike *Dennis*, however, he would have upheld certain restrictions of free speech in this case.

Here the Subversive Activities Control Board, after exhaustive hearings, had found that the Communist Party was being used by a foreign power to make advances in the United States. Other evidence tended to confirm their findings that "espionage, business activities, formation of cells for subversion, as well as the exercise of First Amendment rights," were being used "to pry open our society and make intrusion of a foreign power easy."[123] According to Douglas, these findings raised questions of security beyond the ken of Americans engaged in discussing ideas. The "machinations of a foreign power" added "additional elements" and justified "the bare requirement that the Communist Party register and disclose the names of its officers and directors."[124] Despite the fact that he knew that "the disclosure of membership lists may cause harassment of members and seriously hamper their exercise of First Amendment rights,"[125] Justice Douglas believed his conclusion to be "in line with the most exacting adjudications touching First Amendment activities."[126]

Another constitutional right, however, was involved. Like Justice Brennan and Chief Justice Warren, Justice Douglas would have struck down the registration provision as conflicting with the Fifth Amendment's self-incrimination clause, since the Smith Act made membership in the Communist Party a crime. A 1965 Supreme Court opinion later did exactly that.[127] Nonetheless, Justice Douglas's opinion in the 1961 Subversive Activities Control Board case is important for our purposes. It demonstrates that the preferred freedoms doctrine is exactly what it claims to be: a judicial balance weighted in favor of certain fundamental rights. Our society's heavy interest in those rights, however, can be overborne by demonstrated need for promoting some other important interest. Absent the Smith Act, Justice Douglas believed that the government had demonstrated its need for restricting important First Amendment rights of the Communist Party via the registration provision of the McCarran Act.

United States v. Robel (1967)[128] involved the provision of the 1950 Subversive Activities Control Act making it illegal for a member of the Communist action organization, after it was under final orders to register, to engage in any employment in any defense facility. The opinion for the Court of Chief Justice Warren used the preferred freedoms doctrine to hold that section of the act unconstitutional. As in all opinions using the preferred freedoms doctrine, the Chief Justice saw the issue in terms of competing interests. He quickly established that the judicial accommodation must recognize that "the most cherished of [our democratic] ideals have found expression in the First Amendment,"[129] and that freedom of association was one of those ideals. The Chief Justice also recognized that a legitimate governmental interest was involved—the need to reduce the threat of sabotage and espionage in defense facilities. To him, there was only one constitutional way to achieve an accommodation between this legitimate congressional power and vital individual rights: "It has become axiomatic that [p]recision of regulation must be the touchstone in an area so closely touching our most precious freedoms."[130] No other judicial standard could adequately safeguard our most vital freedoms while still permitting Congress to exercise its constitutional power.

Since the law in question made Robel's continued employment at a defense facility contingent upon his surrendering his membership in the Communist Party, its inhibiting effect on the right of political association was clear. It was equally clear to the Court majority that the statute was indiscriminately broad. It made no distinction between passive, marginal members and active, knowing ones, between types of defense facilities, or between sensitive and nonsensitive positions. Because of the fatal defect of overbreadth, the statute was unnecessarily restrictive of the right of association and therefore unconstitutional.

The preferred freedoms doctrine shows its obvious strengths in this type of case. First, since the doctrine emphasizes the importance of political freedoms such as the right of association, any governmental restrictions of those freedoms must be clearly justified. Chief Justice Warren's opinion did not permit the government's broad assertion of its power and interests to go unchallenged: the "concept of 'national defense' cannot be deemed an end in itself, justifying any exercise of legislative power designed to promote such a goal."[131] Justice Harlan's *Barenblatt* opinion, it will be recalled, had done exactly that.[132] Here, unlike his realist brethren, the Chief Justice's use of the preference doctrine meant he would treat the government's claimed purpose more narrowly—its interest was in reducing the threat of sabotage and espionage at defense plants.

Second, the doctrine does not ignore important societal interests in areas like defense security. Once the congressional goal was specified, the Chief Justice could insist it be achieved by means having a less drastic impact on the continued vitality of First Amendment freedoms. Congress must carefully define the sensitive positions in defense industries. Similarly, it must carefully specify which persons are to be excluded from those positions on security grounds.[133] Such a statute would be constitutional, according to the Chief Justice, despite the fact that even a narrowly drawn statute would have some restrictive impact on the right of association.

Third, and most important, the restrictions of fundamental rights could be limited to areas of demonstrable need. In the name of national security there was no reason to curtail unnecessarily those liberties which made national defense worthwhile. On the contrary, there was every reason to take good care that restrictive legislation was not needlessly expanded.

For the same reasons, the Court eventually used the preferred freedoms doctrine to impose severe limitations on state loyalty oaths. The most informative cases are *Elfbrandt v. Russell* (1966),[134] and *Keyishian v. Board of Regents* (1967).[135] In both cases, the Court majority held that a statute impinging upon the freedom of association protected by the First Amendment must be narrowly drawn. In both cases, the dissenting opinions argued that the Court should continue to use the doctrine based upon realist theory to uphold loyalty oaths.[136] The contrast between the realist and optimalist theories of democracy is clearly drawn in these cases.

The *Elfbrandt* and *Keyishian* decisions did not foreclose all state loyalty-security programs. The latter opinion explicitly acknowledged the legitimacy of a state's interest in protecting its educational system from subversion.[137] Under the same doctrine, presumably the Court would recognize a similar state interest in other areas—law enforcement agencies, for example. The thrust of those opinions, however, is that even within areas of admitted state concern about political activity, great care must be taken that security programs affect only the particular individuals most likely to subvert the state's interest. Hence, not even active, knowing membership in the Communist Party is a sufficient bar to public employment; the state must demonstrate an individual's actual intent to further the party's unlawful aims. Only this type of accommodation, the Court majority believed, adequately recognizes both legitimate governmental interests and a democratic system's necessary interest in political freedom.

The preferred freedoms doctrine did not play a prominent role in judicial decisions involving congressional investigations of suspected Communists and Communist activities. Neither was it entirely absent. Chief Justice Warren's opinion for the Court in *Watkins v. United States* (1957)[138] reversed the contempt of Congress conviction for due process reasons. The opinion stated that the question under inquiry by a House Un-American Activities Subcommittee was not made sufficiently clear to Watkins so that he could determine whether he was within his rights in refusing to answer.[139] The great bulk of Warren's opinion was a sharply worded attack on the type of investigation conducted by the committee, written from the perspective of the preferred freedoms doctrine.

To the Chief Justice the "critical element" was "the existence of, and the weight to be ascribed to, the interest of the Congress in demanding disclosures from an unwilling witness." He was unwilling to assume that every investigation was "justified by a public need" which "overbalances any private rights affected."[140] The asserted governmental interest would have to be closely scrutinized by the judiciary to insure that Congress did not unjustifiably encroach upon an individual's protected freedoms.

The vagueness of the resolution establishing the committee frustrated that inquiry. "Who can define the meaning of 'un-American'?" Warren asked. "What is the single, solitary 'principle of the form of government as guaranteed by our Constitution'?"[141] Nor did the committee's diverse and wide-ranging activities give its jurisdiction and purpose any greater clarity and particularity. The Chief Justice could only conclude that:

> It is impossible in such a situation to ascertain whether any legislative purpose justifies the disclosures sought and, if so, the importance of that information to the Congress in furtherance of its legislative function. The reason no Court can make this critical judgment is that the House of Representatives itself has never made it.[142]

Presumably, then, if Warren had decided *Watkins* on First Amendment grounds, the committee's contempt citation would not have withstood the judicial scrutiny required by the preferred freedoms doctrine. Using that standard, it is extremely doubtful that any investigation by that committee could have survived a challenge in the courts. Since the conviction was actually reversed for due process reasons, however, the Chief Justice's discussion of the First Amendment was only an admonition to Congress.

Precisely because of their adherence to the preferred freedoms doctrine, certain Justices resorted to due process reasons to protect First Amendment rights. In *Wilkinson v. United States* (1961)[143] and *Braden v. United States* (1961),[144] the Supreme Court affirmed contempt of Congress convictions. Among other activities, both Wilkinson and Braden were involved in protesting both the existence of the House Committee on Un-American Activities as well as an investigation by that committee in Atlanta. When subpoenaed to appear at that Atlanta hearing, they each refused to answer the subcommittee's questions about their activities. In both cases Justice Stewart's opinions for the Court relied upon Justice Harlan's *Barenblatt* opinion.[145] Justice Douglas's dissenting opinions[146] argued that the Un-American Activities Committee had failed to lay an adequate foundation at the Atlanta hearing for the questions put to Wilkinson and Braden. "After *Watkins*," Douglas insisted, anyone was entitled to rely on that case's due process "propositions for protection of his First Amendment rights."[147]

As this review indicates, there would have been fewer governmental restrictions on political activity if the Supreme Court had consistently used that doctrine to decide Communist Party cases. It is extremely doubtful that a greater toleration for the politically obnoxious (from the majority's standpoint) would have posed any threat to our security. When the federal and state laws regarding Communists were struck down or drastically limited in the late 1960s our internal security did not suffer. In terms of consequences, political freedom would have been in a healthier condition in the United States had the Supreme Court always shown a decided preference for freedom.

One wonders however whether this preference is enough. To maximize political expression in accordance with optimalist theory requires a widespread acceptance of its exalted position within our constitutional hierarchy of values. Even unanimous acceptance by the judiciary would not be sufficient, for an elected leadership with a different value orientation would still have ample opportunity to restrict speech. Widespread acceptance, in turn, would be achieved only if the preferred freedoms doctrine came to be seen as a binding recommendation.

The very nature of optimalist theory and the preference doctrine mitigates against that possibility. Such political freedoms as speech and association are regarded as vitally important interests in a democratic society; but they are not seen as sacrosanct rights. As Chief Justice Warren said in his *Robel* and *Watkins* opinions, there is a need to accommodate conflicting interests. So, despite the abundance of passionate language about the great importance of free speech, the judicial opinions reflecting optimalist theory teach us that the continued exercise of vital political freedoms depends upon a critical judgment of the competing interest in any given situation.

True enough, the same opinions also seek to teach us how we should exercise that judgment. We must closely scrutinize all governmental claims impinging upon political freedoms; we must never lightly suffer any restrictions in this area. But the structure of an opinion based upon the preferred freedoms doctrine includes a conclusion about whether or not the government has shown a compelling need to infringe individual liberty in that *particular* case. The particular balance automatically limits the prescriptive lesson of any language in a preference opinion glowingly speaking of the vital importance of free speech or association; for, it is arguable in the next case, when the circumstances are different, that the decision should reflect a different accommodation. The limitation on general principles is only emphasized by opinions like Chief Justice Warren's in *Robel*, Justice Brennan's in *Keyishian*, and Justice Douglas's in the 1961 *Subversive Activities Control Board* case which would sustain some governmental infringement of political freedom. The protection to be accorded political freedom necessarily remains an open question.

The judicial adherents of optimalist theory are unlikely to persuade others of the essential correctness of the preferred freedoms doctrine by showing the lack of evidence demonstrating imminent peril. Any complex situation permits a multitude of assessments. The very materials which Chief Justice Vinson found so menacing in *Dennis* were thought by Justice Douglas to be the harmless mutterings of discredited, isolated fanatics. Justice Douglas marshalled "the facts" to support his argument, but, at the time, he persuaded only those already predisposed to believe him. In the end, an individual's value orientation is more likely to color his evaluation of the factual situation than the other way around.

The likelihood of multiple judgments limits still further the persuasiveness of judicial opinions based upon the optimalist theory of democracy. If judges arrive at their decisions by assessing the competing interests, are they not, as Justice Frankfurter always pointed out, engaging in essentially the same process as the legislature? Why, then, should the judicial assessment prevail? Within optimalist theory that question cannot adequately be answered by stressing the Court's role of guardian of our constitutional liberties. The theory is built upon the assumption that other values—such as national security—must enter into the judgment. For the judges then to insist that democracy always requires giving political rights a high priority sounds more like the reiteration of a premise than an argument designed to convince those starting from a different premise. Once the Justices make the constitutional protection accorded political expression depend upon the accommodation of competing interests in a given situation, it becomes very difficult to persuade others that those judges are not merely deciding cases on the basis of their own personal preferences.

The almost classical criticism of the preferred freedoms doctrine has centered around the inability to demonstrate that it is a clearly objective standard for judicial decisions.[148] This criticism does not always seem misplaced. Justice Douglas's apparent willingness in the 1961 *Subversive Activities Control Board* case to permit the registration of Communist Party members is not at all consistent with his other First Amendment opinions.[149] It strikes one as being more like the gesture of a prudent politician: making a concession to the opposition on an essentially minor point to show that you are reasonable. Would he really have held the registration provisions valid under the First Amendment if he did not think that the Fifth Amendment's self-incrimination clause provided a much stronger argument for striking down the law? Given his other opinions, one is entitled to be skeptical.[150] The necessity for accommodation within the preference doctrine can serve more as a cloak for personal predilections than as the basis for reasoned analysis.

Both the lack of persuasiveness and the consequent inability to safeguard political freedom in the long run can also be seen in the cases arising from the black Americans' drive for equal citizenship. The first few NAACP opinions written in the aftermath of the *School Desegregation Decision* placed great stress upon the importance of the political freedoms protected by the First Amendment. The absence of any rational relationship between the stated governmental objective and the actions demanded of the NAACP meant that these cases were actually disposed of on due process grounds.[151] Not until *Shelton v. Tucker* (1960)[152] did the Justices' differences on First Amendment standards become significant. Justice Stewart's opinion for the majority in that case relied upon the preferred freedoms doctrine to sustain the NAACP's claim. The four dissenters, in opinions written by Justices Frankfurter and Harlan, would have upheld the state statute by interpreting the First Amendment according to realist theory.[153]

Justice Stewart began the *Shelton* opinion by stating the competing interests involved. First, "the right of a state to investigate the competence and fitness of those whom it hires to teach in its schools"; second, "the teacher's right of free association, a right closely allied to freedom of speech and a right which, like free speech, lies at the foundation of a free society."[154] Justice Stewart then went on to say that "even though the governmental purpose be legitimate and substantial, that purpose cannot be pursued by means that broadly stifle fundamental personal liberties when the end can be more narrowly achieved."[155]

The Arkansas statute required a teacher to list every organization to which he belonged or contributed over a five year period. Many associational ties—religious, professional, avocational, social—could have no possible bearing upon a person's qualifications to teach. The interference with personal freedom was conspicuously accented by the failure to require that the information be kept confidential, and the history of the act left little doubt it was designed to expose members and supporters of the NAACP and other civil rights organizations. In light of those circumstances, Justice Stewart held that the "statute's comprehensive interference with associational freedom goes far beyond what might be justified in the exercise of the State's legitimate inquiry into the fitness and competency of its teachers."[156]

   NAACP v. Button (1963) [157] involved an aspect of Virginia's "massive resistance" to desegregation. The legislature had sought to stifle lawsuits attacking the racial status quo by revising the barratry laws. Justice Brennan first held that litigation by a group like the NAACP is a form of political expression covered by the First Amendment.[158] The preferred freedoms doctrine supplied one of his reasons for then holding the Virginia law unconstitutional.[159]

   In that part of his opinion, Justice Brennan held that "only a *compelling* State interest in the regulation of a subject within the State's constitutional power to regulate can justify limiting First Amendment freedoms."[160] This view led him to scrutinize closely a state's interest in regulating its bar. Virginia had not shown "a serious danger here of professionally reprehensible conflicts of interest which rules against solicitation frequently seek to prevent."[161] The NAACP and its attorneys provided legal services without charge, so there was no danger of subverting the clients' interests for monetary gain. Lacking any showing to the contrary, it could not be said that the aims and interests of the NAACP were in conflict with those of its members and of nonmember litigants. Justice Brennan, therefore, concluded that while the NAACP had shown that its activities fell within the protections of the First Amendment, Virginia had failed to advance any *substantial* regulatory interests, in the form of substantive evils, which could have justified the broad prohibition it sought to impose.[162] By way of contrast, Justice Harlan, dissenting, would have sustained the Virginia law under the *reasonableness* test used by adherents of the realist theory of democracy.[163]

   In *Gibson v. Florida Legislative Investigation Committee* (1963),[164] the state sought to invade the associational privacy of the NAACP on the grounds that it was investigating Communist activity. The Supreme Court was faced with the problem of reconciling two lines of its own recent precedents. On the one side were the cases upholding the NAACP's right of associational privacy; on the other were precedents denying that right to the Communist party and its members. The situation was tailor-made for Justice Goldberg's use of the preferred freedoms doctrine to uphold the NAACP's First Amendment claim. Once again the opinion for the Court began by stating the conflicting interests—the individual rights of free speech and association and the governmental interest in conducting legislative investigations to inform itself in order to act and protect its legitimate and vital interests.[165]

According to Justice Goldberg, the prior decisions regarding the Communist Party had made a distinction between the investigations of the Party or its members and investigations of organizations like the NAACP and their members. The special character and objectives of the Communist Party caused the governmental interest in controlling subversion to outweigh the right of individual Communists or suspected Communists to conceal party membership or organizational affiliation. However, Justice Goldberg argued, when a nonsubversive organization like the NAACP is involved, it does not automatically forfeit its right of associational privacy simply because the state is investigating Communist activity.[166]

The preferred freedoms doctrine permitted Justice Goldberg to weigh governmental interest differently in the two private associations. When dealing with a nonsubversive organization, government simply had less need for information about its activities. Government, therefore, had a stronger presumption to overcome. It had to *"convincingly* show a *substantial* relation between the information sought and a subject of *overriding* and *compelling* state interest."[167]

Obviously, the key question for Justice Goldberg was whether Florida had shown a substantial connection between the Miami branch of the NAACP and the subversive activities of the Communist Party. If the state could show a substantial connection, it would be an easy task to show a compelling interest in subversive activities. Justice Goldberg carefully scrutinized the record. He found that all the committee could produce was testimony that in years past some fourteen people who were (or were asserted to be) Communists had attended occasional NAACP meetings and were therefore probably members of the Miami branch. The committee could not demonstrate their influence in the chapter (which had a total membership of approximately 1,000), nor could it show that the NAACP, for whatever reason, was engaged in any subversive activities. "The strong associational interest in maintaining the privacy of membership lists of groups engaged in the constitutionally protected free trade in ideas and beliefs may not be substantially infringed upon such a slender showing."[168] Justice Goldberg therefore held that the Florida committee had not laid an adequate foundation for the questions it had asked Gibson, the president of the Miami NAACP.

Justice Goldberg had tried valiantly to stay within the framework of past decisions. The preferred freedoms doctrine, with its emphasis on accommodating the competing interests of a *particular* situation, was admirably suited for that purpose. Nonetheless, Justice Goldberg still could not avoid distorting the precedents, as Justice Harlan, in dissent,[169] was quick to point out. In *Uphaus v. Wyman* (1959),[170] a Supreme Court majority had upheld a legislative inquiry into alleged Communist activity within a pacifist organization, the World Fellowship Camp. Justice Goldberg could not convincingly distinguish *Uphaus* from *Gibson*.

Instead, his effort only served to highlight a change within the Supreme Court. The plain fact was that in 1963 a majority of the Justices were no longer willing to tolerate an infringement of First Amendment rights on nothing more substantial than a claim to be seeking information about Communists. This change was especially important in the South where such claims could be easily used to destroy the nascent civil rights movement. "We cannot," said Justice Goldberg, "close our eyes to the fact that the militant Negro civil rights movement has engendered the intense resentment and opposition of the politically dominant white community."[171]

The same pattern emerges from the majority opinions in *Shelton* and *Button*. Justice Stewart's opinion in the former did not even attempt to distinguish it from previous cases which had pretty much given the states full power to inquire into the personal lives of their teachers.[172] Justice Brennan's opinion in the latter case also did not explain how Virginia's detailed regulation of the bar differed materially from state bar regulations the Court had previously upheld.[173] Lacking such demonstrations, these opinions seem to say more about the majority's desire to protect the NAACP in the South than about their concern with developing principles for a consistent promotion of political freedom. *Shelton, Button*, and *Gibson* would hardly persuade the unconvinced that a Court majority was not simply using the preferred freedoms doctrine to cloak their own political biases.

The civil rights movement, of course, was not restricted to the court-oriented activities of the NAACP. At times, it became a mass protest movement against racial inequality. In large part the success of such demonstrations depends upon their ability to shatter the political tranquility of a community or the nation. The result was frequent legal clashes with the forces of law and order. In these cases, too, Justices of the Supreme Court frequently applied the preferred freedoms doctrine.

The first case, *Edwards v. South Carolina* (1961)[174] is not a clear example of any specific doctrine. The eight-man majority saw the entirely peaceable demonstration at the state capitol in Columbia as "an exercise of basic constitutional rights in their most pristine and classic form." Since there was no evidence to support the breach of peace charge, the majority was not willing to permit South Carolina's vague statute to be used for punishing the demonstrators' "constitutionally protected rights of free speech, free assembly and freedom to petiton for redress of grievances."[175] The absence of evidence in support of the state's action meant there was little need to engage in an extended discussion of the nature of First Amendment rights involved in a mass demonstration.[176] Justice Stewart was clearly more concerned about massing the Court than with doctrinal purity.

The preferred freedoms doctrine did play an essential part in Justice Goldberg's opinion for the Court in *Cox v. Louisiana* (1965).[177] The cases arose from a demonstration by the Committee on Racial Equality protesting the arrests of blacks who had engaged in sit-ins at lunch counters in Baton Rouge. By the time the Supreme Court heard the case, Reverend Cox was charged with breach of the peace, obstructing public passages, and picketing near a courthouse. While the majority reversed the breach of peace conviction by developing an analogy with *Edwards*,[178] they plainly used the preferred freedoms doctrine to dismiss the other two charges.

Justice Goldberg held that the demonstration had indeed obstructed a public sidewalk and that a state and municipality had the right to regulate the use of streets and sidewalks in the interest of public safety and convenience. He "emphatically" rejected the notion that the First Amendment afforded "the same kind of freedom to those who would communicate ideas by conduct such as patrolling, marching and picketing on the streets and highways" as is afforded "to those who communicate ideas by pure speech."[179] No one had an unlimited right to demonstrate at any public place at any time.

Nonetheless, Goldberg considered peaceful demonstrations as within the ambit of constitutionally protected activity. Governmental regulations of public streets and highways, therefore, had to be carefully scrutinized by the Court. Only narrowly drawn, impartially administered, regulations concerning the time, place, duration, or manner of use of streets for public assemblies would be sustained as proper exercises of governmental responsibility.[180] Any less rigorous standard would not afford sufficient protection to our vitally important political freedoms. Broad, vague statutes, like the Louisiana prohibition of obstruction of public sidewalks, permit the authorities too much discretionary power over a constitutionally protected means of expression.[181]

On the third charge—picketing near a courthouse with intent to obstruct justice—the Court divided five to four in favor of reversal. The Justices were not divided, however, about the merits of the statute. There was no question in their minds that it was "a precise, narrowly drawn regulatory statute which proscribes certain specific behavior."[182] Nor was there any disagreement that it dealt with an important interest—protecting judicial proceedings from mob intimidation[183]—therefore, the Court unanimously held that such a narrowly drawn statute was "obviously a safeguard both necessary and appropriate to vindicate the State's interest in assuring justice under law."[184] In this instance, an accommodation of competing interests led the Court to sustain the state law.[185]

Nonetheless, the majority reversed Cox's conviction on this count also. Justice Goldberg argued that when the police had consented to the demonstration across the street from the courthouse, they had made an administrative determination that it was a legal site for a protest meeting. To later charge Cox, after he had refused to disband the demonstration, with violating a statute prohibiting picketing near a courthouse would be entrapment—convicting a citizen for exercising a privilege the state had clearly told him was available to him.[186] Cox's conviction, therefore, had to be reversed as a violation of due process.

Once again a reliance upon the preferred freedoms doctrine was evident. Only a firm belief in maximizing the opportunities for political protest would have led the Court majority to use the entrapment argument to reverse this conviction. It is difficult to imagine any other value for which five Justices would have excused a violation of an admittedly valid and valuable law designed to protect a court from mob interference. At the time of the *Cox* decision, at least, five Justices thought the First Amendment rights present in peaceful civil rights demonstrations should normally be given precedence.

In *Brown v. Louisiana* (1966),[187] the prevailing opinion by Justice Abe Fortas used the preferred freedoms doctrine to overturn convictions resulting from a protest in a small, rural, branch library. The library had a history of operating on a segregated basis, but in this case the five black demonstrators were given all the service they had requested. Nonetheless, they chose to stage a peaceful and orderly "stand-up" in the front room of the two-room library. This act would have prevented others from using the library's books and periodicals. Only because no one else entered the library that Saturday morning was Justice Fortas able to write that "there was no disturbance to others, no disruption of library activities and no violation of any library regulations."[188] The convictions must be reversed, he maintained, because there was no evidence that the Louisiana breach of peace statute had been violated.

Justice Fortas then went on to confirm the impression that he was stretching a bit in order to protect a protest he deemed legitimate. He gave "another and sharper" argument based on the First Amendment. Since the protest action was covered by that Amendment, the Court would be required to assess the constitutional impact of the statute in this situation, *even if* the action were within the statute's scope. Here, the statute was "deliberately and purposefully applied solely to terminate the reasonable, orderly and limited exercise of the right to protest the unconstitutional segregation of a public facility." It was, Justice Fortas concluded, an intolerable interference with a constitutionally protected right.[189]

Justice Goldberg in *Cox* had insisted that the conduct involved in a protest demonstration could be regulated under properly drawn laws. The picketing near the courthouse conviction was overturned not because it was "deliberately and purposefully applied solely to terminate a reasonable, orderly and limited demonstration against segregation," but because the detailed scrutiny required under the preferred freedoms doctrine had led Justice Goldberg to find a violation of due process. Now, in *Brown*, Justice Fortas was arguing that even if a properly drawn statute was correctly applied, it could not be used to squelch a demonstration against segregation. Such peaceful political protests had indeed achieved a preferred position in the constitutional hierarchy of at least three Justices.

A few months later, when *Adderley v. Florida* (1966)[190] was decided, only a minority of the Justices supported the demonstrators' claim that they were engaged in a constitutionally protected activity. The demonstrators had been convicted of trespassing with malicious intent upon the premises of the county jail. Justice Douglas's dissenting opinion made quite clear which doctrine the minority was employing: peaceful assembly, and petitioning for redress of grievances "are preferred rights of the Constitution."[191] Like free speech, these rights were important in our democratic system because they helped inform both officials and other members of the public what some of their fellow citizens expected from government. Protest demonstrations "should not be condemned as tactics of obstruction and harassment as long as the assembly and petition are peaceable."[192]

Despite this language, Justice Douglas indicated that some public facilities were dedicated to purposes which made them unsuitable sites for mass demonstrations. "In other cases it may be necessary to adjust the right to petition for redress of grievances to the other interests inhering in the uses to which the public property is normally put."[193]

The minority did not think either of these limiting factors were present in *Adderly*: "The jailhouse, like an executive mansion, a legislative chamber, a courthouse, or the statehouse itself . . . is one of the seats of government whether it be the Tower of London, the Bastille, or a small county jail. And when it houses political prisoners or those who many think are unjustly held, it is an obvious center for protest."[194] Unlike the majority, the minority did not believe that the demonstrators' conduct had upset the basic functions of the jail; "things went on as they normally would."[195] Given the ambiguous factual record,[196] the minority's interpretation of the events is almost certainly a product of their theoretical approach to mass demonstrations.

The preferred freedoms doctrine, therefore, enabled Justice Douglas to argue that *Adderley* could not be distinguished from *Cox* and *Edwards*. All three cases involved a peaceful petition for the redress of grievances. Like the other cases, the Florida trespass law involved in *Adderley* vested too much discretionary authority in government officials. It permitted the sheriff and similar "custodians" of public property to decide when public places shall be used for expressing ideas via the constitutional rights of assembly and petition. The Florida law thereby gave certain public officials the awesome power to decide whose ideas may be expressed. Such power, Justice Douglas maintained, was out of step with all the Court's previous decisions, including both *Cox* and *Edwards*, which protected First Amendment rights from overly broad grants of discretionary authority.[197]

On Easter Sunday 1965, the late Dr. Martin Luther King conducted a peaceful demonstration in Birmingham, Alabama, without first obtaining a parade permit and in open defiance of a temporary injunction by the state circuit court. The next day, the circuit court judge found Dr. King and some of his colleagues in contempt. In *Walker v. Birmingham* (1967),[198] the United States Supreme Court sustained the state court ruling in a five to four decision.

All the Justices agreed that a mass demonstration creates the need to reconcile First Amendment political freedoms with a municipality's interests in traffic control and the prevention of disorder.[199] There was also agreement that the Birmingham parade ordinance was not a suitable vehicle for accommodating those conflicting interests. Its vague language gave too much discretion to the authorities.[200] Similarly, the Justices unanimously agreed that the injunction suffered from the same defects since it literally incorporated the parade ordinance.[201] Only one issue divided the majority from the minority: could Alabama require a person challenging the constitutionality of a court order to exhaust his legal remedies before violating that order?

The three minority opinions insisted it was perfectly proper to raise a constitutional challenge to an injunction by violating it. Persons seeking to challenge the constitutionality of a statute have often been required to violate it in order to establish standing. The minority could find no reason why a court order should be treated with any greater respect than a statute. This option was particularly important, the minority opinions insisted, when the case involved First Amendment rights.[202] There is good reason why a person should be permitted to challenge a court order impinging upon his First Amendment rights by violating it. Time is often a critical political variable.[203] In both *Cox* and *Adderley* the demonstrations developed overnight in response to the arrests of civil rights activists. In *Walker*, Easter Sunday was of symbolic importance to the Reverend King's Southern Christian Leadership group. The preferred freedoms doctrine helped the *Walker* minority recognize the importance of the time factor.

The doctrine also enhanced the Justices' ability to handle the issue of the legitimacy of demonstrations on public facilities. Because of the emphasis on First Amendment rights, Justices taking this position are unlikely to ignore the importance of protest demonstrations. If all public facilities were totally closed to peaceful protests, the disadvantaged groups in our society would be losing a potent political instrument, perhaps the only means at their disposal for focusing attention on their concerns. As Justice Douglas said in his *Walker* dissent, "The rich can buy advertisements in newspapers, purchase radio or television time, and rent billboard space. Those less affluent are restricted to the use of handbills . . . or petitions, or parades, or mass meetings."[204]

Under the preferred freedoms doctrine, therefore, while limitations may be imposed to protect the principal function of a public facility, government could not constitutionally prohibit all use of its property for mass demonstrations. In a democracy, the importance of political freedom should generally outweigh minor inconveniences to normal patterns. Streets are public facilities dedicated to traffic. Although no city should be expected to submit to paralysis, "it is the city's duty under law, and as a matter of good sense, to make very effort to provide adequate facilities so that the demonstration can be effectively staged, so that it can be conducted without paralyzing the city's life, and to provide protection for the demonstrators."[205]

Courts and jails are admittedly public facilities where the maintenance of orderly processes is of utmost importance. Still, there is no a priori reason why their purposes should totally immunize the *surrounding* area from peaceful demonstrations. The key questions are whether the normal routines were affected and how much. In *Adderley* the evidence showed the demonstration had not caused much more than official irritation at its presence. That being so, the protestors' claims would have been upheld under the preferred freedoms doctrine because "our Constitution and our traditions, as well as practical wisdom, teach us that city officials, police and citizens must be tolerant of mass demonstrations, however large and inconvenient."[206]

In *Cox*, a direct, open use of the preferred freedoms doctrine would have been a distinct advantage. Justic Goldberg's opinion, it will be recalled, upheld the constitutionality of the ordinance regarding picketing near the courthouse. To avoid applying it to Cox, he had to resort to the due process concept of entrapment; yet, the demonstration had clearly taken place "near" the courthouse, within the meaning of a statute designed to protect the judicial process from outside interference. It was near enough for 23 students in the jail section of the building and the 2,000 demonstrators outside to react to each other. In addition, one judge felt compelled to leave his chambers because of the noise. Rather than rely upon a dubious interpretation of the word "near," it would have been far better for the majority to have held the disturbances were not sufficient to warrant a limitation on First Amendment rights. As it is written, Justice Goldberg's opinion cannot help but give the impression that the majority was bending the law to protect a cause they obviously favored.

So for all the impressive evidence these mass demonstration cases provide of the preferred freedoms doctrine's utility in protecting political rights, one must again confront the charge that it is more nearly a device for masking judicial preferences than a neutral legal principle. One would be more comfortable with this doctrine if the Justices employing it occasionally gave some indication they would decide against demonstrations whose causes they favored. After all, the doctrine is based on the idea that interests other than First Amendment rights are involved in such demonstrations.

In *Adderley*, for example, Justice Douglas's opinion for the dissenters said:

> There may be some public places which are so clearly committed to other purposes that their use for the airing of grievances is anomalous . . . A noisy meeting may be out of keeping with the serenity of the statehouse or the quiet of a courthouse. No one, for example, would suggest that the Senate gallery is the proper place for a vociferous protest rally.[207]

The library "stand-up" opinion which Justice Fortas wrote for three of the same four judges[208] makes them seem anything but neutral in applying the preferred freedoms doctrine. Is not a library "so clearly committed" to quiet reading, studying, and reflection that its "use for the airing of grievances is anomalous?" Are only "noisy," "vociferous" protest rallies to be banned? It is difficult to understand why under certain circumstances a silent demonstration could not be just as inconsistent with, and disruptive to, those public facilities which need "quiet" and "serenity." If this observation is true, then the library "standup," by the very standards enunciated by Douglas, should have been condemned by the *Adderley* minority.

Justice Fortas subsequently explained his opinion in *Brown* by emphasizing that the protestors had violated an unconstitutional practice of segregation. Had the library not been segregated, he indicated, the outcome might well have been different.[209] Whatever the library's past history of segregation, however, Brown was given at least normal service. Even a small rural Louisiana parish *may* have brought its practices into conformity with the law of the land; there is no evidence that Brown was the victim of discriminatory practice because of his race.[210] Justice Fortas's subsequent explanation, therefore, only reinforces the impression of one-sided justice.

Even the impression of one-sidedness undermines a judicial position. What had begun as an eight-man majority in the 1961 *Edwards* case had dwindled to a bare five-man majority in the *Cox* case two years later. In the still later *Adderley* and *Walker* cases, the preferred freedoms doctrine had become the minority position. Over this period, the preferred freedoms doctrine did not prove a very reliable protection for those blacks engaged in mass demonstrations, just as in the heyday of the Cold War the doctrine had not provided adequate protection for the political freedoms of American Communists. In any event, the consistent use of the preferred freedoms doctrine in support of those seeking to remedy the injustice of segregation—seemingly without regard for other legitimate interests—calls the doctrine itself into question.

CONCLUSIONS

In the end, any assessment of the relative merits of the preferred freedoms doctrine must turn on its inability to serve as a source of objective standards for handling political problems. This weakness can be traced back to optimalist theory and, beyond that, to the competitive paradigm itself.

Optimalist theory asserts that democracy is a political system based upon the free competition for the free vote. Authority to decide political issues is given to those individuals selected by that process. The judicial authority to intervene is derived from the competitive electoral process because the areas requiring active judicial supervision are defined by their relationship to those processes. The optimalist theory of democracy inevitably focuses one's attention on leadership decisions.

This focus is evident in all three of the areas discussed here. The expatriated American is denied the very right to belong to our society. Judicial opinions applying optimalist theory protect the basic right of citizenship by detailed examination of the government's reasons. The structuring of the electoral process is often decisive in determining which laws shall be made or unmade. Judicial opinions applying optimalist theory would safeguard an ultimately effective majority rule by recognizing an apportionment which reflected an elected leadership's accommodation of all substantial interests. Certain freedoms are essential to the free competition for the free vote. Within optimalist theory, those freedoms are protected by an exacting judicial scrutiny of the interests asserted by the government.

The same focus on decisions of the political leadership can be seen most clearly in the social scientists' proposals for realigning our two-party system. They accept the idea that in modern democracy the people elect their rulers and the rulers govern. The reforms, therefore, center on the types of political programs the competing elites will offer the electorate.

The focus on political elites—their functions, decisions, claims—means that the rights of the citizen are never adequately defined. Citizenship is a basic right in optimalist theory, but except for the right to participate in the electoral process its dimensions are not explored. Political participation is seen as an essential feature of democracy, but its equation with the act of voting removes all the active overtones surrounding the concept of participation and reduces it to the lowest common denominator. Optimalist theory recognizes that the electoral process cannot function without the rights of free speech, petition, and peaceable assembly, but the nature and scope of those rights are left to a case-by-case judicial determination of competing interests. All in all, optimalist theory handles the important rights of a citizen simply by labelling them "important."

Such labelling does, of course, serve a useful function. It creates a rough hierarchy of constitutional values. Like the Realists, Optimalists begin with recognizing that circumstances frequently create a tension or conflict between what the elected rulers deem necessary and what the Constitution may have orginally intended to be protected from government. This conflict is inevitable because the Constitution does not entail a consistent plan of democratic government: the Framers were not democrats. As democrats, the Optimalists maintain, we must interpret the document in light of democratic theory— the struggle for political power through the free competition for the free vote. Unlike the Realists, however, they recognize that the competitive electoral process requires a special consideration for certain individual rights. Although, in optimalist theory, the Constitution has ceased to be an independent source of authority, the theory does point to a particular way of resolving conflicts: governmental actions which impinge upon important individual rights must be clearly justified.

Unlike realist theory, this teaching is reinforced by acknowledging the Supreme Court as the proper agency for resolving those conflicts. The Court must subject governmental claims limiting basic individual rights to the closest possible scrutiny. Only clearly necessary actions which pose the least possible danger to vital freedoms will be sustained. In optimalist theory, the Supreme Court is the principal institution for translating the fundamental values of democracy into our politics.

This view of the Court's function makes the lack of clear, objective standards all the more important. For like the Realists, the Optimalists do not make a distinction between different *types* of claims—principles and rights are regarded as another type of interest. Principles and rights are not invested with any great moral or ethical content; like all other claims they must be treated as means designed to promote certain interests. As a result, optimalist theory offers little encouragement to the individual to think in terms other than his own interests, except insofar as it effectively teaches that certain rights must be granted special treatment by virtue of their importance to the functioning of a democratic system.

That lesson can only be diluted by the lack of clear standards. The absence of objective criteria makes it easy to suspect that principles are being used to cloak personal preferences. The judges using optimalist theory often appear to be deciding cases on the basis of their own political instincts. Such appearances, whether true or not, cannot help but reduce the impact of optimalist theory. A leader perceived as acting to further his own interests cannot expect others to surrender their interests for the greater good.

Even more important, the absence of clear standards emphasizes the element of accommodation within optimalist theory, and the very language of accommodation works against the theory's persuasiveness. We are told that the Justices must decide how much freedom is consistent with the functioning of a democratic political system. It is all very much like an engineer calculating how much stress his physical system can tolerate. The social engineers making this delicate accommodation must calculate how much discord our political system can tolerate. Neither the structural engineer nor the social engineer, however, really wants to subject his system to the maximum feasible stress. Each much prefers to work well within the limits of calculated safety.

It is not surprising, then, that in optimalist theory the most to be expected from our leaders is greater toleration. It is doubtful whether the adherents of that theory themselves do more than tolerate unconventional political activity.[211] Toleration must not be confused with persuasion; it is more like grudging acquiescence than acceptance. The elected leadership is likely to continue pursuing its original restrictive objectives by other means. This action would be probable even among those leaders who granted the Supreme Court's authority to decide such matters. Since the judicial opinions based upon optimalist theory never deny the legitimacy of values other than political freedom, those not sharing the preferred freedoms doctrine could read the judicial opinions as simply requiring more care from the statutory draftsmen. Here, too, the leadership response would not accept the preferred freedoms doctrine of optimalist theory as a binding recommendation.

As for the general public, the lesson they are likely to learn from these judicial opinions is that the extent of their political freedom is bounded by their leaders' toleration. Toleration is a noble sentiment, one no civilized society can do without; but we would do well to recognize its limits. The tolerated act is still accepted only on the sufferance of those with the power to decide otherwise.

Optimalist theory, if consistently adhered to by all leadership groups, extends the boundaries of permitted dissent, but a citizen's own freedom still depends on someone else's critical evaluation of the situation. As Justice Fortas once wrote: "The state must tolerate the individual's dissent, appropriately expressed. The individual must tolerate the majority's verdict when and as it is settled in accordance with the laws and procedures that have been established."[212]

For all the emphasis on individual rights in optimalist theory, this elitist element cannot be overlooked. It means that only the socially acceptable dissidents can feel comfortable. The more unorthodox dissenters know their political activity is merely being tolerated and is subject to restriction when dominant elements in society deem it necessary. "Liberalism is a sentiment, not a program," Andre Malraux has written.[213] The Optimalists' failure to define carefully the nature of the rights they seek to protect means that the radicals' rights are limited by the liberal sentiment of toleration.

The Framers of our Constitution thought they had provided a stronger safeguard for our liberties. Before we accept optimalist theory, we should make sure the Framers' intention cannot be realized. The Constitution was intended to provide firm guidelines, not a noble sentiment, and the original intent is still worth of our best efforts.

III

CONTEMPORARY THEORIES OF DEMOCRACY: NATURAL RIGHTS THEORY

——————————————————————

Eight

LIBERAL NATURAL
RIGHTS THEORY ———————————

The judicial crisis during the New Deal and the Cold War were not the only domestic concerns shaping American constitutional theory. The problems posed by the bureaucratic administrative state, the civil rights movement, and the Vietnam protest movement also had an impact. For most of the Justices and commentators, these later events were accommodated within patterns of thought developed in response to the earlier concerns. This continuity was not the case with Justice William O. Douglas. His mature political theory can best be seen as an unending attempt to frame adequate constitutional protections for the full range of individual liberties. It was nothing less than an effort to reintroduce a natural rights theory of American democracy back into constitutional interpretation.

For a variety of reasons, Justice Douglas's constitutional framework has proved exceedingly elusive. His service on the Supreme Court was longer than any man in history. During his more than thirty six years on the bench he faced the whole range of complex and often novel issues which are the hallmark of contemporary public law. Nor was the Justice noted for his reticence in expressing his individualistic views—he authored more than 1,200 majority, concurring, and dissenting opinions. The changing issues during his long judicial career and the sheer number of his opinions account for part of the elusiveness. He also produced dozens of extrajudicial works—

legal articles, book length essays on civil liberties, essays and broadsides on broad socioeconomic developments at home and abroad, popular magazine pieces, and a two-volume autobiography. The superabundance of extrajudicial material only compounds the already difficult task of systematically analyzing the Justice's constitutional theory.

Moreover, Justice Douglas's felt obligation was to the Constitution, not to its prior interpretation (including his own); an adequate resolution of the issues immediately before the Court was more important to him than doctrinal consistency. Experiences both off and on the Court led him to change his doctrines over time.[1] Then, again, the very style of Justice Douglas's opinions frequently obstructs doctrinal analysis. He was more concerned with reaching the correct public policy than with painstaking legal analysis; he was more interested in illuminating his reasons by reference to the operating social realities than by conventional judicial reasoning.[2] Little wonder, then, that except for computer analyses based on simple-minded programs of "who wins" versus "who loses," Justice Douglas's constitutional ideas have been exceedingly difficult to systematize.

As with any other American political thinker, he shared a common heritage of ideas. Like the scholars and Justices working within the competitive paradigm, he believed in the central importance of free elections to our democracy. As noted in the previous chapter, his opinions frequently reflected an Optimalist's preferred freedoms constitutional interpretation. In time, however, he came to believe that American democracy could not be equated solely with the free competition for the free vote, no matter how broadly the functional requisites of such a system were read. Like Alexander Meiklejohn,[3] he believed the Constitution was an independent source of legitimacy. Yet Douglas maintained that the basic American concern has always been the individual, not the maintenance of a political system of self-government.[4] Like Justice Black,[5] therefore, he believed the Constitution, in all its provisions, seeks to promote the good life for all by assuring the good life of each. Yet Douglas did not share Black's concern with limiting judicial protection to those rights found within the formal pattern outlined by the Framers of the Constitution. Justice Douglas believed that even a broad reading of the Bill of Rights was not enough protection for individual liberty in modern society.[6] If the Constitution is to remain a living, vital force in the affairs of each generation, the Justices could not shirk their obligation to develop *new* constitutional doctrines.[7] Thus most of Douglas's values were held in part by each of the Justices with whom he served during his long career.

This conceptual overlapping, quite natural in America, makes it difficult to perceive the distinct outlines of Douglas's position. His overriding concern with doing justice in each case, and his lack of concern with a careful articulation of the parameters of his position add to the confusion and uncertainty.

Nonetheless, by the late 1950s Douglas had put shared American values together in a distinctive way, at least for that period in our history. The Justice had come to the conclusion that the grand design of the Constitution was the maximum feasible self-fulfillment of each individual. That objective led Justice Douglas to attempt a realistic assessment, in each problem area, of how best to update the traditional natural rights written into our Constitution.

THE GRAND DESIGN OF THE CONSTITUTION

For William O. Douglas it was always self-evident that people do not acquire rights from government; one person does not give another rights. "Man gets his rights from the Creator. They come to him because of the divine spark in every human being."[8] Douglas believed that this premise was the fundamental difference between democratic government and fascist, communist, and authoritarian states.[9] He well knew that few contemporary democrats started with this eighteenth-century axiom, but his upbringing, his early experiences, his education, his professional life, and his world travels confirmed rather than weakened this seemingly old-fashioned notion.[10] Perhaps that sentiment is why he never tired of quoting the Declaration of Independence. Jefferson's words enabled Douglas to maintain that, at least in the American scheme of things, the "starting point has always been the individual not the state."[11] If rights exist—or at least ought to exist—independently of government, then *the* basic purpose of government is to secure and advance those rights. Whatever may be the theory elsewhere, Douglas took the Declaration as proof that government in America was instituted to secure individual rights.[12]

For Justice Douglas, the Constitution has to be read in light of that overriding purpose. Like any legal document, the fundamental American Charter had to be adapted to changing circumstances. If the charter of government is not kept current, it becomes archaic and out of tune with the needs of the day. The Framers would want no less, Douglas maintained. They had established the Constitution to secure the blessings of liberty to themselves *and* to their posterity.[13]

In the constitutional thought of William O. Douglas, securing this liberty was the obligation of *all* branches of government, but the primary responsibility lay with the elected leaders. Douglas never sought to minimize the importance of meeting the basic physical needs of the American people. A strong, efficient, well-balanced national economy was indispensable to American democracy. Socioeconomic policy could only be made by the people's representatives and, increasingly, by administrative agencies. They had the constitutional authority; they were accountable through the electoral process; they had the technical expertise.

In the realm of socioeconomic policy, Justice Douglas consistently adhered to the values he had articulated as a law professor and as chairman of the Securities and Exchange Commission. The judiciary with life tenure must avoid writing their own social and economic creed into the basic Charter, for then the nation would lack the adaptability to meet the changing needs of the people. Change, not fixity, was the inevitable condition of the modern world. Under the Commerce Clause, [14] the Tax Clause, [15] the Due Process Clause, [16] and the Equal Protection Clause[17] Justice Douglas's response was always the same: judges must not interfere with local, state, and federal officials—whether on local government bodies,[18] in state legislatures,[19] in Congress,[20] on zoning boards,[21] in state regulatory agencies,[22] or in federal administrative agencies[23]—in their efforts to manage the material environment. The social and economic problems of the state and nation must be kept under the political management of the people and their elected representatives.

Importantly, however much Justice Douglas believed that elected officials and administrative agencies had the authority to pursue policies *they* thought desirable, his own economic views remained constant. Democracy flourished where individual economic opportunity was a living reality. Others might seek to emulate the economic systems of the social democracies in Western Europe; Douglas always insisted economic prosperity could best be achieved under a capitalism which emphasized competition, individual initiative, and freedom of opportunity. During his first five years in Washington as a member and later chairman of the Securities and Exchange Commission, Douglas became the friend and disciple of Justice Brandeis. Like Brandeis, his speeches at that time frequently deplored the "curse of bigness," whether corporate or governmental.[24] In the first volume of his autobiography written thirty-five years later, Douglas still proclaimed that "free enterprise in the Jeffersonian sense freed the spirit and loosed all men's creative energies."[25] The economic views articulated by Jefferson, which Brandeis had sought to revive, found an outspoken champion in William O. Douglas. Because of Douglas's economic belief, he was always sensitive to the potential danger to human freedom inherent in bureaucratic, administrative power.

Justice Douglas was always seeking to expand individual freedom. Recognition of this objective helps account for many of the seeming inconsistencies in his constitutional theory. Douglas came to the Court believing, as did all New Dealers, that governmental intervention in our social fabric was required to expand individual freedom. When he later perceived that some governmental actions posed a threat as much as a benefit, he began to emphasize *procedural* protections against administrative actions.[26] Since even this emphasis was not enough, he came to be *the* great advocate on the Supreme Court for relaxing the self-imposed limits on the jurisdiction of the federal courts. If the federal courts did not permit citizen and taxpayer suits, how could federal aid to church-related schools be challenged,[27] abuses by the Central Intelligence Agency come to light,[28] or the issue of the President's constitutional authority to declare war be raised in a proper forum?[29] In each of these areas, and many more, Justice Douglas clearly explained the underlying purpose of his position. The sovereign in this nation is the people. By not allowing them to challenge administrative actions in the courts their sovereignty becomes an empty symbol, and a secret bureaucracy would run our affairs.

For all his concern with protecting the individual from administrative excesses, Douglas never retreated from his basic belief that when social and economic policy is involved elected agencies and administrative boards should have maximum flexibility. When no procedural irregularity existed, and when he saw no infringement of a fundamental right guaranteed by the Constitution, he sustained the governmental action. In his very last term on the Court, he wrote the opinion sustaining a local zoning ordinance which greatly infringed the life styles of persons not living in traditional family units.[30]

To survive the modern state, individuality also needed a broad space for autonomous action. In his later years, Justice Douglas came to believe that the preservation of individual autonomy was a special task of the judiciary. In the second volume of his autobiography, he talks repeatedly about the Court's role in keeping government off the people's backs.[31] An expansive judicial view of constitutionally protected individual rights would fence in the government, thereby maintaining, and perhaps enlarging, the sphere of private individual action. Our Constitution authorized just such a private, individual political space under the rubric of individual rights. The Court, in taking an active judicial concern for individual rights, would be fulfilling the special role assigned to it by the Constitution. Note well how he puts it: "So far as the Bill of Rights is concerned, the individual is on his own when it comes to the pursuit of happiness."[32] This statement is quintessential Douglas. Judicial activism on behalf of the Bill of Rights became his principal vehicle for keeping the government out of private domains and thereby exalting individual autonomy.

In the entire canon of his writings, there is no evidence that Justice Douglas ever agonized over the allegedly nondemocratic character of judicial review. That power, he asserted, had become well entrenched; history had made it part of our constitutional fabric. The only issue concerned how the Court used this historically legitimated power. The purpose of democratic government, according to Justice Douglas, was the enhancement of individual freedom. The Constitution sought to promote that objective by ensuring fair procedures and, more importantly, by setting metes and bounds to governmental activity. The basic rationale for the Supreme Court, with its extraordinary power, was its capacity to act as guardian of the Constitution. A readiness to entertain constitutional issues, particularly those involving individual rights, was plainly in the greater interests of American democracy. The judges, "too, must be dynamic components of history if our institutions are to be vital, directive forces in the life of our age".[33]

Justice Douglas had little patience for those like Justices Frankfurter and Harlan who, in the name of democracy, constantly deferred to legislative judgments: "where wrongs to individuals are done by violation of specific guarantees, it is abdication for courts to close their doors." Judicial self-restraint was a "self-inflicted wound." "The citizen should know that in the courts one can get justice, no matter how discriminatory government officials may be . . . When the courts are niggardly in the use of their power and reach great issues only timidly and reluctantly, the force of the Bill of Rights in the life of the nation is greatly weakened."[34]

As might be expected, Justice Douglas was the Court's foremost advocate for developing a constitutional right of privacy. The right to be left alone, to have the freedom to order one's own choices was, to Douglas, a central objective of democratic government. He wrote his first opinion using this concept in 1952,[35] and during his remaining years on the Court Douglas made increasing use of the concept. Justice Douglas served long enough to persuade a majority of his brethren of the constitutional validity, at least for some purposes, of the right of privacy.[36] Characteristically, he then took the opportunity, in a concurring opinion, to give a fuller outline of his own views. In many ways, this opinion was Justice Douglas's most theoretical effort. He even ranks, from his perspective, the individual rights constitutionally guaranteed to American citizens. He began with rights he believed to be protected by the First Amendment and therefore "absolutely" immune from governmental control. Note how he subsumes those rights under a broader concept of personal choice:

> First is the autonomous control over the development and expression of one's intellect, interests, tastes and personality.[37]

Justice Douglas then went on to indicate the type of rights he would deem "fundamental," that is, individual rights subject to some governmental regulation provided there is a compelling interest and the statute, ordinance, or administrative rule is narrowly and precisely drawn:

> Second is freedom of choice in the basic decisions of one's life respecting marriage, divorce, procreation, contraception, and the education and upbringing of children.[38]

Again, this catalogue of fundamental rights is subsumed under Douglas's belief in maximum, individual autonomous actions.

Lastly, he indicated another group of "fundamental" rights also subject to minimal regulation only upon a showing of compelling state interest:

> *Third is the freedom to care for one's health and person, freedom from bodily restraint or compulsion, freedom to walk, stroll or loaf.*[39]

Just how this last grouping is distinguished from the second is not clear from his opinion, nor does he indicate whether a "right" in the third group is entitled to somewhat less judicial protection than those in the second, though that seems to be implied. Again, Justice Douglas does not specifically indicate where the "right to work," which he called fundamental,[40] would be categorized.

Enough has been said to indicate both the range and depth of concern for individual rights in the political theory of Justice Douglas. The theoretical source of that concern has also been indicated. He truly believed that "outside areas of plainly harmful conduct, every American is left to shape his own life as he thinks best, do what he pleases, go where he pleases."[41] The belief in maximum individual choice was based on his theory of American democracy, a natural rights theory akin to Jefferson's. It is time to begin assessing some of the strengths and weaknesses of this liberal natural rights theory for contemporary American society. For that analysis, a discussion of the theory's use in cases dealing with citizenship, political participation, and free speech— key notions in any theory of democracy—will prove most enlightening.

AN ANALYSIS OF LIBERAL NATURAL RIGHTS THEORY

Citizenship

There is an inherent tension between the political-legal concepts of citizenship and natural rights. Citizenship is exclusive. Only members can claim the full range of rights in a given society. Natural rights are, in theory, universal. All individuals are endowed with certain rights simply by virtue of their humanity. To emphasize the importance of citizenship seems to elevate membership rights over universal human rights; it may even imply that rights originate in human arrangements. Abstract rights, however, count for little unless they become part of the operating reality of human beings. To ignore the concept of citizenship is to lose an opportunity—perhaps the only opportunity—for linking the natural rights of man with one agency, the state, which can actually protect and promote those rights.

Classical natural rights theorists like Locke and Jefferson resolved this tension by making the advancement of natural rights the object of civil government. Individuals form civil society precisely in order to promote their individual rights. The social contract embodies the universal, inherent rights of men. Citizenship in such a society entails the enjoyment of natural rights.

Like other natural rights theorists, Justice Douglas recognized citizenship's centrality in the social contract. He plainly believed all governments, as a matter of simple justice, ought to promote basic human rights. He also recognized that the millennium has not yet arrived. At least until that time, the advancement of natural rights will depend upon the action of certain governments. Those governments—Douglas labelled them democracies—could best advance the cause of humanity by being faithful to their own traditions. Through this very traditional route Justice Douglas squared his profound universalism with his unquestioned, deep-seated American nationalism.[42]

United States citizenship, therefore, was never to be treated lightly. It was a prized possession: in the real world it has great tangible value. Denationalization might result in "the loss of all that makes life worth living,"[43] the ability to enjoy the full range of individual rights. For this reason alone, citizenship could never be taken away casually. A naturalization certificate could only be revoked on "clear, unequivocal and convincing" evidence that the person had committed fraud or some other specific illegal act to procure it.[44] Otherwise an American citizen could only be expatriated by the voluntary relinquishment of loyalty to the United States and by the attachment to another country.[45] The issue of voluntariness could only be resolved at a full judicial trial conforming to the Bill of Rights. Congress could provide rules of evidence, but it could not declare that such equivocal acts as service in a foreign army, participation in a foreign election, desertion from our armed forces, or draft evasion established a *conclusive* presumption to renounce American citizenship.[46]

Justice Douglas thought that the manner in which the government of the United States was formed indicated that the "sovereign in this nation is the people."[47] That sovereignty, in turn, meant that the retention of a valid citizenship was essentially beyond legislative control. He supported this position by repeated reference to the provisions of the Fourteenth Amendment. Because the grant of citizenship was clear and explicit, because there was not a single word in the document covering expatriation, and because of citizenship's importance, Justice Douglas thought it "is a grant absolute in terms."[48]

There are matters of style and emphasis in these opinions which well illustrate the strengths and weaknesses of Justice Douglas's decisions. The style of his opinions was far from conventional. Even when writing the opinions for the Court he spent little effort in working out a tight justification for the holding. *Schneider v. Rusk* (1964)[49] was the only majority opinion he wrote dealing with involuntary expatriation. The case involved a law which automatically expatriated naturalized citizens who later returned to and resided for three continuous years in their native country.

After quickly outlining the case, Justice Douglas starts the opinion by positing "the premise that the right of citizenship of the native born and naturalized persons are of the same dignity" and, with a few minor exceptions, "are coextensive." He then proceeds to restate *his* "view that the power of Congress to take away citizenship for the activities of the citizen is nonexistent absent expatriation by the voluntary renunciation of nationality and allegiance." Obviously this standard would resolve the case quickly in favor of Mrs. Schneider; but given the composition of the Court at that time, Justice Douglas is forced to say that *his* reading of the Constitution "has not yet commanded a majority of the entire Court."

As a result, he has to resolve the issue on the due process standard of reasonable relationship which he has just told us he continues to oppose. After briefly indicating the source of that standard in prior cases, he turns to its application. The application was almost cavalier. Justice Douglas maintained that living abroad is not an indication of voluntary renunciation of American allegiance. But voluntariness has little or nothing to do with a reasonableness standard. That standard requires only that Congress have an understandable basis for enacting the statute. As Clark's dissenting opinion[50] shows, there was ample historical and other evidence for a reasonable man to believe that automatic expatriation was the most efficacious way of dealing with the difficulties sometimes created for American foreign policy by naturalized citizens returning to their homelands.

That same argument by Clark also disposes of Douglas's equal protection claim that the citizenship of native-born and naturalized Americans are the same. Conventional equal protection analysis permits the legislature to make reasonable classifications. Only if Justice Douglas had taken the time and effort to bring the whole issue under the then emerging and still controversial "new" equal protection standard[51] would his analysis cohere. That justification would have required him to explain how and why citizenship was a fundamental right and why, in this case at least, there was no compelling state interest sufficient to justify governmental infringement of that fundamental right. Justice Douglas, however, did not bother to do any of that. Once he could not use his criteria, Douglas seems to have lost interest in the doctrinal aspects of the case. At best, Justice Douglas was applying the preferred freedoms doctrine. At worst, he simply disposed of the case.

Douglas's opinions are also replete with practical, pragmatic concerns. We can therefore see more concretely why Douglas placed such a high value on citizenship. Citizenship "carries with it the privilege of full participation in the affairs of our society, including the right to speak freely, to criticize officials and administrators and to promote changes in the laws including the very charter of our government."[52] He feared that a reasonableness test could be used to deprive people of American citizenship for a large number of embarrassing, controversial, or unorthodox views and actions.[53] The very possibility of the loss of citizenship for such acts would place a damper on full and effective participation; it would help promote unobtrusive orthodoxy and retard idiosyncratic individuality. Justice Douglas plainly indicated that, at least for him, citizenship meant full political participation including broad-scale First Amendment rights. We now can begin to understand how, for Justice Douglas, a citizen is distinguished from a mere subject, how a citizen is to function as part of the sovereign authority.

Political Participation

Full and effective participation in the affairs of our nation was a cardinal benefit of American citizenship as envisioned by Justice Douglas. Individuals could participate in a number of ways, but none was more important than the exercise of the franchise. The right to vote was "too precious, too fundamental"[54] to be unduly burdened, because it helped ensure "government of the people, by the people, for the people." The right enabled each voter to seek the kind of society he thought best. Moreover, Justice Douglas knew that "over the years most victories involving the rights of man have been won at the polls or in conventions of the people or in petitions such as produced the Magna Carta,"[55] rather than in the courts. That is why he maintained: "Free and honest elections are the very foundation of our republican form of government."[56]

The electoral process, therefore, was invariably perceived by Justice Douglas in terms of the individual and personal right to vote. There was "more to the right to vote than the right to mark a piece of paper and drop it in a box or the right to pull a lever in a voting booth."[57] The right to vote entailed the right to have the vote count, i.e. to have it matter as much as one's fellow citizens: "Discrimination against any group or class of citizens in the exercise of these constitutionally protected *rights of citizenship* deprives the electoral process of integrity."[58] As a result, the Justice was an early[59] and consistent advocate of using the Equal Protection Clause to impose a "one person, one vote—one vote, one value" standard. Because individual rights were at stake, he opposed those using the "political question" doctrine as a thicket behind which the judiciary could retreat.[60]

When the substantive issue came before the Warren Court, both Black and Douglas had the satisfaction of writing their earlier dissenting opinions as the law of the land. It is instructive to compare those opinions. Justice

Black's 1964 *Wesberry* opinion applied the "one person, one vote" standard to congressional apportionments. The opinion is long on history and short on political theory, yet only with implicit use of contract theory—which he derived from the intention of the Framers—does Justice Black's opinion cohere.[61] Justice Douglas's 1963 *Gray*[62] opinion applied the "one person, one vote" standard to the statewide Democratic primary in Georgia. It utilizes little else than the concept of equal political participation derived from his natural rights theory.

Georgia law provided that county unit votes determined the outcome of a primary election. The winner in the Democratic primary was invariably successful in the general election. Each county was allotted a number of votes ranging from six (for the most populous counties) to two (for the least populous). The system effectively submerged the urban votes in statewide elections.

The district court had sustained the system by analogizing it to the electoral college system for electing the President. In the text of his opinion, Justice Douglas simply dismissed that analogy as inappropriate because the electoral college was the result of specific historical concerns and was an explicit constitutional mechanism. An attached footnote, however, is more revealing. There he noted that the electoral college "was designed by men who did not want the election of the President to be left to the people." For Douglas, the United States had evolved into a democracy based upon the full participation of all adult citizens; the Framers' constricted conception of political equality belonged to a "bygone day" and was irrelevant for determining what the Equal Protection Clause requires in contemporary elections.[63] That same evolutionary conception quickly appears in the text. Justice Douglas used it to say that the Equal Protection Clause requires the "idea that every voter is equal to every other voter in his State, when he casts his ballot in favor of several competing candidates."[64]

The Georgia county unit case claimed to be resolving only the issue of voter equality once the geographical unit for which the representative to be chosen was designated. Nonetheless, Justice Douglas plainly and deliberately used language which indicated how he would resolve all apportionment issues. Hence he agreed with Chief Justice Warren's opinion for the Court in *Reynolds v. Sims* (1964)[65] which held the "one person, one vote—one vote, one value" standard applicable to both houses of a state legislature. In fact, the Chief Justice used language based upon the same natural rights theory as Justice Douglas when he said that "each and every citizen has an *inalienable* right to full and effective participation in the political processes."[66]

As a result of the conception of political equality rooted in his natural rights theory, Justice Douglas's record on apportionment was entirely consistent. He joined the *Kirkpatrick*[67] majority in 1969 when the Court insisted upon a good faith effort to achieve absolute equality among congressional election districts. Any deviation from absolute equality would appear to enhance some people's rights at the expense of others. When, in 1973, a later Court majority applied a more lenient standard, at least to state legislative bodies, he dissented.[68] A belief that each individual voter had an inalienable right to an equally effective voice in a state government made Justice Douglas intolerant of any deviation from perfect equality unless plainly unavoidable.

Similarly, he was part of the Warren Court majority which extended the "one person, one vote" principle to elections at the local level. Once the decision was made to have citizens participate individually by ballot in the selection of officials who carry out governmental functions, the *only* consideration for Justice Douglas was the individual right of each qualified voter to participate on an equal footing in the election process.[69] Again, when a later Court majority permitted deviations from a good faith effort at absolute equality in local elections, he dissented.[70]

Justice Douglas did not believe his firm insistence on the principle of voter equality unduly limited flexibility or experimentation, particularly at the local level. In *Dusch v. Davis* (1967),[71] he wrote the opinion upholding an electoral system which required that seven members of an eleven-member general governmental board be residents of particular boroughs. The boroughs did not contain equal numbers of people. Since all the councilmen were elected by the votes of all the electors, Douglas viewed them as city officials, not as representatives of the particular boroughs wherein they resided. The plan give equal weight to each voter while still ensuring a specific geographic distribution of officials. To Douglas, it indicated how group interests could be partially accommodated to the individualistic demands of the "one person, one vote" principle.

There is, of course, a danger with this plan. Although a popular majority could not completely cancel out the voting strength of geographically concentrated minorities, it could exercise a tacit veto power on their choices. A white majority within the city as a whole, for example, could block the election of a radical black candidate favored by the residents of a largely black borough.

In a companion case, *Sailors v. Board of Education* (1967),[72] Justice Douglas's opinion for the Court emphasized that not all governmental officials need be elected. It was legitimate to provide other methods of selection. To avoid the application of the "one person, one vote" standard, two conditions had to be met. First, the selection process had to be basically appointive rather than elective. Second, the officials had to perform essentially nonlegislative functions. Thus all general legislative bodies in the United States (with the constitutionally mandated exception of the United States Senate) had to be selected via a "one person, one vote" election system. Other officials could be selected by other means. Once the decision was made to employ an election process, however, that decision required the application of the "one person, one vote" principle,[73] for only that principle, Justice Douglas believed, insured the integrity of elections in a democracy.

His concern with the integrity of the electoral process led Douglas to dissent in *Fortson v. Morris* (1966).[74] Justice Black's opinion upheld a provision in the Georgia constitution which provided that if no candidate for governor received a majority of the votes in the general election, then a majority of the General Assembly would elect the governor from the two persons having the highest number of votes. Justice Douglas and the three other dissenters thought it was unrealistic to treat the general election as a discrete event which was now over. Douglas had written the *Gray* opinion which had extended the "one person, one vote" standard into the party primaries on the grounds that they were an integral part of the state's election. The same rationale was applicable to this post-election device. In fact, as Douglas correctly noted, this situation was worse than in *Gray*. Here, the legislators were not even bound to vote for the winner in their constituency. Under party rules, the Democrats who controlled 229 of the 259 seats were almost certain to vote against the Republican gubernatorial candidate who had won a plurality in the general election.

To make matters worse for any adherent to the "one person, one vote" principle, a district court had already found the Georgia legislature to be grossly malapportioned. On a population basis—as distinct from political affiliation—the legislators represented a minority of the voters. For Justice Douglas, the purpose of voting was to give each voter an equally effective way of participating in government. That purpose required the Court to make a close and *realistic* scrutiny of the entire election process. Anything less— as, for example, Justice Black's highly formalistic approach to the electoral process in *Fortson*—was not a sufficient safeguard of the fundamental right to vote.[75]

The same diligent concern for the right to vote can be seen in cases dealing with the issue of who is entitled to vote. Any unjustified discrimination in determining who may participate in political affairs would also undermine the legitimacy of representative government. Malapportioned legislatures or the county unit system diluted the effectiveness of some citizens' votes. Statutes denying the franchise to citizens who are otherwise qualified posed the danger of denying those individuals *any* effective voice in governmental affairs substantially affecting their lives. Once the right to vote was involved, mere rationality was not enough. The fundamental nature of the right demanded that all restrictions on its exercise be subject to exacting judicial scrutiny.

Douglas, therefore, joined Justice Stewart's opinion for the Court in *Carrington v. Rash* (1965)[76] which held that Texas could not bar an otherwise qualified person from voting merely because he was a member of the armed forces. In *Kramer v. Union Free School District* (1969),[77] he joined Chief Justice Warren's opinion holding that New York could not limit the franchise in certain school district elections to owners (or leaseholders) of taxable property and to parents (or guardians) of public school children. In *Cipriano v. City of Houma* (1969),[78] he joined the brief, unsigned Court opinion striking down a state law which gave only property taxpayers the right to vote on the issuance of revenue bonds by a municipality system. Finally, in *Phoenix v. Kolodziejski* (1970),[79] he joined Justice White's opinion for the Court which struck down an Arizona law limiting the right to vote on general election bond issues to real property taxpayers.

In each of these cases there was, at least, arguably, a rational basis for the state classification. Under the traditional equal protection standard that rationality would have been enough to sustain the laws. But, in each case Justice Douglas saw a restriction on the exercise of a fundamental right which, at least for him,[80] required the Court to subject the law to a more exacting scrutiny. Under that equal protection standard, the challenged law almost invariably is held unconstitutional.

Justice Douglas wrote one opinion for the Court dealing with direct restrictions on the exercise of the franchise. *Harper v. Virginia Board of Elections* (1966) [81] held that the payment of a $1.50 annual poll tax was unconstitutional under the Equal Protection Clause. The opinion is a characteristic Douglas effort. While the opinion itself does not attempt a sustained justification for either the standard or the conclusion, the elements, when they are reorganized a bit, present a strong argument. First, as always, Douglas insists that voting is a fundamental right at the heart of a free and democratic society. Second, because it is so fundamental, any classification which might restrain its exercise must be subjected to close judicial scrutiny. Third, by that standard, wealth or fee paying has no compelling relationship to voting qualifications: "Wealth, like race, creed or color, is not germane to one's ability to participate intelligently in the electoral process."[82]

As the three dissenters noted,[83] correctly, Douglas's opinion in *Harper* virtually ignores or repudiates every conventional guide to sound judicial craftsmanship. There is no reliance upon the wording of the Constitution or the intention of the Framers. The long history of the poll tax's use as a condition of voting is passed over in silence. Only the precedents, in which the Court had sustained the poll tax against the same challenges, were "recognized" by Douglas.[84] Douglas simply overrode these precedents—and the traditional equal protection test they embodied—by saying that the Court had never confined itself to historic notions of equality where fundamental rights were concerned: "Notions of what constitutes equal treatment for purposes of the Equal Protection Clause *do* change."[85]

Justice Douglas used *The School Desegregation Cases* to illustrate this evolutionary motion. The recently decided reapportionment cases were used to show that the opportunity for equal participation by all voters in state elections justified the application of the newer, more stringent equal protection standard. Neither line of opinions, however, need be read that way.[86] The connections require more justification than Douglas deigned to supply. That deficiency is why Justice Black thought the opinion reeked of the "old natural-law-due-process formula"; it was long on conclusions based upon that theory and short on sustained arguments.[87] As applied to Justice Douglas, this characterization, as we have seen, is correct.[88]

The strengths of Justice Douglas's theory can be seen not only in the above cases but also in *Oregon v. Mitchell* (1970).[89] The case dealt with the attempt by Congress to lower the voting age to eighteen in all elections. Justice Black's opinion, which proved decisive on the divided Court, held the law valid when applied to federal elections but unconstitutional as applied to state elections. Justice Douglas believed that Congress could enfranchise eighteen-year-olds across the board.[90]

At stake, he argued, was a civil right deeply embedded in our Constitution. He had recently helped lead the Court to the recognition of its obligation to protect this right against various state restrictions, including voter qualifications. In terms of the Constitution, protecting the right to vote had largely been accomplished through the Equal Protection Clause of the Fourteenth Amendment. Justice Douglas now noted that Congress too had a role to play in promoting Fourteenth Amendment rights. The fifth section of that Amendment authorizes Congress to exercise its discretion in determining whether and what legislation is needed to secure the Amendment's guarantees. Congress had concluded that a reduction in voting age from twenty-one to eighteen was needed in the interest of the equal protection of those citizens who bore the more direct burden for our national defense. Congress had made a reasoned judgment. Eighteen-year-olds had a large stake in modern elections. They had the degree of maturity needed to exercise the franchise; therefore, they should have political equality.

Given Justice Douglas's paramount concern for enlarging the scope of individual rights, his opinion was hardly surprising. This approach was particularly appropriate in all areas affecting the right to vote. By insisting that representative bodies conform to the "one person, one vote" standard and that restrictions on participation in the electoral process be kept to an indispensable minimum, Justice Douglas was seeking to maintain the legitimacy of our electoral institutions in terms of their origins. The natural rights theory embedded in our founding documents has made voting central to our notion of self-government. The exercise of the franchise is a principal means of protecting and advancing one's interest. It is also the constitutionally sanctioned method for an individual citizen to participate in decisions affecting his life. Within our inherited political culture, unequal access to the electoral process can only create alienation and erode the legitimacy of our electorally based institutions. In this area, a concern with individual rights dovetails with the legitimacy and stability of the constitutional regime.

Justice Douglas's opinions dealing with participation in the electoral process also reveal some of the inherent weaknesses of his natural rights theory. The fair representation of each citizen in an elected assembly requires more than substantial equality of population within each district. It also requires a coherent and realistic notion of what is meant by voting *power*. If political power is not equalized, then even absolutely equal districts would still defeat the equal rights of each citizen to his full and effective participation in the political system.

The problem is that at the level of dealing with the details of various systems of representation no one really knows how to equalize the citizen's political power. Long ago, Rousseau warned that any system of representation would defeat the objective of equalizing each citizen's political power.[91] We now assume that some form of representation is required by the size of our populations, but the relative virtues of different systems are much debated. Single-member, multi-member, winner-take-all, proportional representation, and cumulative voting, all have their defenders and detractors. Within some systems, it is not clear whether an easily definable interest group—let alone a single citizen of that group—gains by dispersion or concentration. Two cases illustrate the point, and Justice Douglas's dilemma.

In *Wright v. Rockefeller* (1964),[92] the Court rejected a challenge to the single-member congressional districts on Manhattan Island. It was alleged that the districts had been drawn on racial lines so as to concentrate black and Puerto Rican voters in the eighteenth district in order to preserve the seventeeth as the largely white (silk-stocking) district. Because Justice Black's opinion for the Court held that the suit failed for lack of sufficient proof, he could avoid the issue of whether the scheme unconstitutionally "diluted" black voting power.

Justice Douglas, in dissent,[93] thought that sufficient evidence had been presented to establish a prima facie case of designing the electoral districts along racial lines. He thought this action was constitutionally forbidden; in the public sphere, race was, he believed, a forbidden category. Justice Douglas rejected, out of hand, the contention of Representative Adam Clayton Powell and other intervenors about the political advantages of the existing system. They had contended that the concentration of black and Puerto Rican voters in the eighteenth district represented by Mr. Powell added to the effective political power of those groups in Congress. Justice Douglas said that the issue of political power was irrelevant to the problem. Racial districts were at "war with democratic standards." He recognized, of course, that race played "an important role in the choices which individual voters make from among the candidates," but a state could give no encouragement to its citizens to vote for a candidate solely on account of race.

In 1964, then Justice Douglas believed the issue of full and effective political power would have to be resolved within the parameters mandated by our "color-blind" Constitution. This belief was in perfect accord with the *School Desegregation Cases* and the integrationist ideal they contained. This position was also in perfect accord with the individualistic premises of the reapportionment cases.

By 1971, the call for "black power" had pierced the public dialogue in the United States and called into question the integrationist model for achieving full racial equality. In reapportionment cases, the demand for "black power" was raised in *Whitcomb v. Chavis* (1971).[94] Indiana had long used multimember districts to compensate partially for population disparities among its legislative districts. Some Marion County blacks claimed that the system of multimember districts diluted the force and effect of black votes, particularly those from the district's ghetto area. Justice White's opinion for the Court rejected the claim.

The absence of any systematically developed theory of how to equalize each citizen's effective voting power did not stop Justice Douglas from dissenting. Justice White thought the "under-representation" of the ghetto black in terms of the low number of legislators from that area was most probably a result of which party won the most elections. Most ghetto blacks were affiliated with the Democratic Party, but it had lost four of the last five elections. After all, he argued, supporters of losing political candidates—such as adherents of the minority party in safe districts—have no basis for evoking a constitutional remedy for their relative lack of political power. It was a consequence of any form of winner-take-all elections. The Constitution did not mandate proportional representation or cumulative voting to ensure adequate representation of all interests. Justice White was also not prepared to resolve the theoretical issue of whether a group with distinctive interests is better served by having its own safe districts or by being in a position to influence, through bloc voting, an entire multimember delegation. In short, *Whitcomb* majority believed that, within the parameters set by the "one person, one vote" principle, the task of equalizing voting power was best left to other, nonjudicial, agencies.[95]

Justice Douglas thought the Court was obligated to correct a "festering electoral system." The multimember system, at least as it functioned in Marion County, operated in favor of upper middle class and wealthy suburbanites at the expense of an identifiable racial group. The evidence for this bias was in the small number of state representatives residing in the ghetto area. Justice

Douglas did not deal with how to measure actual voting power. He thought that issue irrelevant; the only issue was whether the identity of a racial group was systematically washed out of the system.[96]

A standard to measure actual voting power is *not*, however, irrelevant to the issue Douglas wanted to decide. We must know what we are attempting to equalize before we know whether it has been diluted and before we can fashion an adequate remedy. Justice Douglas was at a loss to address this issue because his theory was inadequate for the problem. Justice Douglas's theory was decidedly individualistic; each *individual* was to be treated alike. Here, the issue was the relative political clout of different *groups*. Douglas's theory led him to call for the aggregation of discrete individuals into numerically equal voting units. It could take him no further. Once the districts have been equalized numerically, as Justice White's opinion plainly shows, many issues about implementing the full and effective political participation of our citizens still remain.

To make matters worse, Justice Douglas's 1972 dissent in *Whitcomb* is patently inconsistent with his 1964 dissent in *Wright*. There he had opposed a system which insured Harlem ghetto residents at least one congressman (and a very powerful one at that) in the following words:

> When racial or religious lines are drawn by the State, the multiracial, multireligious communities that our Constitution seeks to weld together as one become separatist; antagonisms that relate to race or religion rather than to political issues are generated; communities seek not the best representative but the best racial or religious partisan. Since that system is at war with the democratic ideal it should find no footing here.[97]

In *Whitcomb*, Justice Douglas was doing the very thing he had denounced seven years earlier. He now thought the Constitution required distinct minorities to seek the best racial partisan, not necessarily the best representative. With no theoretical basis for determining how a *group* could have its interests most fully and effectively represented, Justice Douglas had no consistent, principled way of resolving such issues. Rather than have the judiciary abstain on the basis that such issues were beyond the Constitution—as Justice Black invariably did—Justice Douglas appeared to adopt the prevailing avant-garde liberal position. Needless to say, such opinions did not strengthen his position. The appearance of partisanship rarely enhances judicial authority.

A passionate commitment to the natural rights of individual citizens can and did help rectify obvious inequalities of access to the political process. When coupled with a strong concern for the operating realities, as was the case with Justice Douglas, it enables one to look behind the legal formalities and deal with actual obstacles to full citizen participation. When the Court opened up the system by removing state-imposed obstacles to individual participation, when it acted, in other words, on premises akin to those of Justice Douglas, it helped restore a sense of legitimacy to our government.

When Justice Douglas sought to go beyond restrictions upon individual participation, his passionate commitment to racial justice exceeded his theory. At the important but complicated level of representation of group interests, Justice Douglas's opinions were inconsistent enough to appear motivated by his personal policy preferences. The basic premises of Lockean theory, no matter how updated, do not produce a clear answer to balancing group interests. A Constitution based upon principles of individual natural rights, and interpreted on that basis, relegates such issues to the area of political accommodation. Justice Douglas's efforts to resolve all the problems of group representation opened him to the standard criticism of any natural rights judicial theory: natural rights theory too easily serves as a cloak for the personal policy commitments of judges; it too easily leads to highly subjective conclusory statements rather than to painstaking and carefully reasoned analysis.

Political Freedom

This perennial problem for natural law theorists haunts Justice Douglas's opinions in other areas as well, most notably those dealing with the First Amendment's Free Speech Clause. That clause, indeed the entire Amendment, was central to the Justice's mature political theory. He saw the Amendment's stark negative commands as performing two indispensable functions in our democracy. By keeping the government out of the most private realms of belief, conscience, and opinion, each American is able to develop his inherent potential. By permitting the fullest exchange of all views, each citizen can make his own individual input into the political process.

Justice Douglas, however, never achieved a systematic theory of political freedom. His natural rights theory led him to a heightened concern for individual privacy and autonomy, but he never clearly indicated what was to be included within that zone. Similarly, his natural rights theory led him to an expanded view of constitutional protections for individual expression, but his definition of expression was so vague as to preclude much sense of its limits. He invariably supported idiosyncratic modes of expression against government claims for order, security, or regulation. As his justifications changed to take account of novel events, Justice Douglas's opinions were frequently open to the charge of being ad hoc, personal responses to important issues.

This apparent lack of consistency among Justice Douglas's later opinions should not be confused with the long-term evolution of his approach to the

First Amendment. He was, after all, largely unconcerned with civil liberties and rights before he was appointed to the Court. His academic specialty at the Columbia and Yale law schools was business and finance, particularly bankruptcy. He became a leading New Dealer through his work on the Securities and Exchange Commission. In fact, the opposition to his appointment as an Associate Justice was articulated in terms of Douglas's insufficient concern for the rights of the common people.[98] Only over the course of his long judicial career, and aided by his close personal association with Justice Black,[99] did he come to see the First Amendment in absolute terms.

When Douglas first joined the Supreme Court, and for many years thereafter, he shared the preferred freedoms doctrine. This view always placed Douglas on the libertarian side but there is no mistaking the preference language of those earlier opinions for his later more absolutist position.[100] As late as 1952 he still summarized his interpretation of the First Amendment this way:

> My view is that if in any case other public interests are to override the plain command of the First Amendment, the peril of speech must be clear and present, leaving no room for argument, raising no doubts as to the necessity of curbing speech in order to prevent disaster.

> The First Amendment is couched in absolute terms—freedom of speech shall not be abridged. Speech has therefore a preferred position as contrasted to some other civil rights.[101]

This same *Beauharnais* dissent, however, also contains a catalogue of Douglas's objections to the way the majority at that time was treating First Amendment cases. The Court was permitting the legislature to regulate First Amendment rights within reasonable limits. The leeway permitted to legislatures in matters relating to business, finance, industrial and labor conditions, health, and public welfare was legitimate, Douglas argued, for there was no guarantee in the Constitution preserving the status quo in those areas. But freedom of speech rested on a different constitutional plane. Justice Douglas saw the Court's deference to legislative judgment in these areas as an "ominous and alarming trend" which sanctioned the imposition of a new orthodoxy.

The Court's deference to legislative judgments in First Amendment cases and Douglas's perception of an emerging official orthodoxy were both related to the Communist Party cases at the onset of the Cold War. *Dennis v. United States* (1951)[102] was clearly the watershed case. The Court majority there abandoned the "clear and present danger" test. Only the dissenters, Justices Black and Douglas, continued to maintain it was applicable even in cases dealing with alleged subversives. The major dissenting opinion by Justice Douglas convincingly shows how the application of the Holmes-Brandeis formula for a First Amendment preference would have reversed the Smith Act convictions of the American Communist Party's eleven top leaders.[103]

When the Court majority then proceeded to use *Dennis* as authority for sustaining a large variety of punitive actions against individuals with "left-wing" political sympathies, Justice Douglas found himself in a distinctly isolated position. His overt response was typified by the *Beauharnais* dissent noted above: a call for a return to the preferred freedoms doctrine; a defense of this doctrine's virtues in terms of the language of the Amendment and the function of free speech in a democratic society; and a note of despair about the future of freedom in our land.

The despair and isolation, however, also caused Justice Douglas to rethink his First Amendment position. By 1957 Douglas was ready to abandon virtually all notions of judicial balancing in First Amendment cases. He had come to believe that most judges, either out of sympathy with the prevailing orthodoxy or because of self-doubts about their authority to intervene, would defer to the judgments of political agencies. The incorporation within our tradition of a more absolutist interpretation of constitutional adjudication seemed, to Douglas, the best prospect for reversing this trend.

In *Brandenburg v. Ohio* (1969),[104] Justice Douglas gave voice to the misgivings which had led him to abandon, a decade earlier, the "clear and present danger" test. The Court's handling of that doctrine from its introduction in *Schenck* (1917) to the *Dennis* era showed, Douglas thought, "how easily 'clear and present danger' is manipulated to crush" the fundamental right of free speech. He therefore saw "no place in the regime of the First Amendment for any 'clear and present danger' test, whether strict and tight as some would make it, or free-wheeling as the Court in *Dennis* rephrased it."[105]

In *Brandenburg*, Justice Douglas also gave voice to what had become his settled interpretation of the First Amendment: "The line between what is permissible and not subject to control and what may be made impermissible and subject to regulation is the line between *ideas* and *overt acts*.[106] Note that Justice Douglas in making that distinction did *not* use language found in the Constitution. For Justice Black the primary justification for the absolute protection of speech was the wording of the First Amendment.[107] Because Justice Douglas was more concerned with protecting the individual's right of expression, he drew the line between ideas and acts, not speech and acts. Douglas knew that "[a]ction is often a method of expression" and he believed such acts to be "within the protection of the First Amendment."[108] Just as "speech brigaded with action" could be treated as action, so symbolic acts should be treated as speech. A realistic appraisal of the actual situations, not a bright line analysis based upon the text, was the cornerstone of Justice Douglas's ultimate interpretation of the First Amendment.

There is no one, single place in which Justice Douglas outlines all the elements underlying his broad, absolutist interpretation of the First Amendment. Once again, however, reading his opinions provides us with a coherent set of substantial, cogent reasons. First, there is the wording of the Amendment itself. That absolute language left, in his view, no room for governmental restraint on conventional speech and press activities.[109] Second, there was the intent of the Framers: "The First Amendment did not build upon existing law; it broke with tradition, set a new standard and exalted freedom of expression."[110] Third, insofar as the Justices are bound by the literal words of the Constitution and the intent of the Framers, the Courts are not authorized to balance First Amendment rights against other societal needs and interests. Douglas argued "that all the 'balancing' was done by those who wrote the Bill of Rights. By casting the First Amendment in absolute terms, they repudiated [all] timid, watered-down emasculated versions of the First Amendment."[111] Of course, Justice Douglas placed his major reliance upon what he perceived to be the objectives underlying the Framers' absolutist language. Here, his primary reliance was upon the individual's inherent natural right to develop his own personality.[112]

Justice Douglas also connected this natural rights interpretation with his view of our democratic society. This connection led him to go beyond a literal reading of the First Amendment; hence, the particular freedoms enumerated in the Amendment became the primary basis for his claim that there was a constitutional right to privacy and autonomy. The "people, as the ultimate governors, must have absolute freedom of, and therefore privacy of, their individual opinions and beliefs regardless of how suspect or strange they may appear to others."[113] The government is *their* agent. Each individual is entitled to first decide how he would want that agent to act. To permit the government to censor or repress ideas by entering the zone of individual autonomy would be to reverse this fundamental relationship between citizens and government. That relationship is why "matters of belief, ideology, religious practices, social philosophy and the like are beyond the pale and of no rightful concern of government."[114]

Moreover, "effective self-government cannot succeed unless the people are immersed in a steady, robust, unimpeded and uncensored flow of opinion and reporting which are continuously subjected to critique, rebuttal and expression."[115] This concern led Douglas to expand the language of the First Amendment to embrace freedom of expression. Through expression we arrive at our ideas; when we communicate those ideas to others we help mobilize our fellow citizens and keep our elected agents informed and accountable. Freedom of expression, protected by the First Amendment, enables the people to exercise their sovereignty. That communication is yet another reason why freedom of expression is fundamental and needs to be protected absolutely—such protection helps insure that it "is the voice of the people who ultimately have the say."[116]

Obviously, the last three reasons advanced by Justice Douglas are not entirely consistent with his first three. He could not place primary reliance upon the absolutist language of the First Amendment because he wanted to cover individual privacy and a broadly defined right of expression. His claim, therefore, that all balancing of competing interests was done by the Framers and that we are bound by the Framers' decision cannot be taken seriously. When Douglas converts speech, assembly, petition, and religious free exercise into privacy and expression, he is doing nothing less than making his own reconciliation of competing interests and rights.

To be sure, Justice Douglas claimed to be making these evolutionary changes in order to keep our Constitution faithful to its overall purposes and objectives. But, as we have seen, at that theoretical level the intent of the Framers is rarely clear; there is more than one possible reading of that history and of the course of American society thereafter. In truth, all that Justice Douglas could accurately claim is that the language and intent of the Framers of the First Amendment permitted (i.e. did not preclude) his broad evolutionary interpretation.

Justice Douglas's interpretation produces a clear approach to many important First Amendment issues. It enabled him to consistently oppose—in defense of the values enumerated above—all the government's attempts to suppress the Communist Party and to penalize its members and other left-wing dissidents. The federal government sought to continue the Smith Act prosecutions under the same provisions the Court had upheld in *Dennis*. In *Yates v. United States* (1957),[117] Douglas joined Justice Black's opinion which called for "complete freedom of expression of ideas, whether we like them or not, concerning the way government should be run and who should run it."[118] In *Scales v. United States* (1961),[119] the Court sustained the Smith Act provisions making membership in an organization that engages in proscribed advocacy a criminal offense. Since no illegal act other than membership was involved, Justice Douglas objected to making mere belief in the Communist creed a crime. All beliefs, ideas, and dogmas were wholly protected by the First Amendment and not subject to inquiry, examination, or prosecution by the government.[120]

Justice Douglas also believed that the First Amendment precluded the government from attaching disabilities to membership in the Communist Party and other proscribed organizations. In 1958, he wrote the opinion for the Court which held that the Secretary of State lacked statutory authority to deny such individuals a passport.[121] Douglas made clear that he, at least, came to that rather narrow holding because of his concern to protect the constitutional right to travel he derived from the First Amendment. Congress reacted by giving the Secretary of State that precise statutory authority. By the time a challenge to the new law came to the Supreme Court, its membership had changed. Justice Goldberg's opinion for the Court in *Aptheker v. Secretary of State* (1964)[122] held the statute unconstitutional because it too broadly and indiscriminately transgressed the right to travel. Justice Douglas wrote a concurring opinion to emphasize that freedom of movement is related to such First Amendment values as knowing, exploring, studying, observing, and even thinking.[123]

Similarly, when the 1961 Court sustained a state bar association's authority to probe into an applicant's organizational affiliations, including possible membership in Communist or other left-wing groups, Douglas dissented.[124] A decade later, he joined Justice Black's plurality opinions which held that the First Amendment forbids a state from excluding a person from practicing a profession *solely* because he is a member of a particular organization or because he holds certain beliefs.[125] In what may have been the nastiest act upheld by the Court during the Cold War, *Flemming v. Nestor* (1960) sustained a 1954 amendment to the Social Security Act which terminated the retirement benefits of an individual deported for membership in the Communist Party. Justice Douglas objected to this legislative confiscation of an individual's *earned* benefits solely because he had once been a Communist.[126]

Justice Douglas also opposed making employment opportunities conditional upon loyalty oaths and security clearances involving inquiries into beliefs and associated memberships.[127] When in 1971, the Court, in striking down a Florida oath for teachers on due process grounds, indicated that "positive oaths" (i.e. oaths indicating support of the state and United States constitutions) were constitutional, Douglas wrote a separate opinion because "beliefs as such cannot be the predicate of governmental action."[128] He was merely reiterating a conclusion he had come to thirteen years earlier: "The realm of belief as opposed to action is one which the First Amendment places beyond the long arm of government."[129] The most Justice Douglas would concede to the government in this area was the possibility of conducting a narrowly focused "security risk" program for those employees of specified, high risk defense establishments.[130]

His commitment to the sanctity of individual beliefs and the privacy of associational membership obviously meant that Justice Douglas thought all legislative inquiries into those matters unconstitutional. During the heyday of the Cold War, he always opposed, on First Amendment grounds, legislative inquiries into possible Communist beliefs or affiliation.[131] This opposition also meant that Justice Douglas, unlike the members of the Court adhering to political theories based upon the competitive paradigm, had no difficulty reconciling his First Amendment opinions dealing with inquiries into the activities of the Communist party with those dealing with inquiries into the activities of the NAACP.[132]

Justice Douglas's views of the First Amendment, as well as his more practical concern to protect NAACP members from the ravages of the massive resistance to school desegregation, led him to support that organization in every case which came before the Court. In 1958 he joined Justice Harlan's opinion for the Court which declared there was a First Amendment right of association and which sustained the NAACP's reliance upon that right against Alabama's efforts to obtain its membership lists.[133] No doubt Justice Douglas would have preferred to see the protection afforded to the right of association cast in more absolutist terms, but when one of the more conservative of our recent judges was willing to lead a unanimous Court in the recognition of a new constitutional right it was hardly surprising that Justice Douglas kept his silence.[134]

Later, when the Supreme Court upheld the NAACP's refusal to give its membership list to the city of Little Rock,[135] Justices Black and Douglas took a firm First Amendment position. Justice Stewart's opinion for the other seven members held that Little Rock had shown no relevant correlation between its occupational license taxes and the compulsory disclosure (and possible publication) of the membership list. Douglas and Black were now willing to declare that First Amendment rights were "beyond abridgment" and that "one of those rights, freedom of assembly, includes of course freedom of association; and it is entitled to no less protection than any other First Amendment right."[136]

In 1963 Justice Brennan's opinion for the Court in *NAACP v. Button* held that the legal activities of the NAACP and its legal staff were modes of expression and association protected by the First Amendment and that this protection precluded Virginia from curtailing those activities under its traditional interest in regulating the state bar.[137] Again, Justice Douglas joined this extension of the First Amendment. He added a brief concurring opinion to indicate what the case was really about: the legislation in question was part of Virginia's systematic effort to crush the NAACP in order to frustrate the implementation of school desegregation.[138]

Finally, when the Court held that a committee of the Florida Legislature had not established a sufficient connection between its request for the membership list of the NAACP's Miami branch and its stated purpose of ferreting out Communists,[139] Douglas filed a long concurring opinion.[140] He restated his view that the type of free society created by the First Amendment meant that the government was powerless to legislate with respect to membership in private associations. Because it could not legislate, government could not investigate in this area, otherwise the provisions of the First Amendment could be easily circumvented. Government can intervene only when belief, thought, or expression moves into the realm of action inimical to society. Justice Douglas ended his opinion by making a strong argument for considering the newly declared right of association as part of a more pervasive right of privacy against government intrusion, a right he thought had not yet been given the recognition it deserved.

Justice Douglas applied the same distinction between overt acts and expression in the area of obscenity. Since Justice Douglas did not believe the First Amendment permitted government to suppress any expression unless it was so closely brigaded with action so as to be a part of that action, his decisions on the obscenity cases were perfectly consistent.[141] He would not have permitted even narrowly drawn laws aimed at restricting the access of the young to pornography.[142] Most probably he would have sustained local ordinances limiting the places where "adult" material could be located. He was no longer on the Court when that issue was squarely raised,[143] but, as noted above, he was highly tolerant of most zoning ordinances.[144]

In sum, Justice Douglas, contrary to many critics, did have doctrinal standards on such matters as the First Amendment. At first glance his interpretation of the First Amendment seems a satisfactory theory for enlarging individual freedoms. If Douglas's natural rights approach to free speech and related matters had ever gained general acceptance and if it were conscientiously followed by the courts, the legally recognized liberties of all Americans would undoubtedly be greater than ever before. We would be well on the way toward institutionalizing the type of free society Douglas saw as the grand design of the Constitution, a society which out of respect for the individual protects the sanctity of thought and belief. Douglas was certainly correct in his insistence that this ideal was no stranger to our political tradition. It was rooted in the ideas of natural rights shared by the Framers; it was a major part of our intellectual tradition at least until the New Deal era; and many commentators continue to see the pervasive influence of individualism in the present era.[145]

The question, then, is why Justice Douglas's position has rarely been treated seriously. The First Amendment positions of Alexander Meiklejohn and Hugo Black have attracted an abundance of commentators, if not followers, in the law reviews and general journals of the intellectual community.[146] Libertarians have consistently failed to treat Douglas's views with the same respect they accorded the others. Liberals were grateful for his support, and frequently quoted a strong passage here or an eloquent phrase there, but they ignored the theory behind Douglas's votes. Since most libertarians share Douglas's deep and abiding commitment to individual liberty, how do we explain this treatment?

The basic problem is the modern intellectual's deep-seated and well-founded skepticism toward natural law doctrines of any sort. Science had led people to question the existence of universal laws stemming from Nature or Nature's God. Perhaps even more serious, the very generality of the concepts of natural law left their application to concrete issues highly problematic. Experience, most contemporary intellectuals believe, has shown that natural law could be used to support a variety of contradictory values. The very ambiguity of the concepts made any sustained justificatory system appear highly subjective, almost arbitrary. Another person starting with the same values could arrive at an equally plausible but contradictory conclusion. That arbitrariness had been the major *theoretical* weakness with the Supreme Court's earlier attempt to defend the natural right of property.

The same dilemma was posed by the liberal natural rights theory of William O. Douglas. There was a remarkable consistency to his opinions dealing with political speech and even the usually troublesome obscenity issue. The consistency was directly traceable to his political theory. The same theory, however, created problems for other First Amendment issues, and he was never quite able to justify his resolution of those issues within the bounds of the theory. That inability, once again, raised the spectre of arbitrary decision making, of personal, highly subjective, almost instinctive conclusions, cloaked with a thin veneer of ambiguous generalities derived from natural rights theory.

Take, for example, the problem of privacy. His first opinion utilizing the right to privacy dealt with another First Amendment issue—the problem posed by a captive audience. The privately owned public transportation company in Washington, D.C. sold the franchise to broadcast in its vehicles to a local radio station. In *Public Utilities Commission v. Pollak* (1952),[147] all members of the Court agreed that the commission's approval meant the scheme should be treated as governmental action subject to constitutional norms. The majority upheld the commission's decision.

Justice Douglas's dissent interprets the liberty protected by the Fifth Amendment in light of First Amendment values—respect for the conscience of the individual and the sanctity of his thought and belief.[148] The company's riders were a captive audience because they were forced to listen to messages selected by the radio station. Douglas questioned the long-term implications of this system and found it wanting by his First Amendment criteria:

> Once privacy is invaded, privacy is gone. Once a man is forced to submit to one type of radio program, he can be forced to submit to another. It may be but a short step from a cultural program to a political program.

If liberty is to flourish, government should never be allowed to force people to listen to any radio program.[149]

Justice Douglas saw privacy as a notion "implicit in a free society" and therefore as part of the "totality of the constitutional scheme under which we live."[150] In his opinion for the Court holding a state prohibition of access to birth control devices unconstitutional,[151] Justice Douglas argued for the recognition of a zone of privacy created by several constitutional guarantees. The specific guarantees in the Bill of Rights, he argued, "have penumbras, formed by emanations from those guarantees that help give them life and substance."[152] In an earlier book he had connected this notion of penumbras and emanations to his basic natural rights theory:

> The penumbra of the Bill of Rights reflects human rights which, though not explicit, are implied from the very nature of man as a child of God . . . Man as a citizen had known oppressive laws from time out of mind and was in revolt. Man, as a child of God, insisted he was accountable not to the state but to his own conscience and to his God.[153]

From this premise in natural rights theory, Justice Douglas became the leading exponent of a constitutional right to privacy.[154] Our interest here focuses on its First Amendment implications. His earliest use of the concept of privacy in *Pollak* as well as such later opinions as his concurrence in *Gibson* obviously squares with his general First Amendment stance.[155] Privacy, however, was also central to the issues posed by another line of First Amendment cases, those relating to libel and defamation. Douglas's opinions in this area were noticeable for their lack of concern for privacy.

The landmark modern case was *New York Times v. Sullivan* (1964).[156] Justice Brennan's opinion for the Court held that the First Amendment prohibited "a public official from recovering damages for defamatory falsehood relating to his official conduct unless he proves that the statement was made with 'actual malice'—that is, with knowledge that it was false or with reckless disregard of whether it was false or not."[157] In light of his previous First Amendment opinions, it was not surprising that Justice Douglas signed the concurring opinions of both Justice Black and Justice Goldberg. The latter argued for an absolute immunity for speech about public officials.[158] The former argued the Goldberg position was only the *minimum* position consistent with First Amendment values; Justice Black had come to believe the First Amendment precluded punishment for libel.[159]

New York Times v. Sullivan was the fountainhead for several decisions in subsequent years. The Court extended the term "public official" to include virtually all persons affiliated with government, including ordinary civil servants,[160] and candidates for public office.[161] Justice Douglas approved of this extension. His support, however, was not keyed to the factor of "public office," rather it was related to his basic belief in the complete freedom to discuss public issues. To him, that freedom was a *minimum* command of the First Amendment.[162]

New York Times v. Sullivan had raised the question of the proper standard for assessing libel actions brought by *private* individuals. The Court has extended the "actual malice" test of that case to cover *public figures*—those persons who by their activities have thrust themselves into the limelight.[163] It is now, however, unwilling to extend the doctrine to cover libel and defamation actions brought by other individuals.[164] Justice Douglas went along with the first development and opposed the second on the theory that the First Amendment covers discussion of matters of public interest,[165] but, since all events are arguably of public interest, little remains of an individual's attempt to protect his privacy.

The cases illustrate this point well. In 1952, James Hill and his family were on the front pages of many newspapers when they were held captive for eighteen hours by three escaped convicts. A 1955 *Life* magazine article, replete with pictures, claimed that a novel and play entitled "The Desperate Hours" dramatized the incident. Unlike the experiences of the Hill family, however, the family in the story was abused by the convicts. The issue before the Court was whether the *New York Times* libel standard should be extended to cover actions brought under New York's Right of Privacy Statute. In *Time, Inc. v. Hill* (1967),[166] Justice Brennan's plurality opinion urged the extension of the *New York Times v. Sullivan* doctrine to cover the privacy issue. Justice Douglas, like Justice Black, acquiesced in that decision only to dispose of the case. He would have preferred to say that the First Amendment precluded Hill's action.[167]

He argued that a fictionalized account of an event was part of the public domain. As such, all discussion of it was totally protected by the First Amendment, for any narrower standard would leave authors and press subject to chancy decisions made by judges and juries. In the process of stating those views, Justice Douglas took a rather cavalier attitude toward privacy:

> It seems to me irrelevant to talk of any right to privacy in this context.
> Here a private person is catapulted into the news by events over
> which he had no control. He and his activities are then in the public
> domain as fully as the matters at issue in *New York Times v. Sullivan*
> . . . Such privacy as a person has ceased when his life has ceased to be
> private.[168]

This statement embodied his well-considered judgment. He reiterated it seven years later. At least as to discussion of public affairs, the First Amendment prohibits all libel action. Public affairs for Douglas included a great deal more than merely political affairs: "Matters of science, economics, business, art, literature, etc. are all matters of interest to the general public. Indeed, any matter of sufficient general interest to prompt media coverage may be said to be a public affair."[169] Again, he was quite explicit about an individual's right to privacy against the media:

> Unlike the right to privacy which, by the terms of the Fourth Amendment, must be accommodated with reasonable searches and seizures and warrants issued by magistrates, the rights of free speech and free press were protected by the Framers in verbiage whose prescription seems clear.[170]

To suffer the slings and arrows of the media for whatever reasons and about any aspect of one's life is the price we pay for our regime of freedom, according to Douglas. To many, this opinion was bound to seem a blatant disregard for the plight of an individual seeking to shun the public spotlight. In no way could Hill, for example, be characterized as a public figure. As a private person he was more vulnerable to injury because he lacked access to the media to rebut charges against him; and an attempt by the private individual to "go public" would merely compound his loss of privacy. Nor was Hill, at the time of *Life*'s publication, a participant in a newsworthy event. It is not clear why the law cannot punish deliberate distortions which might harm individuals involuntarily subjected to media coverage and powerless to otherwise protect themselves. Certainly "notoriety" created by allegedly defamatory media coverage should not suffice to make a private individual a public figure any more than a legislative interest to discover an individual's associational activity should by itself justify inquiries into his private beliefs.

Even so staunch a champion of the system of free expression as Professor Thomas I. Emerson recognizes that defamation of reputation tends to have an impact on an individual like other tortious acts. Emerson, like Douglas, believes that the Constitution fully protects expression (as opposed to only speech), but on the issue of defamation and libel the professor disagreed with his friend, the Justice. Emerson thought defamation could be subjected to civil penalties, under narrowly drawn laws, without doing harm to First Amendment values.[171]

Justice Douglas was unwilling even to deal with the fact that absolute freedom of the press and individual privacy and dignity are not always compatible. Rather than balancing what his *own* opinions taught were competing First Amendment values, he wrote opinions which spoke of an absolutist constitutional right of the press. This viewpoint from the Court's leading advocate of the right of privacy! Moreover, the very tone and style of these opinions by Justice Douglas were bound to be distressing to liberal intellectuals. He made his conclusions sound like self-evident deductions from higher law values embedded in the Constitution, the exact same approach he used to justify constitutional protection for a zone of privacy. At times, Douglas's own opinions seem to serve as the best argument against his natural rights theory.

Justice Douglas's fight to enhance privacy in most areas and his almost callous attitude toward it in the area of libel and defamation was unlikely, by itself, to account for the liberal intellectuals' indifference toward his interpretation of the First Amendment. The cases where Justice Douglas did not support the right of privacy were simply not the important ones when measured against events dominating the last two decades of his service in the Court; rather, commentators focused on the way he proposed handling cases involving "speech plus action." As the civil rights movement gave way to the black protest movement, as opposition to American military operations in Indochina grew more vehement, demonstration became an increasingly important form of political activity. Justice Douglas conceded that demonstrations were a form of conduct, but he also believed the communicative element involved in such activity brought it within the scope of the First Amendment.

The cases early in Justice Douglas's judicial career had held that picketing, marching, and parading were forms of expression entitled to some First Amendment protection.[172] They were noticeably ambiguous in defining the limits which the differences between "pure speech" and "speech plus" would entail in the application of First Amendment principles. By the time the more recent spate of cases arrived on the Court's docket, Justice Douglas had adopted his absolutist interpretation of the First Amendment in areas usually included in the "pure speech" category. Interest was therefore focused on the difference, if any, this interpretation would make in cases involving a mixture of speech and conduct.

In the first three significant cases, Justice Douglas wrote no opinion. In *Edwards v. South Carolina* (1963),[173] he joined Justice Stewart's opinion for the Court which upheld the right of 187 black students to stage a peaceable demonstration on the grounds of the state capitol. In *Cox v. Louisiana* (1965),[174] Justice Douglas was part of the majority which reversed the black civil rights leader's conviction under a general breach of peace statute, a statute forbidding obstruction of a public sidewalk and a statute forbidding picketing near the courthouse. Justice Goldberg's opinion for the Court made the customary distinction between "pure speech" and "speech plus." The conduct elements involved in protest demonstrations, he insisted, could be regulated by properly drafted and applied statutes and ordinances.[175]

The very next year, however, in the "library stand-up" case,[176] three Justices—including Douglas—appeared to argue that even if a properly drawn statute was correctly applied, it could not be used to squelch a protest against segregation. A few months later, when *Adderley v. Florida* (1966)[177] was decided, Justice Douglas found himself writing the minority opinion. Adderley and thirty-one other blacks had been convicted for trespassing with malicious and mischievous intent upon the premises of the county jail. Justice Black's majority opinion proceeded on the premise that demonstrations were conduct, not speech, and as such could be regulated or curtailed by even-handed enforcement of a nondiscriminatory statute.

Justice Douglas's dissent recognized the conduct element inherent in any demonstration, but he stressed the speech element involved. Perhaps because it was the best vehicle for unifying the four dissenters,[178] Douglas's opinion was based upon the preferred freedoms doctrine. He recognized the need to balance other societal interests against the speech values inherent in a public protest, but citizens' First Amendment rights were to be outweighed only upon a clear showing that the demonstration interfered with significant societal functions.[179]

Justice Douglas thus recognized that some public facilities were dedicated to purposes which made them unsuitable sites for mass demonstrations, that some protests were not consistent with other necessary societal functions. He mentions that noisy demonstrations may be out of keeping with the serenity of a statehouse or the quiet of a courthouse;[180] but the library stand-up opinion which he joined makes this part of Douglas's *Adderley* dissent seem less than candid. Is not a library so clearly committed to quiet reading, studying, and reflection that its "use for airing grievances is anomolous?" It is difficult to understand why under certain circumstances a silent demonstration could not be just as inconsistent with, and disruptive to, public facilities which need "quiet" and "serenity." If this is true, then the library "stand-up," by the very standards he enunciated in *Adderley* should have been condemned by Douglas.

Six years later, the Court seemed to have adopted the standard Douglas had called for in his *Adderley* dissent. *Grayned v. City of Rockford* (1972)[181] involved a city antinoise ordinance prohibiting a person, while in the area adjacent to a school, from wilfully making a noise or diversion that disturbs the school session. In his opinion for the Court, Justice Thurgood Marshall held:

> The nature of a place, "the pattern of its normal activities, dictate the kinds of regulations of time, place and manner that are reasonable."
> Although a silent vigil may not unduly interfere with a public library, . . . making a speech in the reading room almost certainly would.

That same speech would be perfectly appropriate in a park. *The crucial question is whether the manner of expression is basically incompatible with the normal activity of a particular place at a particular time.* Our cases make clear that *in assessing the reasonableness of a regulation, we must weigh heavily the fact that communication is involved;* the regulation must be narrowly tailored to further the State's legitimate interest.[182]

On its face, this holding for seven members of the Court would indicate that Douglas had carried the day. Not only was his basic argument (in italics) adopted, even the controversial decision in the library case was reconciled. No wonder such civil libertarians as Professor Lawrence Tribe have hailed it as a "seminal formulation."[183] Yet Douglas alone dissented. The demonstration outside the school involved racial grievances against the school administration. The extent of the disruption within the school was a matter in controversy. Justice Douglas chose to emphasize that although there was noise, most of it was produced by the police loudspeakers, and there was no evidence that Grayned himself was boisterous or rowdy. Unlike the majority, he was unwilling to let the trial court alone determine the factual issue. He certainly was unwilling to have police attempts at maintaining order be used against the protestors whose actions had prompted the presence of the police.[184] In asserting that the entire demonstration "was done in the best First Amendment tradition"—seemingly without regard for other legitimate interests—Justice Douglas once again called into question his natural rights doctrine.

CONCLUSIONS

There is, as we have seen, much to praise in the political theory of Justice Douglas as a vehicle for interpreting the Constitution. His belief in the natural rights of man is deeply rooted in our political tradition, particularly the founding generation. His concern to apply that theory realistically to contemporary problems is also in keeping with the highest goals of our political-constitutional tradition.[185] The Supreme Court's role in shaping a "living," "evolving" Constitution is a stock idea of contemporary American political thought; it is found in all the standard introductory texts. Felix Frankfurter, the high priest of judicial self-restraint in the recent era, also warned of the dangers of literalness, of treating the Constitution as "a piece of outworn parchment instead of being words that have called into being a nation with a past to be preserved for the future."[186] What distinguishes Justice Douglas was not his attitude about the malleability of the Constitution, but his political theory.

His natural rights theory led Justice Douglas to a well-rounded, if generalized, view of the nature of American citizenship. A government formed by individuals in order to promote their natural rights, by definition, vests sovereignty in the people, not the government; therefore, retention of citizenship was beyond legislative control. More important, this sovereignty meant each individual was to participate fully in the decisions affecting the polity and life styles of its citizens. Finally, his commitment to the natural rights of the individual American citizen led him to interpret the First Amendment in a way which recognized both its instrumental role in a system of self-government, and as an end in itself—as an essential component in the dignity of man, his personal autonomy, and his unending quest for self-realization. Justice Douglas has been one of the few recent proponents of liberty to conceive freedom of speech from this dual perspective. The opinions which derived from that perspective unquestionably sought to enhance human freedom.

We should not, solely on the basis of remembrances of things past, automatically be distressed by the judicial activism of Justice Douglas. His goals were not the values of the Old Guard Court. "The natural rights of which I speak are different," wrote Douglas. "They have a broad base in morality and religion to protect man, his individuality, and his conscience against direct and indirect interference by government."[187] Many commentators have argued that the essential function of the American Supreme Court lies in its efforts to keep our society true to its own fundamental principles.[188] In seeking to enhance the political freedom of all Americans, to ensure their full access to the political process, and to protect the citizenship of those groups whose rights are occasionally submerged in that process, Justice Douglas was attempting to secure the integrity of democratic society.[189] Activism on behalf of such values is hardly a vice.

There is reason, however, to be troubled by Douglas's constitutional interpretations. Natural rights theory is as ambiguous in its specific prescriptions as it is clear in its objectives. In two of the areas we have canvassed, those ambiguities, when coupled with Douglas's active pursuit of justice, created problems. The problems posed by the expatriation cases were sufficiently general so as to pose few problems for a natural rights interpretation of the Constitution. Once we seek to implement the objective of full citizen participation, however, the theory yields no clear answer to the detailed problems. A theory based upon individual rights could not take him beyond "one person-one vote," yet any *realistic* assessment of an individual's voting power must also account for the relative political power of distinct groups. His theory was inadequate for that purpose and Douglas appeared to be acting on his instinctive support for the underdog without even being sure he was actually helping.

Similarly, in his interpretation of the First Amendment, Douglas's concern for the communicative aspects of protest demonstrations always seemed to override all other values and interests. He never fully reconciled the dual premises of his interpretation of the First Amendment—its functional role in self-government and its intrinsic quality for the dignity of man—hence, his inability to recognize the right of privacy in the libel cases. Occasionally, in his later years, he spoke of the "Society of the Dialogue" as a way of reconciling the participatory and private aspects of his First Amendment theory;[190] but he never refined that notion sufficiently for it to provide any guidance for his, let alone our, decisionmaking. As a result, when he opted for the participatory strand in the libel-privacy cases, it once again seemed to reflect his instinctive reactions.

The instinctive reactions of Justice Douglas can rarely be faulted and never easily, because they were based on our traditional ideas. The American political heritage has always assumed that the struggle for power is a persistent fact of social life and that too much concentrated power—whether it be economic, religious, or political—is the mortal enemy of individual liberty. Douglas used his contract theory to argue that America had been created precisely to secure the blessings of liberty, to protect the individual from the coercive effects of concentrated power. Rights were to be granted special treatment by virtue of their importance in this age-old quest to implement the moral dignity of man. Natural rights theory enabled Justice Douglas to articulate his basic values in clear, forthright, and, to an American, easily understandable terms.

The same theory reinforced Justice Douglas's uninhibited willingness to use the Court as a principal agency for insuring the continuing relevance of those values fundamental to our polity. All institutions in the United States, he believed, should be striving to implement the moral ideals of the Declaration and the Preamble. The legal order existed to advance the notions of justice outlined in those documents. The judiciary, therefore, should seek to do this in each case at hand. This approach rarely lent itself to an overt concern for systemic factors. Justice Douglas seemed to operate on the premise that it was sufficient unto the day to grant justice in each case. As the courts pursued this policy and simultaneously took a broad, flexible view of their jurisdiction, they would incrementally advance American society. Moreover, to Justice Douglas the moral dignity of the individual was apparently too important to be sacrificed on the altar of long-term systemic considerations. If all we know about the future is that in the long run we shall all be dead, such trade-offs are foolish in the extreme. Finally, Justice Douglas obviously hoped other institutions, and the American people in general, would respond to the just acts of the Court. The very rhetoric of his opinions indicates this concern to involve the public, as does his habitual utilization of nonlegal, popularly accessible sources and his extensive lecturing and writing. This popularization was all part of his attempt to renew our commitment and spread the word. As a moral crusader he was second to none. The natural rights of man found a true champion in William O. Douglas.

Both the substance and the style of his jurisprudence thus flowed from his political theory. It is to the adequacy of that theory as an aid in constitutional interpretation that we must now turn. Natural rights theory, even one rooted in our Whig heritage, finds few adherents in America today. There are several reasons for this unpopularity and Justice Douglas's theory is vulnerable on all counts. First, there is the jurisprudential, philosophical skepticism about the very existence of "natural rights." Several centuries of diligent work by intelligent people have produced as much diversity as agreement. Even the proponents of such theories are not agreed as to the contents of man's natural rights.[191] As noted above, Justice Douglas himself was aware of this factor; he was quick to distinguish his liberal natural rights theory from that held by his more conservative predecessors such as Justice Field. That response, however, is not adequate to a query about the very existence of natural rights. Little wonder, then, that the bulk of legal and social theorists no longer hold certain values to be inherent in the very nature of things and, for that reason alone, to be accorded transcendental importance.

Awareness of this criticism has led contemporary natural law theorists to shift their argument to its functional utility. Precisely because it is premised on an indissoluable intersection between law and morals, natural law requires that law be examined in terms of its full impact on human development.[192] By holding certain moral values absolute, it is argued, a theory of natural rights helps ensure their continued operational relevance. This argument assumes the theory will be more specific than the Ten Commandments or Kant's categorical imperative; to be politically and socially useful, a theory must go beyond mere moral exhortation. That assumption, of course, raises the issue discussed above: which values are "natural" to man?

In this sense Justice Douglas was fortunate. The values embedded in our founding documents enabled him to bypass the problem in its most abstract, philosophical form. He could assert that the natural rights of man, at least for American society, were those we conventionally label as Lockean. He had more difficulty asserting the primacy of the Jeffersonian version of those rights, but that never seemed to bother him and it need not detain us. Even those rights are notoriously ambiguous. If the Bill of Rights is to be interpreted as a code of natural rights, it must still be made applicable to the cases at hand. A mere enunciation of the moral goals does not automatically dictate the means. Outlining these means was Justice Douglas's problem in the area of political participation. Once the cases got beyond the equal right of each individual to full and effective participation in the electoral process, his theory could provide no guidance about how best to implement that principle. Rather than serving a useful function, Justice Douglas's theory seemed to hide the need for difficult choices and careful analysis even from him.

It is sometimes argued that natural rights theory can at least serve the function of establishing our priorities. Granted that difficult choices will have to be made about how best to implement agreed-upon values, nonetheless, that is a choice among relative goods. With the moral ends beyond debate, we can at least take comfort in the fact that our prior consensus shields us from straying too far from the correct, just, path of action. Would that it were so! Unfortunately, it is difficult to accept this argument, at least as applied to a theory of natural rights, for frequently choices must be made between competing rights. At that point, guidance is needed in making a difficult choice, and a theory which emphasizes the *absolute* rights of man tends to stunt our critical faculties.

A conflict of basic values indicates there can never be a too rigid separation of ends and means. True, means must be selected with certain values in mind, but those goals must be critically assessed and reassessed in terms of the consequences of the means necessary for their achievement. Choice and reconciliation require detailed analysis, with full recognition that trade offs must be made among competing rights. Choice and reconciliation mean that no rights can ever be truly absolute.[193] Failure to recognize this fact leads to embarrassing positions akin to Justice Douglas's problem with the right of privacy. When a Justice is expected to apply general principles to concrete problems, it is encumbent upon him to explain how he arrived at his standard. Again, a theory of natural rights, because it begins by asserting certain absolute values, encourages pronouncement rather than justification. Faced with a conflict between his absolutist notion of freedom of expression and his equally absolutist notion of privacy, Justice Douglas simply ignored the latter value.

Finally, it is sometimes argued that a theory of natural rights serves an indispensable educational function. The theory permits its adherents to enunciate the values necessary for the dignity of man in a bold, clear manner and thereby helps to inculcate those ideals among other political actors and the general population. Whatever the merits of this argument in general, it is a plainly inadequate prescription for an American Supreme Court Justice. The agency on which he serves operates through the articulation of rules (derived from general standards) which other institutions and actors are expected to follow. Other than an obvious concern with a just (by his standards) resolution of the case at hand, Justice Douglas's concern was to move the law in the correct policy direction. For an appellate court, however, policy objectives are closely aligned to doctrine because it participates in the policy-making process precisely by establishing legal norms controlling a particular issue.

Douglas's frequent disregard for conventional legal analysis and for theoretical clarity served to weaken his long-range objectives.

Moreover, the great authority we bestow on our appellate judges stems from their ability to convince us—at least most of the time—that they are more concerned with enunciating generally applicable standards than with who wins the immediate case at hand. Failure to provide adequate justification makes it easy to suspect that abstract principles are being manipulated to cloak personal preferences. Justice Douglas was particularly vulnerable on this count and the vague ambiguous generalities of his natural rights theory provided a too easy avoidance mechanism. A judge who cannot explain, even *after* a decision, why one party deserves constitutional vindication, can expect, at most, grudging acceptance. Far better that he explain *before* the decision what standards were applicable to a particular line of cases and why. Then the law could truly serve to guide and educate our citizenry.

As indicated above, a theory of natural rights, without more focus and direction, cannot provide this justification. The mere assertion of values is no substitute for a careful explanation of why those values are so important and how equally important values should be reconciled when they conflict. For this type of functional analysis, opening the philosophical debate about which rights are "natural" may not be necessary. It is certainly never sufficient. For this reason contemporary scholars most concerned with individual rights have not followed Justice Douglas. Instead, they have sought to elaborate upon the importance of those rights in modern society, to work through the implications of those rights for a political system, and to derive specific legal doctrines for governing concrete issues.[194] For modern man, belief rests upon acceptance, acceptance upon persuasion, and persuasion upon good reasons.

IV

CONTEMPORARY THEORIES OF DEMOCRACY: THE CONTRACT THEORIES

The Functional Contract _____

In the years immediately after World War II, a few scholars began questioning the wisdom of the competitive paradigm for democracy. They were troubled by the social science emphasis on observable political behavior at the expense of normative political questions. These scholars, however, did not believe natural law theories could advance the discussion of such questions. Like the social scientists, they were unwilling to rest their arguments upon a metaphysical claim about Nature or Nature's God. Instead, they turned once again to the idea of a political contract.

According to their theory, all Americans, beginning with the constitutional generation, have entered into an agreement to be self-governing. The unique feature of democracy is that the people are simultaneously rulers and ruled. As the ruled we are subject to governmental authority. As the rulers We, the People, have certain absolute freedoms—those liberties directly related to self-government must be protected absolutely. The instrumental branches of government cannot destroy the functional requisites of the fourth and sovereign branch. This democratic theory was intended both to aid our understanding of democracy and to guide our interpretation of the Constitution. According to the functional contract theory, the Constitution, in all its provisions, looks forward to a self-governing polity.

ALEXANDER MEIKLEJOHN AND JOSEPH TUSSMAN

In 1948 the distinguished educator and philosopher, Alexander Meiklejohn, published a series of lectures entitled *Free Speech and Its Relation to Self-Government*.[1] He was plainly opposed to the contemporary dominance of the "scientific method" in the study of our political life. While the social scientists were doing useful work, he argued, their efforts could play only a secondary part in our understanding of a free society. A total reliance upon social science minimizes the essential distinction between democracy and other forms of government because it reduces our understanding of politics to an accurate description of contending forces. To understand the American plan of government, Dr. Meiklejohn contended, we must create and use methods of inquiry suitable to the study of men as self-governing persons, of men using their minds to give direction to their behavior.[2]

A dozen years later, Joseph Tussman's *Obligation and the Body Politic* was published. A student and disciple of Meiklejohn, he too was bothered by the predominance of the social science perspective. In the name of scientific objectivity, Tussman claimed, we are increasingly reducing our study of the American political life to a purely descriptive and predictive account of our behavior. This stategy has helped us understand existing situations, but social science cannot teach us what we should do; it has not provided decision makers with the necessary guidance. Social science cannot provide a sufficient education for self-governing men.[3]

For both men the problem with seeing our democracy solely in terms of pluralistic forces was that it said nothing about political freedom. It substituted the control of our elected rulers for the idea of self-government. It meant the Americans' belief that they were "free" was merely a myth by which the masses could be manipulated, cajoled, or driven into action without knowing what they were doing. Neither Meiklejohn nor Tussman denied that social scientists had provided an accurate description of how our political system actually operates;[4] but, they believed, the Constitution gave the American people the authority to govern ourselves. They sought to provide us with a political theory which would encourage them to claim that authority.

The Agreement of the People

At the core of Meiklejohn and Tussman's theory is the notion that the American plan of government is based upon a social compact. Alexander Meiklejohn defined the terms of the agreement:

We the People of the United States, are a body politic. Under the Constitution, we are agreed together that we will be, by corporate action, self-governed. We are agreed that as free men, politically equal, we alone will make the laws and that, as loyal citizens, equal before the laws, we will obey them. That is our social compact—the source both of our freedoms and our obligations.[5]

Let us explore the nature of this agreement. First, it defines the nature of our political relatedness. As Tussman notes, "A body politic, on this view, is a group of persons related by a system of agreements; to be a member of a body politic is to be party to the system of agreements."[6]

Second, the Constitution is the basic expression of that agreement. It defines the purposes for which we entered into the body politic and describes how we chose to organize it. People enter into a social compact for a purpose and that purpose is the common good or the public interest.[7]

The most important facet of the agreement, however, is how the American people chose to organize themselves for pursuing those substantive goals. The words "We, the People," mean that "it is agreed, and with every passing moment it is reagreed, that the people of the United States shall be self-governed. To that fundamental enactment all other provisions of the Constitution, all statutes, all administrative decrees, are subsidiary and dependent."[8]

Third, to give meaning to the idea of self-government, We, the People, must be recognized as the supreme governing agency of the United States. "All political authority, whether delegated or not, belongs, constitutionally, to us. If any one else has political authority, we are lending it to him."[9] Some of this sovereign power has been delegated in the Constitution to legislative, executive, and judicial agencies. We, the People, have recognized that we can govern ourselves, in so complex a society as ours, only by delegating certain of our powers. The agencies we have created, however, are the subordinate branches of government. Their powers, tasks, and decisions are always subject to review and reversal.[10]

For, We, the People, have reserved powers to ourselves as well as delegated them. We have retained the power of direct participation in the work of governing. By establishing ourselves as an active electorate, we have become the Fourth Branch of government. In retaining the power of voting, of choosing by joint action those representatives to whom we have entrusted certain of our powers, we have kept for ourselves the most fundamental of all powers. We, the People, are the Fourth and highest branch of government. In a real sense we are the government.[11]

Fourth, in another very real way we are also the governed. When we entered into the social compact, we agreed to subordinate our private judgment to the public judgment. Self-government would be impossible if the "self" which governed could not make its will effective.[12]

Unlike the competitive paradigm, this theory does not make a sharp distinction between rulers and ruled. In our public capacity, acting together either directly or through our agents, we make and administer law. In our private capacity, acting alone or in groups, we are subject to the law. We, the People, are both rulers and ruled.

Fifth, the compact to be self-governing is the basis of political freedom. Political freedom requires voluntary consent and participation; it does not mean the absence of public control or an individual's veto power over all laws. We are politically free when we have voluntarily agreed to participate in making public policy. Tussman put it well when he wrote, "In this tradition 'political freedom' does not turn on the absence of law but on whether the law is 'self-imposed.'"[13]

In broad terms, this assessment is the way Meiklejohn and Tussman perceive the basic agreement of the people. It is based, of course, on that aspect of the American political tradition which runs from the Mayflower Compact through the Declaration of Independence to the Constitution. In large measure, Meiklejohn and Tussman are simply trying to get us to take that doctrine seriously again.[14] They cannot and will not base their claim primarily on the authority of history, however. That predicate would mean we are being governed by the dead hand of the past. The lessons of history are significant only insofar as they help us understand what it means to be self-governing. The basic claim of Meiklejohn and Tussman is that only a contract theory like theirs can give meaning to that idea of democracy.[15]

The Absoluteness of the First Amendment

While the nature of the basic agreement is familiar stuff, the concept of the Fourth Branch of government is novel. Especially as developed by Meiklejohn, the concept lead to a novel interpretation of the Constitution. The Constitution does not mention the people as the Fourth Branch of government. Its words seem to limit the political activity of the people to casting a ballot. With the aid of a few quotations from The Federalist Papers[16] and that aspect of the American political tradition mentioned above, however, Dr. Meiklejohn was able to argue that "in the deeper meaning of the Constitution, voting is merely the external expression of a wide and diverse number of activities" required by a system of self-government.[17]

To govern in a responsible manner, We, the People, need to understand the problems and issues confronting our nation. We must also pass judgment upon the decisions our agents have made in handling those issues. Finally, we too must help devise new ideas, plans, and methods for advancing our common interest. These activities, in all their diversity, are the substance of political freedom. These activities, according to Meiklejohn's interpretation, are given absolute, unqualified protection by the First Amendment.[18]

Dr. Meiklejohn found support for this reading of the Amendment in other sections of the Constitution. The two provisions he thought had the most direct bearing on the "inviolability of the powers of the Fourth Branch" were the Tenth Amendment and Article I, section 2(1).[19] He used the Tenth Amendment to support his argument that the people had retained their sovereign authority. He used Article I, section 2(1) to draw an analogy between the powers of Congress and the powers of the people. Since that provision gave the people's legislative agents absolute freedom of speech to discuss public policy, the sovereign people must also be free to exercise their reserved powers.[20]

He also relied upon the sharp, resolute, and absolute wording of the First Amendment itself, but the wording created so many problems for him he was forced to recognize that "the text of the Amendment is, with respect to its meaning, partial and incomplete."[21] Many activities which Meiklejohn believed to be protected by it did not actually conform to a literal reading of the text. For example, he included the freedom to vote within the scope of the First Amendment, even though that right is not mentioned in the Amendment.[22]

On the other hand, he believed the First Amendment afforded no protection to many forms of speech. For, if it was designed to protect political freedom, the Amendment "cannot have been, and obviously was not, intended to give immunity to every possible use of language."[23] Libel, blasphemy, obscenity, counselling of crimes, offensive and provocative remarks are all abuses of speech whose regulation is not a violation of the Amendment's intention.[24]

This interpretation led Dr. Meiklejohn to his famous thesis that under the Constitution there are two different protections for speech rather than only one. There is a "freedom of speech" about *public* matters. That right is the political freedom necessary for self-government which the First Amendment declares to be absolutely nonabridgable. Individuals also have a *private* right of speech, the liberty to speak their minds on a whole range of matters not related to the governing of society. This right is the "liberty of speech" the Fifth Amendment protects. Private speech, therefore, is protected by the Due Process Clause and may be regulated, "though such limitations may not be imposed unnecessarily or unequally.[25]

The absoluteness of the First Amendment in this contract theory is not based upon "a sentimental vagary about the 'natural rights' of individuals."[26] "It is not a Law of Nature or of Reason in the abstract. It is a deduction from the basic American agreement that public issues shall be decided by universal suffrage."[27] The absolute protection which Meiklejohn would accord

political freedom is based upon his examination of the structure and functioning of our political system.

The absoluteness of the First Amendment does not mean, however, that
every governmental regulation affecting public speech and related political
freedoms is unconstitutional. When self-governing people demand political
freedom, they are not saying every individual has an inalienable right to
participate in the political process whenever, wherever, however he chooses.
Using the town meeting as his basic example, Meiklejohn reasoned that the
ultimate interest of the self-governing process was not unregulated political
activity but wise decisions. Reasonable regulations which furthered that aim
were perfectly proper even though they barred citizens from speaking, *provided*, however, no regulation was imposed to curtail a particular suggestion
of policy. No plan of action could be outlawed because it was thought unwise,
false, dangerous, unfair, etc.—that prohibition would be a mutilation of the
community's thinking process. Politically neutral regulations of individual
political actions, however, were often required to maintain a functioning
system of self-government.[28]

There are thus two boundaries to the absoluteness of the First Amendment. One is based on the dichotomy between "public" and "private" speech.
The other is based on the analogy between our democratic system and a
town meeting, and is embodied in the notion that public decision making
often requires politically neutral regulations to facilitate political participation.

These and other boundaries created by the public contract theory will
be the primary focus of the remainder of this chapter, for, if the basic agreement is a purposive act, that purpose sets limits to actions made in the name
of the body politic. Since both Meiklejohn and Tussman insist the basic
American agreement was to establish a system of self-government, the boundaries imposed by their political contract are set by the functional requisites
of a system of self-government. An analysis of boundaries therefore yields a
greater understanding of the Meiklejohn-Tussman idea of democracy.

More important, such analysis will lead to a better comprehension of
the truly novel feature of this democratic theory—the way Meiklejohn and
Tussman establish an absolutist conception of political freedom. They do not
rely upon the American tradition of inalienable natural rights.[28] Instead, their
arguments are based upon the functional requisites of the Fourth and sovereign branch of government. Natural rights theorists in the Lockean tradition
use contract theory to establish government's obligation to protect individual
rights; that protection is the reason men entered into the political contract.
In the political theory of Meiklejohn and Tussman, Americans entered into
the political contract to create a self-governing system; the contract is used
to establish government's obligation to maintain that democratic system. A
shift has been made. Individual rights are not to be protected solely because

they are individual rights; they are to be protected only insofar as they are functional requisites of a self-governing political system. As we examine the functional contract theory, then, we must seek to discover whether a political theory with this systemic focus is compatible with the absolutist protection of individual rights.

JUSTICE BRENNAN AND THE FIRST AMENDMENT

Before turning to the applicability of functional contract theory, however, some further explication is necessary. As in previous chapters, the analysis of this political theory will rely heavily on Supreme Court opinions. Meiklejohn and Tussman would heartily approve; they both recommend a close study of Supreme Court opinions. The Court, wrote Meiklejohn "is commissioned to interpret to us our own purposes, our own meanings."[29] It does so by applying principles to facts and values, not merely in the abstract, but in their bearing upon the concrete, immediate problems confronting our polity.

In the functional contract theory, the Supreme Court has a clearly legitimate role to play in our democracy. Unlike the competitive theories, democracy is not equated with the electoral process; rather, the entire governing process created in our political contract is called democratic.[30] Like Congress and the Presidency, the Supreme Court is a fully authorized agency of our government; it too is mentioned in the Constitution. We, the People, have assigned to this particular agency the delicate and important task of interpreting our laws, including the supreme law itself. A Justice adhering to this theory of democracy should feel no hesitancy in exercising the full range of judicial powers. He is merely doing his authorized task. Since this authority comes directly from the sovereign people via the Constitution, the exercise of judicial review is perfectly compatible with democracy.

In performing his assigned task, one contemporary member of the Supreme Court, Justice William J. Brennan, Jr., has placed great reliance upon Meiklejohn's interpretation of the First Amendment.[31] The clearest example of this reliance is found in *New York Times v. Sullivan* (1964).[32] To assist a civil rights campaign in Montgomery, Alabama, Dr. Martin Luther King's Southern Christian Leadership Conference had taken a full page advertisement attacking Police Commissioner Sullivan's handling of the demonstrations. The commissioner brought a civil libel action against the newspaper and four of the conference's leaders because the advertisement allegedly contained defamatory statements. Justice Brennan's opinion for the Supreme Court reversed a $500,000 judgment to Sullivan by the Alabama courts.

The Justice later said that "the case presented a classic example of an activity that Dr. Meiklejohn called an activity of 'governing importance' within the powers reserved to the people and made invulnerable to sanctions imposed by their agency-governments."³³ Like Meiklejohn, Brennan's "general proposition [was] that freedom of expression upon public questions is secured by the First Amendment."³⁴ He developed that general proposition by following two lines of argument long advocated by Meiklejohn.

The first was an historical argument. Justice Frankfurter and others frequently asserted that the Bill of Rights was not intended to lay down novel principles, but simply to embody certain common-law guarantees inherited from our English ancestors.³⁵ To counter this argument, Meiklejohn maintained that no revolutionary transfer of authority in the history of mankind surpasses in novelty, or in importance, that achievement of the body politic we call, "We, the People of the United States."³⁶

Justice Brennan bypasses the argument about the Framers' intent in 1787–1789 by maintaining that "a national awareness of the central meaning of the First Amendment" was "first crystallized" in "the great controversy over the Sedition Act of 1798."³⁷ A series of quotations from James Madison during that period enables the Justice to come down squarely on the side of Meiklejohn:

> [Madison's] premise was that the Constitution created a form of government under which "The people, not the government, possess the absolute sovereignty" . . . Earlier, in a debate in the House of Representatives, Madison had said: "If we advert to the nature of Republican government we shall find that the censorial power is in the people over the Government, and not in the Government over the people" . . . The right of free public discussions of the stewardship of public affairs was thus, in Madison's view, a fundamental principle of the American form of government.³⁸

Commenting on this language, Professor Harry Kalven, Jr., correctly noted the parallel with Meiklejohn's interpretation. For the first time a judicial opinion had asserted that the "(First) Amendment has a 'central meaning'— a core of protection of speech without which democracy cannot function, without which, in Madison's phrase, 'The censorial power' would be in the Government over the people and not 'in the people over the Government.'"³⁹

The second line of argument used by Justice Brennan to support that general proposition was based on an analogy to *Barr v. Matteo* (1959).⁴⁰ There the Court majority had held an utterance of a federal official to be absolutely privileged if made "within the outer perimeter" of his duties, because the threat of damage suits would "otherwise inhibit the fearless, vigorous, and effective administration of policies of government" and "dampen the ardor of all but the most resolute, or the most irresponsible, in the unflinching discharge of their duties."⁴¹ In the *New York Times* case, Justice Brennan held that "[a]nalogous considerations support the privilege for the citizen-critic of government. It is as much his duty to criticize as it is the official's duty to administer."⁴²

This analogy is, of course, the same one Meiklejohn made using Article 1, section 2(1) of the Constitution. Except for his failure to refer to the people as the Fourth Branch, Justice Brennan's opinion at this point is pure Meiklejohn.⁴³ Little wonder, then, that Professor Kalven could report the following exchange with Dr. Meiklejohn: "Before I had disclosed my own views, I asked him for his judgment of the *Times* case. 'It is,' he said, 'an occasion for dancing in the streets.'"⁴⁴

The holding of *New York Times* did not establish an absolute bar to civil or criminal libel actions brought by public officials. In *Garrison v. Louisiana* (1964),⁴⁵ Justice Brennan explained why he did not favor a total prohibition of such suits:

> The use of calculated falsehood . . . would put a different cast on the constitutional question. Although honest utterance, even if inaccurate, may further the fruitful exercise of the right of free speech, it does not follow that the lie, knowingly and deliberately published about a public official, should enjoy a like immunity . . . Calculated falsehood falls into a class of utterances which "are no essential part of any exposition of ideas and are of such slight social value as a step to truth that any benefit that may be derived from them is clearly outweighed by the social interest in order and morality" . . . Hence the knowingly false statement and the false statement made with reckless disregard of the truth, do not enjoy constitutional protection.⁴⁶

For Brennan, as for Meiklejohn, the limits of the protection afforded by the First Amendment were determined by the functional relationship between speech and self-government. The governing importance of speech entitled it to the absolute protection of the First Amendment. Speech which had no relation to the governing process, or which hindered that process, could be regulated by due process of law.⁴⁷

We shall presently evaluate the merits of this notion. We shall have to determine whether it is consistent with the idea of "a profound national commitment to the principle that debate on public issues should be uninhibited, robust, and wide-open."⁴⁸ The discussion of political freedom, however, is best postponed until we complete an analysis of the concepts of citizenship and political participation in this democratic theory.

AN ANALYSIS OF THE FUNCTIONAL CONTRACT THEORY

Citizenship

When we turn to the concept of citizenship in this political theory we must rely upon the work of Professor Tussman. Dr. Meiklejohn was primarily interested in questions of political freedom, and no Justice of the Supreme Court has squarely followed the functional contract theory in dealing with citizenship cases.

In any contract theory, a citizen is defined as a party to the basic social compact creating the body politic. The agreement of the people defines their political relatedness: it establishes the nature of their rights and obligations.

A contract theory also tells us something about how a person becomes a member of the body politic. The political theory of Meiklejohn and Tussman is no exception. The whole conception of an agreement to be self-governing demands that entry into the body politic be voluntarily and knowingly made. Any other treatment would render meaningless those aspects of political relatedness which most concern Meiklejohn and Tussman. In their theory, political freedom requires the voluntary agreement to participate in making public policy.[49]

Neither Meiklejohn nor Tussman can treat the process of consenting to the basic agreement as a myth, a fiction, or even as an ideal. Their argument that the United States is a self-governing polity requires *our* acceptance of the governmental purposes and structures of the Constitution.[50] Only in this way could the American people be regarded as self-governing.

Predicating citizenship upon a knowing and voluntary consent creates problems, as Professor Tussman admits. There is of course no question that the naturalized citizen's entry into the American body politic required such consent. The naturalization process demands an explicit recognition of the authority of our political arrangements. A person becomes a naturalized citizen by voluntarily and knowingly declaring himself "a party to the system of agreements which constitute the body politic."[51]

With a native-born person, however, this conception creates impressive difficulties. For him there are no commonly accepted rites of passage into American citizenship. Dr. Tussman is compelled to fall back upon the notion of tacit consent. He must then define the acts he regards as signifying that a person has tacitly become a party to the system of agreements which constitute the body politic. His difficulty lies in the fact that if tacit consent is to be treated as the full equivalent of express consent, it cannot be an unconscious or accidental act.[52]

No action of American citizens, however, seems to imply a knowing and voluntary agreement to join the body politic. Little wonder, then, that Tuss-

man decries our practice of robbing the "pledge of allegiance" of any significance by making it a ritual.[53] We have neglected to teach our native-born
what it means to be a citizen in a self-governing polity.[54] Tussman laments
this situation, but he will not cut his political theory to fit the facts. Only to
the extent that membership in a body politic involves a knowing and voluntary
consent can he speak meaningfully about political freedom and self-government.

The insistence upon consent also creates problems for Professor Tussman
when he discusses a person's separation from the body politic. He recognizes
that "the quality of freedom in our membership" is enhanced "if, in addition
to its being voluntarily entered into, there is a continuing option of withdrawal."[55] Consent, then, appears to be in a process of constant renewal. This
enrichment of freedom leads Tussman to accept the idea of voluntary
withdrawal.

He would, however, place some limitations on the right of an individual
to withdraw from the body politic. To protect the integrity of the individual's
decision, the government can create procedures which will ensure it was a
deliberate as opposed to a hasty act.[56] Tussman also believes the right of
withdrawal cannot be used to avoid the obligations of citizenship.[57] The
refusal to surrender one's private judgment and interest to this public judgment about the public interest can only lead to anarchy. If, therefore, the
appropriate governmental agencies have established a selective service system
to meet a public need, the individual is obligated to recognize the legitimacy
of that decision.[58] To protect the integrity of the body politic, Tussman would
impose limitations on the individual choice to withdraw from society. Systemic needs have curtailed the very option he saw as enhancing the quality
of freedom.

It is not surprising, then, that Tussman finds the problem raised by the
expatriation cases a complicated one. On the one hand he does not wish to
surrender the *individual's* right to accept or reject membership in the American
body politic; despite the fact that his actions may embarrass or offend us,
the choice should still be his. On the other hand, Dr. Tussman's concern for
the needs of our political system makes it difficult for him to accept the idea
that there is nothing a person may do by which he forfeits his citizenship.[59]
In the end he is unable to resolve this problem created by the tensions within
his theory.

Although the functional contract theory cannot provide clear guidance
for handling the issue of expatriation, it does have a concept of citizenship
not found in the competitive theories of democracy. "Its basic assertion is
that every citizen has two distinct roles to play. Each is a member, a subject,
a private person free within the common limits to pursue his own ends. But
each is also an agent of the body politic, a ruler, a member of the sovereign

tribunal with all of the duties, obligations, and responsibilities that go with that role."[60]

In this theory, a citizen and a subject, at least in a democracy, are not regarded as equivalent. The latter is subjected to decisions in the making of which he had no effective share. He is not self-governing; he is not politically free. A citizen is more than a subject; he is a participant in the governing process.[61]

Political Participation

Like the competitive theories of democracy, then, functional contract theory uses the concept of political participation to distinguish a citizen from a subject. If, in Tussman's words, "the *essential* feature of a democratic polity is its concern for the participation of the member in the process by which the community is governed,"[62] that concept cannot be reduced, as in the competitive theories, to the act of voting. A too close identification of political participation with the exercise of the franchise lends itself, as we have seen, to a marked distinction between the rulers and ruled. That dichotomy is incompatible with functional contract theory which asserts that We, the People, are both the rulers and the ruled. The sovereign people are not to be thought of as passive, slumbering subjects but as active participating rulers— the Fourth and highest branch of government.

Unfortunately, Meiklejohn never adequately explored the institutional changes which would be necessary to sustain any mass political participation going significantly beyond the act of voting. Dr. Meiklejohn did little more with his conception of the Fourth Branch than to stress the importance of recognizing the sovereign authority of the people and the absolute nature of our political freedoms. He was not opposed to institutional changes; he just thought them secondary to a reordering of our political values.[63]

Insofar as Meiklejohn had reference to anything other than existing institutions, it was to the New England town meeting. He regarded that institution "as a model by which free political procedures may be measured."[64] The democracy envisioned by functional contract theorists is obviously based on their conception of that institution: private men come to the public forum and determine public policy by asserting, justifying, and deciding claims in terms of the public interest.

In focusing on that institution, however, Meiklejohn tended to ignore the society upon which it was based. The town meeting flourished in a remarkably unified society where private claims differed in degree, not in kind. The New England Puritan went into the town meeting with full knowledge of the unity of his community and was far from hospitable to radically divergent opinions. The focus on the public interest was more a "given" created by the nature of society than a product of that type of forum. The pluralism which accompanied industrialization destroyed the town meeting. The community was fragmented by powerful and widely divergent private interests. Pluralistic man went into the public forum to assert his claims, and the intense competitive nature of these claims destroyed the sense of community. Pluralistic compromise became the price of unity. That contention at least has been the argument of most American social theorists since the last quarter of the nineteenth century.[65] Meiklejohn never explained why they were wrong.

Dr. Meiklejohn always deplored the submersion of the public good in the scramble for private interest. In foregoing a discussion of institutional changes, however, he provided little guidance for reasserting the primacy of a commitment to the public interest. Moreover, in the one institution he does mention, he blithely overlooked the tension between his participatory theory of democracy and the social conformity which in the past had been required to support that forum. As a result, exhortation became a substitute for analytic and/or imaginative suggestions for enhancing the quality of political participation. Exhortation is not the most enlightening approach for a self-proclaimed effort at political education.

In *Obligation and the Body Politic*, Professor Tussman also shunned a discussion of structural changes. He argued that only a proper political education will enable us "to transform ourselves from domestic into political animals."[66] The goal was clear. It was nothing less than "the reshaping of the electorate into a genuinely deliberative tribunal capable of dealing responsibly with fundamental issues."[67] He did not, in that work, discuss the methods, tools, and structures for achieving that goal. Instead of talking about innovative means for enhancing popular participation in the political process, he emphasized the necessity of delegation. In a society as complex as ours, technology begets specialization and specialization begets delegation. Tussman insisted that popular participation should not be viewed as an alternative to delegation; there must be sufficient participation to maintain the credibility of the idea of self-government. The free citizen, Tussman urged, should "persist in the demand for *constitutionality* which, with all its complexity, reflects the vitality of the demand that government be the creature of agreement."[68]

Professor Tussman thus stripped the concept of political participation of its claim to an independent birthright; he made it the handmaiden of the demand for constitutional government. This act was only the first step in Dr. Tussman's exposition. In the next, as the quotation indicates, he related the refusal to abdicate self-government to the delegation of authority. We are bound by our representatives' actions only insofar as they are truly taken on behalf of the body politic.[69] The discussion which began with the citizen's *participation* now focused on the *representatives'* duty to subordinate private interest to public interest. When our agents accept that responsibility, government remains "a creature of agreement," the "demand for constitutionality" is satisfied, and the sovereign authority of the people is maintained. The problem for Tussman, then, was one of ensuring that our agents will remain faithful to their charge.

So a theorist who stressed the self-governing nature of the American polity saw the principal need of our political system as "agent[s] who by endowment and the training of mind and character can play the public role."[70] Only those cast in the mold of Plato's Guardians could satisfactorily function as Tussman's representatives. Since people who combine wisdom, character, and power in the right measure are currently in short supply, he fell back upon a call for confronting "our greatest unmet . . . challenge"—"the education of the ruler, of the political agent."[71]

Our comprehension would have been increased had Professor Tussman fully explored the ways people would participate in a self-governing polity and discussed the structural changes required by this theory. Madison's Constitution has been our principal educator. We have learned our political values from the spirit of our laws.[72] Tussman was deeply upset by our political values. He saw the need for reform, but he did not identify that need with specific institutional changes. He did not indicate how we can overcome the structural bias which leads us to staff the public tribunals with individuals he deems spiritually alien to their functions and purposes. Instead, Tussman identified participation with the demand for constitutionality and left unresolved the tension between Madison's Constitution and the functional contract of democracy. It will take more than novel sentiments to overcome the values legitimized by our current institutional patterns. New tribunals will be required to shape new values, to nourish popular participation on behalf of public values. Without them, we lack a way of educating ourselves for the demands of self-government.

Fortunately, in a later work, *Government and the Mind* (1977), Professor Tussman did address the need to create new institutional patterns for nourishing public participation. That work adds a significant dimension to functional contract theory. Though it is far from a complete blueprint of needed changes, it is a welcome beginning. The work is discussed in chapter 11. Here it is only important to realize that without substantial institutional changes, functional contract theory, for all its rhetoric, could not plausibly establish the people as the Fourth and sovereign branch.

Functional contract theory has had no observable impact on Supreme Court opinions dealing with such structural aspects of political participation as reapportionment. The emphasis within the theory on full participation certainly points in the direction of the Court's "one person, one vote" standard; so, too, does Dr. Meiklejohn's view that an individual's right to vote is absolutely protected by the First Amendment. Dr. Tussman interprets equal protection to mean the "equal claim of each private person to public consideration," the denial "that there are first-class and second-class citizens," and the prohibition of "discrimination or special favor" by the body politic.[73] It is therefore not surprising that Justice Brennan, the leading judicial adherent of the functional contract theory, wrote several significant opinions based upon the "one person, one vote" standard.[74]

The cases which established that standard, however, were authored by Justices who cannot easily be classified as adherents of functional contract theory of democracy. The Court's reapportionment revolution, therefore, including Justice Brennan's contributions, are discussed in chapters 8 and 10.[75]

The functional contract theory, as found in the works of Professors Meiklejohn and Tussman discussed here and in the opinions of Justice Brennan, supports the equal population standard. It is a significant, positive element of the theory, for, as Chief Justice Burger said, "The voting rights cases . . . have represented the Court's efforts to strengthen the political system by assuring a higher level of fairness and responsiveness to the political process."[76] It should be noted, however, that until Professor Tussman undertook to investigate the full dimensions of political participation the theory's most distinctive aspect was lost. Its central focus is the citizen's role in a democratic society. Unlike the competition theories of democracy, functional contract theory uses the concept of citizenship for emphasizing the importance of actively belonging to a democratic society.

Political Freedom

Professor Tussman has only recently begun to talk about institutional changes. For exactly the same reason as the competitive theories of democracy—the failure to present a meaningful picture of a self-governing mass society—the ultimate justification for the functional contract theory turns on the concept of political freedom. Fortunately, we are in a good position to evaluate this part of the theory. Dr. Meiklejohn was primarily concerned with issues of political freedom. His extensive writings on that subject have had a significant impact on our constitutional law. Supreme Court cases, therefore, provide an excellent vehicle for comprehending this aspect of the functional contract theory of democracy.

All the major cases involving the Communist Party with which we have been concerned were decided before 1964, that is, before Meiklejohn's interpretation of the First Amendment had any visible impact on the Justices. Nonetheless, in one or another of his many articles Dr. Meiklejohn commented on each of those cases. There is no doubt how a Justice sharing his democratic theory would have decided those cases or what his opinion would have said.

Like Justice Frankfurter, Meiklejohn did not doubt that such laws as the Smith Act, the Subversive Activities Control Act of 1950, and the Security Act of 1954 restricted the exercise of free speech and assembly. Also like the Justice, he recognized that the fundamental problem the acts raised was one of reconciling the conflicting claims of national security and political freedom.[77] Unlike Frankfurter, however, Meiklejohn always insisted that the "essential meaning of the First Amendment is that, already, in the making and maintaining of the Constitution, the procedure of 'balancing' has been undertaken and completed."[78]

To Meiklejohn the Constitution's meaning was straightforward and clear. "Congress is not the Government. It is one of three *subordinate* agencies established by the Government with limited and specific powers." We, the People, in exercising our sovereign authority, have directed Congress to use its powers to "prevent evils;" but, we have not given Congress the power to abridge political freedom. On the contrary, the sovereign governing body "has clearly and unequivocally, on the basis of long deliberation, declared that *Congress* shall *not* have, shall *not* exercise, that authority."[79] Only the sovereign tribunal can make that determination when, in its judgment, a limitation seems advisable.

Until that time, our governing decisions should be made in accordance with the Constitution, and the "Constitution of the United States, as it was adopted and as it now stands, does not give equal status to the duty of self-preservation and the duty of maintaining Political Freedom. On the contrary, our 'experiment' in self-government makes that freedom an absolute, while self-preservation is a conditional and relative consequence of it."[80] Political freedom is an absolute because our whole history, according to Meiklejohn, tells us that the ultimate, though not the only, interest of our Constitution is that of creating and maintaining a self-governing polity. Self-preservation has actually been a consequence of the First Amendment. Despite the undoubted risks involved, whatever the apparent balance of immediate gains and losses, history has justified the belief that political freedom gives a better assurance of national security than does any program of political repression.[81]

Congress may, of course, legislate against forceful or violent action against the government and the overt preparation for such an act. Congress may even prohibit *incitement* to such action—an utterance so closely related to a specific overt act that it may be regarded and treated as part of the act itself. These activities have nothing to do with the political activities by which free men govern themselves, and are not protected by the First Amendment.[82] "An advocacy, on the other hand, even up to the limit of arguing and planning for the violent overthrow of the existing form of government, is one of those opinion-forming, judgment-making expressions which free men need to utter and to hear as citizens responsible for the governing of the nation."[83]

Unlike Justice Harlan,[84] Dr. Meiklejohn did not believe the advocacy of ideas was protected by the First Amendment while advocacy of action could be regulated. For him, the distinction upon which the application of the First Amendment rested was between advocacy of action and "incitement to action." Advocacy was protected no matter what was advocated; incitement could be regulated and/or proscribed.

Dr. Meiklejohn, therefore, would have upheld the defendants' claims in the *Dennis*[85] and *Yates*[86] cases. To "make the advocacy of revolution a criminal offense, as the Smith Act does, is to violate the basic principle of political freedom."[87] Rather than saying, as Justice Frankfurter did, that the advocacy of Communist Party doctrine must necessarily rank low in any scale of constitutional values,[88] Dr. Meiklejohn made it part of the fundamental political process of self-government.

Since Meiklejohn did not believe the First Amendment permitted Congress to outlaw an association, group, or party because it advocated a policy of violent overthrow of the existing government, the only additional factor posed by the 1961 *Subversive Activities Control Board* case was whether the allegation that the Communist Party was subservient to some foreign country could justify the registration provision of the 1950 Subversive Activities Control Act. Justice Frankfurter, in his opinion for the Court, had made much of that second factor in upholding the statute.[89] Meiklejohn, however, would have rejected the very administrative and legislative "findings" upon which Frankfurter relied.

By his standards, the evidence did not prove "control" by a foreign power, only ideological agreement. In the Soviet Union, the government can control the Communist Party because it can enforce its orders through the police and military. In the United States, however, the Soviet government can only "enforce" its "orders" by dismissals from the Party. In fact, in the United States, membership in the Party is a disability and resignation often brings rewards. This situation led Dr. Meiklejohn to conclude that people "do not accept Communist beliefs because they are members of the party. They are members of the party because they accept Communist beliefs."[90]

Similarly, he maintained that the membership sections of the Smith Act involved in the *Scales*[91] and *Noto*[92] cases were unconstitutional. Since he did not think the federal government had demonstrated that the Communist Party as an association was engaged in illegal acts, he argued that membership in the Communist Party was protected by the First Amendment.

Over the years, Meiklejohn found many reasons for opposing legislative attempts to compel testimony from alleged Communists. He objected to the vagueness of the committees' authorizations,[93] and to their procedures.[94] Nor could he understand why Justices like Frankfurter and Harlan were willing to accept the Fifth Amendment's privilege against self-incrimination as a ban to further inquiry but were unwilling to institute the same ban for claims based on the First Amendment. Such an interpretation gave the Fifth Amendment clause a superior constitutional status to the First Amendment. When a person sought to avoid his *own* self-incrimination his claim was not balanced away. This interpretation of the Fifth Amendment contradicted a fundamental premise of Frankfurter and Harlan that no constitutional provision was absolute. It also, Meiklejohn noted, reflected a distorted sense of constitutional priorities.[95]

His fundamental objection, however, was that the First Amendment forbids any subordinate agency of government from asking, under compulsion to answer, for a citizen's political commitments. It is an invasion of the "reserved" governing powers of the people. To ask a man, "Are you now or have you ever been a Communist?" violates the constitutional authority of "one who governs to make up his own mind without fear or favor, with the independence and freedom in which self-government consists."[96]

There is no doubt that a Justice employing functional contract theory would have held unconstitutional the legislative investigations involved in *Watkins*,[97] *Barenblatt*,[98] and *Gibson*.[99] When Congress "supervises" the political activity of the citizen—his speech, his advocacy, his memberships—the priority of public necessity over private expression is not asserted; rather, the relation between the subordinate branches and the Fourth branch of government is radically altered.

For the same reasons, Meiklejohn's interpretation of the First Amendment would bar any citizen, under threat of penalty, from being required to take an oath as to his beliefs. Under this interpretation, the loyalty oaths involved in *Cramp v. Board of Public Instruction* (1961),[100] *Baggett v. Bullitt* (1964),[101] and *Elfbrandt v. Russell* (1966)[102] were unconstitutional, not for the reasons stated in the Court opinions, but simply because no agency is authorized to inquire into the political ideas of the citizenry. Similarly, the loyalty program involved in *Keyishian v. Board of Regents* (1967)[103] would not have been held unconstitutional for the statutes' vagueness and overbreadth, but solely because the political activities of the citizenry are protected by the First Amendment.[104]

Not that either Meiklejohn or Tussman would interpret the Constitution as barring all loyalty-security type programs. Their concern for the functional necessities of government clearly indicates that narrowly drawn regulations, designed for specifically demarcated "sensitive" positions and based upon the requirement of *loyalty* in action, would be constitutional. But "loyalty may never be tested on grounds of adherence to, or rejection of, any *belief*."[105]

Under this standard, it would have been impossible for the federal government to have impugned the loyalty of the distinguished nuclear physicist, J. Robert Oppenheimer, by denying him security clearance after conceding his proven loyalty to this nation.[106]

The pattern emerging from Dr. Meiklejohn's comments on our various post–World War II, anti-Communist programs is quite unlike the democratic theories based upon the competitive paradigm. It is not like the balancing doctrine of the Realists which all too frequently subordinated political freedom to governmental claims about the need for self-preservation; nor is it like the Optimalists' willingness to tolerate only as much political freedom as they deem consistent with the needs of an orderly society. Of course, Meiklejohn's approach has nothing at all in common with the fear of political diversity usually found among our most rabid anti-Communist witch-hunters. Rather, Meiklejohn's interpretation of the First Amendment is based upon his faith that our real security lies in the complete, total, and absolute political freedom of our people, and a political theory which makes that freedom the core of democratic self-government.

The same commitment to the "principle that debate on public issues should be uninhibited, robust and wide-open" emerges from an analysis of the NAACP cases. Meiklejohn applauded Justice Harlan's opinion in *NAACP v. Alabama* (1958)[107] which explicitly held, for the first time, that the right of association was protected by the First Amendment. Similarly, he supported the Court opinions which protected the privacy of membership in that association against Southern efforts to compel disclosure.[108] Meiklejohn did not agree with the balancing and preference doctrines found in those opinions and he never did understand why the Court persisted in applying one First Amendment rule to the NAACP and another to the Communist Party. Still, he recognized the Court had succeeded in thwarting the Southern attack on the NAACP and that, as a result, political freedom in America was enhanced.

Meiklejohn's distinctive interpretation of the First Amendment begins to emerge in Justice Brennan's opinion for the Court in *NAACP v. Button* (1963).[109] In holding that Virginia's attempt to stifle law suits against the status quo was unconstitutional, Justice Brennan first held that litigation by a group like the NAACP is a form of political expression covered by the First Amendment. "Groups which find themselves unable to achieve their objectives through the ballot frequently turn to the courts . . . And under the conditions of modern government, litigation may well be the sole practicable avenue open to a minority to petition for redress of grievances."[110] The concern for enhancing the political freedom of all our citizens led Justice Brennan, like Meiklejohn, to expand the scope of the First Amendment.

The same concern led Justice Brennan to hold that the Court would not uphold vague statutes that impinge upon First Amendment rights. In the area of political expression the standards for permissible statutory vagueness must be strict. The threat of sanctions may deter political freedom almost as potently as the applications of sanctions. "Because First Amendment freedoms need *breathing space* to survive, government may regulate in the area only with narrow specificity."[111] Justice Brennan then held that the Virginia statute, on its face, did not provide ample "breathing space" for political freedoms.[112]

Justice Brennan had thus not only extended the scope of activities covered by the First Amendment, he had also developed a metaphor—the "breathing space" notion—to protect all political freedoms. Although he then went on to use the preferred freedoms doctrine as an alternate basis for holding the Virginia law unconstitutional,[113] Justice Brennan was clearly approaching Meiklejohn's interpretation in the first part of his opinion. That he had not quite arrived at that view of the First Amendment is evident from his reliance on the vagueness doctrine; for, under Meiklejohn's interpretation, once an activity is protected by the First Amendment it cannot be limited even by a precisely worded ordinance.

In *Dombrowski v. Pfister* (1965),[114] Justice Brennan extended the "breathing space" notion to a point where it was hard to distinguish it from the Meiklejohn interpretation enunciated in his *New York Times* opinion of the previous year. Dombrowski and other individuals were connected with the Southern Conference Educational Fund, a civil rights organization. They sought to restrain Louisiana officials from prosecuting or threatening to prosecute the fund or its officers for alleged violation of Louisiana's Subversive Activities and Communist Control Law, and Communist Propaganda Law.

The threshold question was whether federal courts could issue injunctive relief against *threatened* state prosecutions in order to protect free expression. The traditional answer, the one given by the District Court and by Justices Harlan and Clark in dissent, was that in order to spare our federal system from premature federal judicial interference, the injunction should not be issued. A possible narrowing construction by the state courts might adequately protect the First Amendment rights involved. If not, those rights could be vindicated in the course of the normal adjudication of state criminal prosecution, including an appeal to the United States Supreme Court.

Justice Brennan's opinion for the Court claimed this was a situation in which a defense in a state criminal prosecution would not assure adequate vindication of those constitutional rights. "For free expression—of transcendent value to all society and not merely to those exercising their rights—might be the loser . . . The *chilling effect* upon the exercise of First Amendment rights may derive from the fact of prosecution, unaffected by the prospects of its success or failure."[115] When vaguely drawn state statutes impinge upon First Amendment rights, the federal courts should not abstain.

By citing his own *Button* opinion as authority for the last sentence, Justice Brennan was indicating a new, enlarged view of the constitutional protections afforded political freedoms. Not only did those rights need "breathing space," he now believed their sensitive nature required the Court to shield them from the "chilling effects" of governmental actions. If he had applied that criterion in the earlier case, he would have had no reason to employ the preferred freedoms doctrine in *Button* even as an alternate line of reasoning. The latter doctrine is, after all, one type of balance test, while the "chilling effect" metaphor suggests that no government action having a deleterious impact on political freedom could be sustained regardless of the weight of competing interests. In his *Dombrowski* opinion, Justice Brennan had no recourse to any balancing. The "chilling effect" notion seems indistinguishable from Meiklejohn's position.

Justice Brennan was merging his "breathing space" metaphor into Meiklejohn's interpretation. The right of free expression in his *Dombrowski* opinion was seen as a transcendent societal value and not merely as the private interest of a single individual. That viewpoint is pure Meiklejohn. As authority for that statement, Justice Brennan cited his own opinion in *Garrison*, a case in which he had applied the *New York Times* standard and a case which he himself has cited as following the Meiklejohn interpretation of the First Amendment.[116]

Upon first analysis, then, the functional contract theory seems capable of fulfilling the most important claim of its proponents: an enhancement of our political freedom. It may be doubted that this enlarged view of First Amendment rights is sufficient to provide, by itself, a meaningful concept of citizenship or the stimulus for greater public political participation. Nonetheless, the conceptual achievement—Meiklejohn's interpretation of the First Amendment—should not be minimized. If that standard were conscientiously followed by our public officials, the liberties of all Americans would be in a healthier condition. The right of Communists and other radicals to propagate their views would never be in jeopardy of being balanced away. The political freedom of dissident racial minorities to press for a change would not be limited by the toleration of the majority—it would be theirs as a matter of constitutionally protected and legally enforceable right. The vast majority of Americans would benefit from a fuller, more varied expression of public issues. These are not small benefits, and their attainment seems feasible upon adoption of the functional contract theory.

Committed civil libertarians, however, have not rushed to embrace Meiklejohn's theory. While the cases analyzed above may show that interpretation to its best advantage, they do not exhaust the full range of issues involving political freedoms. When other lines of cases are considered, problems begin to emerge. With those problems comes a hesitancy about the wholesale adoption of the functional contract theory.

The first problem deals with the difficulty in defining the boundaries of the political freedoms entitled to absolute protection. While one of the appealing features of the functional contract theory is the attempt to create an area of absolute freedom, that freedom is limited to the public realm. What is the nature of public expression covered by the First Amendment as distinct from the private speech covered by the Due Process Clauses? We are by no means sure where public speech begins and private expression ends.

Take, for example, the constitutional problem raised in obscenity cases. Professor Kalven, surely a friendly and knowledgeable interpreter, believed that under Meiklejohn's interpretation not all art and belles lettres were covered by the First Amendment. If the people need free speech primarily in order to govern themselves, Kalven reasoned, not all forms of communication have a governing importance. Any speech without a governing importance presumably would be subject to regulations conforming to due process.[117]

The parallel between this reading of the functional contract theory and the opinions of Justice Brennan in the obscenity cases is striking. In his opinion for the Court in *Roth v. United States* (1957),[118] Justice Brennan argued that the constitutional "protection given speech and press was fashioned to assure unfettered interchange of ideas for the bringing about of political and social changes desired by the people."[119] All ideas having even the slightest redeeming social importance—however unorthodox, controversial, or even hateful to the prevailing climate of opinion—have the full protection of the First Amendment. Because obscenity is utterly without redeeming social importance, it is not within the area of constitutionally protected speech or press.[120]

Given this interpretation of the First Amendment, Justice Brennan correctly recognized the importance of creating a standard for judging obscenity which would also provide an adequate safeguard for nonobscene material. Unfortunately, neither Justice Brennan nor any other Justice has been able to provide such a standard, and the resulting confusion has led one commentator to dub the obscenity opinions the "Grapes of Roth."[121]

The chief difficulty, of course, has been the attempt to maintain that obscenity is without the slightest redeeming social importance. Obscenity may be used as a critical device to attack public policies—witness the comedy routines of the late Lenny Bruce.[122] Obscenity may also be used to undermine broad social attitudes which affect public policies—witness the attacks on Puritan morality in much of our contemporary literature. Art, music, and entertainment shape men's minds at least as much as political discussions. To allow governmental regulation of even part of those forms of communication is to limit the range of ideas available to the public. For this last reason

Meiklejohn eventually came to argue that all forms of art and literature are protected by the First Amendment.[123] For essentially the same reasons, Justice Brennan also came eventually to that conclusion.[124]

It is only right and proper that Meiklejohn have the last say about what his interpretation means. The fact remains, however, that two such sympathetic and knowledgeable supporters as Professor Kalven and Justice Brennan reasonably thought obscenity was not of governing importance. That fact indicates that Meiklejohn's boundaries between "public" and "private" speech are far from clear.

The boundary problem also emerges in the area of libel. In his last major paper, Professor Meiklejohn argued that libel provided a good example of the distinction he had in mind. In cases of a private action—when one individual damages another by tongue or pen—the First Amendment affords no protection to the persons sued because the attack has no relation to the business of governing. If, however, the same thing was said to demonstrate a person's unfitness for public office, the act should properly be regarded as a type of citizen participation in government protected by the First Amendment. "Though private libel is subject to legislative control, political or seditious libel is not."[125] This reasoning lies behind the standard employed by Justice Brennan in his *New York Times* opinion. When, however, is a person acting in his public capacity and when is he solely a private man? What, in other words, are the boundaries of the "public conduct" concept?

In the *New York Times* case, the attack on Commissioner Sullivan clearly related to his activities as supervisor of the Montgomery Police Department. The *Garrison* case clearly involved the New Orleans District Attorney's criticism of the official conduct of certain state court judges.[126] In *Rosenblatt v. Baer* (1966),[127] however, the scope of the "public official" designation under *New York Times* was itself at issue. Some of Rosenblatt's columns in the *Laconia Evening Citizen* were sharply critical of the way the Belknap Recreation Area had been managed by Baer and the county commissioners by whom he was employed. Justice Brennan's opinion for the Court rejected the argument that the *New York Times* rule should apply only to elected officials:

> Criticism of government is at the very center of the constitutionally protected area of free discussion. Criticism of those responsible for government operations must be free, lest criticism of government be penalized. It is clear, therefore, that the "public official" designation applies at the very least to those among the hierarchy of government employees who have, or appear to the public to have, substantial responsibility for or control over the conduct of governmental affairs.[128]

Quite obviously, Justice Brennan was willing to apply the *New York Times* standard to cover the official conduct of almost any minor governmental official. To recover damages for libel that official would have to prove that the attacks upon his conduct were false and that they were made with a knowledge of their falsity or with a reckless disregard of their veracity.[129]

Confusion reigned among the judges on federal and state courts. Some courts limited the *New York Times* libel standard to actual public officials.[130] Others applied it to cover politically controversial activities of well-known individuals such as General Edwin Walker and Linus Pauling.[131] Some judges read the *New York Times* rule as prohibiting awards for libel in any case involving the discussion of public issues unless actual malice was proved,[132] while other judges limited that test to public officials and to those who by their own actions thrust themselves into the vortex of public controversy.[133]

In the midst of this confusion the Supreme Court decided *Time, Inc. v. Hill* (1967).[134] In the prevailing opinion, Justice Brennan did not read the *New York Times* standard as applying only to comment about public officials or even to political expression.[135] To fulfill their function in this democracy, the constitutional guarantees of speech and press "must embrace all issues about which information is needed or appropriate to enable the members of society to cope with the exigencies of their period."[136] Nor could any meaningful distinction be made between fiction and nonfiction. An exception for fiction would deprive a great deal of valuable communication of its constitutional protection.[137] The *New York Times* actual malice test must be applied to all communications of public concern.

Unfortunately, Justice Brennan's opinion was far from clear when it came to indicating the criteria distinguishing matters of public concern from those concerning only private individuals. What made the incident involving the Hill family a matter of public concern? After all, Hill was a private individual, not a public official. He had not deliberately thrust his family into the public arena. Far from it, he had done all within his power, including moving from Pennsylvania to Connecticut, to protect the privacy of his family life. Furthermore, the incident involving Hill was two and a half years old when the *Life* article was published, so it does not readily lend itself to being called a newsworthy event which should automatically be considered a matter of public interest. Justice Brennan dealt with none of these factors and, therefore, he did not adequately explain why a magazine's sensationalized account about the opening of a Broadway play had made this part of Hill's life a matter of public concern.[138]

Perhaps Justice Brennan had come to accept fully Meiklejohn's contention that all forms of art and literature are of governing importance. By definition, then, discussions in works of art which dealt with actual incidents would be considered public matters and would be entitled to the protection of the *New York Times* standard. Only in libel cases involving comments about the private lives of individuals would that stringent standard not apply.[139]

If this rationale was indeed behind Justice Brennan's language, it cannot provide an intelligible standard for distinguishing public discussion from private comment. On the one hand, he was unwilling to automatically exclude fictionalized material from the protection of the *New York Times* standard on the perfectly understandable grounds that such communication is often of public concern. On the other hand, he seemed unwilling to treat comments in works of art or comments about such works in the same manner he treated other statements dealing with an individual's private life. All three types of communication, however, can have the same destructive impact on the private realm. Because Justice Brennan's opinion did not come to grips with this possibility, four Justices refused to sign his opinion; they did not think he had adequately protected the right of privacy.[140]

The distinction between public and private sphere is central to the functional contract theory. That distinction should be one of the theory's most attractive features. Defining an area of individual privacy has become a primary need in modern society. Neither Meiklejohn nor Brennan, however, provided a meaningful boundary, and that failure made people skeptical of the theory's utility. Justices Harlan, Clark, Stewart, and Fortas, for example, shared their brother Brennan's concern for protecting the right of privacy; yet these Justices came to believe that *New York Times* did not provide a rational standard for handling libel cases. In light of the *Hill* case, these men did not think that standard gave adequate protection to society's pervasive and strong interest in preventing and redressing attacks upon private reputations.[141] Since none of these Justices shared Brennan's theory of democracy,[142] it is hardly surprising that his inability to make a sharp and clear distinction between public and private spheres made it impossible for him to lead the Court. His brethren proposed other tests to protect the right of privacy.[143] On the issues posed by libel cases, Justice Brennan became an army of one.[144]

The most difficult problem confronting proponents of the functional contract theory has been delimiting the public forum. Meiklejohn himself was unwilling to have the discussion of public issues confined to formal assemblies. In this country, he maintained, the facilities for active discussions among members of our self-governing society were virtually nonexistent. He thought it imperative that we enlarge freedom by establishing cultural centers in every village, town, and district, where all citizens, as they may choose, could meet together for the consideration of public policy. Largely because of the failure to make such provisions for free and unhindered public discussion, streets, parks, and similar community facilities must be considered public forums.[145]

Professor Kalven attempted to develop a concept of the public forum which encompassed this idea.[146] His thesis took the form of three interrelated propositions. First, parks and streets should be considered public communication facilities analogous to public meeting halls. For support, he relied on the cases which dealt with Justice Roberts's famous dictum that when a citizen goes into the streets to communicate his thoughts about public questions he is exercising an immemorial right of a free man.[147] If Kalven had chosen to develop his argument without relying upon these cases, he surely would have based it on the principle that minorities must enjoy as easy access to public opinion as the majority. A demonstration has significant publicity advantages over more conventional forms of political expression, since it can attract extensive news coverage and thereby arouse widespread interest. As a result, for persons with an unpopular position or without financial resources, a demonstration or mass meeting may be the only effective means to publicize their message. Nor is it sufficient to provide an American version of London's Hyde Park, an area deliberately designed to isolate spokesmen for minority viewpoints. The people must truly be able to communicate with each other and, absent other facilities, the streets and parks must serve as public forums. This line of argument explains why Kalven can say that the "generosity and empathy with which such facilities are made available is an index of freedom."

Second, to view streets, parks, and other public places as suitable sites for political communication means that the people have a constitutional right to engage in political activity at such locations. While the government may impose certain regulations on the use of those facilities, it may not ban all political activity from the streets and parks. Professor Kalven thus rejected the distinction between "pure speech" and "speech plus"—i.e. expression inextricably intertwined with conduct. Kalven believed that the very category called "speech plus" indicated that this form of political activity was "summarily subject to regulation."[148] He knew that if the streets could be used as a public forum, then any use of that kind of facility necessarily involved "speech plus." You do not take to the streets to raise a fine point of political theory in quiet discussion or through a learned journal. The open forum demands that one be outspoken whether in the use of oratory, pamphlets, or picket signs. In that kind of arena, there is no intelligible rationale for distinguishing "pure speech" from "speech plus." "If it is oral, it is noise and may interrupt someone else; if it's written, it may be litter."[149] In either case there are collateral consequences which invite regulation just as mass demonstrations do. The important thing is what they have in common—the communication of ideas.

Since the groups most likely to resort to the public forum were those lacking easy access to institutionalized communication media, such regulation could be used to prevent certain points of view from being expressed at all.

In the interests of furthering political freedom, it was much better, Kalven maintained, to treat *all* means of communicating ideas simply as speech.

His concern for giving a hearing to all points of view led Professor Kalven to his third proposition in which he made a distinction between regulations like Roberts' Rules of Order and regulation of content. Following Meiklejohn, he thought time, manner, and place regulations were essential for "the rational use of speech resources."[150] Despite the differences between streets and parks on the one hand, and a town meeting (Meiklejohn's example of a public forum) on the other, Kalven thought that "Roberts' Rules are a happy analogy because they make it so clear that the concern ought not to be with censorship, or with the content of what is said; what is needed is a phasing or timing of the activity, not a ban on it."[151]

The problems posed by Kalven's enlarged view of what constitutes a public forum become apparent in the Supreme Court cases involving mass demonstrations against racial inequality. For example, the second issue in *Cox v. Louisiana* (1965)[152] involved a conviction for violating a state law forbidding obstruction of a public sidewalk. There was no doubt among the Justices that the mass demonstration had indeed obstructed the public sidewalks. In his opinion for the five-man majority, Justice Goldberg argued that mass demonstrations were "speech plus." In reversing the Reverend Cox's conviction, Goldberg had indicated the judicial necessity for accommodating the competing interests—Cox's fundamental right of free speech and the state's need to maintain orderly traffic patterns.[153] To Professor Kalven, the Court majority clearly did not subscribe to his concept of the public forum. He thought this part of *Cox* should have been decided on the theory which holds that orderly mass demonstrations are a method of communication as fully protected by the First Amendment as any other form of expression. Although demonstrations may interfere with the public use of the streets for transportation, the right to the streets is such that demonstrations cannot be totally prohibited and they can be regulated only for weighty reasons.[154]

How weighty these reasons have to be is evident from Professor Kalven's unhappiness with the way the Court disposed of the third conviction in the *Cox* case, involving the charge of picketing near a courthouse. The Court, it will be recalled, was united in the belief that this statute was a proper means of protecting judicial proceedings from mob intimidation.[155] Kalven thought the Court's blanket endorsement of this limitation on the public forum unpersuasive. Not all demonstrations near a courthouse are designed to, or actually do, interfere with the judicial process.[156]

What saved this aspect of the *Cox* opinions, according to Kalven, was the explicit stress on the narrowness and precision of the statute.[157] While the Court should take due notice of specific legislative judgments, the Justices should not let that factor automatically override a democratic society's interest in a wide-open, robust debate. Maintaining and protecting that forum, Kalven was saying, should receive the highest judicial priority.

With this emphasis, Kalven undoubtedly would have disagreed with Justice Black's opinion for the Court in *Adderley v. Florida* (1966),[158] which upheld convictions for trespassing with malicious intent upon the premises of the county jail. In fact, in making his argument, Kalven would have used language very much like that found in Justice Douglas's dissent. He, too, would have had the Court recall the importance of the public forum to minority groups in our society, and therefore the importance of remembering that not all demonstrations should "be condemned as tactics of obstruction and harassment as long as the assembly and petition are peaceable."[159]

Similarly, Professor Kalven would surely have agreed with the dissenting Justices that there was nothing anomalous about staging a protest demonstration on the grounds of the county jail.[160] If courthouse grounds were not automatically precluded as sites for demonstrations, there is not much justification for categorically prohibiting all protests in areas adjacent to jails. The key question would be whether the demonstrators had actually upset the basic functions of the jail. Given the ambiguous factual record in *Adderley*, and the high priority Kalven gave to the concept of public forum, he would surely have favored overturning the convictions.

Furthermore, Adderley and her fellow demonstrators were convicted under a very general Florida law forbidding trespass with malicious and mischievous intent. The law certainly did not represent the kind of "deliberate, specific and relevant legislative judgement" which, Kalven thought, had saved the picketing near the courthouse statute in *Cox*. Like Justice Douglas, he would undoubtedly have objected that the Florida statute gave the "custodian of public property" arbitrary power to suppress ideas.[161] A general trespass statute should not be used to curtail access to the public forum.

Similarly, Professor Kalven would not have agreed with the majority opinion in *Walker v. Birmingham* (1967).[162] The injunction in *Walker* which sought to restrain the Southern Christian Leadership Conference from parading without first obtaining prior approval was as vague as the Birmingham parade ordinance incorporated within it. Professor Kalven's concern for the public forum would make him just as fearful of vague judicial orders as other forms of governmental regulation.

What, then, of his attitude toward the library "stand-up" case, *Brown v. Louisiana* (1966)?[163] The demonstrators were convicted under the same general breach of peace statute involved in the first indictment of the *Cox* case. Justice Fortas's plurality opinion began by noting that *Brown* was the fourth time in little more than four years that the Supreme Court was reviewing convictions of civil rights demonstrators under the Louisiana law, and in not one of the cases was there evidence of planned or intended disorder.[164] Professor Kalven's dislike of vague laws which permit arbitrary official curtailment of dissent would probably have led him to a similar response.

Justice Fortas had gone on to argue that the Constitution protected the right to conduct a peaceful and orderly protest against segregation even within a library.[165] Professor Kalven would surely have agreed about the importance of peaceful and orderly protests—*against* segregation and, also, *for* segregation. The Constitution was designed to permit the free expression of all views about public issues. Professor Kalven, however, would also have had deep reservations about the appropriateness of a library as a site for a demonstration. In the article outlining his position, Kalven wrote, "certainly it is easy to think of public places, swimming pools, for example, so clearly dedicated to a recreational use that talk of their use as a public forum would in general be totally unpersuasive."[166] Justice Fortas viewed a public library as "a place dedicated to quiet, to knowledge and to beauty."[167] That function made it even a more unlikely place for a demonstration than a swimming pool. With a specifically drawn, narrowly worded statute, Kalven would no doubt have argued against this protest. As it was, however, the vagueness of the statute would probably have led him to side with the Court majorty.

Professor Kalven's call for statutory specificity makes an almost impossible demand on government. With the exception of streets and parks, no government is likely to know beforehand which facility will be the site of a protest demonstration. One day the demonstration is outside a courthouse; the next, it is at the jailhouse grounds; the third time it can take place inside a library. Each of these facilities is dedicated to a different, specialized function. Each site would therefore require a different accommodation between the protestors' need for an appropriate forum and a society's interests in maintaining the functions of government. It would take an ability to read the future bordering upon omniscience for a legislature to work out detailed guidelines beforehand. Government must resort to general trespass and breach of peace ordinances.

Kalven recognized this problem when he wrote that the "judgments of time, place, and manner required must be so linked to the factual situation as to make detailed legislative regulation a clumsy, inflexible device."[168] He thought the matter may best be handled via licensing requirements. Professor Kalven well knew, however, that an absolute insistence upon obtaining prior permission can also frustrate much important, spontaneous protest; avoiding this frustration was one of his reasons for advocating the concept of the public forum. For example, he did not fault the demonstrators in either *Cox* or *Edwards* for failing to obtain a parade permit. In short, his comments about the specificity of regulations cannot be taken too literally.

His comments are better seen as one device for the courts to use in protecting access to the public forum. In general, he recognized the need for the courts to weigh the speech interest in the public forum against the other uses of public places. That comparison, of course, is a balancing test of sorts, but one in which Professor Kalven thought the thumb of the Court should permanently be placed on the speech side of the scales.[169] His call for narrowly drawn regulations are, in context, a measure of how far he would go in protecting protest demonstrations.

Professor Kalven's argument here may make it difficult to perceive why he had so many misgivings about the preferred freedoms doctrine used in *Cox*. After all, that doctrine too is based upon a judicial balance favoring political freedom, and the Justices who used the preferred freedoms doctrine generally came to the same conclusions as Kalven. His reluctance to endorse an outright balancing test like the preferred freedoms doctrine is best explained by a case like *Cameron v. Johnson* (1968).[170] The case arose from a voter registration drive in Forrest County, Mississippi. Beginning in January, 1964, civil rights organizations had maintained a daily picket line on the grounds of the county courthouse in Hattiesburg where the registrar of voters was located. On April 8, the state of Mississippi enacted an antipicketing law which went into effect immediately. Two days later, Cameron and his associates were arrested for violating that statute.

The Court's holding that the Mississippi statute was not void on its face was a critical element in its decision not to intervene,[171] and the *Cox* opinion made that holding in *Cameron* all but inevitable. If the First Amendment does not "afford the same amount of freedom to those who would communicate ideas by conduct such as patrolling, marching, and picketing on streets and highways, as [it] afford[s] to those who communicate ideas by pure speech,"[172] and if picketing is therefore "subject to regulation even though intertwined with expression and association,"[173] then the Mississippi statute was clearly not void on its face.

If the judicial balancing process began with Kalven's concept of the public forum, however, the judges would almost certainly arrive at a different conclusion. If citizens have a constitutionally protected right to use the streets and sidewalks for peaceably advocating public policy, then the government can interfere with this First Amendment right only for the most important reasons. A federal court would be obligated to determine whether a criminal law had been invoked merely to harass and disrupt the exercise of that First Amendment right. This obligation certainly could not be avoided by presuming, as the Court did in *Cameron*, that picketing was subject to regulation. Professor Kalven was arguing that the presumption must lie *against* the application of an antipicketing statute in order to protect the public forum.

Judicial adherence to this line of reasoning would have meant that, at the very least, a federal injunction should have been issued to prevent Mississippi officials from applying their antipicketing law to Cameron and his associates. There is no evidence that the pickets were disorderly or had obstructed use of the sidewalks or access to the courthouse. When the picketing began in January, the sheriff had used barricades to set off a small "march route." The barricades remained in place until April 9 (the day after the enactment of the antipicketing law) and during all this time the protestors had confined their picketing to the "march route." The protest was thereby confined to the same area.[174] In this situation, the state had not shown any compelling reason to justify interfering with the citizens' access to the public forum.

On the other hand, one of the troubles with Meiklejohn's interpretation is his insistence that the First Amendment requires absolute neutrality about the *content* of the speech involved in those demonstrations. Whatever the propriety of governmental regulations of the time, manner, and place of demonstrations, officials—including judges—ought not to be concerned with the content of the protest. The citizen's ideas about any socially important problem are not to be censored.[175] It is difficult, however, to maintain that the content of the political speech involved is never a relevant factor for evaluating mass demonstration. Since demonstrations are designed to provoke a reaction, the possibility of violent conflict must be faced. That mass demonstrations under certain circumstances have the potentiality for erupting into violence is conceded by all.

Why then, should their political content be ignored? Surely not because words have no impact. Meiklejohn's whole rationale for protecting speech is premised upon his belief that ideas do matter, that speech plays an active role in moving people toward political commitments and actions. *What* is said may often be as important as *how* it is said. H. Rap Brown's speech may not have started a race riot in Cambridge, Maryland, in 1967,[176] but it takes little imagination to conceive of a situation in which speech could incite a riot or contribute to its continuation.[177] To regard the content as a forbidden category for regulating mass demonstrations would preclude the Court from developing legal criteria for when officials may intervene to avert impending dangers.[178]

If this point has merit, it points toward a more fundamental objection to the functional contract theory. The problem of applying an absolutist conception of the First Amendment to protest demonstrations stems from the difficulty in making a sensible distinction between speech and conduct in that situation. Meiklejohn and his followers are able to argue for the absolute freedom of public speech only because they admit the validity of regulating action. The mass demonstration cases indicate that, while it is always analytically conceivable to make a distinction between speech and action, it is not always empirically possible to do so. Since the Justices, according to this group of theorists, are to apply principles to facts and values in concrete cases, the soundness of Meiklejohn's interpretation is called into question. In the end, it may be wiser to recognize, with Justice Holmes, "that the character of every act depends upon the circumstances in which it is done,"[179] and that we should not impose rigid categories upon complex phenomena.

CONCLUSIONS

The same conclusion emerges when we recall the difficulties in defining the boundaries between public and private speech. Functional contract theorists insist that speech which may have an impact upon the self-governing process is an action requiring the absolute protection of the First Amendment. Speech which is not of governing importance need not be granted total immunity from reasonable regulation. Once again, a clear analytic distinction can be and has been made. Once again, it was not always empirically possible to apply that distinction in a sensible manner. The obscenity cases, and especially the libel cases, indicate that a rigid dichotomy between public and private realms does not lead to a sensible grasp of the complexities of modern life. People do not function in airtight compartments marked public and private. This fact is made even more true if we view democracy, as the public contract theorists urge, as a political system in which We, the People, have important public functions. Rather than imposing a rigid dichotomy on a nondichotomous situation, we might be well advised to assess the competing values at stake in a particular situation.

Still, any such assessment requires a prior ranking of competing values. The ultimate utility of the functional contract theory, at least in these borderline cases, would then lie in its emphasis on the overriding importance of public speech in a system of self-governance. The theory compels an individual, in the area of libel, to justify his claim for private rights in terms of the public needs of a democracy. In the area of mass demonstrations, as seen by Professor Kalven's position, the theory requires judicial support for activities of governing importance unless contrary considerations can be clearly shown to be more important. In both libel and demonstration cases, the force of the argument, in the context of the functional contract theory, depends upon the reasons advanced for absolutely protecting the clear case of political speech. A formal, public speech about governmental policy is the core example of Meiklejohn's position. Unless we accept the reasons for handling the core example, there can be no justification for applying the priorities derived from it to the problems of the penumbra.

The First Amendment, in this theory, provides total immunity from governmental regulation for all political discussion, because that freedom is required in a system of self-government. The instrumental branches of government cannot destroy the fundamental, functional requisites of the Fourth and sovereign branch. If our liberties are dependent upon the functional requisites of democracy, however, why are certain freedoms absolute? The functional contract theorists may read the Constitution as a consistent plan which requires absolute political freedom, but circumstances are not always consistent. At certain times, other requisites of the system, such as its physical survival, may seem important enough to override absolute freedoms.

Systems analysis leads to weighing competing social needs rather than to an absolute adherence to any one component of the system. By building their argument for an absolutist interpretation of the First Amendment upon the functional requisites of a system, even a democratic system, these contract theorists have built upon sand. The political theory behind systems analysis simply cannot support an absolutist view of the political process or any of its components.[180]

Anyone familiar with modern social science literature will find it almost impossible to accept an absolutist interpretation of the First Amendment, the fundamental tenet of the functional contract theory. It might be thought that this criticism is beside the point since Meiklejohn and Tussman were both frankly distressed by much of what passes for social science. They sought to create a political theory whose primary purpose was the political education of the citizen. Perhaps, only criticism directed toward the theory's educational utility is relevant.

There is no doubt that the functional contract theory fares better when viewed in this light. If American officials were persuaded to adhere to this theory, the political freedom of all Americans would suffer fewer governmental restrictions. If the American people became convinced of the rightness of this theory and learned to internalize its prescriptions into their behavior, they would benefit from a fuller, more varied expression of public issues. More importantly, the vast majority of citizens might be encouraged to participate more actively in our governing processes.

Our whole perception of "normal" political life might also change. In the functional contract theory the public interest is invariably regarded as something different than, though not necessarily opposed to, private interest. "Rights" in the areas of private activity are not absolutes but a matter of political wisdom and prudence. Attention is thereby focused on differing claims about the public interest. Because there is no question that private property may be regulated, the debate would center upon whether any particular regulation is desirable. The theory leads the individual to justify his claim for private rights solely in terms of the public interest of a democracy. The public interest is not merely the sum of private interests; it is something apart. Recall the distinction between public and private speech. The functional contract theory thus encourages us to develop a distinct concern for the polity which shapes our lives.

The educational force of this theory, however, is also plagued by difficulties. There is, first of all, the internal inconsistency created by a functional interpretation of the American political system which is coupled with an absolutist insistence upon the inviolability of one particular function—speech about public matters. Those who instruct are also required to offer a coherent theory. Without it, they cannot hope to persuade.

Second, the functional contract theory of democracy assumes the desirability of vast popular participation going significantly beyond the act of voting. Social scientists have challenged this populistic assumption; technological society precludes it, they assert. At the very least, then, a theory which fundamentally departs from the existing social science paradigm should address itself to this point. Meiklejohn, however, never explored the institutional changes necessary to make mass political participation function in the modern world, and Tussman has only recently begun to discuss institutional changes. An educational theory must also instruct. Without specific guidance, it is difficult to learn.

Without concrete, detailed institutional analysis, the functional contract theorists fail to come to grips with another concern raised by social scientists. This concern goes to the very heart of any theory based upon vast popular participation in the decision-making process beyond the act of voting. Since the bulk of recent social science data indicates mass apathy and ignorance,[181] the *wisdom* of such a participatory theory is called into question. Neither Meiklejohn nor Tussman provides a satisfactory answer. The existing condition of the American citizenry may indeed be the result of generations of poor education with a misconceived theory of democracy, as the functional contract theorists claim. The answer may, indeed, be the proper education regarding the obligations of self-government. But are we to build our institutions and our lives around the distant prospect of that glorious day when we are all properly educated? The few public-spirited men we have today may reasonably be excused for believing we would do better to recognize existing competencies and build upon them.

In sum, public contract theory has much to teach us about the American polity, and it offers many intriguing suggestions for improvement. In its present stage of development, however, the theory does not present a coherent and totally plausible view of our political system.

THE INDIVIDUALISTIC CONTRACT _____

As the domestic ramifications of the Cold War gradually emerged, some of the proponents of the First Amendment preference standard began seeking a firmer intellectual position from which to defend individual freedom. One such position was provided by the functional contract theory; but, the proponents of that theory were not the only Americans questioning the conventional wisdom of the competitive paradigm for democracy. In particular, the erosion of liberties which took place in the early years of the Cold War led one member of the Supreme Court to rethink some of his most basic conceptions of democracy. What emerged in the opinions, lectures, and speeches of Justice Hugo L. Black was a bold and distinct theory of democracy.[1]

The American government, in Justice Black's political theory, is the best means for achieving the fundamental purpose of all just government: the enhancement of individual freedom. That purpose was central to the contract which created this nation—the Constitution. Our fundamental Charter promotes individual liberty by both its positive and negative provisions. With its positive provisions, the Constitution furthers individual liberty by giving each person the right to participate in the government of his society. Through its negative clauses the Constitution shields individuals by limiting governmental power and authority. According to Justice Black, the Constitution, in all its provisions, seeks to promote the good life for all by assuring the individual freedom of each.

THE CHARTER OF INDIVIDUAL LIBERTY

The Justice's political theory stressed the importance of our Constitution.[2] It marked "a virtual revolution in the history of the government of nations."[3] While the Constitution obviously reflects the Framers' experience with English history and law, it cannot be seen primarily as a codification of late eighteenth-century English practices. That view would undermine the revolution on which the American nation was founded. It also runs counter to the founding generation's belief in the importance of our written Constitution. Like Alexander Meiklejohn and William Douglas, but unlike Justice Frankfurter, Justice Black believed the Constitution established a unique and better governmental system.

What makes the American plan of government unique are those features reflecting the Framers' fear of arbitrary government. To the republicans of 1789, the great enemy of freedom was tyranny—arbitrary, lawless rulers.[4] Hugo Black's reading of history led him to fear the same evil; thus, he believed that the key features of the American Constitution were designed to protect us from tyrannical rulers—the written nature of the Constitution, the fact that it is the supreme law, the internal division of governmental authority, and the establishment of an independent judiciary.[5]

A written constitution, by its very nature, defines and limits governmental powers to ensure the government does not act as it pleases.[6] The separation of powers, with the system of checks and balances, was designed to prevent any branch from infringing individual liberties.[7] Finally, a really independent judiciary was necessary to give force and effect to constitutional liberties and limitations on governmental authority.[8] In short, the basic plan and purpose of the Constitution, according to Justice Black, was the promotion of individual liberty by preventing arbitrary government.

This conception of the Constitution is intimately connected with Black's view of judicial function. Since he thought an independent judiciary, exercising the power of judicial review, is an essential feature of our type of free government, he had little difficulty believing, despite the absence of an explicit grant of power and the paucity of historical material, that judicial review was fully understood by the Framers and certainly by those who most carefully considered the problem.[9] In turn, this view meant that Justice Black, like Justice Douglas, did not believe the courts should "restrict their usefulness in protecting constitutional rights by creating artificial judicial obstacles to the full performance of their duty. The essential protection of the liberty of our people should not be denied them by the invocation of a doctrine of so-called judicial self-restraint."[10] When judges have a constitutional question before them, and the public interest calls for its decision, refusal to decide that question is an evasion of responsibility. In that sense Justice Black was a judicial activist.

Justice Black, however, did not belong to that school of judicial activists who would hold unconstitutional those laws they consider politically undesirable. He objected to the Court's use of the Due Process Clauses to strike down federal and state laws which a majority found "unreasonable," "capricious," "arbitrary," or "contrary to a fundamental sense of civilized justice." Since the cornerstone of Justice Black's "constitutional faith [was] a basic belief that the Constitution was designed to prevent putting too much uncontrollable power in the hands of any one or more public officials," he could not subscribe to such a loose interpretation of due process.[11] To avoid that traditional conception, he developed his famous argument in *Adamson v. California* (1947).[12] The Due Process Clause of the Fourteenth Amendment should be interpreted as a shorthand summary of the specific provisions of the first Eight Amendments. The judges, too, are to be bound by the written Constitution.

Like other members of the New Deal generation, the decisions of the Old Guard Court made Hugo Black doubt the wisdom of placing too great a reliance upon the courts. He never believed that the Constitution prevented the people's representatives from enacting social welfare legislation.[13] By insisting that substantive due process was really only a shorthand summary of the specific provisions of the first Eight Amendments, Justice Black sought to prevent the courts from substituting their definition of constitutionality for the prescriptions of our written Constitution. He was never under the illusion that his prescription would end division among the judges or eliminate the courts' policy-making function,[14] but he did believe his approach would affect the very nature of judicial decision making:

> To pass upon the constitutionality of statutes by looking to the particular standards enumerated in the Bill of Rights and other parts of the Constitution is one thing; to invalidate statutes because of application of "natural law" deemed to be above and undefined by the Constitution is another. In the one instance, courts proceeding within clearly marked constitutional boundaries seek to execute policies written into the Constitution; in the other, they roam at will in the limitless area of their own beliefs as to reasonableness and actually select policies, a responsibility which the Constitution entrusts to the legislative representatives of the people.[15]

Due process was not the only area in which Black sought to confine the judges to an exploration of the meanings of the Constitution's literal text. The same approach characterized his opinions touching all other clauses, including Commerce,[16] Equal Protection,[17] and even the Contract Clause.[18] Nowhere is this approach more evident than in his opinions dealing with the First Amendment. Justice Black insisted that the Supreme Court give full force to its absolute command. In explaining this now famous position, he once said:

> But when I get down to the really basic reason why I believe that "no law" means no law, I presume it could come to this, that I took an obligation to support and defend the Constitution as I understand it. And being a rather backward country fellow, I understand it to mean what the words say.[19]

Though rather tongue in cheek, this statement was clearly derived from Justice Black's belief that "the history and language of the Constitution and the Bill of Rights . . . make it plain that one of the primary purposes of the Constitution with its amendments was to withdraw from the Government *all* power to act in certain areas—whatever the scope of those areas may be."[20]

Justice Black developed an internally consistent approach to the Constitution. The First Amendment is to be treated like all the other clauses. Language and history are the crucial factors influencing his interpretation of the Constitution—not reasonableness or desirability as determined by Justices of the Supreme Court.[21] He summarized the central belief of his constitutional faith this way:

> The courts should always try faithfully to follow the true meaning of the Constitution and other laws as actually written, leaving to Congress changes in its statutes, and leaving the problem of adapting the Constitution to meet new needs to constitutional amendments approved by the people under constitutional procedures.[22]

For Justice Black the Constitution was the source of all authority in our polity. "The United States is entirely a creature of the Constitution. Its power and authority have no other sources."[23] Unlike Professor Meiklejohn, however, he did not see the Constitution primarily as the basic contract of a self-governing society, but rather as a fundamental charter of individual liberty. "[That] great document is the unique American contribution to man's continuing search for a society in which individual liberty is secure against governmental oppression."[24] To be sure, the difference between Black and

Meiklejohn on this point was one of emphasis, for the Justice believed that "the right of each man to participate in the self-government of his society" is "perhaps the most fundamental individual liberty of our people."[25]

The difference, however, is not unimportant. Meiklejohn's emphasis meant that proponents of the functional contract theory stress the mutual obligations and common purposes which unite members of any political community. Black's emphasis on individual liberty gave an atomistic cast to his political theory. His emphasis on the literal wording of the Constitution and the history which led to the Framers' using those particular words also led to some unique features in his democratic theory. We shall now turn to a detailed analysis of some of those features.

AN ANALYSIS OF THE INDIVIDUALISTIC CONTRACT THEORY

Citizenship

As with any contract theorist, Justice Black thought of a citizen as a party to the basic social contract creating the body politic. Unlike other countries where existing sovereign governments came, over time, to recognize more of their people as citizens, in the United States the people created the nation. "Its citizenry is the country and the country is its citizenry."[26] In "our country the people are sovereign"[27] because they created the government.

If the Constitution which created our nation was the deliberate, conscious act of the people, then citizenship must be thought of in the same way. When membership in the body politic is seen as agreement with the fundamental contract, citizenship becomes synonymous with participation in that deliberate act of creation. The very conception of a government created by an agreement of the people means that citizenship will be thought of as a knowing, voluntary act.

Unlike Professor Tussman, Justice Black did not attempt a full exploration of the implications of citizenship within his political theory. He did not, for example, discuss how a native born American *consciously* joins the political community. As a judge he simply dealt with those aspects of citizenship which emerged in the cases before the Court. This meant, in practice, that his concern with citizenship revolved around the issue of expatriation. Nonetheless, his reliance upon contract theory was unmistakable.

His basic position was that under our form of government, as established by the Constitution, the citizenship of the lawfully naturalized and the native born cannot be taken away. Citizenship may be voluntarily relinquished, but the "Government cannot sever its relationship to the people by taking away their citizenship."[28] Justice Black began, as always, with the text of the Constitution. The right of citizenship is found in the first sentence of the Fourteenth Amendment. The Constitution by its own terms can qualify any right. But there is no word in that document which deals with expatriation; so, "the Amendment can most reasonably be read as defining a citizenship which a citizen keeps unless he voluntarily relinquishes it."[29] The *American* Constitution is controlling, Justice Black insisted, not notions drawn from an implied attribute of the sovereignty possessed by all nations.[30]

Justice Black's theory of the judicial function required more than an exclusive reliance upon the words of the text; he also sought to understand the meaning of those words by a careful examination of their history. In this area, historical analysis could not be avoided in any event, since the government's claim (supported by Justices like Frankfurter and Harlan) was that expatriation was always seen as a necessary and proper adjunct of the power to regulate foreign and military affairs and was not precluded.[31] In his reading of our political history, Justice Black found support for his conclusion that what "the Constitution has conferred neither the Congress, nor the Executive, nor the Judiciary, nor all these in concert, may strip away."[32]

Justice Black recognized, as does everyone else, that the Fourteenth Amendment's framers were concerned with making the citizenship of the blacks permanent and secure, not with the problem of expatriation. Their fear was that some later Congress might take away the citizenship conferred on the blacks by the 1866 Civil Rights Act. Nonetheless, Justice Black argued that the method they chose for accomplishing that purpose has great significance for the problem of expatriation: "it seems undeniable from the language they used that they wanted to put citizenship beyond the power of any governmental unit to destroy."[33] He found legislative and judicial statements to support his position,[34] but he recognized conflicting inferences can be drawn from the historical materials.[35]

In areas such as due process Justice Black would defer to legislative judgments. To treat expatriation as a social welfare regulation, however, ran counter to his basic political theory. In addition to the explicit language of the Fourteenth Amendment, the "very nature of our free government makes it completely incongruous to have a rule of law under which a group of citizens temporarily in office can deprive another group of citizens of their citizenship."[36] Moreover, because it was a precious right, American citizenship should not be made dependent upon the Supreme Court's passing notions of what constitutes "fair," "reasonable," or "arbitrary."[37] With such interpretation, there would have been little need for the founders to draft a written Constitution or a later generation to add a Citizenship Clause.

Justice Black, therefore, opposed all governmental efforts to expatriate unwilling American citizens. In *Perez v. Brownell* (1958),[38] Justice Frankfurter's opinion for the Court sustained Congress's authority to expatriate an

American citizen for voting in a foreign election. Justice Black joined the dissenting opinion of Chief Justice Warren as well as that of Justice Douglas.[39] Congress may not declare that such an equivocal act as voting in a foreign election established a *conclusive* presumption of intention to throw off American nationality. When the same issue came before the Court nine years later, Justice Black wrote the *Afroyim* opinion which overturned *Perez.*[40]

For the same reason, Justice Black agreed in *Trop v. Dulles* (1958)[41] that a loss of American citizenship could not be made the automatic consequence of a conviction and dishonorable discharge for wartime desertion. Desertion, however reprehensible it may be, was not unambiguous evidence of voluntary renunciation or abandonment of citizenship. The Citizenship Clause also means, according to Justice Black, the government cannot expatriate men who leave the country or remain outside for the purpose of avoiding military service.[42] The dereliction of duty could be punished, but not by the deprivation of citizenship.

Nor did Justice Black see a distinction between the rights of citizenship of the native born and those of the naturalized person. He joined the majority in *Schneider v. Rusk* (1964) which precluded the government from expatriating Mrs. Schneider for having continuously resided for three years in the foreign state of which she was formerly a national.[43] Similarly, he dissented when a new Court majority began to make inroads into the Black-Douglas-Warren view of citizenship by making a distinction between the citizenship rights of the native born and at least some naturalized Americans. He could not accept an interpretation of the Citizenship Clause which excluded from its protections all those acquiring United States citizenship while abroad. Nor did he believe the Constitution permitted Congress to treat such persons as "provisional" citizens—to accept them as citizens subject to later revocation if durational residency requirements are not met. That interpretation, he claimed, rested on the Court's own view of what was fair, reasonable, and right, and it did not preclude a later Congress from making such provisional citizens meet additional requirements.[44]

In sum, Justice Black's reading of the Constitution led him to believe that the power of Congress to take away citizenship for activities of the citizen is nonexistent. Expatriation can come about only by the voluntary renunciation of nationality and allegiance. He knew this view was not compelled by either the language or the history of our Constitution. The expatriation cases clearly reveal an area where Justice Black made his interpretation of the Constitution and its history the servant of his political theory.

Unfortunately, this line of cases does not clearly indicate all the theoretical dimensions of Justice Black's conception of citizenship; he said that "citizenship in this Nation is a part of a cooperative affair."[45] He never spelled out the nature of that cooperative effort, however. Clearly, Justice Black saw

Americans as citizens, not subjects; they are each entitled to the sovereign authority of our body politic. A fuller account of how he envisioned a citizen's role in our polity awaits a discussion of his concept of political participation. We shall then be in a position to comprehend how a member is to exercise his share of the sovereign authority, how a citizen is to function in Justice Black's political theory.

Political Participation

For all his reliance on contract theory, Justice Black never abandoned a notion of political participation he had earlier developed when he held the optimalist theory of democracy.[46] In that competitive theory, it will be re- called, political participation is identified with the act of voting. The free exercise of the free vote enables the mass of people to influence political decisions, but only the elected leaders actually participate in the decision- making process. Although Justice Black recognized the need for other mech- anisms of popular *influence* on government—most notably through the ex- ercise of First Amendment rights—he never developed a cooperative, communitarian concept of political participation. He did not, like the func- tional contract theorists, see democracy as each citizen's participation in a common exploration for the public good. Instead, he believed the American "government envisions a system under which its policies are the result of reasoned decisions made by public officials chosen in the way the laws provide."[47]

To Justice Black, "the right of each man to participate in the self-gov- ernment of his society"[48] is equivalent to "having a voice in the election of those who make the laws under which, as good citizens, we must live."[49] Representative government is the essence of self-government. Reliance upon elected officials is required not only because the size of our polity means most citizens can participate politically only as qualified voters, but, more impor- tantly, because our federal and state constitutions and our laws have estab- lished representative institutions as *the* way Americans are to participate politically. Our basic laws legitimize representation as the American way of practicing self-government.

Justice Black never explicitly relied upon contract theory when talking about voting, political participation, and representative government. Instead, he articulated the commonly accepted judicial view that "the political franchise of voting" is a "fundamental political right, because preservative of all rights."[50] Through the ballot the citizen can hold government officials accountable and can advance and protect his interests. That outlook is precisely the way po- litical participation (voting) is viewed in the competitive theories of democ- racy.[51] That idea is what Justice Black meant when he said, "No right is more precious in a free country . . . Other rights, even the most basic, are illusory if the right to vote is undermined."[52]

Despite this language, I do not think Justice Black's position in the reapportionment and voting rights cases can be understood apart from contract theory. As we have seen, it is possible to make the claim that an individual's interests are best advanced by an apportionment plan explicitly recognizing a group basis for politics. Justice Black, on the other hand, always stressed the individual *right* to vote rather than the *benefits* to be derived from the political power of the franchise. Apportionment plans, he insisted, must recognize the right of each qualified voter to cast a vote of equal importance to that of every other voter regardless of the consequences or the power of competing interest. The only limiting factors on this equality among voters are to be found in the fundamental charter, the Constitution. Both factors— the equal right of individual voters and the limits imposed on that right by the constitutional text—are more easily derived from contract theory than from the competitive paradigm.

Justice Black's position began to emerge in the very first of the modern apportionment cases, *Colegrove v. Green* (1946).[53] Justice Frankfurter, in the plurality opinion, argued that apportionment was a political question and therefore not meet for judicial determination. Justice Black disagreed and wrote the dissenting opinion which was joined by Justices Douglas and Murphy. While voting is part of elections, and elections are "political," the basic issue involved the right to vote guaranteed by the federal Constitution. Article I, section 2, provides that congressmen "shall be . . . chosen . . . by the people of the several states." It thus gives those *qualified* a right to vote and a right to have their vote counted. Justice Black could see no reason why the federal courts should avoid handling a case which involved the national right to choose representatives.[54]

The theoretical difference between Justices Frankfurter and Black, then, was clear as early as 1946. The former saw apportionment cases as an inextricable part of the struggle for power among competing societal interests; hence, it was a political question. Justice Black, however, saw apportionment in terms of its impact on the *individual's* right to vote and to have that vote counted. He also thought that "the constitutionally guaranteed right to vote and the right to have one's vote counted clearly imply the policy that state election systems, no matter what their form, should be designed to give approximately equal weight to each vote cast."[55]

In 1964, Justice Black had the satisfaction of writing one of his dissents into law. *Wesberry v. Sanders* (1964)[56] overruled *Colegrove* by holding that "construed in its historical context, the command of Art. I, Sec. 2, that Representatives be chosen 'by the People of the several States' means that as nearly as is practicable one man's vote in a congressional election is to be worth as much as another's."[57] Justice Black maintained that an apportionment plan which made a vote in one district worth more than in another was "counter to our fundamental ideas of democratic government."[58] He chose not to elaborate this idea; he did not explain how our fundamental democratic ideas required congressional districts with relatively equal populations. He chose, instead, to deal only with the notion that malapportionment "would cast aside the principle of a House of Representatives elected 'by the people,' a principle tenaciously fought for and established at the Constitutional Convention."[59] Thus, unlike his dissent in *Colegrove*, Justice Black's opinion for the Court in *Wesberry* did not rely upon the Fourteenth Amendment and dealt with democratic ideas only in passing references.

His use of history is, nonetheless, quite revealing, especially when contrasted with Justice Harlan's. Black maintained that when the delegates at the Philadelphia Convention "agreed that the House should represent 'people' they intended that in allocating Congressmen the number assigned to each State should be determined solely by the number of the State's inhabitants."[60] Hence, the constitutional requirement of a census. Such an argument, Justice Harlan insisted, confused two issues: direct election of representatives and the apportionment of representatives among the states:

> The Great Compromise concerned representation *of the States* in the Congress. In all the discussion surrounding the basis of representation of the House and all of the discussion whether Representatives should be elected by the legislatures or the people of the States, there is nothing which suggests even remotely that the delegates had in mind the problem of districting within a State.[61]

Notice how Justice Harlan completely ignored the *reasons* advanced by those favoring election by the people. For him, the Great Compromise involved issues of state power and political interests. While Madison, Wilson, Mason et al. were surely not unconcerned with questions of power and interest, they also believed it necessary to stay within the confines of Whig theory. Power and interest had to be reconciled with popular sovereignty, for the people were the acknowledged fount of all authority. Unless the new government was directly grounded on the support of the people, it would remain—like the government created by the Articles of Confederation—a mere creature of the states. Direct election of at least one branch of the legislature was needed to establish the legitimacy of the federal government, and this principle was embedded in the Great Compromise.[62] When these *reasons* are considered, Justice Black's opinion makes good sense. In Whig theory, the legitimacy of a government could be "diluted" just as much by gross malapportionment as by other devices for curtailing an adequate representation of the population.[63]

Justice Black's primary concern was in maintaining the legitimacy of the representative system of government created by the Constitution. For this reason he immediately translated a reapportionment question into one dealing with individual voters and government. In contract theory, the government is founded on the consent of each individual citizen. A logical way to sustain that consent is through participation in the election of representatives. Since each individual is regarded as the equal of every other, our Constitution's plain objective must be equal representation for equal numbers of people in the House of Representatives, the grand depository of the democratic principle in the government created by the Constitution. Justice, common sense, and the continued legitimacy of the system required that standard.

These same theoretical assumptions were the decisive factor in *Reynolds v. Sims* (1964).[64] Chief Justice Warren's opinion for the Court saw state legislative apportionment in terms of an individual right. In explaining this position, Chief Justice Warren, like Justice Black in *Wesberry*, turned to the nature of the governmental system:

> [R]epresentative government is in essence self-government through the medium of elected representatives of the people, and each and every citizen has an inalienable right to full and effective participation in the political processes of his State's legislative bodies. Most citizens can achieve this participation only as qualified voters through the election of legislators to represent them. Full and effective participation by all citizens in state government requires, therefore, that each citizen has an equally effective voice in the election of members of his state legislature.[65]

Once apportionment was seen as an *individual* right to participate, an equal protection standard like "one person, one vote, in substantially equal population districts" was inevitable. The Court has traditionally held that clause as requiring the uniform treatment of persons standing in the same relation to the challenged governmental action. In *Reynolds*, the Court majority viewed the relationship established by a state legislative apportionment scheme exactly as Justices Black and Douglas had seen it eighteen years earlier in *Colegrove*: like the right to vote itself, apportionment was a mechanism for *individual* participation in the political process. From this perspective, any distinction between voters is bound to be seen as invidious, arbitrary, or irrational because each individual voter has an equal claim to exercise that right in the same manner as his fellow citizens. "Since legislatures are responsible for enacting laws by which all citizens are to be governed," Chief

Justice Warren wrote in *Reynolds*, then with "respect to the allocation of legislative representation, all voters, as citizens of a State, stand in the same relation regardless of where they live."[66]

Because apportionment involves "an individual citizen's ability to exercise an effective voice in the only instrument of state government directly representative of the people,"[67] both houses of a bicameral state legislature must be apportioned on an equal population basis. The *Reynolds* majority recognized that the right of a citizen to equal representation would amount to little if the states could effectively submerge the equal population principle in one house of a bicameral legislature: "In all too many cases the . . . probable result would be frustration of the majority will through minority veto in the house not apportioned on a population basis."[68] In short, the Court held that since legislative apportionment involved an individual's right to participate politically, both houses of a bicameral legislature must be apportioned on an equal population basis. To do otherwise would impair the rights of some citizens as compared with citizens living in other parts of the state.

To the argument that some departures from a strict population standard were necessary to protect minority interests, the *Reynolds* majority replied, in essence, that there was no constitutional basis for exempting any particular *interest* (as opposed to certain individual *rights*) from the democratic process of majority rule. Like Madison and the Justices in the minority, they saw the principle task of modern legislatures as forming policy in light of the various and competing interests in society. In the democractic theory of the *Reynolds* majority, however, all societal interests were subject to majority rule.[69]

Besides, the *Reynolds* majority did not really think there was any great danger to minority *rights*, at least not as long as the Court remained vigilant. They plainly believed the whole issue of minority *rights* was a red herring thrown up to insulate the very *interests* gaining from malapportionment. Thus Chief Justice Warren could dismiss the whole issue by saying: "Our constitutional system amply provides for the protection of minorities by means other than giving them majority control of state legislatures . . . a denial of constitutionally protected *rights* demands judicial protection."[70]

The same point arose in a slightly different context in the companion case of *Lucas v. Colorado General Assembly* (1964).[71] Chief Justice Warren's opinion for the six-man majority found the Colorado apportionment plan unconstitutional. Since an individual right to equal participation was involved, the fact that the apportionment plan was approved by the electorate was without significance.[72] The fundamental purpose of our Constitution was to put individual rights (as opposed to interests) beyond reach of the political process. Not surprisingly then, the fact that Colorado law provided readily available political remedies—via referendum and initiative—meant only that a court might await the outcome of those procedures before acting, for those remedies still left individual rights in the hands of the majority. "Courts," not the political process, "sit to adjudicate controversies involving alleged denial of constitutional *rights*."[73]

From the perspective of a political theory which saw apportionment as an individual right to equal political participation, any distinction between voters is bound to be seen as invidious, arbitrary, or irrational. This viewpoint is amply demonstrated by a 1969 case involving the application of the *Reynolds* doctrine of "one person, one vote, in substantially equal population districts." The question raised regarded the phrase "substantially equal." In *Reynolds*, Chief Justice Warren had indicated the Court would sustain minor deviations from the equal population standard based on "legitimate considerations incident to the effectuation of a rational state policy."[74] The Court then went on to reject several factors usually central to pre-*Baker* apportionment plans: history, geography, economic, or other group interests. Explicitly mentioned as the type of considerations the Court would consider legitimate were the desire to insure some voice for political subdivisions, and the desire to balance off minor inequities in one house by arranging minor deviations from the equal population standard in the other.[75]

In 1967, Missouri had brought its congressional districts to numerical equivalences which would have delighted pre-*Baker* critics of legislative malapportionment. The most populous district was only 3.13 percent above the mathematical ideal of perfect equality and the least populous was only 2.83 percent below. Yet, in *Kirkpatrick v. Preisler* (1969),[76] the Supreme Court rejected the effort.

Justice Brennan's opinion for the five-man majority rejected out of hand the argument that there is a fixed percentage population variance small enough to be considered *de minimis* (too small to matter legally). Because apportionment involved an individual right, the Court majority could see "no non-arbitrary way to pick a cutoff point at which population variances suddenly became *de minimis*."[77] Furthermore, the majority Justices were fearful that acceptance of a certain range of deviation would simply encourage legislators to strive for that range rather than equality as nearly as practicable. Because equal representation for equal numbers of people was a formula designed to prevent debasement of individual voting power and diminution of each voter's influence on his elected representatives, toleration of even small deviations on principle rather than from necessity would detract from those purposes. The democratic ideal of full and effective political representation permitted only such limited population variances among districts as were "unavoidable despite a good-faith effort to achieve absolute equality, or for which justification [was] shown."[78] Missouri could not seriously contend that the disparities among its congressional districts were unavoidable by this standard, for it conceded it had not made a "good-faith effort to achieve absolute equality." Nor would the Court majority accept the justifications Missouri offered for the population disparities including the representation of local government units explicitly mentioned by the *Reynolds* majority.[79]

The internal logic of the democratic theory which had led to "one person, one vote" had now led the majority to take a critical view of *any* departure from absolute population equality among legislative districts. Not only had the Court interpreted "as nearly as practicable" to mean that a state was required to "make a good faith effort to achieve precise mathematical equality," but it had also required that any remaining population disparities, "no matter how small," be justified.

When the Court then proceeded to reject every justification that had been—and possibly every one that could be—advanced, it was too much for Justice Fortas. As a supporter of the *Reynolds* doctrine, he agreed that the states should be required to make a "good faith" effort to achieve population equality, but he thought it unwise to insist upon mathematical precision when population figures are always approximations.[80] While Justice Fortas was unwilling to fix a percentage figure for permissible variation, that was precisely the approach recommended by another supporter of the *Reynolds* doctrine, Justice White. White would not, except in unusual circumstances, quibble with an apportionment plan if the variations between districts were acceptably small (which he defined as a variation between the largest and smallest districts of 10 to 15 percent).[81] Both Justices were obviously seeking to temper the democratic ideals behind *Reynolds* with a small dose of pragmatism. They were suggesting ways which would minimize confrontations between the courts and legislatures while still requiring the states to approach the ideal derived from a democratic theory stressing individual rights. After all, they argued, in a state like Missouri with more than 4.3 million people, in congressional districts of approximately 432,000 people, it is difficult to see how a 1.06 ratio between the largest and smallest district "debases" the "weight" of any individual vote.

As Justice Brennan's opinion indicates, however, there is no nonarbitrary way to make such an accommodation within democratic theory requiring each individual to have an equal right to full and effective political representation. In that framework, any deviation from absolute equality enhances some people's rights at the expense of other individuals. The *Kirkpatrick* majority was bound to feel more comfortable accepting only those variances arising from factors beyond the conscious control of the legislature—inaccuracies in the census data, population changes since the last census, and such variations as emerged from a "good faith" effort at absolute equality. Whatever inequality of voting power still persisted could not then be ascribed to government favoring one person over another.

Unfortunately, the realities of American two-party politics belie that assumption. Even within an apportionment plan based on a good faith effort at absolute equality among districts, effective voting power is not going to be distributed among the electorate in a random or accidental way. *Kirkpatrick* does not proscribe gerrymandering—the deliberate distortion of district boundaries for partisan or personal political purposes. An insistence upon a "good faith" effort to achieve absolute equality may, of course, make partisan gerrymander more difficult;[82] it cannot eliminate the practice. The standard looks only at the numbers of people, religiously ignoring their other attributes. At least one characteristic however—party registration—is never ignored by our political parties. In normal two-party politics, the party controlling the state government at reapportionment time will do all in its power to create "safe" districts for itself. So long as the dominant mode of electing representatives is from single-member constituencies, the most powerless voters will continue to be those members of a preordained minority party within a safe district.

It is not clear how Justice Black would have responded to the issue of partisan apportionment plans which otherwise meet the Court's standards. He died before the *Gaffney v. Cummings* (1973) decision upholding such apportionments.[83] From earlier cases, where partisan districting was a tangential factor, he apparantly would have agreed with Justice White that partisan considerations are an inevitable part of legislative districting.[84] From the perspective of Justice Black's theory, partisan apportionments are unlike plans based on economic, social, or geographic interests. The nonideological character of our parties rarely commits them to a definite course of action, certainly not for long periods of time. Partisan apportionment does not, like interest-based plans, necessarily create almost permanent advantages or liabilities for one political policy. Within the confines of a partisan apportionment plan, the voters may still have meaningful opportunity to effect government programs. Moreover, a voter's partisan affiliation is voluntarily assumed to advance his own concerns. Party affiliation, unlike race or sex, is not a permanent, ascriptive characteristic. The voter can not only press for his objectives within his chosen party, he may also shift his loyalties when he sees fit. Unlike interest-based apportionment plans, partisan districting can be viewed as still leaving the voter a considerable range of options.

Gaffney was also one of a series of 1973 cases in which the Court majority accepted a *de minimis* standard for apportionment of state legislatures.[85] Deviations of less than 10 percent required no justification. On this point, it is hardly likely that Justice Black would have agreed with the Court. For the reasons stated above, he was more likely to have agreed with the dissenters in *Gaffney*—the three remaining members of the *Kirkpatrick* majority: "The conclusion that a State may, without any articulated justification, deliberately

weight some persons' votes more heavily than others, seems to me fundamentally at odds with the purpose and rationale of our reapportionment
decisions."[86] *(Kirkpatrick's* requirement of a good faith effort at absolute equality still applies to congressional districting plans.)[87]

Justice Black's ideas about representative institutions also led him to apply
the "one person, one vote" standard to elected units of local government.
Here, too, the electoral process is the basis of legitimacy. The process is a
way of claiming that local institutions act with the consent of the governed,
of the people within their constituencies. He thus joined Justice White's
opinion for the Court in *Avery v. Midland County, Texas* (1968).[88] The majority
did not insist that the Constitution required a single, uniform mechanism for
meeting local needs, though they realized that the states, in providing for
the government of their towns, cities, and districts, have usually mandated
representative forms of government.[89] The *Avery* majority did require, however, that when the "State delegates lawmaking power to local government
and provides for the election of local officials from districts specified by statute,
ordinance or local charter, it must insure that those qualified to vote have
the right to an equally effective voice in the election process."[90] A body which
claims to represent all the people in a county must give each voter a full and
effective right to select its members.

Justice Black's opinion for the Court in *Hadley v. Junior College District*
(1970)[91] made this line of reasoning even more explicit. Given his ideas about
the reasons we resort to the electoral process, Justice Black believed that
elections themselves are the best single way for distinguishing one governmental function from another. The very fact that a state decided to have
certain officials selected by popular vote was a good indication of a position's
significance. From the voter's perspective, the harm from unequal treatment
is the same in any election, regardless of the officials selected.[92] From a systemic
perspective, voter equity is also important. "This is so because in our country
popular election has traditionally been the method followed when government
by the people is most desired."[93] Justice Black always insisted that the desire
to legitimate an agency by connecting it to American ideas of popular sovereignty could be frustrated by an apportionment which does not treat members of the public equally.

Once again, Black's opinion for the Court made it clear that considerable
latitude still remained with the state. Justice White's *Avery* opinion had not
foreclosed the use of specialized governmental units.[94] Justice Black's *Hadley*
opinion also recalled that the Court had previously upheld, in *Dusch v. Davis*
(1967),[95] an election scheme which required that candidates for a general
governmental unit be residents of particular boroughs.

More important were two other qualifications in Justice Black's opinion
in *Hadley*. First, he used an earlier case to remind the states that when they

select officials by appointment rather than popular election, and that choice does not itself offend the Constitution, the officials need not "represent" equal numbers of people.[96] To Justice Black there was nothing in the Constitution which compelled a state to select its officers through elections rather than by appointment. That statement was the basis of his controversial opinion in *Fortson v. Morris* (1966).[97]

The key to Justice Black's opinion for the five-man *Fortson* majority was his belief that this was not a voting case at all. He saw the popular election as a discrete event which was now over. He claimed there were actually two distinct ways of selecting a governor under the Georgia constitution. The first and preferred one was election by a majority of the voters. That having failed, the state was now preparing to use the second, or alternate, method, election by the legislature.

Since he believed a state could, if it wished, permit its legislature to select its governor, he had no difficulty sustaining the alternate method. "A method which would be valid if initially employed is equally valid when employed as an alternative."[98] So long as the state chose another method for selecting its officials, Justice Black saw no need to impose on it criteria designed to insure the legitimacy of the electoral process. He found no provision in the federal Constitution "which either expressly or impliedly dictates the method a State must use to select its Governor."[99]

As Justice Black noted in his *Hadley* opinion, this reliance upon a prior state choice of method certainly simplifies the judicial task. Whether it provides a sensible approach is another matter entirely. In *Fortson*, for example, it is far from clear that the election process was over. In other cases the Court had extended the "one person, one vote" standard into the preelection primaries, which selected the candidates for the general election, on the grounds that they were an integral part of the state's election.[100] The same rationale seems applicable to postelection methods.[101]

Justice Black made no attempt to deny that if the legislature determined the outcome of the election the votes cast in the general election would be weighted in a way that was contrary to the principle of "one person, one vote." To dismiss this concern, as Justice Black did, on the formal grounds that the general election was over seems highly arbitrary. This election method does the very thing Justice Black had so long opposed—it makes voting the mere mechanical casting and counting of ballots without regard to the effectiveness of the vote. The purpose of voting, Justice Black taught us, is to give each voter an equally effective way of participating in government. At the very least, each voter should have an equally effective impact on the individuals claiming to represent him.[102]

The other major qualification in Justice Black's *Hadley* opinion is even more puzzling. While all members of a relevant electorate must be treated equally, the state, he maintained, had great leeway in designating the class of voters and specifying their qualifications.[103] Justice Black had been a moving force in the *Reynolds* decision which maintained that because the right to vote legitimated institutions of representative government, any alleged infringement had to be carefully and meticulously scrutinized. A majority of the Warren Court believed the same factors were at work in voter qualification cases as in the apportionment decisions: "Any unjustified discrimination in determining who may participate in political affairs or in the selection of public officials *undermines* the legitimacy of representative government."[104]

At first glance it is difficult to see why Justice Black should disagree. He never denied that the substantive factors involved in the two lines of cases were the same. What he objected to was the majority's use of a "natural law" formulation of equal protection to strike down state voter requirements they believed to be irrational, irrelevant, unreasonable, arbitrary, or invidious.[105] His objection here was exactly the same as his opposition to the way the Court has frequently used substantive due process.

When the majority struck down Virginia's poll tax law because they could see no relation between voter qualifications and wealth,[106] Justice Black dissented. He interpreted the equal protection notion of rationality as requiring the Court to uphold a law if any set of facts can reasonably be conceived to justify it. He thought a state's desire to collect revenue and a belief that voters paying a poll tax will have a greater interest in state affairs were sufficiently reasonable policies.[107] Significantly, he never explicitly took exception to the analogy with the apportionment cases found in the majority opinion of Justice Douglas.

This is not to say that Justice Black invariably rejected constitutional challenges to state voter qualifications. When a state failed to provide any reasonable justification for limiting the franchise, he joined opinions holding those laws unconstitutional.[108] The voter classification had to be clearly relevant to the state's objectives.[109]

The difference in Justice Black's handling of the voting cases involving apportionment plans and those involving state-imposed limitations on the franchise was based on his attitude toward the judicial standards involved in each area. In the apportionment cases, Justice Black was apparently satisfied that the "one man, one vote" standard, especially as refined in *Kirkpatrick*, was precise enough to restrain judges. In the voter qualification cases which did not involve federal statutory law, however, the majority used vague terms like "arbitrary" and "invidious" to strike down state laws.[110] Having finally helped to lead the Court majority toward a rigorous, clear standard in the apportionment cases, he was reluctant to resort to standards considerably more ambiguous in the voter qualification cases. That ambiguity would run afoul of his basic attitude about the role of the judiciary in our constitutional democracy. Yet in terms of the substantive issue involved in both lines of cases—the individual's right to vote—the distinction is extremely difficult to sustain.

In the framework of Justice Black's own political theory, he should not have let his concern for the role of the judiciary override the substantive claims involved. When he placed primary reliance upon that concern rather than with enhancing a constitutionally recognized right, he sounded more like Justice Frankfurter than the Justice Black who once wrote: "It has always been the rule that where a federally protected right has been invaded the federal courts will provide a remedy to rectify the wrong done."[111]

What all these opinions in voting cases indicate is that Justice Black's position cannot properly be understood apart from his political theory. As always, Justice Black sought to interpret the Constitution in light of his reading of history; this reading supplied the basis for his political ideas.

Because of the Framers' Lockean presuppositions, Justice Black's position was perforce cast in terms of individualist contract theory. If an individual is to see a representative institution as a mechanism for self-government, he must believe that the law affords him a meaningful opportunity to elect the members of that body. Only then will he give his consent to that institution, only then will he agree it is his authorized representative. Since consent is necessarily individual, each citizen must be treated equally; hence, Justice Black's constitutional standard for elective representatives: one person, one vote; one vote, one value. Because his position is derived from an attempt to grasp the requisites of the political theory embedded in our constitutional structure, he is also willing to abide by the limitations imposed by that structure.

The strengths of this position should be apparent by now. Justice Black used his individualist contract theory to help destroy a great institutional hypocrisy. No longer may representative institutions claim to speak for the people while systematically discounting large numbers of people through malapportionment. By insisting that representative bodies conform to the one person, one vote standard, Justice Black sought to restore their legitimacy. Legitimacy may not, in itself, be sufficient to insure the equal effectiveness of each participant in the political process, or, for that matter, the viability of legislative bodies themselves. But surely a concern for the legitimacy of the representative process is essential for those other goals.

Justice Black also stressed the centrality of voting to any notion of self-government. Not only did he see the franchise as a means of protecting and advancing one's interests, he saw it as the principal vehicle for an individual to participate in the governmental decisions affecting his life. Whatever other mechanisms we may think desirable for extending the democratic idea of self-government in our postindustrial society, the need for free and open elections will not diminish. Hugo L. Black's recognition of this simple truth and his long fight for judiciary protection of this "most precious right" enhanced the political freedom of all Americans.

Ironically, this same concern with our constitutional system points to some of the limitations of Justice Black's political theory. The judges, too, are to be limited by the Constitution. The best way to achieve that desirable result is for the judges to adhere to the meaning of the Constitution. Unless a governmental action runs afoul of the historically intended meaning of specific clauses or of the historically intended functions of specifically mentioned institutions, it is presumed constitutional. Justice Black's position is sensible for a man in his position. A judge must indeed be cognizant of his *own* role in the constitutional structure as well as the ends posited for the rest of our system. Not all ends are to be achieved through judicial power; that action, too, would destroy the idea of self-government through elected representatives. There was frequently a need for Justice Black to weigh his concern for the constitutionally authorized system of elective self-government against his idea of judicial rectitude.

As his opinions in the voter qualification cases indicate, Justice Black's concern for maintaining the proper judicial role sometimes precluded acting to enlarge political participation. Because he came to his concern for democratic theory through his judicial role, his intellectual endeavors invariably began and ended with the written Constitution. For all his concern for self-government, there is no sustained discussion anywhere in his writings about what that concept could possibly mean in a large, technologically oriented, bureaucratically organized society. He gives us no clues on how we can adapt eighteenth-century institutions of self-government to our radically different circumstances.

Both the strengths and limitations of Justice Black's conception of political participation are well illustrated by his opinion in *Oregon v. Mitchell* (1970).[112] He arrived at his conclusions by seeking to understand the relationships created by our constitutional structure. His examination of historical materials led him to conclude the Framers could not have expected the newly created national government to survive without the ultimate power to control itself and fill its offices under its own laws. The Constitution authorized the states to make laws regarding national elections; but it also provided that if Congress became dissatisfied with those state laws, Congress could alter them. He treated Congress's decision to lower the voting age to eighteen in congressional elections as evidence of its dissatisfaction with the age requirements of most state laws. Black concluded, as had prior cases, that Congress has ultimate supervisory power over congressional elections.[113]

Similarly, Justice Black did not think it could be seriously contended that Congress has less power over presidential elections than it has over congressional elections. Acting under its broad authority to create and maintain a national government, he thought Congress unquestionably had the power under the Constitution to lower the voting age to eighteeen for all elections to federal offices, and to remove state residence requirements for presidential elections.[114]

On the other hand, he thought the Constitution plainly intended the states to have the power to maintain their own separate and independent governments, except insofar as the Constitution commanded otherwise. He took the Tenth Amendment as indicating that the Framers never imagined the national Congress could set qualifications for state and local elections. "No function is more essential to the separate and independent existence of the States and their governments than the power to determine within the limits of the Constitution the qualifications of their own voters for state, county, and municipal offices and the nature of their machinery for filling local public offices."[115] Justice Black thus thought Congress's attempt to lower the voting age for state elections unconstitutional.

The Civil War Amendments, according to Justice Black, did give Congress the power to end discrimination, however trifling, on account of race. In forbidding the use of literacy tests, Congress, on the basis of its hearings, determined that they reduced voter participation in a discriminatory manner throughout the nation. In the poll tax case, he had explicitly stated his belief that Congress had the power under section 5 of the Fourteenth Amendment to abolish that state regulation if it believed it was being used as a racially discriminatory device. He had objected because the Court majority, not Congress, had acted. He maintained, there and in this case also, that section 5, in accordance with our constitutional structure of government, authorizes Congress to pass definitive legislation to protect Fourteenth Amendment rights. Congress had here made the necessary determination that banning literacy tests was an appropriate means to guard against racial discrimination. Justice Black would not upset that determination.[116]

The strength of this opinion lies in Justice Black's clear vision of the relationship between voting and government and the Constitution. Voting is the constitutionally authorized means for citizen participation in government. It is the way we Americans govern ourselves. Since our Constitution recognizes two distinct levels of government, that relationship must pertain to both state and national government. If the two levels are to remain distinct, however, they must have their own independent roots in the source of all authority, the people. Within the specific parameters set by the Constitution, the states cannot have ultimate control over the federal electorate nor must the Congress determine who the states may enfranchise. The clarity of Justice Black's position in this case stems from his focus on the structural requisites implied by our federal system.

The problems with his opinion also arise from that focus. Justice Black's opinion seems sensible only until one realizes he was talking about that most precious of all democratic rights, political participation. *Oregon v. Mitchell* does not deal with a state's authority to pursue some substantive policy, some result of the democratic process. It deals with the essence of that process—public participation, however limited, in our decision-making institutions. Justice Black agreed when the Court said as much in *Reynolds*. Surely the lesson of that case should be that an individual's right to vote is as important at the state level as at the national level. Like his right of free speech, it should not be made dependent upon the agency of government with which he is dealing. Voting, no less than free speech, should be a right pertaining to the individual as a citizen of a free society. He should not be less of a citizen in his city or state than in his nation. When Congress acts to enlarge the franchise, it is acting in our best tradition; it is seeking to extend one of the great benefits of citizenship to other members of our society.

Justice Black's opinion in *Oregon v. Mitchell* indicates that however passionately he advocated self-government through representative institutions, he lacked a comprehensive theoretical conception of citizenship. His concept of citizenship was not large enough to embrace political participation as well as membership in a society. He treated them as isolated concerns because they are in different clauses of the Constitution. Because he lacked a coherent, overriding conception of citizenship, Justice Black was sometimes prone to let his concern for the jurisdictional arrangements override the more central issue—the value of citizenship in a free society.[117]

Political Freedom

The absence of a well-integrated theory of democractic citizenship also undermines the most famous doctrine of Justice Black's political theory—his insistence that the First Amendment is an absolute. No notion was more important to Justice Black. In many ways, all his mature political ideas developed from his concern with the condition of free speech in our society. Though he developed a clear, articulate doctrine of free speech, he never consciously connected that doctrine to other aspects of political participation in a democracy. That missing link is the source of whatever weaknesses adhere in his otherwise strong defense of our political freedom.

Hugo Black did not always have an absolutist interpretation of the First Amendment. When the New Deal Senator from Alabama first joined the Supreme Court, and for many years thereafter, he shared the preferred freedoms doctrine. Although he quickly gave voice to extemely libertarian views, there is no mistaking the balancing language of those opinions as opposed to his later absolutist viewpoints. He continued to hold this view in the immediate post–World War II period.[118]

When the Court majority began to take a less libertarian position on free speech issues during the onset of the Cold War, Justice Black began to have serious misgivings about any judicial balancing test. In the 1951 *Dennis* case, he noted his basic disagreement with the majority's constitutional approach; but he did not claim the First Amendment afforded an absolute protection to speech. Instead, he reiterated his belief that First Amendment freedoms belong in a "high preferred place . . . in a free society."[119]

As Justice Black came to feel that the court majority was balancing away vital political freedoms, his own position grew more rigid, more uncompromising. By 1952 he was expressing his belief that no judicial balancing test could be depended upon in "the present period of fear." At least as to speech in the political realm, his language began to take on absolutist overtones. "[T]he right to speak on matters of public concern must be wholly free or eventually be wholly lost."[120] What had started as a disagreement about the proper emphasis to be accorded free speech ended with Justice Black articulating a novel constitutional doctrine. No longer did he talk about the high preferred place of the First Amendment. He now spoke of the absoluteness of those rights.

Once again, Justice Black did not explicitly ground his constitutional interpretation in contract theory. Once more I think his position cannot properly be understood outside that context. Witness how Justice Black defended his idea of First Amendment absolutes: "I do not want anybody who is my servant, who is my agent, elected by me and others like me, to tell me [what] I can or cannot do."[121] The Constitution is the written manifestation of the contract establishing this relationship between the people and the government. It is the means by which the people grant authority to their rulers. When the Constitution says to public officials "Thou shall not," Justice Black believed the words mean what they say. The Framers used absolutist language to withdraw from their agents all authority for acting in those areas.[122]

As always, Justice Black used history to support his interpretation of the language. Sometimes, he referred in broad, sweeping strokes to the age-old struggle of people to curb the dangerous power of their governors.[123] More often he referred to the particular American history surrounding the adoption of the Bill of Rights.[124] Most frequently he emphasized the words of James Madison who drafted the Bill of Rights: "The right of freedom of speech is secured; the liberty of the press is expressly declared to be *beyond the reach of this Government*."[125] Black's reading of history thus confirmed his analysis of the language: "Nothing that I have read in the Congressional debates on the

Bill of Rights indicates that there was any belief that the First Amendment contained any qualifications."[126]

The Justice was well aware that most of his contemporaries both on and off the Court maintained that a belief in absolutes derives from an impossible quest for certainty in an inherently uncertain universe. The imperatives of individual liberties were seen as colliding with the imperatives dictated by the need for the effective functioning of our complex modern government. Only a pragmatic concern for consequences, it was held, can indicate the best course of action in any context.

Black did not neglect to answer his critics in kind. He pointed to the consequences of the balancing approach to the liberties safeguarded by the Bill of Rights. He was frightened by the prospects of the judiciary balancing away the constitutional rights of Americans. When the individual citizen most needs judicial protection of his constitutional rights, "balancing" would provide the least security.[127] Besides, if balancing is inevitable, Justice Black contended the Framers themselves had provided the definitive accommodation. The Framers balanced the freedoms of religion, speech, press, assembly, and petition against the needs of a powerful central government, and decided our nation's true security lay in those First Amendment freedoms.[128]

This statement about the original and authentic constitutional balance enabled Justice Black to shift his argument away from a pragmatic discussion of consequences. He was now once again focusing upon the ark of our national covenant. The ultimate evil of individual balancing was not even the probable erosion of individual rights. It was the known impact such an approach will have on what, to Black, is our greatest national treasure, our written Constitution. "In effect," he contended, balancing "changes the direction of our form of government from a government of limited powers to a government in which Congress may do anything that courts believe to be 'reasonable.'"[129] Balancing disregards the very feature the Framers thought was the unique American contribution to the science of government—a written constitution. For this reason, the judges should not tamper with the Constitution in the name of "reason," for they would then be undermining the very foundation of our Republic, the great Charter which called the American nation into being and gave it a special character.

Justice Black, therefore, had a clear position in all those cases posing no problems about the scope of First Amendment freedoms. He simply did not believe that liberties admittedly covered by the Amendment can nevertheless be abridged for the sake of some claimed superior public interest. This abridgment is exactly what happened, of course, in the 1951 *Dennis* case.[130] The interest in national security, the majority claimed, justified the infringement of free speech. The same sections of the Smith Act were involved in the *Yates*[131] case, and by 1957 Justice Black had reformulated his position. Unlike his dissent in *Dennis*,[132] his separate opinion in *Yates* has no references to the preferred freedoms doctrine. Instead, he called for "complete freedom for expression of all ideas, whether we like them or not, concerning the way government should be run and who shall run it."[133]

The theme of his dissent in *Communist Party v. Subversive Activities Control Board* (1961)[134] was that the 1950 act set the United States on the road toward outlawing groups preaching doctrines nearly all Americans detest. He thought banning an association because it advocates hated ideas violated the fundamental tenets of our Constitution. He did not see the registration provisions—the actual sections of the 1950 act involved in the Subversive Activities Control Board case—as furthering the people's need for useful information. Information would be the legitimate objective of any true registration law, Black claimed. Here the objective was to make it impossible for any organization to function once a registration order was issued against it. Justice Black was surely correct about this objective. No reading of the law or of its legislative history could support any other conclusion. Justice Black's opinion contained procedural and constitutional arguments, but he insisted they be seen as parts of a larger plan which threatened our liberties. That focus gave great strength to this dissent.[135]

By far, the largest part of his opinion was devoted to his belief that the act violated the First Amendment. Justice Black did not neglect to point out the historical parallels to both the 1950 Subversive Activities Control Act and the Smith Act,[136] and the decision of the Framers to reject that approach.[137] He again noted the evils of the balancing approach used by the majority to sustain this law under the First Amendment.[138] All those arguments, however, were subordinated to his central concern. He simply did not think that, under the Amendment, Congress had the power to outlaw an association, group, or party because it advocates a policy of violent overthrow of the existing government.[139]

He continued this "essay" in his dissenting opinion in *Scales v. United States*[140] and his concurring opinion in *Noto v. United States*,[141] the two Smith Act membership cases decided that same day. In *Scales*, he devoted most of his own dissent to castigating the "freedom-destroying nature of the balancing test."[142] In *Noto*, he preferred to rest his opinion not on the lack of sufficient evidence introduced at the trial, but on the "more solid ground that the First Amendment forbids the Government to abridge the rights of freedom of speech, press and assembly."[143]

The core of Justice Black's position was that membership in a political organization or belief in a political ideology cannot be punished by government. He viewed any governmental action which injures an individual or deprives him of something valuable as a punishment. He did not believe a person can be denied public employment,[144] tax exemptions,[145] social security benefits,[146] or even the privilege of remaining in the United States[147] solely on the basis of his political activities or beliefs. When a state seeks to prevent a person from practicing law, it must accord him the same rights, including his First Amendment rights, as when it seeks to deprive him of any other property.[148] In short, the "First Amendment's protection of association prohibits [government] from excluding a person from a profession or punishing him solely because he is a member of a particular political organization or because he holds certain beliefs."[149]

It therefore followed that government should not be able to conduct investigations into an individual's political beliefs and associations. There is no legitimate purpose for government to conduct an inquisition into a person's beliefs and affiliations. The First Amendment would, in Justice Black's view, bar the use of any information obtained. Moreover, inquiries into these protected areas discourage citizens from exercising rights protected by the Constitution. The freedom envisioned by the Framers, according to Black, requires more than orthodox, time-serving, government-fearing individuals. Such freedom requires people who are fearless enough to think as they please and to say what they think. For this reason, Justice Black believed the First Amendment is a complete ban on any governmental inquiry into the realm of speech and association.[150]

Justice Black's absolutism made him a bold and seemingly fearless defender of an individual's political beliefs; yet we are entitled to ask whether his sharp distinction between conduct and ideas can satisfactorily deal with the complexities of contemporary American life. How, for example, is the government to protect military security if it cannot screen the personnel with access to secret information? Since World War II, Communists and Communist sympathizers—in the United States, Britain, and Canada—have been the most frequent betrayers of military secrets. Justice Black's unqualified dichotomy would not permit even a narrowly focused inquiry into the political beliefs of the relatively few individuals dealing with military security.

Justice Black probably recognized his theory's inadequacies for dealing with the hard realities of our security interests. Professor Sylvia Snowiss has noted that Justice Black invariably refrained from articulating his absolutist position in the cases where the government could raise a legitimate security interest. Instead, he simply noted his concurrence with opinions which used the preferred freedoms approach to call for narrowly drawn, specific, and limited loyalty-security programs.[151] Justice Black's "silence" permitted him to retain a theoretical consistency; it did not, however, strengthen the credibility of his absolutism.

When we shift our attention from the First Amendment cases involving the Communist Party to those involving the NAACP, the same pattern emerges from Justice Black's opinions. He joined Justice Harlan's opinion for the Court in *NAACP v. Alabama* (1958)[152] which declared there was a First Amendment right of association and which sustained the NAACP's reliance upon that right against Alabama's efforts to obtain its membership lists.

When the Supreme Court upheld the NAACP's refusal to give its membership lists to the city of Little Rock,[153] Justices Black and Douglas filed a joint concurrence. Justice Stewart's opinion for the other seven members held that Little Rock had shown no relevant correlation between its occupation license taxes and the compulsory disclosure and publication of those membership lists. Black and Douglas took a firmer First Amendment position. First Amendment rights they declared, were "beyond abridgement either by legislation that directly restrains their exercise or by suppression or impairment through harassment, humiliation, or exposure by government."[154]

When the Court held a committee of the Florida legislature had not established a sufficient connection between its request for the membership list of the Miami branch of the NAACP and its stated purpose of ferreting out Communists, Justice Black again filed a separate concurring opinion.[155] In his view, the constitutional right of association included the privilege of any person to associate with Communists or anti-Communists, Socialists or anti-Socialists, or, for that matter, with people of all kinds of beliefs, popular or unpopular.

As with Meiklejohn's interpretation, then, Justice Black's absolutist interpretation of the First Amendment seems, at first glance, capable of enhancing our political freedom. Here, too, we may well doubt that this enlarged view of First Amendment rights is sufficient, by itself, to encompass a meaningful concept of citizenship or to provide the stimulus for greater public political participation. Nonetheless, if Justice Black's views about free speech ever gained general acceptance and were conscientiously followed, the liberties of all Americans would undoubtedly be in a healthier condition. That fact is clearly shown by these cases.

It is important to stress that the First Amendment rights Justice Black sought to cloak in absolute immunity from governmental abridgement are rights he saw as belonging to all Americans, not just dissident minorities. His opinions appeared in cases involving activists in minority causes, but Black always saw the political freedom of all Americans concretely intertwined with the right of a pacifist to resist inquiries about the guests at his summer camp,[156] with a teacher's refusal to tell a congressional committee about his alleged Communist affiliations,[157] and with the refusal by candidates for admission to the bar to reveal or explain their political beliefs and affiliations.[158] To Justice Black, the real importance of these cases was more than the personal rights of the individuals involved. It was *"the interest of the people* as a whole in being able to join organizations, advocate causes and make political 'mistakes' without later being subjected to governmental penalties for having dared to think for themselves."[159]

The best illustration of how Justice Black's absolutist interpretation of the First Amendment enhances political freedom for all Americans is to be found in the celebrated *Pentagon Papers* case.[160] In the late spring of 1971, the *New York Times* and the *Washington Post* began publishing stories based on a classified Pentagon study of American involvement in the war in Indochina. The newspapers also published some of the classified documents found in that study. The federal government sought a permanent injunction against the continued publication of those articles and documents without prior clearance from the government. Six Justices signed a *per curiam* opinion for the Court which held that under the First Amendment any prior restraint of publication bears a heavy presumption against its constitutional validity and that the government had not shown sufficient justification for imposing such a restraint in this instance.

Although the newspapers were able to resume publication, the case can hardly be viewed as a complete vindication of the right of a free press to publish whatever it pleases. Even without a congressional statute, three Justices thought the executive's claim to be acting on behalf of American national security outweighed the traditional right of the press to be free from prior restraints.[161] Their opinions reflect the realist theory of democracy discussed in chapter 6. Two Justices joined the majority only because they felt the government had not met the extraordinary burden required to impose a prior restraint, and they went on to suggest the newspapers might be subject to criminal prosecutions (after the fact) for publishing classified information.[162] Justice Marshall's concurring opinion discussed only the absence of congressional law.[163] These three opinions reflect the optimalist theory of democracy discussed in chapter 7.

In the end, then, only Justices Black, Douglas, and Brennan stated that the First Amendment barred all prior restraints on the right to publish news;[164] and, only Justice Black, in an opinion Justice Douglas joined, made it clear that the central issue was the right of all Americans to learn what their agents—the government—were doing. Relying, as always, upon both the words of the Constitution and the history surrounding their adoption, Justice Black plainly stated his understanding of why the founding fathers wrote freedom of the press into the First Amendment:"The press was to serve the governed, not the governors. The Government's power to censor the press was abolished so that the press could remain forever free to censure the Government. The press was protected so that it could bare the secrets of government and inform the people."[165]

This discussion of the role of a free press in our political system was the core of Justice Black's opinion. He totally rejected the Solicitor General's argument that, despite the language and history of the First Amendment, the President's authority in foreign affairs and as commander in chief justified this effort to enjoin the publication of current news in the name of national security.[166] The government's argument and its acceptance by some of his judicial brethren served to confirm to Justice Black the Framers' wisdom and the correctness of his own position. Only an absolute interpretation of the First Amendment could "preserve inviolate the constitutional rights of free speech, free press, and free assembly in order to maintain the opportunity for free political discussion, to the end that government may be responsive to the will of the people. Therein," Justice Black concluded, "lies the true security of the Republic, the very foundation of constitutional government."[167]

In the context of our national agony over the Indochina War, Justice Black's opinion in this case was faultless. By 1971 that war had been an overriding concern of American politics for more years than anyone wanted to recall. Its past, present, and future impact on our society approached the incalculable. To have denied the public information about that war—information which no official could show as creating direct, immediate, and irreparable damage to our nation or its people—was to deny the very ingredients necessary for democratic government. The newspapers served to make public reaction to the war more informed, more enlightened.

Hugo L. Black always knew that an informed public is vital to our political system because democracy is predicated upon debate and discussion. In the course of his long career he learned that this essential element is most threatened, is most in jeopardy of being curtailed, precisely when it is most needed by our democracy—when our society and its leaders must make major decisions which will shape our future. For this reason, Justice Black now came to believe that only the firmest judicial defense of the First Amendment can preserve the freedoms for a wide-open and robust *public* discussion of those decisions. On the evidence of events like those surrounding the *Pentagon Papers* case, Justice Black has a most persuasive position.

The question, then, is why more of the intellectual community has not come to espouse Justice Black's absolutist interpretation of the First Amendment. Most share Black's deep and abiding commitment to liberal values and see democracy as inextricably linked with the freedoms embodied in the First Amendment. Like Alexander Meiklejohn, however, Justice Black was unable to rally a significant segment of the intellectual community to his position. If anything, the absolutist interpretation of Justice Black has attracted fewer supporters than Meiklejohn's interpretation. In the law reviews, in the professional journals of political science and philosophy, and in the general quarterlies and magazines of the intellectual community, Justice Black's views are invariably treated with the respect reserved for an honorable, but mistaken, position.

As with Meiklejohn's position, this treatment stems largely from Justice Black's inability to handle important problems arising at the boundaries of his conception of free speech. He was not, of course, plagued by exactly the same difficulties as the proponents of the functional contract theory. Since Justice Black made no distinction between public and private speech he had no difficulty framing a constitutional standard for handling obscenity. He believed that:

> There is nothing in the language of the First Amendment to indicate that it protects only *political* speech . . . Since the language of the Amendment contains no exceptions, I have continuously voted to strike down all laws dealing with so-called obscene materials since I believe such laws act to establish a system of censorship in violation of the First Amendment . . . Censorship, even under the guise of protecting people from books or plays or motion pictures that other people think are obscene, shows a fear that people cannot judge for themselves.[168]

Justice Black found it difficult to comprehend how talk about sex can be placed under any kind of "censorship" without risking even greater dangers—attempts to tell people how and what to think. Given the Supreme Court's evident inability to frame an adequate standard for handling obscenity and pornography, and given the general libertarian bias of the American intellectual community, Justice Black's position in this area certainly did not diminish the attractiveness of his absolutist doctrine.

In the context of the 1950s and 1960s, I do not believe many people failed to support Justice Black's theory because of its inadequacies in dealing with genuine national security needs. The nation's loyalty-security programs put in place during the Cold War hysteria were too broad and plainly helped sustain ideological witch-hunts.[169] In that environment, it was easier to interpret Justice Black's absolutism as a strength rather than a weakness. His was a clarion call for a return to first principles. In the context of the fight against McCarthyism, the full implications of Justice Black's absolutism were ignored,[170] or his theory was regarded as a tactical position; once the hysteria was over, it was assumed he would modify his theory to sustain properly drawn and administered security programs.[171] We must look elsewhere for the cause of the cool reception accorded Justice Black's interpretation of the First Amendment.

One such area regards the status of libel and slander laws. Justice Black's apparent disregard of these ancient and universally accepted laws formed a major part of the criticism leveled at his famous lecture on the Bill of Rights. Two years later, he defended his belief that the First Amendment "was not intended to authorize damage suits for mere words as distinguished from conduct." He maintained "that it is time enough for government to step in to regulate people when they *do* something, not when the *say* something, and I do not believe myself that there is *any* halfway ground if you enforce the protections of the First Amendment."[172]

When the Court, in *New York Times v. Sullivan* (1964),[173] first imposed substantive restrictions on state defamation laws, Justice Black noted his reservation in a separate concurring opinion. At the very least, Justice Black thought, the First Amendment left the people and the press absolutely free to criticize officials and discuss public affairs with impunity. An unconditional right to say what one pleases about public affairs was only a *minimal* guarantee of the First Amendment. He would have preferred to decide this case on the grounds that the people and the press had an absolute, unconditional right to speak and publish.[174]

When Justice Brennan sought to apply the *New York Times* "actual malice" standard to libel cases involving public figures (as opposed to public officials) and to libel actions brought by a private individual involving events of public or general interest, he could no longer muster a majority of the Court.[175] To Justice Black, his brother Brennan's experience indicated that the *New York Times* doctrine would plunge the Court into the same quagmire as in the field of obscenity. He was confident that experience with the "actual malice" doctrine would prove its inadequacy to protect freedom of the press from destruction in libel cases. The words "malicious" and "reckless disregard of the truth" could never serve, according to Black, as effective substitutes for the absolute "no" of the First Amendment.[176]

Justice Black had good reason to fear that freedom of speech and press would not be adequately protected by the "actual malice" exception. Knowing or reckless falsity are elusive concepts and necessarily give a jury broad scope and much discretion. A trial is a chancy thing to begin with, no matter what standards the Supreme Court imposes. To let a jury using the "actual malice" standard choose a verdict and impose damages as it sees fit and proper, is to make vital First Amendment rights dependent upon emotions and preju-dices.[177] The Court has held that the freedoms of speech and press "may not be submitted to vote; they depend on the outcome of no election."[178] It is difficult indeed to see why those rights should be made dependent upon a jury's decision. For this reason, I do not think the concern about the cor-rupting effect of falsehood has been the major source of dissatisfaction with Black's position. Much as democrats dislike having the political process distorted by misleading statements, as the inheritors of the liberal tradition they fear suppression of unpopular ideas even more.

What really troubled people about Justice Black's adamant opposition to all libel and defamation laws was his apparent lack of concern for individual privacy. As long ago as 1890, Samuel D. Warren and Louis D. Brandeis, in the most famous of all law review articles, emphasized the importance of "the right to privacy."[179] Since then, the forces shaping modern society have contracted our sense of physical space. The more difficult it has become to escape from both the unavoidable and deliberate intrusions on our lives, the more vehemently Americans have asserted the right to be left alone, to live their lives as they choose. It was their concern for the right to privacy which led some of the libertarian Justices to oppose an extension of the *New York Times* doctrine[180] and make them reluctant to embrace Justice Black's interpretation of the First Amendment.

Justice Brandeis once called privacy "the most comprehensive of rights and the right most valued by civilized man.[181] Justice Black, on the other hand, consistently and persistently refused to recognize privacy as a claim entitled to constitutional protection. His insistence upon sticking to the plain language of the Constitution precluded him from talking as though there was some constitutional provision prohibiting any and all governmental invasions of individual privacy. Only certain aspects of privacy were protected, he maintained; not all of them were protected in the same way.

The First Amendment thus afforded an absolute protection to an individual's beliefs and associations, while the Fourth Amendment protected his house and property only from unreasonable search and seizures.[182] Similarly, Justice Black did not think judges had the authority to protect an individual from intrusions emanating from the private sector by creating a right equal to or superior to the right of free press the Constitution had created. Because the right of free press was enshrined in the Constitution, Justice Black was unwilling to have a claim based upon that right rejected in favor of a legislatively created "right" to privacy.[183] In his judicial theory, neither the judges nor the legislature could shield the individual from the media.

Why this position would trouble the growing number of people concerned about the need for privacy in our society is well illustrated by Justice Black's opinion in *Time, Inc. v. Hill* (1967).[184] Justice Brennan's plurality opinion would have permitted a retrial, for he thought the error lay in the trial judge's failure to use the "actual malice" test explicitly in his instructions to the jury. Justice Black's separate opinion urged both reversal and dismissal of the suit. He believed the First Amendment precluded any law limiting the press.

Differing attitudes toward privacy are reflected in the two opinions. Justice Brennan recognized the existence of both a public right of communication and a zone of individual privacy. His "actual malice" test was designed to reconcile these two claims, and although it was heavily weighted in favor of the First Amendment right of free press, he was willing to countenance some limitations in the name of the individual's claim to be left alone. Justice Black, on the other hand, saw only one right involved—that of the press. He displayed no concern whatever for the way the media discussed events and for the damage to individual lives which might result.

In such circumstances, it is difficult to see what great damage could result from permitting a jury to determine whether or not the error was incidental. In cases brought by private individuals—persons whose conduct comes to public attention *only* because of the action of the media—compensation can be limited to proved, actual damages, caused by statements shown to be defamatory. If juries are unable to grant essentially unlimited awards for punitive damages, the media need not fear it will be punished simply because it expounds unorthodox views. Given the power of the media in our society, such a rule appears more likely to encourage responsibility than to engender fear and timidity. From the perspective of the individual involuntarily thrust into the limelight, even Justice Brennan's "actual malice" test might seem too lenient, but he, at least, recognizes that absolute press freedom and individual privacy and dignity are not always compatible. Justice Black's theory seemed unable to admit that possibility.

The absence of an explicit right to privacy in the Constitution created a blind spot for Justice Black. He consistently adhered to his constitutional theory; he was faithful to the text. Most Americans concerned with privacy were unwilling to ignore that individual right merely for the sake of theoretical consistency. If the theory ignored that right, they were bound to question the theory.

I think, however, there was another reason Justice Black's position did not attract wider support in the intellectual community. In the 1960s, the primary disagreement with Justice Black's interpretation of the First Amendment was the sharp distinction he made between "speech" and "conduct" in the demonstration cases. More than anything else, this focus was dictated by the course of events. As the civil rights movement gave way to the black protest movement and as opposition to American military operations in Indochina grew more vehement, demonstrations became an increasingly important form of political activity.

Political liberals tended to see those protests primarily as a form of communication. To Justice Black, demonstrations were forms of conduct. Liberals believed the communicative element involved in such activity brought it within the scope of the First Amendment. Justice Black maintained such conduct was only marginally protected by the Speech and Assembly Clauses. He believed government could substantially regulate demonstrations, while the liberals thought the Constitution precluded all but minimal government intervention.

Since the liberals generally supported the goals, if not always the tactics, of the protestors they became increasingly disenchanted with Justice Black's position.[185] No longer, as when "communism" was the primary First Amendment issue, did the liberals stress the virtues of Justice Black's absolutist defense of the First Amendment. Conservatives, on the other hand, began to develop a newfound appreciation for his judicial integrity. Both groups, of course, were influenced by the substantive results which would have followed from his interpretations. Still, their reactions indicate how important this problem is to a proper evaluation of Justice Black's interpretation of the Constitution.

As soon as Justice Black began to insist upon the absolute nature of the First Amendment he recognized the need to make a *sharp* distinction between speech and conduct.[186] He made the distinction in his famous *Barenblatt* dissent.[187] Since the point was peripheral to the main issue of *Barenblatt*, however, this element of Justice Black's interpretation of the First Amendment did not receive much attention. It became a more prominent feature in 1964 when the Court decided *Bell v. Maryland*.[188] The case involved a 1960 "sit-in" at a Baltimore restaurant to protest the management's policy of excluding blacks. The fifteen to twenty protestors were peaceful and orderly but they refused to leave when they were denied service solely on the basis of their race. After an hour and a half, they were arrested for violating the Maryland trespass statute.

One of the issues involved in the case was the protestors' claim that their actions were protected by the First Amendment. Although the Court did not decide this or any other substantive issue involved in the case, Justice Black, in dissent, rejected out of hand the contention "that a person's right to freedom of expression carries with it a right to force a private property owner to furnish his property as a platform to criticize the property owner's use of that property."[189] The Maryland statute, he insisted, was directed not against what Bell and his associates *said*, but what they *did*—remaining on the premises of another after being warned to leave.

The protestors' First Amendment claim was an extension of an argument Justice Harlan had made in *Garner v. Louisiana* (1961).[190] Harlan had suggested that a peaceful, orderly, sit-in demonstration was as much a part of the free trade in ideas as verbal expression, more commonly thought of as speech. Such a demonstration appeals to others just as much as, if not more than, a public oration delivered from a soap box at a street corner. Moreover, Justice Harlan had argued, the Court had never limited the right of speech to mere verbal expression.

Harlan had been careful to qualify his view of the relationship between protest demonstrations and the First Amendment by denying the Constitution protected demonstrations conducted on private property over the objection of the owner. This qualification was, of course, at the heart of the *Bell* case. As we have just seen, Justice Black's dissent made much of it. He and Justice Harlan, who joined his dissent, were in agreement on this point. They differed significantly on the relationship between the First Amendment and demonstrations, however. Justice Harlan's flexible balancing approach enabled him to treat demonstrations as a form of expression, for his position also permitted him to say that not all expression was constitutionally protected. Justice Black preferred to keep his categories pure. Speech must be totally free; demonstrations should be classified as conduct for they often require regulation.

Bell v. Maryland was not resolved upon First Amendment grounds, so it was not until *Cox v. Louisiana* (1965)[191] that Justice Black's distinction between speech and conduct became clearly visible. Because Justice Black saw standing, patrolling, and picketing as conduct, not speech, he did not doubt that government could regulate or even prohibit that conduct.[192] A state could bar all picketing on its streets and highways. He repeated his statement from *Barenblatt* that when passing upon the validity of such a regulation, which may *indirectly* infringe on free speech, the Court would have to weigh the circumstances to protect, not destroy, First Amendment freedoms. In context, however, he clearly would sustain a properly drawn and applied statute curbing demonstrations. He explicitly stated the streets and highways were basically dedicated to facilitating travel from one place to another. Government, therefore, had a proper concern with anything interfering with this basic purpose. Moreover, Justice Black thought the government was not constitutionally required to supply a place for people to exercise freedom of speech or assembly. In this "balance" Justice Black would be weighing a proper governmental interest against a nonexistent private right. There can be little doubt about how he would decide a case involving a properly drawn and applied statute.

What kind of statute would meet Justice Black's criteria in this area? *Cox* itself begins to supply the answer. He agreed with the Court majority in reversing Reverend Cox's conviction for breach of the peace. He thought it was based on a statute which on its face and as construed by the Louisiana Supreme Court was unconstitutionally vague. Justice Black would not permit the government to suppress particular ideas under the guise of regulating conduct.[193]

Moreover, the Louisiana breach of the peace statute, like its law against obstructing streets and sidewalks, explicitly exempted labor organizations. By specifically permitting picketing for the expression of labor union views, the state was attempting to pick and choose the views it was willing to have discussed on its streets. Black believed that if the streets of a town are open to some views, they must be open to all. In agreeing with the majority that Cox's conviction for obstructing public passages must be overturned, Justice Black again indicated that regulations of conduct which affect speech cannot deal with the content of the ideas.[194]

The third statute involved in *Cox* illustrates the kind of regulation Black would have government use in handling protest demonstrations. It flatly prohibited anyone from picketing or parading near a courthouse, residence, or other buildings used by a judge, juror, witness, or court officer "with the intent of influencing" them. Black constructed a judicial balance since the statute aimed at conduct impinging on speech. He found a legitimate state purpose, even more important than the maintenance of orderly traffic patterns. The law was enacted to promote the orderly processes of justice, to free court procedures from intimidation by crowds. Justice Black recognized no individual right for the other side of the balance. Citizens did not have an automatic right to use the streets for protest.[195] Justice Black therefore concluded the Louisiana statute prohibiting picketing near a courthouse was a narrowly drawn regulation of conduct designed to achieve a legitimate state purpose and well within its constitutional authority.

Justice Black, unlike the Court majority, also thought the law had been properly applied against Cox. There could be no question that the 2,000 or so demonstrators had intended to influence court officials; that pressure, after all, was the purpose of the protest. Nor could there be any question that the demonstration had taken place "near" the courthouse, within the meaning of the statute. In addition, one judge had felt impelled to leave the building. To Black and the other dissenters, Cox had engaged in precisely the kind of activity the statute proscribed.[196]

Justice Black's opinion in *Cox* illustrates that his sharp distinction between speech and conduct was only the starting point for his analysis. Since few, if any, jurisdictions totally forbid all picketing or marching, his own formulation meant he had to weigh the circumstances involved in the particular demonstration. It would not do, however, to minimize the importance of the differences he saw between verbal and nonverbal expression. The distinction set the presumption of his "balance." Once the Justice was convinced an activity could properly be labelled conduct, he would sustain virtually any governmental regulation which did not on its face or in its application threaten discriminatory treatment based upon content. This approach enabled him to carry over to the demonstration cases a key element in his interpretation of the First Amendment—governmental neutrality toward all ideas. This approach also enabled him to suggest a wider latitude for governmental control of activity he viewed as potentially deleterious.

In *Brown v. Louisiana* (1966)[197] Justice Black, in dissent, noted that discriminatory enforcement, which had contaminated the public street phrase of the state breach of the peace statute in *Cox*, was not present in the public buildings section of the statutes. The public buildings section created no exception for labor organizations; on its face, it flatly prohibited any person or group to remain in a public building when requested to leave by competent authorities. Justice Black also did not believe this section, especially when applied to a library, suffered from the vice of vagueness. Whatever the disagreement about the range of activities permitted on a street or highway, public buildings like a library are maintained to perform certain specific functions. A library is dedicated to circulating books and reading. Those purposes limited the discretion of the authorities—they could not legitimately ask someone to leave who was actually attempting to use the facility to read, study, or obtain material. Similarly, the purposes of the facility provided the public was a clear indication of the kind of activity which would not be sanctioned. Individuals not using a public library for library purposes had no right to stay there over the protest of the librarian. To Justice Black, this section of the Louisiana breach of the peace statute was a narrow, specific, ideologically neutral regulation of conduct and was therefore constitutional.

Moreover, Justice Black could find no fault with the way Louisiana applied the statute in this case. Given the extremely small size of the rural branch library, the Louisiana courts had ample grounds for concluding that even a peaceful, orderly "stand-up" by only five men disrupted the library's normal, quiet functioning. In sum, he could see no reason to overturn the convictions.

When the Court decided *Adderley v. Florida* (1966),[198] Justice Black finally had the opportunity to write his views into a majority opinion. Adderley and thirty one other blacks had been convicted of trespassing upon the grounds outside the county jail. Justice Black proceeded on the premise that the demonstration was conduct, not speech, and as such could be regulated or curtailed by evenhanded enforcement of a nondiscriminatory statute.

The major constitutional issue, at least for Justice Black, was whether the statute was so general as to suffer from the vice of vagueness. Justice Black again used the idea of property being dedicated to specific purposes as a way of rejecting the vagueness claim. The state capitol grounds in *Edwards* are open to the public; jails, built for security purposes, are not. Streets and highways, as in *Cox*, are sometimes used for marching and picketing; a jail serves a clearly demarcated and widely understood function.

Having found the statute constitutional on its face, the only remaining issue of significance for Justice Black was whether it had been applied in an evenhanded manner. His examination of the record satisfied him there was absolutely no indication that Florida officials had acted because they objected to what was being sung or said by the demonstrators or because they disagreed with the objectives of the protest. They objected only to the demonstrators' presence on property reserved for jail uses. Justice Black could therefore find no reason for overturning the convictions.[199]

Justice Black's treatment of the demonstration cases revealed an insensitivity to protest politics in contemporary American society. Peaceful and orderly demonstrations provide politically disadvantaged groups with one of their most potent political instruments. To those with an unpopular position or without financial resources, a demonstration is often the only effective means to publicize their message.[200]

The limitation on political participation of groups protesting the status quo was more than a speculative possibility in Justice Black's theory. His sharp distinction between speech and conduct permitted governmental authorities to forbid all picketing, patrolling, and marching on all public facilities. Neither the First Amendment nor any other constitutional provision, according to Black, compels government to provide a place for people to speak, write, or assemble.[201] A blanket prohibition against using streets and parks for political purposes suggests an appealing governmental neutrality; but, underneath that formal equality lurks a systematic discrimination in practice. Those who feel most aggrieved, the very people who feel that the formal institutions and mechanisms of government are not responsive to their rights and interests, would lose an opportunity to call for change.[202]

When, late in his judicial career, Black failed to recognize the importance of peaceful demonstrations as a form of political expression, he committed the very error his earlier opinions had warned against. He, too, easily transformed "minor inconveniences into major evils of such magnitude as to warrant the curtailment of the liberty of expression."[203] Actually, the demonstrations in *Cox* and *Adderley* are best seen as minor inconveniences. In *Cox*, the demonstration across the street from the courthouse could not have resulted in the unfair administration of justice. No one arrested for participating in a sit-in (the "injustice" being protested) was then on trial, and even the judge interrupted by the noise outside the building suffered no more than a temporary inconvenience. Reverend Cox and the students gave no indication of staying indefinitely. The plight of the judge, taken at face value, was of about the same magnitude as the public's temporary lack of access to the state capitol in *Edwards*, which Black had recognized as entirely legitimate. In *Adderley*, there was no evidence that the protest on the grounds *outside* the jailhouse had upset any of the procedures for dealing with prisoners *inside* the building. At most, there was some minor, and presumably temporary, inconvenience of access to the jail, and even that point was in dispute.[204]

Obviously, some public facilities may be dedicated to purposes completely alien to any mass protest—a hospital, for example. Other public facilities may normally be used for purposes which make most demonstrations anomalous[205]—a library for example. The latter example is what makes Justice

Black's dissent in the library stand-up case so persuasive. The five demonstrators were peaceful, but their very presence completely disrupted a facility dedicated to quiet reading, study, and reflection. Nor did they give any indication of leaving soon; rather, as their professed model was the lunch counter sit-ins, they were likely to remain as long as the facility was open. Unlike the situations which led to the sit-ins, however, they had been given all the service available at the local branch library.

One does not need Justice Black's sharp distinction between speech and conduct, however, to recognize that Black had come to the sounder conclusion in the library stand-up case. Justice Douglas, using a preferred freedoms approach, conceded as much in his *Adderley* dissent.[206] The preferred freedoms approach, precisely because it is a balancing test, seems better suited to reconcile, by detailed analysis of the *facts*, a democracy's need for maximum political expression with a society's legitimate interests in orderly traffic patterns, quiet residential areas, secure jails, and fair trials. Justice Black's approach provided him with rigid categories that proved insensitive to the First Amendment claims involved in mass demonstrations.[207]

The central point for analysis, then, must be why, relatively late in his career, Justice Black sought to define political expression so narrowly. He knew an absolutist interpretation did not automatically preclude some flexibility at the margins. Like the followers of Alexander Meiklejohn, Justice Black could have argued that the mixture of speech and conduct involved in demonstrations required some judicial balancing. Justice Black himself had suggested as much in his *Barenblatt* dissent, in the very opinion in which he first fully articulated his absolutist interpretation of the First Amendment. Justice Black was well aware that absolutism did not require a narrow view of political expression.

A re-reading of Justice Black's opinions shows that the critical factor was his belief that the protest politics of the 1960s posed a serious threat to American democracy. Beginning with *Bell v. Maryland* (1964), the spectre of anarchy looms large in his opinions. Heretofore, his First Amendment opinions dealing with the Communist Party, the NAACP, obscenity, and libel had focused on the content of ideas being voiced by various Americans. That focus gave the impression that Justice Black saw the processes by which ideas are expressed and opinion mobilized as being beyond the scope of governmental regulation. It had appeared that Justice Black thought citizen participation in these activities was beyond the concern of the government.

At the close of his *Bell* dissent, however, he emphasized that the great purpose of freedom of speech and press was to settle disputes peaceably, without resort to intimidation, force, or violence, and that therefore some limitation on the *means* of expression was not only permissible, but essential in a well-ordered democracy. He still maintained, of course, that our system did not sanction any interference with the widest possible exchange of ideas. The *content* of communications was absolutely protected by the First Amendment; but our national plan also required a restraint on any means of communication which threatened others. Government could and should channel the expression of ideas into certain prescribed channels. The best way—Justice Black came close to saying the only way—to achieve a good society, including racial justice, was through the orderly procedures of representative government and the judicial system.[208] A person with this view of the democratic political process was bound to see the seeds of disintegration in the continual resort to protest demonstrations.

A year later, in *Cox*, Justice Black returned to this point with even more passion.[209] Thereafter, his hostility towards protest demonstrations became a settled part of Black's jurisprudence.[210] The clearest statement is to be found in his Carpentier Lectures at the Columbia University School of Law. The orderly processes of representative government are compared to the clamorous, tumultuous, potentially riotous demonstration; the reasoned decisions of governmental agencies are contrasted with the peremptory, shouting, emotional demands of the protestors; responsible officials selected by all the people through the ballot box are juxtaposed to the self-appointed spokesmen for particularized interests; peaceful accommodation within the system is seen as an alternative to the hate-breeding divisiveness produced by taking to the streets. Peace, order, and the rational pursuit of justice are identified with the existing institutional processes; tumult, potential anarchy, emotional appeals to narrow self-interest are seen as inherent in mass demonstrations.[211]

Another indication of Justice Black's antagonism toward the protest politics which began to emerge in the 1960s can be found by his great concern with a factor he had not stressed in other contexts and at other times—privacy. His original position, it will be recalled, stemmed from his refusal to acknowledge that a general right of privacy could be judicially created from separate clauses in the Constitution.[212] At an earlier time, when Justice Black saw the domestic political scene as essentially tranquil and orderly, he was quite willing to tolerate intrusions into the serenity of private homes occasioned by loudspeakers[213] or door to door solicitation.[214] A municipality, he then believed, could not protect the tranquility of its streets and homes at the expense of stifling the dissemination of ideas.

By 1969, however, Justice Black saw a person's home as a bastion of domestic tranquility wherein one could escape the hurly-burly of the outside business and political world. He urged legislatures to enact narrowly drawn statutes regulating the conduct of demonstrators so that the people would not be subjected to the "uncontrollable whim and arrogance of speakers, writers, protestors and grievance bearers." He now believed there was no constitutional necessity to sacrifice the home, that "sacred retreat to which families repair for their privacy," to the desires of those who wish "to convert the occupants to new views, new morals, and a new way of life."[215]

At the end of his long career, Justice Black had thus clearly come to believe that the political action involved in protest demonstrations was *outside* and *opposed* to the political system established by the Constitution. For this reason, he did not believe such activity was encompassed within the protections of the First Amendment. Insofar as the Amendment was designed to serve a political function, it was to enhance the people's choice at the ballot box and their representatives' decisions in public office. A continual resort to protest demonstrations jeopardized the very goals he believed the First Amendment was designed to advance—peace, order, and justice.[216]

CONCLUSIONS

Once again, then, we are back to the point raised by Justice Black's opinions in the denaturalization and reapportionment cases—his theoretical conception of American democracy. Despite the occasional use of language suggesting the contrary, Justice Black's opinions are permeated with an individualistic conception of man in society. "Citizenship in this Nation is a part of a cooperative affair," he wrote in *Afroyim*, but nowhere did he elaborate upon a cooperative concept of citizenship. Instead, his focus on *individual* rights precluded that development. He always believed the Constitution was designed to protect against arbitrary uses of governmental authority so that each individual could pursue his own vision of the good life.

His First Amendment opinions, when read against the background provided by his reapportionment opinions, well illustrate the point. It will be recalled that Justice Black's absolutist interpretation of the Free Speech Clause was intrinsically individualistic. Individuals have the absolute right to speak and that right cannot be abridged by government acting as an agent of society. Societal concerns for certain aspects of individual privacy could not be sustained against another person's First Amendment right to free speech. Justice Black saw this individually held right of free speech as giving the people a great influence over governmental policy.

In his opinions primarily concerned with how that influence is to be made manifest, we saw that his central concern was in insuring equal weighting of each individual's vote. Again, there was an all but exclusive focus on a right adhering to discrete individuals. The only way he talked about citizens participating in self-government was through the mechanisms of representative government. His focus on individual rights led him to see society as composed of almost atomistic individuals engaging in the enterprise of self-government through representative institutions. Each citizen's participation in the electoral process seems to be the extent of cooperation inherent in Justice Black's conception of American citizenship.

Justice Black's limited conception of joint public endeavors is strikingly similar to the ideas of the Framers. The Framers of the Constitition also saw governmental institutions as providing the minimum cooperation necessary to maintain a society. The primary activities of men were seen as taking place outside the reach of government and their civic role took on a decidedly secondary importance. The political order was seen as an instrument for the protection of personal interests. Essentially privatized individuals were to have conflicting interests filtered through the formal arrangements of government; their interests would be protected by a system which permitted only mutually tolerated policies to emerge.[217] Hugo L. Black's extensive search for the intent of the Framers—an activity which occupied him throughout his thirty five years as a Justice—was bound to reinforce the already strong emphasis on individualism he had expressed as a populist politician before taking his seat on the Court.[218]

It is surely more than coincidental, for example, that Justice Black's opposition to street protests paralleled Madison's dread of factions. Madison feared factions because their passionate pursuit of their own interests made them intolerant of others. We have just seen Black raise the same objection to the politics of mass demonstrations: it made compromise within the system all but impossible. Like the Framers, Justice Black saw passionate attachments forged *outside* the system as jeopardizing peaceful cooperation *within*.

When a concern about the potentially harmful effects of human solidarity are seen in conjunction with a theory emphasizing the private and personal pursuit of the good life, it is understandable why Justice Black's opinions never explore the dimensions of how we are cooperatively to govern ourselves. An individual may, of course, choose to see his interests in communal terms, but the only common interest Justice Black recognized as inherent in our governmental system is the institutional arrangements for organizing individual inputs. This idea is not peculiar to the thought of Justice Black; on the contrary, as we saw in the historical survey in Part I, it is the dominant mode of American political thought. It does mean, however, that for all of Justice Black's expressed concern for enhancing self-government, he viewed political participation in much the same way as the adherents of the competitive theories of democracy. He offered us no new vision of community purpose and democratic citizenship.

The same point can be made another way. Because Justice Black came to his concern for democratic theory through his judicial role, his intellectual endeavors started and ended with the written Constitution. This approach was his great strength as a judge. It was also his weakness as a political theorist. He believed the Constitution was central to the American political system.

He sought to interpret the Constitution in a way that would keep it faithful to what he believed to have been the intent of the Framers and relevant to our current situation. By insisting our government was without authority to take away a person's citizenship, Justice Black was trying to insure that an old idea—government as the agent of the sovereign people—would have a functioning importance in the American polity of today. When Justice Black insisted that our representative bodies conform to the "one person, one vote" standard, he sought to restore legislatures as an important means of self-government, while simultaneously reinvigorating a most precious right of democratic citizenship—the right to vote. He saw his absolutist interpretation of the First Amendment as a way of achieving an age-old dream of freedom: to give all citizens the right to speak their minds, join organizations, and peaceably advocate causes without fear of governmental penalties.

Perhaps most important of all, Justice Black sought to restore importance to the very idea of a written constitution. Judges interpreting the Constitution in the light of one or the other of the competitive theories of democracy were always a majority during Justice Black's long tenure on the Court. He came to believe that those approaches—even the more libertarian, preferred freedoms approach—drained the Constitution of meaning. If a judge must balance competing interests, if he must weigh the supposedly enduring principles embodied in the written document against the needs seen as compelling by the government, then the Constitution is empty until the Court decides to put a particular content into it. Since issues, circumstances, etc. vary from case to case and from time to time, a balancing approach builds vagueness into the Constitution. The document becomes inherently incapable of saying anything lasting and enduring to the American people. If words have no stable meanings, why have a written Constitution?

Justice Black saw the Constitution as more than a set of vague admonitions subject to judicial manipulation. He saw it as the very foundation of our polity. To him, the Constitution gave life to our society. Like the founding generation, he saw the written Constitution as shaping and molding the essential nature of American democracy. For the Constitution to function in this manner, Justice Black saw the judicial role as giving fairly precise meaning to the constitutional text. The judges were not to engage in the same kind of endeavor as the people who made the original, necessarily pragmatic decision under review. The judges were to keep the Constitution as an active, shaping factor in American politics by defining the constitutional clauses so as to give them substantive meaning in light of the Framers' intentions. Not only would the resulting substantive definitions give the judges a distinctive foundation for evaluating decisions under review, it would also keep this nation on its historic course. By defining the scope of constitutional clauses, Justice Black sought to make the Constitution known and knowable. The document could then truly be the fundamental law of the land; it would shape and guide our political decisions.

Though Justice Black, in his reading and thought, constantly went back to the same body of ideas—the intent of the Framers—he invariably stopped his exploration when he arrived at a way of handling the issues which came before him. It is no accident that he called his summary lectures *A Constitutional Faith*. When he did theorize beyond particular constitutional clauses, he invariably did so in terms of the theme found in those lectures—the judge's role in our society and the importance of our written Constitution. He developed no theory of political life separate from, apart from, the institutional arrangement dictated by the Constitution.

Justice Black never used the latent implications of contract theory to explore new ways of organizing American society, as both Meiklejohn and Tussman did. If our inherited arrangements are not sufficient for a meaningful democracy in post-industrial American society, we cannot turn to the writings of Justice Black for guidance. He sought to restore, not to innovate. He was a great conservative, and one of the ironies of our times is that Hugo Black was so often seen as a radical. Granted the nobility of this ancient vision, and even its liberating features, we may still question whether an essentially atomistic conception of political man is adequate in a technologically integrated society. The alienation and anomie around us suggest it is not.

V

CONCLUSION

Eleven

THE UTILITY OF REASON

For more than a century the American people have viewed the Constitution of the United States as the basic charter of a democratic nation. This long-standing consensus has led to a peculiarly American phenomenon. All the basic concerns about the nature of our polity—e.g. the distribution of power and the limits of power—are discussed within the parameters of democratic theory. Those boundaries are admittedly wide. Nonetheless they narrow the range of political discourse. Americans are not like Spaniards in the post-Franco era. We do not seriously discuss whether our country would be better served by a government dominated by a military junta or a church. Most Americans simply assume that we are, and ought to be, ruled by a government whose authority is derived from the will of the people as expressed, at least in part, through free, periodic elections.

American thinkers are not, however, in agreement about the meaning of democracy. There is no single, authoritative American theory of democracy. The Constitution was drafted by adherents of republican, not democratic theory.[1] Instead of scrapping the Constitution and drafting a new one when democracy became the prevailing political creed, Americans since the time of Jefferson have interpreted the republican Constitution in light of their democratic ideas.[2] The United States is not like France. Except for the Civil War Amendments,[3] basic changes have not produced a fundamental change in the

American Constitution. The legitimacy of the Constitution itself has plainly been sustained by its historical acceptance, but because it was drafted by adherents of republican theory, the Constitution cannot legitimate any particular democratic theory.

Moreover, the interpretative processes by which the Constitution was sustained as the country became a democracy led to a variety of theories. Americans frequently incorporated elements of the country's republican past into their conceptions of democracy. In other societies, Great Britain for example, democracy became equated with majoritarianism, and any limit on majority rule bears the onus of being called undemocratic. In the United States, a variety of elements other than majoritarianism have been accepted as compatible with democracy. Our intellectual history, like the Constitution, is unable to legitimate a single theory of democracy. The very abundance of democratic theories neutralizes whatever authority historical experience provides.[4]

Today, the democratic theories being used to interpret the Constitution are based upon three distinct paradigms. Though the natural rights, contract, and competitive paradigms are similar in many ways, the differences among them are significant. The political theories based on those paradigms also differ in important matters. Stressing different ideas, each democratic theory leads to a different constellation of concepts for evaluating important political questions. Each democratic theory leads to a different interpretation of the Constitution, a different constitutional theory.

Now, as in the past, Supreme Court Justices have resolved major issues by relying upon their political theories. Justice Frankfurter put it this way:

> It is most revealing that members of the Court are frequently admonished by their associates not to read their economic and social views into the neutral language of the Constitution. But the process of constitutional interpretation compels the translation of policy into judgement and *the controlling conceptions of the Justices are their idealized political pictures of the existing social order.*

We were thus able to analyze judicial interpretations as expressions of more widely held theories of democracy. Analyzing Supreme Court opinions in terms of the Justices' theories gave us a clearer picture of the political implications involved in that agency's decisions. Similarly, we gained a clearer understanding of each theory by examining it in terms of the concrete situations presented by Court cases. We were thereby able to assess the relative merits of each democratic theory utilized by Supreme Court Justices in the post–World War II era.

In trying to discover what would be gained and what would be lost by adopting each theory, no one position seemed without flaws. The principal weakness of the realist theory of democracy discussed in chapter 5 was the absence of a clear notion of constitutionalism. Realist theorists do not fully understand how the Constitution was intended by the Framers to shape the American polity in terms of certain first principles. When all political authority in democracy is seen as emanating from the free vote, "constitutional rules are not crucial independent factors maintaining democracy; rather the rules themselves seem to be functions of underlying nonconstitutional factors."[6]

In realist theory, the Constitution is important because it contains the procedures for selecting our temporary rulers and the procedures those rulers must follow in making public policy. The explicit values embedded in the text serve as admonitions to our elected leaders; they are historically rooted concerns which ought to be seriously considered. The Constitution, however, provides no abiding values which necessarily ought to shape government policy: "In this day and age the Constitution is a fallible guide to national policymaking."[7] We, the people, elect our rulers, and those elected leaders must decide basic policy.

This view leads realist theorists to abnegate the power of judicial review, and, in the process, the functional importance of the Constitution. They are unwilling to vest the Supreme Court with significant authority, because it is a nondemocratic (i.e. nonelected) body. Because the Realists offer no other institutional mechanism, they are left without a means for inculcating the values embedded in the Constitution into the feelings, thoughts, and actions of American citizens. Even the very values necessary to sustain the free competition for the free vote are, in the last analysis, defined by the individuals and agencies politically accountable to the electoral majority. The Realists' interpretation of the Constitution all but deprives it of the substantive norms supposedly making the United States a democracy.

Much the same weakness in optimalist theory discussed in chapter 6 can be traced to the same source: the competitive paradigm. Like the Realists, the central focus of the Optimalists is on the policy-making process related to the electoral system. The Optimalists, however, explicitly assert that the competitive electoral process requires special consideration for such individual rights as voting, speech, and association. The protection of those rights is the distinctive function of the courts, particularly the Supreme Court. American democracy requires, according to the Optimalists, that government policies limiting the functional requisites of the free competitive electoral system withstand exacting judicial scrutiny.

As a result, not all values are treated as theoretically equal interests. A ranking springs from the Optimalists' interpretation of the functional requisites of a democracy based upon the competitive paradigm. Claims are considered important because of the systematic needs of democracy, not because of their derivation from a higher moral tradition or from the Constitution. The ultimate measure of importance is the needs of the system as defined by the competitive paradigm. All claims—rights, principles, interests—are to be accommodated within that matrix.

Understandably then, the Justices employing optimalist theory cannot articulate clear standards. Principles and rights have no independent value per se. No right, despite the language of the First Amendment, can be absolute. The rights of an individual must be treated as the means to promote certain important societal interests and must be balanced against other legitimate interests. Accommodation requires a sensitivity to the complex factual differences distinguishing one situation from the next. The rights of individuals, therefore, still depend upon the Court's evaluation of complex situations. The best that judges employing optimalist theory can do is to articulate a stance: preferred freedoms or exacting scrutiny.

The Optimalists' failure to define carefully the nature of the rights they seek to protect means that those rights are, in practice, limited by the toleration of the Justices. The Optimalists have identified the Supreme Court as the principal institution for translating the fundamental values of democracy into our polity. The Justices employing that theory, however, teach the American people two things: that certain rights are important and ought to be heavily weighted in the policy-making process; and that they, the judges, will assess the exercise of our rights in terms of *their* appraisal of the dangers posed. The consequence of optimalist theory is that the American people soon learn more about the power of the Supreme Court—or the preferences of the Justices—than about the substance of their own rights.

If the constitutional theories derived from the competitive paradigm suffer from their utilitarian, pragmatic premises, they nonetheless bear all the hallmarks of contemporary political theories. Both the realist and optimalist theories are well-developed, carefully thought-out, systemic theories of democracy. The absence of those characteristics is the central weakness of the liberal natural rights theory discussed in chapter 8. Considering this absence, it is not clear how the moral concerns evoked by the latter theory are to be translated into standards for governing our polity.

A liberal theory of natural rights cannot be accused of providing a narrow, restricted view of the Constitution. As evidenced by the opinions of Justice Douglas, the theory offers a way of shaping American society in terms of fundamental principles rooted in our Whig heritage. It does so by making a sharp distinction between rights and interests. Interests may be balanced and accommodated in the pursuit of social policies; individual rights, because they are the basic values for which this society was founded, are exempt from that process. The distinction permits us to understand the Constitution as authorizing wide-ranging policies so long as they are consistent with the rights necessary in any just society. If achievable, this theory could generate a society where the nurturing of human rights was an integral part of our national goals. In liberal natural rights theory, the Constitution is plainly intended to make a difference.

Nonetheless, the theory has limited utility in a constitutional regime. While liberal natural rights theory permits its adherents to enunciate values necessary for human dignity, those values are notoriously ambiguous. The grand principles must be made applicable to the complex problems of American society. Here the theory provides little, if any, guidance about the scope of individual rights and the need to make trade-offs among competing rights. Failure to provide this kind of guidance for the implementation of cherished values is a serious weakness in any proposed constitutional theory.

Historically, constitutionalism emerged as a fence against personal, potentially arbitrary, government.[8] While constitutionalism has come to mean more, it has not thereby ceased to reflect that initial concern. Therefore, publicly articulated standards of action are at the heart of the enterprise. Standards are the mechanism by which the abstract principles of political theory and the general language of the Constitution are to be applied to the nation's ongoing concerns. The content of a proposed set of constitutional standards determined the actual limits to be placed on government and also how the public comes to understand the basic values of society.

If constitutionalism requires the articulation of relatively clear standards for directing a polity, liberal natural rights theory must be found wanting. We may intuitively (or culturally) agree with the theory's general principles, but constitutionalism requires more. It requires that those principles be refined into more concrete, relevant standards and that those standards be consistently followed. Absent that specificity and consistency, we are always haunted by the all too familiar possibility of abstract principles being manipulated to cloak personal preferences. That kind of subjectivist politics is what constitutionalism was designed to prevent. Unfortunately, the opinions of Justice Douglas do nothing to lay this ancient fear to rest. In that most recent effort for promoting inalienable human rights we still only dimly glimpse the actual, operating norms being proposed for our society.

In light of the above criticisms, the strengths of Justice Black's constitutional theory should be apparent. Unlike the competitive theories, his constitutionalism does not suffer from the absence of a clearly defined concept of rights. Individual rights are central to his notion of constitutionalism and they are to be protected in an absolutist fashion. Unlike the liberal natural rights theory of his brother Douglas, Justice Black's positivism enabled him to develop clear, sharp, constitutional standards.

Because Justice Black saw the Constitution as *the* basic element of our polity, he came to believe that interpretations based upon the competitive paradigm were inadequate. Even the more libertarian optimalist theory drained the Constitution of meaning. If a judge must balance competing interests, if he must weigh the supposedly enduring principles embodied in the written document against the needs seen as compelling by the government, then the Constitution is empty until the Court puts a particular content into it. Since issues and circumstances vary from case to case, balancing builds vagueness into the Constitution. It becomes inherently incapable of saying anything lasting and enduring to the American people.

That weakness is why Justice Black was also critical of natural law interpretations of the Constitution. Like the Founding generation, he saw the document as shaping and molding the essential nature of the American polity. For the Constitution to function in this manner, Justice Black saw the necessity of giving a fairly precise meaning to the fundamental text. He believed that natural law theories—whether of the Old Guard Court or of the liberal Justice Douglas—hindered the development of such standards. The vague general principles of natural law permitted the judges to make essentially the same kind of pragmatic decisions as the legislatures. And unlike the competitive theories, natural law doctrines tended to hide this process in moralistic rhetoric. Neither the competitive paradigm nor natural law facilitated the prime task of the United States Supreme Court: defining the Constitution.

By defining the scope of constitutional clauses, Justice Black sought to make the Constitution known and knowable. The judges were to keep the Constitution an active factor in American politics by fashioning relatively fixed standards. Having given the document substantive meaning, the judges were to apply the standards in a consistent manner. Not only would this approach give those values an ongoing applicability, it would also permit the judges to explicate the very real limits our Constitution puts on public policy on behalf of certain individual rights. The Constitution could then truly be the fundamental law of the land: it would shape and guide our political thinking and our policies.

Justice Black, then, cannot be faulted for the absence or the weakness of his constitutional vision. He was the premier constitutionalist to serve on the Supreme Court in the post–World War II era. As the years dim the memories of racial and antiwar demonstrations and riots, Black's theory has attracted renewed attention.[9] We should not, however, forget the problems posed by his particular constitutional theory.

As noted in chapter 10, Justice Black sought to create his constitutional standards by turning to the language and history of the document. His search for the intent of the Framers reinforced the already strong emphasis on individualism he had expressed as a populist politician. He saw the American society created by the Constitution as composed of almost atomistic individuals engaging in self-government through elected, representative institutions. To sustain this kind of society, the Constitution granted individuals a variety of rights. Some of these rights—like those in the First Amendment—were so important to the type of polity sought by the Constitution that they were granted absolute immunity. Against such rights, societal concerns for social welfare, efficiency, and even national security could not be sustained. Justice Black believed the Constitution was designed to protect against arbitrary uses of governmental authority so that each individual could pursue his own vision of the good life.

We must seriously question whether the individualism inherent in Justice Black's theory is adequate for contemporary America. In our complex society the range of issues requiring governmental decisions borders on the infinite. The technical complexity and the number of governmental policies all but preclude widespread and sustained participation by the general public.[10] Instead, effective political participation is normally pursued through narrowly defined, interest-based groups and associations. The power of private, self-seeking interests frequently dominates our politics.[11]

In such a situation, we can no longer assume, if we ever could, that governmental institutions will be able to transmute private interest into policies reflecting the public good. A political theory which, for all its honorable and ancient lineage, cannot get beyond an essentially atomistic conception of political man is probably inadequate. At the very least, the problem must be confronted in an open and direct manner. Justice Black's historically oriented constitutionalism does not even perceive the need to fashion an overriding conception of the public good. Social theory should not proceed by such inadvertence.

A strong case could be made that Justice Black was merely presenting an updated version of the constitutional thought of the founding fathers. The Framers also saw the primary activities of individuals as taking place outside the reach of government. From this perspective, the American political order was created as an instrument for protecting personal interests. Essentially privatized individuals were to have conflicting interests filtered through the formal arrangements of government. Their interests would be protected by a system which permitted only mutually tolerable policies to emerge. That agreement is the extent of joint public endeavors. It could be argued that a notion of the public good distinct from this concern with private interests is not to be found in the constitutional thought of the founding fathers.[12]

The Framers did indeed assume that individual liberty dictated a society in which people pursued their own private interests. The architects of the American Constitution took man as they saw him. Their purpose was not to create a "new man," a virtuous citizen; it was to design a set of political institutions for imperfect human beings.[13] Men were not angels, said Madison,[14] and it was "vain to say that enlightened statesmen will be able to adjust these clashing interests, and render them all subservient to the public good. Enlightened statesmen will not always be at the helm."[15] Plainly, the Framers did not believe private passions and interests could be excluded from government.

Individualism was inescapable in a polity founded on the protection and promotion of natural rights. Individualism was only one component of the Framers' political theory however. Eighteenth-century natural rights theory—the shared, common perspective of all American leadership elements in 1787–1788[16]—contained implicit limits to individualism. Those limits were expressed by the idea of reason upon which the whole artifice of eighteenth-century natural rights theory was constructed. The participants at the Constitutional Convention and the authors of the *Federalist Papers*, therefore, never provided a detailed specification of their conception of the public interest: the true public interest was the result of applying reason to public problems. Too often, recent examinations of the American Constitution have not given sufficient weight to the appeal to reason inherent in the document. By largely ignoring that feature of our constitutionalism, many recent commentators have downplayed the Framers' principal vehicle for shaping political values and attitudes.[17]

By now, it is a commonplace that the founding fathers were full participating members in the "Age of Reason." Two generations ago, Carl Becker and other luminaries explored the efforts of Madison, Jefferson, Hamilton, Adams, Franklin, et. al. to construct a political system grounded on reason.[18] Reason had three analytically distinct meanings in eighteenth-century America: reason as a quality of the universe; reason as a faculty of man; reason as a temper in the conduct of human affairs.[19] For our purposes, there is no need to once again trace the development of the idea that the universe is governed by the laws of Nature or Nature's God.[20] It is sufficient for us to recognize that at the time the Constitution was drafted, it was simply taken for granted that there was a "natural order" of things in the world. This unquestioned axiom meant there was a rational plan to the physical universe and that its laws were open to discovery by human reason.

Human reason, therefore, corresponded to and was part of the reason which permeated the universe. Not only was it the faculty which enabled human understanding of the natural law, it also permitted individuals to bring human institutions into harmony with the natural order. Though this idea, too, had long antedated the Age of Reason, it took on a novel meaning during that period. There was virtually a religious faith in man's ability to comprehend and plan his world. This belief still carried with it the aura of sanctity inherent in the medieval notion of the working of natural reason, but the secular political theorists of the eighteenth century had great confidence in the adequacy of human reason to comprehend natural law. As A. P. D'Entreves has put it: "Reason to the Roman lawyer was perhaps only another name for experience. For the medieval philosopher it was the gift of God. In both cases the evidence of reason had to be implemented, and indeed confirmed, by some other evidence—of fact or faith. But *now the evidence of reason* was *in itself sufficient.*"[21]

Reason, in this sense, underlay the founding generation's belief in their ability to fashion a science of politics adequate for the foundation of a constitutional republic. If human reason was to provide its own source of validation, political theories had to strive for clarity and coherence. That is why science was the model for all systems of thought.[22] A science of politics was not only possible, it already existed albeit in an incomplete form. In this realm of thought, as in all others, the lessons of experience were useful to confirm logical deductions from first principles. Prudential wisdom, however, could not by itself create a science of politics. That task was the function of human reason.

The authors of *The Federalist Papers* believed that the science of politics, like most others, had made great progress.[23] It was still far from perfection. Principles were not as certain in moral and political sciences as in geometry. This relative backwardness was the result either of some defect in human perception or the consequence of strong interest, passion, or prejudice. Plainly, the latter factor was more important: "Obscurity is much oftener in the passions and prejudices of the reasoner than in the subject."[24] For all that, the science of politics had much better claims than any other approach. Reason makes humans capable of managing their own affairs.

This argument brings us to the third meaning: reason as a temper in the conduct of human affairs. In this sense, reason was always contrasted by the founding generation to passion—powerful, self-interested, volatile concerns and actions. The "cool and deliberate sense of the community," wrote Madison, "ought [to prevail] in all governments."[25]

Reasoning together as a method of conducting public affairs did not presuppose unanimity. Given the ambiguities inherent in social conditions, the imperfection of human faculties, and the inadequacies of words to convey complex ideas,[26] when "men exercise their reason coolly and freely on a variety of distinct questions, they inevitably fall into different opinions on some of them."[27] True consultation, the matching of mind with mind in the common quest for truth, was the *only* method to make ultimate and universal truths accessible, in some measure, to fallible human beings.[28]

The Framers of the Constitution operated on the assumption that the "reason of man, like man himself, is timid and cautious."[29] We must not forget, wrote Hamilton, that "men are ambitious, vindictive, and rapacious";[30] therefore, argued Madison, "the mild voice of reason, pleading the cause of an enlarged and permanent interest, is but too often drowned, before public bodies as well as individuals, by the clamors of an impatient avidity for immediate and immoderate gain."[31] Nonetheless, just "as there is a degree of depravity in mankind which requires a certain degree of circumspection and distrust, so there are other qualities in human nature which justify a certain portion of esteem and confidence."[32] Paramount among these beneficient qualities was the faculty to conduct human affairs in a cool, deliberate, reflective manner. In the words of Madison: "It is the reason, alone, of the public, that ought to control and regulate the government. The passions ought to be controlled and regulated by the government."[33]

With this understanding of the widely held belief regarding reason in human affairs, we can obtain a clearer perspective of how the Framers perceived their task. The primary purpose of the famous "auxiliary precautions"[34] was to curb the irrational tendencies of man so that reason might flourish. Reason, they believed, permitted them to fashion a science of politics adequate for the foundation of a constitutional republic. It also led the founders to believe that rational policies *could* emerge from properly structured institutions. In both instances, the founders recognized the tension and conflict between self-interest and the classical conception of public virtue;[35] yet, the American leadership in 1787–1788 continued to believe the application of reason made pursuit of the common good possible. Despite Jefferson's misgivings about certain parts of the documents,[36] the Constitutional Convention itself elicited his admiration because it demonstrated the utility of reason:

> We are yet able to send our wise and good men together to talk over our form of government . . . with the same *sang-froid* as they would a subject of agriculture. The example we have given the world is single, that of changing our form of government under the authority of reason only, without bloodshed.[37]

The Framers did not see virtue and self-interest as mutually exclusive. Man's nature was an amalgam of both elements. They sought to curb the influence of passion and self-interest so that reason could prevail. In their scenario, the reason inherent in human nature was to substitute for the virtuous citizenry of classical republican theory. When reason prevailed, people were led "by a deep conviction of the necessity of sacrificing private opinions and partial interests to the common good."[38]

The appeal to reason is not popular today. An Age of Anxiety has replaced the easy confidence of the Age of Reason. Recent interpretations of American constitutionalism bespeak that newer mood. They start from the assumption that the Constitution, because it is devoid of a substantive, policy-oriented notion of the public good, is in large measure responsible for the forces which have produced a current crisis of legitimacy and authority.[39]

We are indeed in the midst of some such crisis. Our public life is marked by widespread alienation and anomie. Nonvoting in presidential elections now approaches 50 percent of the eligible electorate. Under such circumstances, no successful presidential candidate can enter office with a majority mandate. The position of all other elected officials is much worse. It is now almost impossible to maintain a belief in the citizens' ability to hold governing elites responsible.[40] Our survey in chapters 1–5 indicates that this notion is the lowest common denominator for sustaining authority and legitimacy in contemporary theories of democracy.

It is far from clear, however, that the source of discomfort can be traced to the Constitution rather than to our own inadequacies in operating the system it created. The American Constitution was not designed to create a system in which men were free to engage in a loosely umpired struggle for the accumulation of property. Economic liberty was an important human right to the Framers. To that extent, the Constitution may indeed be responsible for a materialistic American ethos; but, as we saw in chapter 1, that concern was not the central issue of the debates in 1787–1788. The historical material better supports the proposition that the Framers were primarily concerned with establishing an enduring republic to protect individual liberties.[41] The Framers did accept a rather Hobbesian view of man and made no direct effort to change human nature. But that fact cuts both ways. Though they did not directly seek to raise man to Aristotelian heights of civic virtue, neither did they directly seek to shape man in the image of Adam Smith. There was a great deal more openness in the constitutional system created by the Framers. It was not value neutral, but neither did it completely predestine the future direction of the American polity.

The course of American history demonstrates how that open texture has been utilized to sustain a variety of constitutional orders. As we saw in chapters 2, 3, and 4, the constitutional norms of agrarian America gave way to those of an emerging industrialism; the constitutional order of nineteenth-century capitalism was very different from that sustaining today's welfare state. At each period of transition, Americans had to rethink basic concepts in terms of a new perception of the public good.

At no time did many of them ever conceive of some mystical public realm divorced from, yet somehow dominating, private concerns. An autonomous public realm has never seemed sufficiently real, sufficiently concrete. Rather than pursuing such an historical ideal, Americans continued to share the Framers' belief that any conception of the public realm must take account of private concerns—of the rights and interests by which individuals pursue their own, private, vision of happiness. Like Madison, they believed that if "justice is the end of government," if it is "the end of civil society,"[42] then "good government implies . . . fidelity to the object of government, which is the happiness of the people."[43]

As they went about the business of reshaping the dominant paradigms of their day, earlier generations of Americans used the processes created by the Constitution. Those processes insured that private interests could not be ignored in fashioning a new constitutional order with its own conception of the public good. They gave reason the space and the time to combine those interests in a new way. Once a new conception of the public good emerged in the statutes, it was sooner or later legitimated by the Supreme Court. As such, the new conception became part of the supreme law of the land, and created a new constitutional order. That constitutional order functioned as written constitutions were intended by the Framers: it set metes and bounds, it transcended the realm of ordinary politics and gave it a shape—until a new constitutional order emerged.

We appear to be in the throes of yet another transition. I do not think it Pollyannaish to suggest that we shall have to solve our problem by the same processes institutionalized within our Constitution by the Framers. We shall have to utilize our reason to fashion a new conception of the public interest sufficient unto our own day. We no longer share the optimistic faith of the Age of Reason. Yet, if Nature appears indifferent and the gods unavailing, our fate is all the more in our own hands. We are no longer certain that our reason, our intelligence, is adequate to the task. Adequate or not, we must rely upon it, since it is the only guide we have.

That is why I find the functional contract theory of Alexander Meiklejohn and Joseph Tussman attractive. According to that theory, all Americans, beginning with the constitutional generation, have entered into an agreement to be self-governing. The Constitution gives us, the American people, the authority and responsibility to govern ourselves. The functional contract theory encourages us to claim that authority—by exercising our reason.

The functional contract theory differs from the highly individualistic theory of Justice Black in the area where his constitutionalism is most troublesome. Justice Black's theory sees self-government as a necessary artifice for controlling self-interest; self-interest is a presumed "given" of human nature. There is no common public interest—no community—only individual interest limited by governmental restraints. The functional contract theory starts with the notion that in the process of forming our government, Americans created a community with a common public interest. When people act politically in this theory, they *should* make their decisions in terms of that common interest. Justice Black sees policy largely as the aggregation of particular interests; the functional contract theory portrays it as the search for the public good.

Quite obviously, this search requires an explicit emphasis on the social importance of reason. Notice how Professor Tussman discusses democracy in his most recent book:

> At its core is the significance it gives to universal (normal adult) participation in the political process, and the faith that all men can, if encouraged and given opportunity, develop the arts, the skills, the habits necessary for the life of responsible deliberation and decision-making. Democracy seeks to universalize the parliamentary state of mind.[44]

Tussman recognizes that this process "takes some doing." Reason is not a natural or universal habit of mind; it is a cultivated behavior pattern. That belief sets this theory apart from the natural rights theory of Justice Douglas. Tussman, for example, argues that freedom of speech lies at the end of a long social road, not in a state of nature. It is not a primitive right, but was wrested from ruling elites. Its history is not that of constant attempts to limit an inalienable right, but that of gaining the ability to participate in self-government.[45] If we wish to maintain democracy, Tussman insists, we cannot neglect the constant cultivation of human reason.

Government, therefore, has a serious and legitimate concern with the mind of the citizen. It has a tutelary responsibility to prepare citizens for, and to enable them to participate in, the process of self-government. Government does this preparation through its role in formal education, and through its relation to the public forum. Tussman uses the concept of forum not only to refer to particular places where communication occurs, but also to the whole range of institutions and situations of public communication. Through structures and rules, opportunities and protections, the forum gives meaning to an essentially civic conception of free speech.[46]

I think we can reasonably read Professor Tussman's work as an attempt to address the kind of criticism made about the functional contract theory at the close of chapter 9. He views the First Amendment, as Professor Meiklejohn did,[47] not only as a protection against certain types of governmental actions, but also as a mandate to engage in the heavy and basic responsibility of cultivating the general intelligence upon which the success of self-government depends.

This concern for institutions is not the only change and addition I think should be made in the functional contract theory outlined in chapter 9, but none of my proposals do any violence to the theory's basic tenets. Professor Meiklejohn's insistence upon the absoluteness of the First Amendment also has to be modified. Precisely because this is a *functional* theory, rights cannot be absolute. It can be said that certain rights—like the First Amendment—

are so essential to the functioning of our democracy they can only be balanced against rights of the same magnitude or the direct, immediate need to protect a vital aspect of national security. These basic structural rights—and the direct security interest of the entire system—can never be sacrificed for less significant matters.[48] In this way, the priorities correctly asserted by Meiklejohn can be maintained within the logic of functional analysis. As modified, the analysis provides a strong theory of American constitutionalism. To demonstrate the relative strengths of the functional contract theory, let us return once again to the concepts of citizenship, political participation, and political freedom.

CITIZENSHIP

A theory based upon an agreement to be self-governing best explains why we intuitively believe citizenship is important. In the functional contract theory, citizenship is something other than a mere summation of the rights we hold under American law; rather, it is an indication of our acceptance of the fundamental agreement. Any society conditions the lives of its members. Because we have agreed to become part of American society we have consented to those constraints. Membership, therefore, becomes part of our very identities. Citizenship is more than a legal status; it is an integral part of an individual's self-definition. For this reason, citizenship is an important right.

Plainly, such a theory requires that consent to an important agreement be voluntarily and knowingly made. Just as plainly, there are problems in calibrating the theory to our current practices. At least in terms of our native born citizenry—the bulk of our population—no action even clearly implies a knowing and voluntary consent to join the body politic. Tussman's recent emphasis on the tutelary function of government provides a way of addressing the situation. After teaching our native born what it means to be a citizen in a self-governing society, we could properly institute a ceremony where young adults, like our naturalized citizens, explicitly declared themselves parties to the system of agreements constituting our body politic. Such a procedure would reinforce a person's right of voluntary withdrawal from our body politic. The individual would be reminded of the right of free emigration, a human right continuously recognized throughout American history. The quality of membership would be enhanced both by an explicit voluntary entrance into society and by the continuous option of withdrawal. The ideas of consent and freedom would thereby be strengthened.

An individual should also be permitted to renounce American citizenship, yet remain as a resident alien. As is current practice, a resident alien should have virtually the same legal obligations as a citizen. He should be required to pay taxes and serve in the armed forces on the same basis as a citizen. As is also current practice, a resident alien should be entitled to most of our constitutional protections. An individual does not cease being a member of the human race when he is no longer a member of a particular society. Classifications based upon alienage should be inherently suspect and subject to close judicial scrutiny.[49]

A resident alien, however, should be precluded from certain carefully defined positions which relate to this country as a self-governing community. Citizenship should be a qualification for voting, for holding elective office, and for certain, nonelected positions connected with public policy formulation.[50] This standard, an exception to the general repugnance of classifications based upon alienage, rests upon the theoretical distinction made above. Citizenship, whether by birth or naturalization, denotes a significant association with the American polity. It is based upon a faith in our fellow citizens' intentions and abilities to further our joint venture. Every other citizen is an equal with whom we have agreed to share rights and obligations. He is to be treated as a peer, respected as a co-ruler. "Citizen" is an important and honored title in the functional contract theory of democracy.

The right of citizenship, then, is a prerequisite for entrance into this relationship of peers. As such, it must be jealously protected. It is not a status carrying no obligations. The right to be a citizen is a claim to be part of the democratic enterprise, to exercise the power and to hold the obligations of a ruler. As such, while it must not be lightly forfeited, citizenship may be revoked when the people (through their elected agents) find that a person claiming to be a citizen has blatantly and intentionally neglected a significant obligation related to national survival. National survival is the only social objective against which a basic individual right might be balanced. Those offenses plainly showing an abdication of responsibility to the polity (e.g. treason) could warrant expatriation. Expatriation statutes would be subject to the closest judicial scrutiny. Only governmental allegation and proof that the activity inevitably and directly imperils the body politic would justify expatriation; anything less can be punished by ordinary criminal sanctions.

Thus modified, the functional contract theory would become the proper vehicle for handling such cases as *Perez, Trop, Mendoza-Martinez,* and *Afroyim.*[51] It would thereby "teach" a conception of citizenship not found in the competitive theories of democracy. A citizen is more than a subject; he is a participant in the governing process.

POLITICAL PARTICIPATION

In the functional contract theory, then, a citizen is distinguished by the quality of political participation. In chapter 9, I criticized the theory's two principal proponents for their lack of sustained discussion about the institutional changes made necessary by their emphasis on citizen participation. In *Government and the Mind*, Professor Tussman began to redress that imbalance. Not surprisingly, he builds upon the model of the town meeting suggested by Dr. Meiklejohn. Tussman treats that "semi-mythical council" as the paradigm for the highly structured artifact he calls the forum. It is a *necessary* institution for the community to develop its mind or policies through the exchange of ideas. Both opportunity (access) and protection (immunity) must be provided. Since such provision is normally through law, government is involved in the very fabric of the forum. The forum is not something we have before government acts. It is a system in which government is a constitutive element.[52]

Admittedly, this public policy "recommendation" derived from the functional contract theory is vague. The problems of architecture, city planning, programming, etc. remain to be worked out. Recent Supreme Court cases involving the FCC's regulation of the broadcasting industry indicate the complexities.[53] It is surely not beyond our capacities, however, to move in the direction of creating an adequate forum network. Moreover, this institutional need is placed within the context of a theory which not only legitimizes government support for such practices, but which, through its tutelary emphasis, also seeks to encourage citizens to use those facilities. In this way, the functional contract theory can begin to talk about ways of popular participation in the political process.

A reshaped functional contract theory would also support a consistent pattern of interpretation in the reapportionment decisions. The emphasis on full participation requires the application of the one person, one vote standard. This standard would apply equally at *all* levels of government. National, state, and local institutions seek legitimacy and authority through the electoral process precisely because of our acceptance of contract theory. If we are engaged in the process of self-government, then all eligible individuals must have equal access to the system. All laws hindering participation in that process must be subject to strict judicial scrutiny.

The theory is concerned with self-government, not a fair and effective representation of all interests. If the latter were the objective—as in competitive theories—there would be factors other than numbers with which the states could be legitimately concerned. The objective of individual participation in self-government is only a good faith effort to achieve precise mathematical equality. Contrary to Justice Brennan, however, equal participation does not mean an automatic rejection of all *de minimus* criteria.[54] He is surely correct in insisting there is no nonarbitrary way to pick a cutoff point at which population variances become *de minimus*. The theory is premised upon absolute equality of *each* individual's participation; yet, the theory also requires self-government. Judges appointed for life terms cannot be the primary agents of self-government. Moreover, in the age of computers it is always possible to grind out yet another apportionment plan with still a smaller deviation from absolute equality.[55] The pursuit of that theoretically worthy objective must be tempered by the realization that the census data—although the best available statistics—are inaccurate when collected and worsen throughout the decade of a normal apportionment plan's lifetime. Practical considerations undergird the notion of decadal reapportionments. Practical considerations would also suggest that some minor deviations from zero deviation could escape judicial scrutiny.[56] The notion of a good faith effort surely grants elected agencies some play at the joints even in this area.

POLITICAL FREEDOM

As significant as the act of voting is within the functional contract theory, speech is even more important. Institutions like the forum are important because they provide opportunities for discussion. When we vote we each act as individuals; our reasons, motives, and intentions are private. When we speak, we take on a more communal function; communication necessarily involves others. We have the opportunity to enlighten, persuade, inspire. Reason and deliberation function through communication. In short, communication is the means by which we maintain a self-governing society.

Alexander Meiklejohn was basically correct in his interpretation of the First Amendment. If We, The People, are to function as the fourth and highest branch, debate on matters of governing importance must be uninhibited, wide open, and robust. If, for reasons discussed in chapter 9 and summarized above, we cannot accept Meiklejohn's absolutism, we do need a virtually absolutist interpretation of the First Amendment.

The functional contract theory can provide clear, consistent, viable standards in this area. For questions involving communication of governing importance—public speech—Justice Brennan has already provided the standard. In the *Pentagon Papers* case,[57] he did not join the absolutist opinions of Justices Black and Douglas. He recognized that national security may at times justify even a prior restraint on such speech. Justice Brennan would permit restraints on public speech only upon "governmental allegation and proof that publication must inevitably, directly and immediately cause the occurrence of an event kindred to imperilling the safety of a (troop) transport already at sea . . . "[58] This type of balancing—restricted to matters *directly* and *demonstrably* touching the survival of our political system—is quite consistent with functional contract theory.

This method avoids balancing a wide variety of social needs against the individual's right to participate in political discussions, inherent in the competitive theories of democracy. By consistently applying Justice Brennan's standard, the courts would help educate the people about their right (and obligation) to discuss public matters. By giving more than rhetorical support to all kinds of public speech, the courts would also ensure the people that their First Amendment rights were protected in virtually all circumstances. By permitting some balancing, the proposed standard avoids the logical contradiction posed by any absolute within a systemic, functional theory. It also avoids the obvious practical difficulties created by any absolutist right: events do not come in neatly labelled categories. A constitutional theory must provide a standard for handling real emergencies without jeopardizing our core values.

It is sometimes suggested it is necessary to balance two fundamental individual rights. While this balancing would be permissible under the functional contract theory, the theory cautions against a too-ready acceptance of this notion. Fundamental rights are not to be lightly surrendered, even for other rights. The classic example is the "conflict" between the Sixth Amendment's guarantee of a fair trial and the First Amendment's right of freedom of the press. A fair trial is obviously essential in a democratic society; it is a necessary means of safeguarding personal liberty against potential governmental oppression. As Justice Brennan has demonstrated, however, the choice between rights usually need not be made: "Judges possess adequate tools (short of injunctions against reporting) for relieving that tension."[59]

The libel-privacy cases illustrate, however, that some balancing may occasionally be necessary. Two rights, equally fundamental in a democracy, are involved: communication about matters of public concern and the individual's need to be left alone in order to maintain a sense of dignity and autonomy. Although in chapter 9 I criticized Justice Brennan for a lack of sensitivity to the privacy claims in such cases as *Time, Inc. v. Hill* (1967),[60] his actual malice test[61] certainly provides a better balance of these competing rights than the current court standards.[62] In this text, I also noted other standards giving fair recognition to both our right to communicate and our right to privacy.[63] These standards, too, are compatible with a functional contract theory of democracy.

There still remains, of course, the problem of defining public expression. If We, The People, need communication in order to govern ourselves, not all forms of communication have a governing importance. Under the functional contract theory, communication within the public realm is to be given a First Amendment protection approaching absolute immunity. Communication without a governing importance would be subject to regulations conforming to due process. The line between the two types of communication, therefore, is of some importance.

As we saw in chapter 9, Justice Brennan's attempt to use the distinction between public and private speech in the obscenity-pornography cases was a dismal failure.[64] Sexually offensive communication is simply too subjective. Obscenity lies in the eyes of the beholder. Any definition of such elusive matters is bound to elude clear constitutional standards. Justice Brennan recognized this fact himself when he later adopted an absolute protection of all forms of art and literature.[65]

The basic rationale behind Justice Brennan's original standard, however, still merits some consideration. Not all communication is of the same value. We may be unable to formulate a standard permitting us to regulate pornography without threatening the range of ideas available to the public, but it is important to recognize that failure for what it is. It is failure of practical implementation. Theoretically, hard core pornography still remains socially less desirable and less necessary than discussions of public policy. For this reason, under the functional contract theory, there should be no objection to zoning ordinances limiting the places where sexually explicit material is available.[66] Censorship based upon subjective criteria is thereby avoided; yet, the community is able to take some measures to protect the social environment and personal sensitivities.

The most difficult problem posed by the functional contract theory has been that of delimiting the public forum. In the absence of established facilities in every community, people frequently use the streets and parks as public forums. The functional contract theory is sympathetic to such activity. To view streets, parks, and similar public places as suitable sites for political communication means that people have a constitutional right to engage in political activity at such locations. While the government may impose certain regulations on the use of those facilities, it may not ban all political activity from such public places. The problem centers upon the type of regulation to be permitted.

Usually, proponents of the functional contract theory argue that only content-neutral regulations of time, manner, and place are compatible with the kind of free speech required in a democracy. As we saw in chapter 9, there is great difficulty in extending Meiklejohn's interpretation of the First Amendment to meetings and demonstrations in public places. Since these meetings are frequently designed to provoke a reaction, the possibility of violent conflict must be faced. To regard *content* as a forbidden category would preclude the government from developing legal criteria for intervening to avert impending dangers.

Professor Tussman has suggested a variety of factors for developing such criteria. He uses the familiar time, manner, and place categories, but, while his suggestions appear to be content-neutral, they can be used to evaluate the content of speech in public places without jeopardizing its critical function. This evaluation is possible because Tussman insists that recognizing the need for a public forum requires an awareness of its place within our system.[67] The forum is important because of its function—the need for people to communicate and to deliberate. That function should dictate the legal criteria governing the forum. When conditions preclude deliberations, as in times of overwhelming disorder, the forum should be suspended. When the manner of discussion threatens to disintegrate into mob rule and violence, there is a similar justification for suspending the forum.[68] When a public forum would threaten other significant activities, the forum right may have to accommodate to the special characteristics of the place or the primary purpose of the facility.[69] The need for an adequate forum cannot be transmuted into a claim for a ubiquitous forum.

Professor John Hart Ely has recently made a similar suggestion. When the evil the government seeks to avert is directly related to the content of the message, he would utilize a standard which immunizes all expression save that which demonstrably falls within a few clearly and narrowly defined categories. Those categories must be designated in advance, Ely believes, if the First Amendment is to serve its central function of assuring an open political dialogue and process.[70] Professor Ely's suggestion is entirely compatible with Justice Brennan's criteria in *The Pentagon Papers* case. As indicated above, this approach to speech of governing importance readily fits into the functional contract theory of democracy.

When the evil the government is seeking to avert is independent of the message being regulated, Professor Ely believes a balancing approach is unavoidable. Here, the government's concern primarily relates to factors like time, manner, and place. Like Tussman, Ely recognizes that measures concerned "merely" with noise control, traffic control, and the like may not be intelligibly reviewable by any approach excluding the consideration of context.[71]

Both Ely and Tussman maintain that governmental restraints on the use of the public forum have the potential for seriously disabling communication. Courts may, of necessity, be required to use a balancing test of sorts, but it should be one in which the thumb of the Court is permanently placed on the speech side of the scales. The Court should apply an exacting scrutiny test. If citizens have a constitutionally protected right to use the streets and parks for peaceably advocating public policy, then the government can interfere with this First Amendment right only for important and immediately obvious reasons.

The virtue of the functional contract theory is that it can explain our critical need for adequate public means of communication and deliberation. In so doing, however, it does not blind us to the need to make contextual distinctions. Virtually absolutist immunity should be granted to communication in traditional forums—halls, pamphlets, books, the press. These forums do not directly impinge upon the system's other needs. When speech does take place in a situation not specifically dedicated to use as a public forum, other criteria are indeed appropriate. All criteria governing political speech, however, must be fashioned with an explicit emphasis on the overriding importance of public speech in a system of self-governance.

Plainly, this brief sketch of a functional contract theory of democracy cannot provide a definitive resolution of all the problems besetting our democracy. I have, however, attempted to show that it is an adequate theory to inform our view of democratic politics and our interpretation of the Constitution. In the last analysis, it is the emphasis on self-governance which distinguishes the functional contract theory. Self-government, in turn, requires a firm commitment to the utility of reason.

We must continue to believe—and to act upon the belief—that man can, by deliberate intention and rational direction, shape the world of social relations. We must hold to it, if not from the assured conviction of the Framers, then from clear necessity. The only alternatives are cynicism, despair, and a headlong retreat from the experiment of self-government. The Framers rightly saw the Constitution as a noble, yet fragile, experiment. Benjamin Franklin, after the Convention, was asked what form of government it had designed. "A republic, if you can keep it," he replied.[72] In attempting to keep the democracy the Constitution spawned, we must continue to rely upon the very same human faculty as the Framers. We have no choice but to continue to insist upon the utility of reason.

NOTES

INTRODUCTION

1. When the basic principles of democracy were put in abstract terms, Prothro and Griggs found the "degree of agreement on these principles ranges from 94.7 to 98.0 percent, which appears to represent consensus in a truly meaningful sense. The agreement transcends community, educational, economic, age, sex, party, and other common bases of differences in opinion." Prothro and Griggs, *Fundamental Principles of Democracy: Bases of Agreement and Disagreement*, 22 J. OF POLITICS 276 (1960), 284–286.

2. Ibid.; McClosky, *Consensus and Ideology in American Politics*, 58 AMER. POL. SCI. REV. 361 (1964).

3. Ranney and Kendall, *Democracy: Confusion and Agreement*, 4 WEST. POL. Q. 430 (1951); J. PENNOCK, DEMOCRATIC POLITICAL THEORY (1979), xiii, vii-xviii, 1–15.

4. See T. KUHN, THE STRUCTURE OF SCIENTIFIC REVOLUTIONS (1962).

5. Pennock says that democracy "has quite properly been called a 'loosely knit family of ideas.'" DEMOCRATIC POLITICAL THEORY (1979), xviii. Throughout his book, Pennock illustrates the limitations imposed upon the universe of political ideas by even such vague boundaries.

6. W. MURPHY, THE ELEMENTS OF JUDICIAL STRATEGY (1964).

7. Ibid. In exploring the various strategies hypothetically available to a Supreme Court Justice, Murphy always clearly indicates the limitations imposed by the ideological position of the Justice and his colleagues.

314   DEMOCRATIC THEORIES AND THE CONSTITUTION

1. THE REPUBLICAN CONSTITUTION

1. L. HARTZ, THE LIBERAL TRADITION IN AMERICA (1955); C. ROSSITER, SEEDTIME OF THE REPUBLIC (1953), Part 3.

2. B. BAILYN, THE IDEOLOGICAL ORIGINS OF THE AMERICAN REVOLUTION (1967); G. WOOD, THE CREATION OF THE AMERICAN REPUBLIC, 1776–1787 (Norton, ed., 1972).

3. Shoemaker, *"Democracy" and "Republic" as Understood in Late Eighteenth Century America*, 41 AMER. SPEECH 83 (1966).

4. Lokken, *The Concept of Democracy in Colonial Political Thought*, 16 WILLIAM AND MARY Q. (3rd ser.) 570 (1959).

5. Shoemaker, 83. James Wilson defined a "republican or democratic" government as one in which "the people at large retain supreme power."

6. Ibid, 83. John Adams complained about the way "the words republic, commonwealth [or] popular states" were used by "writers who mean by them a democracy." See also Palmer, *Notes on the Use of the Word "Democracy", 1789–1799*, 68 POL. SCI. Q. 203 (1953).

7. Democracy in colonial America certainly did not automatically entail, as it does today, universal adult suffrage. The colonists operated with their own set of assumptions. The exclusion of women and slaves was so axiomatic it was not even discussed. Paying taxes or property qualifications for exercising the franchise were accepted as evidence of a proper attachment to the community. Religious qualifications were imposed for the same communitarian interest. Despite these restrictions, the franchise in colonial America was more broadly based than anywhere else in the world at the time, and those restrictions were not regarded as a denial of the existence of democracy. C. WILLIAMSON, AMERICAN SUFFRAGE: FROM PROPERTY TO DEMOCRACY (1960); WOOD, 167–169.

8. Shoemaker, 95; T. PAINE, THE RIGHTS OF MAN (Dolphin, ed., 1961), 415.

9. Wood, 162–196; H. PITKIN, THE CONCEPT OF REPRESENTATION (1967) contains a full discussion of the theoretical differences between actual and virtual representation.

10. R. H. Lee *Letters of a Federal Farmer, V*, in P. FORD, ed., PAMPHLETS ON THE CONSTITUTION OF THE UNITED STATES, 1787–1788 (1888), 325.

11. Kenyon, *Men of Little Faith: The Anti-Federalists on the Nature of Representative Government*, 12 WILLIAM AND MARY Q. (3rd ser.) 3 (1955).

12. M. FARRAND, ed., THE RECORDS OF THE FEDERAL CONVENTION OF 1787 (1937 ed.), Vol. 1, 48.

13. A. HAMILTON, J. JAY, and J. MADISON, THE FEDERALIST (E. M. Earle, ed., n.d., no. 9), 49.

14. MADISON, THE FEDERALIST, (no. 63), 409.

15. Ibid., (nos. 10 and 51).

16. J. ELLIOT, ed., THE DEBATES IN THE SEVERAL STATE CONVENTIONS ON THE FEDERAL CONSTITUTION (1941 reprint), vol. 2, 327.

17. See James Wilson's statements on this point at the Pennsylvania Ratifying Convention in ELLIOT, vol. 2, 433–434; and Robert Livingston's statement at the New York convention, ibid., vol. 2, 209–210.

18. MADISON, THE FEDERALIST, (no. 10), 59. See also Madison's opposition to a proposed amendment enabling the people "to instruct their Representatives," 1 ANNALS OF CONGRESS 763 (1789).

19. FARRAND, vol.1, 50.

20. Ibid., vol. 1, 447.

21. See statements made by Wilson, ELLIOT, vol. 2, 429; M. Smith, ibid., vol.2, 311; Cadwell, ibid., vol. 4, 9; and Spencer, ibid., vol. 4, 137. Also see statements by Gerry in FORD, PAMPHLETS, 8; and R. H. Lee, ibid., 290.

22. FARRAND, vol. 1, 250, 314, 324, 335, 437, 446, 450.

23. Luther Martin refused to sign the final draft of the Constitution and later opposed its ratification. See his "Address to the Maryland House of Representatives", ibid., vol. 3, 151–159.

24. ELLIOT, vol. 4, 10. See also, WOOD, 282–291.

25. Quoted in WOOD, 290.

26. HAMILTON, THE FEDERALIST (no. 78), 506.

27. Madison and Wilson, FARRAND, vol. 1, 250, 314, 324, 355, 437, 446, 450.

28. HAMILTON, THE FEDERALIST (no. 84), 561.

29. J. ANDREWS, ed., THE WORKS OF JAMES WILSON (1896), 374. The same idea is expressed by T. PAINE in THE RIGHTS OF MAN, 420–445 and by HAMILTON in THE FEDERALIST (no. 81), 524.

2. THE CONSTITUTION CONSTRUED AND DEMOCRATIC THEORIES VINDICATED

1. The consensus was the result of many factors including peace, prosperity, and the authority given the new system by the towering prestige of the first President, George Washington. Madison's political strategy also helped. The state ratifying conventions of 1787–1788 had shown that a Bill of Rights would greatly increase support for the new government; so despite the indifference of many of the original supporters of the Constitution who now had the government they wanted, and even though he then personally thought a Bill of Rights unnecessary in the federal Constitution, Madison insisted upon submitting a series of amendments to the states. 1 ANNALS OF CONGRESS 440–460 (1789). As Madison had hoped, the Bill of Rights quieted the fears many moderate democrats had about the Constitution.

2. Paine, the radical democrat, illustrates this attitude change well. See, PAINE, 420–445.

3. Jefferson to Francis Hopkinson (13 March 1789), in FORD, ed., THE WRITINGS OF THOMAS JEFFERSON, vol. 5, (1899), 456.

4. Jefferson to Colonel William S. Smith (13 November 1787), ibid., vol. 5, 360; and Jefferson to Madison (20 December 1787), ibid., vol. 5, 368.

5. Jefferson to Madison (31 July 1788), ibid., vol. 5, 456. Jefferson's two principal objections to the work of the Philadelphia Convention were the absence of a Bill of Rights and the failure to provide for rotation of the presidency. The addition of the first ten amendments and the customary observance of a two-term limitation by our Presidents cemented Jefferson's adherence to the Constitution.

6. Jefferson, "Notes on Virginia", in A. KOCH and W. PEDEN, ed., LIFE AND WRITINGS OF THOMAS JEFFERSON (1944), 236–245; Jefferson to John Taylor (28 May 1816), FORD, vol. 11, 527; Jefferson to the Marquis de Lafayette (14 February 1815), ibid., vol. 11, 454; and Jefferson to John Adams (5 July 1814), ibid., vol. 11, 393.

7. Jefferson to Madison (20 December 1816), Ford, vol. 5, 368.

8. Jefferson to John Taylor (28 May 1816), ibid., vol. 11, 527.

9. The differences in the political ideas of Jefferson and Madison are developed in A. KOCH, JEFFERSON and MADISON (1950).

10. Ibid.; Jefferson to John Jay (23 August 1785), FORD, vol. 4, 449.

11. Jefferson to Joseph Cabell (2 February 1816) in KOCH and PEDEN, 661; Jefferson to John Tyler (26 May 1810), ibid., 604; "Notes on Virginia," ibid., 262.

12. "He himself was forced into dissent in only one constitutional decision, that of Ogden v. Saunders, 12 Wheat. 213 (1827)." L. FRIEDMAN and F. ISRAEL, THE JUSTICES OF THE UNITED STATES SUPREME COURT, 1789–1969 (1970), 301. The Great Chief Justice served thirty four years, 1801–1835.

13. McCulloch v. Maryland, 4 Wheat. 316, 405 (1819); Cohens v. Virginia, 6 Wheat. 264, 380–448 (1821); Gibbons v. Ogden, 9 Wheat. 1, 4–5 (1824). The same reasoning permeates all of Marshall's constitutional opinions.

14. Fletcher v. Peck, 6 Cranch. 87 (1810); Dartmouth College v. Woodward, 4 Wheat. 518 (1819); McCulloch v. Maryland, 4 Wheat. 316 (1819); Gibbons v. Ogden, 9 Wheat. 1 (1824); Cherokee Nation v. Georgia, 5 Pet. 1 (1831); Worcester v. Georgia, 6 Pet. 515 (1832).

15. Compare the position of Marshall (Marbury v. Madison, 1 Cranch. 137 [1803]; Cohens v. Virginia, 6 Wheat. 264 [1821]) with that of Madison (Madison to Edward Everett [30 August 1830] in G. HUNT, ed., THE WRITINGS OF JAMES MADISON [1900-1910] vol. 9, 383) and with that of Jefferson (Jefferson to Taylor [28 May 1816], in FORD, WRITINGS, vol. 11, 527 and Jefferson to Major John Cartwright [5 June 1824] in KOCH and PEDEN, 714). For a discussion of Jefferson's distrust of judicial review, see KOCH, 227–229.

16. WOOD, 291–305; E. S. CORWIN, THE "HIGHER LAW" BACKGROUND OF AMERICAN CONSTITUTIONAL LAW (1955).

17. "We believe, then, in the principle of *democratic republicanism*, in its strongest and purest sense. We have an abiding confidence in the virtue, intelligence, and full capacity for self-government, of the great mass of our people, our industrious, honest, manly, intelligent millions of freemen." Quoted in J. BLAU, ed., SOCIAL THEORIES OF JACKSONIAN DEMOCRACY (1954), 22.

18. WILLIAMSON, 192–207.

19. J. D. RICHARDSON, A COMPILATION OF THE MESSAGES AND PAPERS OF THE PRESIDENTS, 1789–1897 (1897), vol. 2, 448. Alexis de Tocqueville saw this theory being translated into practice. See TOCQUEVILLE, DEMOCRACY IN AMERICA (1954), vol. 1, 265.

20. R. HOFSTADTER, THE AMERICAN POLITICAL TRADITION (1955), 56.

21. L. HARTZ, ECONOMIC POLICY AND DEMOCRATIC THOUGHT: PENNSYLVANIA 1776– 1860 (1948) esp. Part 4; B. HAMMOND, BANKS AND POLITICS IN AMERICA: FROM

THE REVOLUTION TO THE CIVIL WAR (1957); A. M. SCHLESINGER, JR., THE AGE OF JACKSON (1950), 337–339.

22. Charles River Bridge v. Warren River Bridge, 11 Pet. 420 (1837). For an illuminating account of legal developments in the states favorable to entrepreneurial interests, see M. HORWITZ, THE TRANSFORMATION OF AMERICAN LAW, 1780–1860 (1977).

23. J. STORY, MISCELLANEOUS WRITINGS (1852), 66 and 228; J. STORY, COMMENTARIES ON THE CONSTITUTION (5th ed., 1891), I, 111, sec. 148, 350–387, sec. 457–517, I, 390–91, sec. 521, I, 407–421, especially 414–415, sec. 557–558, II, 241–274, sec. 1374–1400; Charles River Bridge v. Warren Bridge, 11 Pet. 420, 639 (1837) (dissenting opinion); Swift v. Tyson, 16 Pet. 1 (1842).

24. Luther v. Borden, 7 How. 1 (1849), esp. 50–54 (dissenting opinion of Woodbury).

25. Wilkinson v. Leland, 2 Pet. 627, 626–7 (1829) (Argument of Counsel). Webster believed that property gave men a stake in society; property, therefore, was a key element in his political theory. E. EVERETT, ed., THE WORKS OF DANIEL WEBSTER, vol. 3 (10th ed., 1857), 13–16.

26. EVERETT, 104.

27. HARTZ, THE LIBERAL TRADITION, 89–113. See also R. CURRENT, DANIEL WEBSTER AND THE RISE OF NATIONAL CONSERVATISM (1955).

28. R. BASLER, ed., THE COLLECTED WORKS OF ABRAHAM LINCOLN (1953), vol. 7, 259.

29. HARTZ, THE LIBERAL TRADITION, 145–178. For the Southern interpretation of the Constitution in the light of this political theory see John C. Calhoun, *Disquisition on Government* and *A Discourse on the Constitution and Government of the United States*, in R. CRAILLE, ed., WORKS OF JOHN C. CALHOUN (1883).

30. WILLIAMSON, 281.

31. W. Hamilton, *Constitutionalism*, 4 ENCYCLOPAEDIA OF THE SOCIAL SCIENCES 255–256 (1930 ed.). Jefferson's famous comment at the beginning of this change was: "Some men look at constitutions with sanctimonious reverence, and they deem them like the ark of the covenant, too sacred to be touched. They ascribe to men of the preceding age a wisdom more than human, and suppose what they did to be beyond amendment. I knew that age well, I belonged to it and labored with it . . . It was very like the present, but without the experience of the present." Jefferson to Kercheval (12 July 1816), FORD, WRITINGS, vol. 12, 3.

32. Hamilton, 256–257.

3. CONSTITUTIONAL EXEGESIS OLD AND NEW

1. The Slaughter-House Cases, 16 Wall. 36 (1873); Munn v. Illinois, 94 U.S. 113, 126 (1877); The Granger Railroad Cases, 94 U.S. 155–187 (1877).

2. STORY, MISCELLANEOUS WRITINGS, 228. The Court did employ the Fourteenth Amendment to impose some nonracial restrictions on the states. Pumpelly v. Green Bay Co., 13 Wall. 166 (1872).

3. T. COOLEY, CONSTITUTIONAL LIMITATIONS (6th ed., 1890) iii, 68–69.

4. T. TWISS, LAWYERS AND THE CONSTITUTION (1942), 19.

5. Munn v. Illinois, 94 U.S. 113, 142 (1877) (dissenting opinion).

6. Ibid., 136, 141, 145, 140. See also his dissent in The Granger Railroad Cases, 94 U.S. 155–187, at 183–187 (1877).
7. "Address of Justice Field at the Centennial Celebration of the Organization of the Federal Judiciary," (4 February 1890), in S. Field, Opinions and Papers of Justice Field (n.d.), vol. 1, 237.
8. R. Hofstadter, Social Darwinism in American Thought (1955), 7.
9. Justice David J. Brewer, "Address to New York State Bar Association," (1893), in A. Westin, ed., An Autobiography of the Supreme Court (1963), 122.
10. Budd v. New York, 143 U.S. 517, 551 (1892).
11. The comment on this theory is, of course, from Justice Holmes's famous dissent in Lochner v. New York, 198 U.S. 45, 75 (1905).
12. Statement by Chief Justice Morrison R. Waite before the beginning of oral argument in Santa Clara v. Southern Pacific, 118 U.S. 394, 396 (1886). The Court thereby accepted the argument made at its bar by Roscoe Conklin in San Mateo v. Southern Pacific, 116 U.S. 138 (1885).
13. Chicago, Milwaukee & St. Paul R.R. v. Minnesota, 134 U.S. 418, 457, 461 (1890).
14. Coppage v. Kansas, 236 U.S. 1, 14 (1915). By this time Justice Pitney was restating the accepted judicial doctrine of the period, not enunciating a new one. The Court had first adopted the doctrine in Allgeyer v. Louisiana, 165 U.S. 578 (1897).
15. Pound, Liberty of Contract, 18 Yale L. J. 454 (1909). Compare Holden v. Hardy, 169 U.S. 366 (1898) which upheld a maximum hours statute for miners with Lochner v. New York, 198 U.S. 45 (1905) which struck down a similar statute involving the hours of bakers.
16. Gibbons v. Ogden, 9 Wheat. 1 (1824).
17. United States v. E. C. Knight Co., 156 U.S. 1 (1895).
18. Employers' Liability Cases, 207 U.S. 463 (1908).
19. Adair v. United States, 208 U.S. 161 (1908).
20. Leisy v. Hardin, 135 U.S. 100 (1890).
21. Lerner, The Supreme Court and American Capitalism, 42 Yale L. J. 668 (1933).
22. Cooley, 68.
23. For the wavering back and forth on the liberty of contract doctrine compare Muller v. Oregon, 208 U.S. 412 (1908) with Adkins v. Children's Hospital, 261 U.S. 525 (1923). For the same process with the commerce clause, compare the broad view in the Shreveport Rate Cases, 234 U.S. 342 (1914) and Stafford v. Wallace, 258 U.S. 495 (1922) with the restricted view in Hammer v. Dagenhart, 247 U.S. 251 (1918).
24. G. Gilmore, The Ages of American Law (1977), ch. 3.
25. Truax v. Corrigan, 257 U.S. 312 (1921).
26. E. Goldman, Rendezvous with Destiny (1956), 40. There was also a "darker side" to Populism. Populist rhetoric contained a xenophobic element that was sometimes expressed in an overtly antisemitic or racist manner. See R. Hofstadter, The Age of Reform (1960), particularly ch. 3.
27. "Omaha Platform, 1892", appendix F, in G. Hicks, The Populist Revolt (1931). See also ch. 15 and the other appendices.
28. Goldman, 59–65.
29. Hofstadter, The Age of Reform, 131–212.

30. About the nature of the reforms necessary for the restoration of opportunity there was considerable disagreement among the Progressives. Compare WOODROW WILSON, THE NEW FREEDOM (1913) with THEODORE ROOSEVELT, THE NEW NATIONALISM (1910). Both Presidents, however, placed great emphasis on expertise to reconcile competing interests in order to further equal opportunity.

31. See A. LIEF, ed., THE SOCIAL AND ECONOMIC VIEWS OF MR. JUSTICE BRANDEIS (1930); A. T. MASON, BRANDEIS: A FREE MAN'S LIFE (1946); E. POLLACK, ed., THE BRANDEIS READER (1956).

32. Brief, Muller v. Oregon, 208 U.S. 412 (1908), 2.

33. Jay Burns Baking Co. v. Bryan, 264 U.S. 504, 520 (1924) (dissenting opinion).

34. New State Ice Co. v. Liebmann, 285 U.S. 262, 331 (1932) (dissenting opinion).

35. Brandeis, *The Living Law*, 80 ILL. L. REV. 461, 467 (1916).

36. Pierce v. United States, 252 U.S. 239, 273 (1920) (dissenting opinion).

37. Whitney v. California, 274 U.S. 357, 373 (1927) (concurring opinion).

38. Olmstead v. United States, 277 U.S. 438, 478 (1928) (dissenting opinion). See also his classic article with Samuel D. Warren, Brandeis and Warren, *The Right to Privacy*, 4 HARV. L. REV. 193 (1890).

4. THE CHALLENGE TO TRADITION

1. In his Cambridge, Massachusetts, intellectual circle, the Metaphysical Club—which included Chauncey Wright, Charles Peirce, Henry and William James—Holmes took part in the discussions on the experimental nature of Darwinian theory, and he remained a Darwinian, with Darwin's emphasis on Malthus *not* excluded, for the rest of his life. Dewey clearly saw the experimental implications of Darwin. See *Evolution and Ethics*, 8 Monist 321–341 (1898); and THE INFLUENCE OF DARWIN ON PHILOSOPHY AND OTHER ESSAYS (1910), 1–19.

2. R. ARON, GERMAN SOCIOLOGY, trans. by M. and T. Bottomore, (1957); S. WOLIN, POLITICS AND VISION (1960), ch. 10.

3. M. WHITE, THE ORIGINS OF DEWEY'S INSTRUMENTALISM (1943); J. DEWEY, THE QUEST FOR CERTAINTY (1960 ed.), 273–274.

4. Dewey, THE QUEST FOR CERTAINTY, 266.

5. Ibid., 260.

6. J. DEWEY and J. TUFTS, ETHICS (1908), 437.

7. J. DEWEY, THE PUBLIC AND ITS PROBLEMS (1927), 15–16.

8. Ibid., 31–32.

9. Ibid., 45, also 169–170.

10. The phrase is the subtitle of M. White's SOCIAL THOUGHT IN AMERICA (1957).

11. DEWEY, THE PUBLIC, 82.

12. Ibid., 206–209.

13. WHITE, SOCIAL THOUGHT, 244.

14. O. W. HOLMES, SPEECHES BY OLIVER WENDELL HOLMES (1913), 102.

15. O. W. HOLMES, COLLECTED LEGAL PAPERS (1921), 306. See also, M. HOWE, ed., HOLMES-LASKI LETTERS, (1953), vol. 1, 207.

16. HOWE, HOLMES-LASKI, vol. 1, 165.

17. HOLMES, COLLECTED LEGAL, 306.
18. M. HOWE, ed., HOLMES-POLLACK LETTERS (1941), vol. 2, 36.
19. HOLMES, COLLECTED LEGAL, 313. Holmes makes the same point in THE COMMON LAW (1881), 44, 48.
20. HOWE, HOLMES-LASKI, vol. 1, 264.
21. HOLMES, COLLECTED LEGAL, 311. See also 304–305.
22. HOWE, HOLMES-LASKI, vol. 1, 8.
23. HOLMES, COLLECTED LEGAL, 313–314.
24. Ibid., 181. See also 186–198.
25. Vegelahan v. Gunter, 167 Mass. 92, 104 (1896); Tyson & Brother v. Banton, 273 U.S. 418, 446 (1927) (dissenting opinion).
26. Missouri v. Holland, 252 U.S. 416, 433 (1920); Gompers v. United States, 233 U.S. 604, 610 (1914). All the commentators have concluded that his experiences as a soldier were a significant influence on Holmes's thinking. He was a thrice-wounded veteran of the Civil War. Edmund Wilson, in a brilliant essay, most clearly relates the Civil War's impact on Holmes to the legal scholar's early acceptance of Darwinism, pragmatism, and Comte's social science. E. WILSON, PATRIOTIC GORE (1962), 743–796, especially 762–763.
27. Lochner v. New York, 198 U.S. 45, 75 (1905) (dissenting opinion).
28. Lochner v. New York, 198 U.S. 45, 76 (1905) (dissenting opinion).
29. Adkins v. Children's Hospital, 261 U.S. 525, 568 (1923) (dissenting opinion).
30. Rogat, *Mr. Justice Holmes: The Judge as Spectator*, 31 CHI. L. REV. 213–256 (1964); GILMORE, 48–56.
    There is an old chestnut about Justice Holmes which summarizes his position well. Asked by his law clerk about his general theory of the Constitution, the Justice replied, "Long ago I decided I was not God. When a state came here and wanted to build a slaughterhouse, I looked at the Constitution and didn't find anything in there that said a state could not build a slaughterhouse. I said to myself, if they want to build a slaughterhouse, God dammit, let them build it." This tale is found everywhere in the accounts of Justice Holmes and an authoritative citation is nowhere to be found. It became part of our folklore because it is so much in character with all we know about Holmes.
31. Schenck v. United States, 249 U.S. 47 (1919).
32. Abrams v. United States, 250 U.S. 616, 630 (1919) (dissenting opinion).
33. "The question in every case is whether the words used are used in such circumstances and are of such a nature as to create a clear and present danger that they will bring about the substantive evils that Congress has the right to prevent. It is a question of proximity and degree." Schenck v. United States, 249 U.S. 47, 52 (1919). In Abrams he said: "While that experiment (the First Amendment) is part of our system, I think we should be eternally vigilant against attempts to check the expression of opinions that we loathe and believe fraught with death, unless they so imminently threaten immediate interference with the lawful and pressing progress of law that an immediate check is required to save the country." 250 U.S. 616, 630 (1919) (dissenting opinion).

34. McAuliffe v. New Bedford, 155 Mass. 216 (1892); Davis v. Commonwealth, 162 Mass. 510 (1895); Bartels v. Iowa, 262 U.S. 404, 412 (1923) (dissenting opinion).
35. Debs v. United States, 249 U.S. 211 (1919).
36. Frohwerk v. United States, 249 U.S. 204 (1919).
37. S. KONEFSKY, THE LEGACY OF HOLMES AND BRANDEIS (1961), 187.
38. Debs v. United States, 249 U.S. 211 (1919); Frohwerk v. United States, 249 U.S. 204 (1919); Abrams v. United States, 250 U.S. 616, 630 (1919) (dissenting opinion); Gitlow v. New York, 268 U.S. 652, 673 (1925) (dissenting opinion).
39. United States. v. Schwimmer, 279 U.S. 644, 654–655 (1929) (dissenting opinion).
40. HOLMES, COLLECTED LEGAL, 307.
41. M. WEBER, LAW IN ECONOMY AND SOCIETY, M. Rheinstein, ed., trans. by M. Rheinstein and E. Shils (1954), 298.
42. Home Bldg. and Loan Association v. Blaisdell, 290 U.S. 398 (1934); Nebbia v. New York, 291 U.S. 502 (1934).
43. R. MCCLOSKEY, THE AMERICAN SUPREME COURT (1960), 164.
44. Carter v. Carter Coal Co., 298 U.S. 238 (1936); Schechter Poultry Co. v. United States, 295 U.S. 495 (1935); United States v. Butler, 297 U.S. 1 (1936).
45. Morehead v. Tipaldo, 298 U.S. 587 (1936).
46. West Coast Hotel v. Parrish, 300 U.S. 379 (1937).
47. NLRB v. Jones and Laughlin, 301 U.S. 1 (1937).
48. Steward Machine Co. v. Davis, 301 U.S. 548 (1937).
49. United States v. Darby Lumber Co., 312 U.S. 100 (1941) and Wickard v. Filburn, 317 U.S. 111 (1942) can be taken as the logical working out of this revolution and as marking its end.

5. THE COMPETITIVE PARADIGM FOR DEMOCRACY

1. J. SCHUMPETER, CAPITALISM, SOCIALISM, AND DEMOCRACY, 3rd ed. (1962), 269.
2. The "decision to reject one paradigm is always simultaneously the decision to accept another, and the judgment leading to that decision involves the comparison of both paradigms with nature and with each other." KUHN, 77.
3. For example, D. TRUMAN, THE GOVERNMENTAL PROCESS (1951), 502. V. O. KEY, JR., PUBLIC OPINION AND AMERICAN DEMOCRACY (1961), 7.
4. This theory may seem just too simple-minded for sophisticated social scientists; yet, it was the basis for the model used by P. Lazerfeld, B. Berelson, and H. Gaudet in their pioneering study of the 1940 Presidential election, THE PEOPLE'S CHOICE (1944). See Rossi, *Four Landmarks in Voting Research*, in E. BURDICK and A. BRODBECK, eds., AMERICAN VOTING BEHAVIOR (1959), 15–16. Pennock calls this a populist theory of democracy; PENNOCK, 163.
5. KEY, PUBLIC OPINION, 78.
6. A. CAMPBELL, P. CONVERSE, W. MILLER, and D. STOKES, THE AMERICAN VOTER (1960), 227–249; Stokes and Miller, *Party Government and the Saliency of Congress*, 26 PUBLIC OPINION Q. 531–6 (1962).

7. S. ELDERSVELD, POLITICAL PARTIES: A BEHAVIORAL ANALYSIS (1964), 486–7.

8. Stokes and Miller, 535.

9. For example, The President's Commission on National Goals, GOALS FOR AMERICANS (1960).

10. SCHUMPETER, 254.

11. Kuhn discusses the adoption of a new paradigm in terms of its utility in solving the problem which led to the crisis and its utility to guide future research, KUHN, 152–153.

12. A. DOWNS, AN ECONOMIC THEORY OF DEMOCRACY (1957), 82–95.

13. Ibid.

14. SCHUMPETER, 271.

15. McClosky, Hoffman, O'Hara, *Issue Conflict and Consensus Among Party Leaders and Followers*, 54 AMER. POL. SCI. REV. 406, 423 (1960).

16. E. E. SCHATTSCHNEIDER, THE SEMISOVEREIGN PEOPLE (1960).

17. Compare L. VON MISES, BUREAUCRACY (1944) with D. WALDO, THE ADMINISTRATIVE STATE (1948).

18. Key, *A Theory of Critical Elections*, 17 J. OF POLITICS 3 (1955); Key, *Secular Realignment of the Party System*, 22 J. OF POLITICS 198 (1959); Key, *Public Opinion*, 558; SCHATTSCHNEIDER, 78-96; CAMPBELL ET AL., THE AMERICAN VOTER, 531-538; A. CAMPBELL, P. CONVERSE, W. MILLER and D. STOKES, ELECTIONS AND THE POLITICAL ORDER (1966) 63-124.

19. SCHUMPETER, 271–272. He was well aware that the average citizen lacked the resources to compete for political office, but he thought the formal recognition of the possibility was significant for individual freedom.

20. Ibid., 273.

21. S. M. LIPSET, POLITICAL MAN (1959); G. SARTORI, DEMOCRATIC THEORY (1962).

22. For example, T. L. THORSON, THE LOGIC OF DEMOCRACY (1962).

23. R. MACIVER, THE WEB OF GOVERNMENT (1947), 198–199; and ibid., THE RAMPARTS WE GUARD (1950), 27–30; LIPSET, 45.

24. KEY, PUBLIC OPINION, ch. 21; R. DAHL, A PREFACE TO DEMOCRATIC THEORY (1956), 131; TRUMAN, ch. 16.

25. SCHATTSCHNEIDER, 141.

26. Campbell et al. THE AMERICAN VOTER; McClosky, *Consensus and Ideology in American Politics*, 58 AMER. POL. SCI. REV. 361 (1964).

27. J. M. BURNS and J. W. PELTASON, GOVERNMENT BY THE PEOPLE, 6th. ed. (1966), 8; C. ADRIAN and C. PRESS, THE AMERICAN POLITICAL PROCESS (1965), 84–85; M. IRISH and J. PROTHRO, THE POLITICS OF AMERICAN DEMOCRACY, 3d ed. (1965), 55–58. For the significant role of textbooks in establishing a new paradigm within the scientific community, see KUHN, ch. 11.

6. REALIST THEORY

1. SCHUMPETER, 240–243

2. DAHL, A PREFACE, 131, n. 12.
3. MacIver, The Web, 213; Lipset, Political Man, 220. In developing his argument Lipset cites MacIver, The Web, 215–216.
4. Lipset, 403.
5. Dahl, *The City in the Future of Democracy*, 61 Amer. Pol. Sci. Rev. 953 (1967).
6. DAHL, A PREFACE, 130. V. O. Key, The Responsible Electorate (1966), 2–3 (this work was published posthumously, and the final draft of several chapters was done by M. Cummings, Jr.).
7. Key, The Responsible, 62.
8. Ibid.
9. Ibid., DAHL, A PREFACE, 130–131.
10. DAHL, A PREFACE, 131; Key, Public Opinion, 553.
11. Key, The Responsible, 58–60.
12. DAHL, A PREFACE, 146.
13. Ibid., 125–132. See also DAHL, Modern Political Analysis (1963), 8; Key, Public Opinion, 553.
14. S. Hook, Reason, Social Myths and Democracy (1940), 295–296; ibid., Political Power and Personal Freedom (1962), 59–82.
15. Hook, Reason, Social Myths, 285.
16. Ibid., 285.
17. Ibid., 286; Hook, Political Power, 57–58.
18. Schumpeter, 269; Sartori; H. Mayo, An Introduction to Democratic Theory (1960).
19. S. Hook, The Paradoxes of Freedom (1964), 105; ibid., Political Power, 74–77.
20. Hook, Political Power, 54.
21. Ibid., 74.
22. Ibid., 61–62, 75.
23. Ibid., 77.
24. Ibid., 98.
25. Ibid., 31, 74.
26. Ibid., 74.
27. Ibid., 46.
28. Ibid., 48–49. "The dictatorship of the majority [is a] bugaboo which haunts the books of political theorists but has never been found in the flesh in modern history." Hook, The Paradoxes, 66.
29. Hook, The Paradoxes, 91–93.
30. Ibid., 96; Hook, Political Power, 47.
31. Hook, The Paradoxes, 97.
32. Ibid., 103.
33. Ibid.
34. Ibid.,104
35. Compare Poe v. Ullman, 367 U.S. 497 (1961), 498–509 (plurality opinion of Frankfurter) with ibid., 522–555 (dissenting opinion of Harlan).
36. F. Frankfurter, The Public and Its Government (1930), 160.

324 DEMOCRATIC THEORIES AND THE CONSTITUTION

37. American Federation of Labor v. American Sash & Door Co., 335 U.S. 538, 557 (1949) (concurring opinion).
38. Ibid. (Frankfurter).
39. Reynolds v. Sims, 377 U.S. 533, 623–624 (1964) (dissenting opinion). Emphasis added.
40. FRANKFURTER, 161.
41. American Federation of Labor v. American Sash & Door Co., 335 U.S. 538, 555 (1949) (concurring opinion).
42. West Virginia v. Barnette, 319 U.S. 624, 670 (1943) (dissenting opinion).
43. Reynolds v. Sims, 377 U.S. 533, 624 (1964) (dissenting opinion).
44. American Federation of Labor v. American Sash & Door Co., 355 U.S. 538, 553 (1949) (concurring opinion of Frankfurter).
45. Ibid., 556–557.
46. West Virginia Board of Education v. Barnette, 319 U.S. 624, 652 (1943) (dissenting opinion).
47. American Federation of Labor v. American Sash & Door Co., 335 U.S. 538, 555 (1949) (concurring opinion of Frankfurter).
48. HOOK, THE PARADOXES, 102.
49. A. BICKEL, THE MORALITY OF CONSENT (1975), 33–54.
50. Kleindienst v. Mandel, 408 U.S. 753 (1972).
51. For example, Knauff v. Shaughnessy, 338 U.S. 537 (1950).
52. Brinkman, *Citizenship*, 3 ENCYCLOPAEDIA OF THE SOCIAL SCIENCES 471–474 (1930 ed.); Gordon, *The Citizen and the State: Power of Congress to Expatriate American Citizens*, 53 GEO. L. J. 315 (1965).
53. J. KENT, COMMENTARIES ON AMERICAN LAW (6th ed., 1848) vol. 2, 258, note. The leading case, United States v. Wong Kim Ark, 169 U.S. 649 (1898), contains an elaborate discussion of the Anglo-American legal concept of citizenship.
54. For example, H. ARENDT, THE HUMAN CONDITION (1958); M. WALZER, OBLIGATIONS (1970).
55. W. MCWILLIAMS, THE IDEA OF FRATERNITY IN AMERICA (1973); Karst, *Foreward: Equal Citizenship under the Fourteenth Amendment*, 91 HARV. L. REV. 1 (1977).
56. All states and localities impose some residence and registration requirements which undoubtedly can temporarily frustrate a citizen's desire to vote. Most states also exclude mentally incapacitated citizens and convicted felons; some even disenfranchise former felons for a period of years.
57. The discussion here does not deal with whether illegally procured United States citizenship can be revoked, as in Schneiderman v. United States, 320 U.S. 118 (1943), or with the criteria for determining whether such citizenship has been illegally procured, as in Fedorenko v. United States, 449 U.S. 490 (1981).
58. Slaughter-House Cases, 16 Wall. 36 (1873).
59. Dred Scott v. Sandford, 19 How. 393 (1857).
60. Slaughter-House Cases, 16 Wall. 36 (1873).
61. United States v. Wong Kim Ark, 169 U.S. 649 (1898).
62. Ibid.
63. Ibid.; Elk v. Wilkins, 112 U.S. 94 (1884).

64. 8 U.S.C. sec. 1401 (1924).
65. Afroyim v. Rusk, 387 U.S. 253 (1967).
66. See the Nationality Act of 1940. The pertinent provisions are discussed in Roche, *The Expatriation Cases*, 1963 SUP. CT. REV. 325–326. See also, Mackenzie v. Hare, 239 U.S. 299 (1915): Congress may expatriate a woman citizen for the duration of her marriage to a foreign citizen.
67. Afroyim v. Rusk, 387 U.S. 253, 292 (1967) (dissenting opinion of Harlan).
68. Perez v. Brownell, 356 U.S. 44 (1958). (Harlan joined Frankfurter's majority opinion.)
69. Ibid., 60–61; Afroyim v. Rusk, 387 U.S. 253, 268–270, (1967).
70. Trop v. Dulles, 356 U.S. 86 (1958).
71. Ibid., 122.
72. Ibid., 121. Frankfurter used a quotation from an opinion by Justice Holmes, naturally. Jacobson v. Massachusetts, 197 U.S. 11, 29 (1905).
73. BICKEL, THE MORALITY, 33.
74. Ibid., 53–54.
75. Perez v. Brownell, 356 U.S. 44, 84–85 (1958).
76. Roche, 345. See also HOOK, THE PARADOXES, 49–51.
77. Trop v. Dulles, 356 U.S. 86, 124 (1958), (dissenting opinion of Frankfurter).
78. Ibid., 125.
79. H. ARENDT, ORIGINS OF TOTALITARIANISM (1951), 287–289.
80. LIPSET, POLITICAL MAN, 79.
81. KEY, PUBLIC OPINION, 527; R. DAHL, WHO GOVERNS? (1961), ch. 25, 26. Dahl does not stop with stating the fact that most people do not participate in group affairs; he also contends that an increase in such participation would not add much to democratic politics on a societal level. Dahl, *The City*, 962.
82. H. KARIEL, THE DECLINE OF AMERICAN PLURALISM (1961), Part I.
83. KEY, PUBLIC OPINION, 513.
84. Ibid., 514.
85. M. HARRINGTON, THE OTHER AMERICA (1962).
86. KEY, PUBLIC OPINION, 514; DAHL, WHO GOVERNS?, 226–228, and ibid.,A PREFACE, 146–148.
87. DAHL, WHO GOVERNS?, 226–228. While this is a community power study, Dahl's last two chapters, 27 and 28, make it clear that he viewed his analysis as applying to national politics. See also his PLURALISTIC DEMOCRACY IN THE UNITED STATES (1967).
88. DAHL, WHO GOVERNS?, 228.
89. Later, Professor Dahl recognized that one of the costs of the present system is that it "makes it easy for political leaders to ignore groups of people whose problems lie outside the attention, loyalties, values, and identifications of the great mass of voters, particularly if these groups lack bargaining power because of poor organization, low status, isolation, ignorance, lack of political incentives, and so on." R. DAHL, POLITICAL OPPOSITIONS IN WESTERN DEMOCRACIES (1966), 64.
90. DAHL, WHO GOVERNS?, 286–293.

91. Burnham, *The Changing Shape of the American Political Universe*, 59 AMER. POL. SCI. REV. 7 (1965); E. E. SCHATTSCHNEIDER, THE SEMISOVEREIGN PEOPLE, ch. 3.
92. DAHL, WHO GOVERNS? 223–226, 293–294. Dahl also indicates that in our political culture, which assigns individual achievement and nongovernmental techniques high priority, people may never turn to politics for solutions to individual problems. ibid., 279-280. This idea does not square with either his own theory of pluralistic democracy—minorities rule—or with the political history of this country. It was just an alternate attempt to make political apathy into a middle-class phenomenon.
93. Dahl later gave greater emphasis to these factors, *The City*, 967.
94. DAHL, A PREFACE, 145. Key made a similar statement in PUBLIC OPINION, 527.
95. KEY, PUBLIC OPINION, 558.
96. Baker v. Carr, 369 U.S. 186, 300 (1962) (dissenting opinion). A similar statement is made by Justice Harlan. ibid., 333 (dissenting opinion).
97. Colegrove v. Green, 328 U.S. 549 (1946) (opinion of Frankfurter). See also Baker v. Carr, 369 U.S. 186, 266 and 330 (1962) (dissenting opinions of Frankfurter and Harlan).
98. Baker v. Carr, 369 U.S. 186, 278–297 (1962) (dissenting opinion of Frankfurter).
99. Ibid., 285. In *Colegrove*, Frankfurter's discussion of this factor implied that the lack of individual standing was also involved. His *Baker* dissent does not mention this point.
100. Brown v. Board of Education, 347 U.S. 483 (1954).
101. Baker v. Carr. 369 U.S. 186, 327–328 (1962) (dissenting opinion of Frankfurter).
102. Ibid., 301–324.
103. Reynolds v. Sims, 377 U.S. 533, 590–591 (1964).
104. R. DIXON, DEMOCRATIC REPRESENTATION (1968); A. DEGRAZIA, ESSAY ON APPORTIONMENT AND REPRESENTATIVE GOVERNMENT (1963).
105. R. MCKAY, REAPPORTIONMENT: THE LAW AND POLITICS OF EQUAL REPRESENTATION (1965), 9–35; R. HANSON, THE POLITICAL THICKET: REAPPORTIONMENT AND CONSTITUTIONAL DEMOCRACY (1966), 4–17; Advisory Commission on Intergovernmental Relations, APPORTIONMENT OF STATE LEGISLATURES (1962).
106. Reynolds v. Sims, 377 U.S. 533, 590–591 (1964) (dissenting opinion).
107. Cooper v. Aaron, 358 U.S. 1 (1958).
108. See especially, Griswold v. Connecticut, 381 U.S. 479, 499 (1965) (concurring opinion); Poe v. Ullman, 367 U.S. 479, 522 (1961) (dissenting opinion).
109. Baker v. Carr, 369 U.S. 186, 324 (1962) (dissenting opinion of Frankfurter). See also, Reynolds v. Sims, 377 U.S. 533, 620 (1964) (dissenting opinion of Harlan).
110. Baker v. Carr, 369 U.S. 186, 337 (1962) (dissenting opinion of Harlan).
111. Article IV, Sect. 4. The leading cases are: Luther v. Borden, 7 How. 1 (1849); Pacific Telephone v. Oregon, 223 U.S. 118 (1912); Ohio v. Akron Park District, 281 U.S. 74 (1930).

112. Baker v. Carr, 369 U.S. 186, 299 (1962) (dissenting opinion of Frankfurter).
113. Ibid., 270. See also Reynolds v. Sims, 377 U.S. 533, 624–625 (1964) (dissenting opinion of Harlan).
114. Baker v. Carr, 369 U.S. 186, 331 (1962) (dissenting opinion).
115. Ibid., 334. Emphasis added.
116. Ibid., 336–339.
117. Ibid., 258 (concurring opinion).
118. Colegrove v. Green, 328 U.S. 549, 556 (1946) (opinion of Frankfurter).
119. Baker v. Carr, 369 U.S. 186, 270 (1962) (dissenting opinion of Frankfurter).
120. Ibid.
121. Advisory Commission on Intergovernmental Relations, APPORTIONMENT OF STATE LEGISLATURES (1962).
122. Baker v. Carr, 369 U.S. 186, 267 (1962) (dissenting opinion of Frankfurter).
123. Ibid., 251 (concurring opinion of Clark); ibid., 265 (concurring opinion of Stewart); Reynolds v. Sims, 377 U.S. 533 (1964) (concurring opinion of Clark); ibid., 588 (concurring opinion of Stewart); Lucas v. Colorado, 377 U.S. 713, 741 (1964) (dissenting opinion of Clark); ibid., 744 (dissenting opinion of Stewart). The Clark-Stewart standard is discussed in ch. 7.
124. Baker v. Carr, 369 U.S. 186, 262 (1962).
125. DAHL, A PREFACE, 138.
126. S. HOOK, HERESY, YES—CONSPIRACY, NO! (1953), 104–105.
127. S. STOUFFER, COMMUNISM, CONFORMITY AND CIVIL LIBERTIES (1955); Prothro and Griggs; McClosky.
128. DAHL, WHO GOVERNS? 324. See also KEY, PUBLIC OPINION, ch. 28.
129. Auerbach, The Communist Control Act of 1954: A Proposed Legal-Political Theory of Free Speech, 23 CHI. L. REV. 173 (1956).
130. DAHL, A PREFACE, 138.
131. Ibid., 135.
132. Ibid., 137.
133. Dennis v. United States, 341 U.S. 494 (1951).
134. Ibid., 521 (concurring opinion).
135. Ibid., 524.
136. Ibid., 510, quoting United States v. Dennis, 183 F. 2d 201, 212 (1950).
137. Ibid., 527.
138. Ibid., 524–525.
139. Ibid., 519, quoting THE FEDERALIST PAPERS, no. 41.
140. Ibid.
141. Ibid., 525
142. Ibid.
143. Ibid., 525–526.
144. Ibid., 539–540.
145. Ibid., 555.
146. Ibid., 550.
147. Barenblatt, v. United States 360 U.S. 109 (1959). Justice Frankfurter joined this opinion.

148. Ibid., 126.
149. Ibid., 121. Emphasis added. The quoted phrase, "The ultimate value in any society" comes from Dennis, 341 U.S. 494, 509 (1951) (opinion of Chief Justice Vinson). The formal expression of Congress is the Subversive Activities Control Act, Title I of the Internal Security Act of 1950.
150. Barenblatt v. United States, 360 U.S. 109, 134.
151. Ibid., 132–133.
152. Communist Party v. Subversive Activities Control Board, 367 U.S. 1 (1961). Justice Harlan joined the majority opinion by Frankfurter.
153. The act's registration provisions (Sec. 7) required the listing of the names, aliases and addresses of the organization's officers and members, and the listing of all printing presses in the possession or control of the organization or its members. Sec. 9 required the attorney general to keep this information, to make it available to the public, and to submit a yearly report containing this information to the President and Congress. The Subversive Activities Control Act is Title I of the Internal Security Act of 1950.
154. Ibid., 91, also 92–97. In addition to citing Dennis as authority for this statement, Frankfurter also cited Schenck. Since the latter case is the origin of Holmes's clear and present danger test, this is another indication that Frankfurter sees that test as just another way of saying that competing interests must be balanced.
155. Ibid., 90.
156. Ibid., 89–90.
157. Scales v. United States, 367 U.S. 203, 228 (1961).
158. The membership clause made it a felony to acquire or hold a membership in any organization which advocates the overthrow of the government of the United States by force or violence. To avoid a due process issue the Court held this clause applied only to active, knowing membership.
159. Ibid., 228–229.
160. Wilkinson v. United States, 365 U.S. 399, 414 (1961). The opinion for the Court was by Justice Stewart, but, as the quotation indicates, in these cases he followed the Frankfurter-Harlan balancing doctrine and both Justices joined the opinion.
161. Ibid., Braden v. United States, 365 U.S. 431 (1961).
162. Uphaus v. Wyman, 360 U.S. 72 (1959). The Court's opinion by Justice Clark relied upon the Frankfurter-Harlan balancing doctrine and both Justices joined it. Gibson v. Florida Legislative Investigation Committee, 372 U.S. 539, 576 (1963) (dissenting opinion of Harlan). DeGregory v. Attorney General of New Hampshire, 383 U.S. 825, 830 (1966) (dissenting opinion of Harlan).
163. For example, the federal government could not force the leaders of the CPUSA to register because that would automatically provide enough evidence to incriminate them under the Smith Act. This result was a clear violation of the Fifth Amendment's Self-Incrimination Clause. Albertson v. Subversive Activities Control Board, 382 U.S 70 (1965). The likelihood of the Court taking this position was mentioned by Frankfurter in Communist Party v. Subversive Activities

Control Board, 367 U.S. l, 105–110 (1961); but he refused to decide the constitutionality of the act on that likelihood.

164. For example, the evidence must be sufficiently strong and persuasive to enable the jury to conclude that the Communist Party is *presently* advocating the overthrow of the government by force and violence since that intent makes knowing, active membership in it a crime. Noto v. United States, 367 U.S. 290 (1961) (opinion for the Court by Harlan).

165. Ibid., 299–300.

166. Watkins v. United States, 354 U.S. 178, 217 (1957) (concurring opinion of Frankfurter). Harlan's dissenting opinion in Russell v. United States, 369 U.S. 749, 781 (1962) indicates the limits he put on this strict construction of the statute.

167. Yates v. United States, 354 U.S. 298, 303–312 (1957). Justice Harlan construed the term "to organize" strictly and came to the conclusion that it meant "to form." By so holding, convictions for "organizing" the CPUSA were no longer operable under the statute of limitations.

168. Joint Anti-Fascist Refugee Committee v. McGrath, 341 U.S. 123, 149 (1951) (opinion of Frankfurter). Peters v. Hobby, 349 U.S. 331 (1955)—Chief Justice Warren's opinion for the Court was joined by Justices Frankfurter and Harlan. The limits of narrowly construing administrative orders can be illustrated by comparing Justice Harlan's opinion for the Court in Vitarelli v. Seaton, 359 U.S. 535 (1959) with Frankfurter's separate opinion in that case, ibid., 546.

169. Sweezy v. New Hampshire, 354 U.S. 256 (1957) (concurring opinion of Frankfurter); American Communications Association v. Douds, 339 U.S. 382 (1950) (separate opinion of Frankfurter).

170. For areas not covered here, see C. JACOBS, JUSTICE FRANKFURTER AND CIVIL LIBERTIES (1961). ch. 3–6. Jacobs, a supporter of Frankfurter's self-restraint, came to the conclusion that the Justice saw the limits on government primarily in terms of procedural due process.

171. NAACP v. Alabama, 357 U.S. 449 (1958).

172. Ibid., 460.

173. Ibid., 459.

174. Ibid., 462.

175. Ibid., 463.

176. Ibid., 463. The Frankfurter opinion was Sweezy v. New Hampshire, 354 U.S. 256, 265 (1957) (concurring opinion).

177. NAACP v. Alabama, 357 U.S. 449 (1958), 464–466.

178. NAACP v. Alabama, 377 U.S. 288 (1964).

179. Ibid., 296.

180. Ibid., 297.

181. Ibid., 302–310.

182. Bates v. Little Rock, 361 U.S. 516 (1960).

183. Ibid., 524–526.

184. Shelton v. Tucker, 364 U.S. 479, 490–491 (1960) (dissenting opinion of Frankfurter which Harlan joined); ibid., 498 (dissenting opinion of Harlan which Frankfurter joined).
185. Ibid.
186. Ibid., 490.
187. Ibid., 490. Emphasis added.
188. Ibid., 494. Emphasis added.
189. Ibid., 496.
190. Ibid., 497.
191. Ibid., 497-498. Emphasis added.
192. Ibid., 498 (dissenting opinion of Harlan).
193. Ibid., 499 (dissenting opinion of Harlan).
194. Ibid., 496 (dissenting opinion of Frankfurter).
195. NAACP v. Button, 371 U.S. 415 (1963).
196. Ibid., 429. Emphasis added.
197. Ibid., 453.
198. Ibid., 455. Emphasis in original.
199. Ibid. Emphasis added.
200. Ibid. Emphasis added.
201. Ibid.
202. Ibid., 464–465.
203. Gibson v. Florida Legislative Investigation Committee, 372 U.S. 539 (1963).
204. Ibid., 552–555.
205. Ibid., 579, citing Barenblatt, Wilkinson, Braden and Russell. Emphasis added.
206. Ibid., 580.
207. Uphaus v. Wyman, 360 U.S. 72 (1959).
208. See Dombrowski v. Pfister, 380 U.S. 479 (1965).
209. HOOK, THE PARADOXES, 22–37; Mendelson, *On the Meaning of the First Amendment: Absolutes in the Balance*, 50 CAL. L. REV. 821 (1962).
210. Mendelson, 825. See also HOOK, THE PARADOXES, 53. This point was also part of Frankfurter's argument in Dennis.
211. Frantz, *Is the First Amendment Law?* 51 CAL. L. REV. 729, 733 (1963).
212. For the difficulties in defining the extent of state action see L. TRIBE, AMERICAN CONSTITUTIONAL LAW (1978), ch. 18 and the cases cited therein.
213. The classic example in our system has been cases in which a person's claim to the right to fair trial conflicted with the free press right to comment on that trial. Bridges v. California, 314 U.S. 252 (1941); Craig v. Harney, 331 U.S. 367 (1947); Nebraska Press Association v. Stuart, 427 U.S. 539 (1976); Richmond Newspaper v. Virginia, 448 U.S. 555 (1980).
214. For example, the economic interests of both labor and management are recognized in our labor relations laws, but they often go to court to resolve their competing claims under the law. See NLRB v. Yeshiva University, 444 U.S. 672 (1980).
215. For example, American Communications Association v. Douds, 339 U.S. 382 (1950). The right was free speech and association; the interest was an unobstructed interstate commerce.

216. R. Dworkin, Taking Rights Seriously (1977).

217. Frantz, *The First Amendment in the Balance*, 71 Yale L. J. 1424 (1962).

218. Compare the opinions of Justices Stewart and White in New York Times v. United States, 423 U.S. 714, 727–740 (1971) with the dissenting opinions of Chief Justice Burger, ibid., 748; Justice Harlan, ibid., 752; and Justice Blackmun ibid., 759.

219. Mendelson, 825–826.

220. Wechsler, *Toward Neutral Principles of Constitutional Law*, 73 Harv. L. Rev. 1, 15 (1959).

221. Smith v. Allwright, 321 U.S. 649, 699 (1944) (dissenting opinion).

222. Watkins v. United States 354 U.S. 178 (1957).

223. Ibid., 216–217.

224. Barenblatt v. United States, 360 U.S. 109, 116–126 (1959). Compare Justice Black's opinion for the dissenters of this point, Ibid., 138–141.

225. Murphy, Congress; C. H. Pritchett, Congress versus the Supreme Court, 1957–1960 (1961).

226. Yates v. United States, 354 U.S. 298 (1957).

227. Ibid., 323–328.

228. Ibid., 350.

229. McCloskey, 220–321; A. Bickel, The Least Dangerous Branch (1962), ch. 3–5.

230. Hook, Heresy, Yes, 105. This passage is a defense of Frankfurter's "remarkable" concurrence in *Dennis*.

231. West Virginia Board of Education v. Barnette, 319 U.S. 624, 655 (1943) (dissenting opinion).

232. Dahl, A Preface, 137.

233. Hook, The Paradoxes, 62.

234. Dennis v. United States, 341 U.S. 494, 521 (1951) (concurring opinion).

235. L. Hand, The Bill of Rights (1958).

236. C. Black, Jr., The People and the Court (1960).

237. Compare Hook, Heresy, Yes, 91–119 with ibid., The Paradoxes, 63–106.

238. Wechsler, 14.

239. Dennis v. United States, 341 U.S. 494, 556 (1951) (concurring opinion of Frankfurter).

240. Hook, Political Power, 104.

241. Dennis v. United States, 341 U.S. 494, 556 (1951) (concurring opinion of Frankfurter).

242. Dahl, Who Governs? 325.

243. Ibid., See also Key, Public Opinion, 557–558.

244. Truman, 512-535.

245. Truman, *The American System in Crisis*, 74 Pol. Sci. Q. 481 (1959).

246. Senator, later President, John F. Kennedy.

7. OPTIMALIST THEORY

1. A. Ranney, The Doctrine of Responsible Party Government (1962), 12.
2. Schattschneider, The Semisovereign, 141.
3. Ranney, 10. Emphasis added.
4. Ranney, 15. The fragmentation of power created by the Constitution has been much criticized by optimalist social scientists. J. M. Burns, Congress on Trial (1949); and ibid., The Deadlock of Democracy (rev. ed., 1963), Parts I and II.
5. Ranney, 15. There is a systematic review of the empirical studies in Choper, *The Supreme Court and the Political Branches: Democratic Theory and Practice*, 122 U. Pa. L. Rev. 810 (1974).
6. E. E. Schattschneider, Party Government (1942), 210. A more extreme statement is found in ibid., Toward a More Responsible Two-Party System (1950), 93–95. On the growth of presidential power, see A. Schlesinger, Jr., The Imperial Presidency (1973).
7. Schattschneider, Party Government, 210. The detailed proposals for change are beyond the scope of this book. Although the Optimalists are agreed on the need for party realignment, they are not always in agreement about the specific changes necessary. Compare Schattschneider, Toward a More, with Burns, Deadlock .
8. Schattschneider, Party Government; also, ibid., The Semisovereign, 129–142; and ibid., Toward a More.
9. Schattschneider, Toward a More, 1–2.
10. Schattschneider, Party Government, 210.
11. Ibid., 206–209. Burns, The Deadlock, 18–24.
12. Schattschneider, Toward a More, 35–36.
13. Thorson (1962).
14. Ibid., 119.
15. Ibid., 120. The quotation comes from Peirce's *Scientific Attitude and Fallibilism*, in J. Buchler, ed., Philosophical Writings of Peirce (1940), 54.
16. Thorson, 139.
17. Ibid., 142. Emphasis added.
18. Ibid., 158.
19. Ibid.
20. Ibid., 157.
21. Ibid., 158. Emphasis added.
22. Ibid., 161.
23. United States v. Carolene Products, 304 U.S. 144, 152–154, n. 4 (1938).
24. Thomas v. Collins, 323 U.S. 515, 530–532 (1945); Marsh v. Alabama, 326 U.S. 501, 509 (1946); Kovacs v. Cooper, 336 U.S. 77, 88, 90 (1949).
25. C. H. Pritchett, The Roosevelt Court (1963).
26. Kovacs v. Cooper, 336 U.S. 77, 90–96 (1949) (concurring opinion of Frankfurter).

27. See Dennis v. United States, 341 U.S. 494, 581 (1951) (dissenting opinion of Black).
28. Murphy, *Deeds Under a Doctrine: Civil Liberties in the 1963 Term*, 59 AMER. POL. SCI. REV. 64 (1965); J. ELY, DEMOCRACY AND DISTRUST (1980), 73–75.
29. NAACP v. Button, 371 U.S. 415, 428–436 (1963); Kennedy v. Mendoza-Martinez, 372 U.S. 144, 159 (1963); Wesberry v. Sanders, 376 U.S. 1, 17 (1964); Bagget v. Bullitt, 377 U.S. 360, 379 (1964).
30. One of the exceptions was Justice Douglas's dissent in Adderley v. Florida, 385 U.S. 39, 48–49 (1966).
31. McKay, *The Preference for Freedom*, 34 NYU L. REV. 1182, 1193–1194 (1959); Mason, *The Core of Free Government, 1938–40: Mr. Justice Stone and Preferred Freedoms*, 65 YALE L. J. 598, 627 (1956).
32. Murphy, 64.
33. McKay, 1190.
34. A. T. MASON, HARLAN FISKE STONE (1956), 514.
35. Ibid., 514–515.
36. See, for example, the per curiam opinion of the Court in the Pentagon Papers case, New York Times Co. v. United States, 403 U.S. 713 (1971).
37. Schneider v. Rusk, 377 U.S. 163 (1964).
38. Ibid., 166.
39. Part II of Chief Justice Warren's opinion in Trop v. Dulles, 356 U.S. 86, 93 (1958) also makes this clear. In Part I, the Chief Justice argued citizenship could not be divested by the exercise of governmental power. Part II was written to show that even if one did not accept that argument, the government still could not denationalize Trop. Presumably, the second section was added to enable Justice Whittaker to join the Chief Justice and Justices Black and Douglas in deciding for Trop. Justice Brennan also decided for Trop on preferred freedoms rationale, but he wrote a separate opinion, ibid., 105.
40. Afroyim v. Rusk, 387 U.S. 253. (1967).
41. Kennedy v. Mendoza-Martinez, 372 U.S. 144, 159 (1963).
42. Ibid., 160–161.
43. Ibid., 163–171; Trop v. Dulles, 356 U.S. 86, 99–102 (1958); ibid., 108–112 (concurring opinion of Brennan).
44. Trop v. Dulles, 356 U.S. 86, 111 (1958) (concurring opinion of Brennan).
45. Kennedy v. Mendoza-Martinez, 372 U.S. 144, 160 (1963).
46. Perez v. Brownell, 356 U.S. 44, 84 (1958) (memorandum of Whittaker); Trop v. Dulles, 356 U.S. 86, 106 (1958) (concurring opinion of Brennan).
47. Trop v. Dulles, 356 U.S. 86, 111 (1958) (concurring opinion of Brennan).
48. Kennedy v. Mendoza-Martinez, 372 U.S. 144, 188–189 (1963).
49. Perez v. Brownell, 356 U.S. 44, 84 (1958).
50. Trop v. Dulles, 356 U.S. 86, 114 (1958).
51. Ibid., 114.
52. Ibid.
53. Kennedy v. Mendoza-Martinez, 372 U.S. 144, 187–188 (1963) (concurring opinion).

54. Trop v. Dulles, 356 U.S. 86, 114 (1958) (concurring opinion). Emphasis added.
55. Kennedy v. Mendoza-Martinez, 372 U.S. 144 (1963).
56. Ibid., 164–184.
57. Ibid., 186.
58. Schneider v. Rusk, 377 U.S. 163, 169 (1964). Justices Harlan and White signed Clark's dissenting opinion which was squarely rooted in the realist theory of democracy discussed in ch. 6 above.
59. Ibid., 168.
60. Trop v. Dulles, 356 U.S. 86, 106–107 (1958) (concurring opinion).
61. SCHATTSCHNEIDER, THE SEMISOVEREIGN, 112.
62. BURNS, THE DEADLOCK, 228.
63. Ibid., 340.
64. Ibid., 1. See also, 227–228.
65. SCHATTSCHNEIDER, THE SEMISOVEREIGN, 112.
66. R. LANE, POLITICAL LIFE (1959), 16–26, analyzes the changing patterns of electoral turnout through 1952. S. VERBA and N. NIE, PARTICIPATION IN AMERICA (1972), discuss turnout through the 1968 election, as well as providing the most systematic treatment of the various factors affecting turnout. For the 1980 estimate, see New York Times, 6 Nov. 1980, p. 1. The argument that turnout is directly related to programmatic differences between the major parties is most forcefully made by W. D. BURNHAM, CRITICAL ELECTIONS AND THE MAINSPRINGS OF AMERICAN POLITICS (1970).
67. BURNS, THE DEADLOCK, 228.
68. SHATTSCHNEIDER, THE SEMISOVEREIGN, 104.
69. McClosky, et al.
70. SCHATTSCHNEIDER, THE SEMISOVEREIGN, 110. Emphasis in original.
71. R. McKENZIE, BRITISH POLITICAL PARTIES (2nd ed., 1964).
72. Ibid.; S. E. FINER, H. BERRINGTON, and D. BARTHOLOMEW, BACKBENCH OPINION IN THE HOUSE OF COMMONS, 1955–1959 (1961); Rose, *The Political Ideas of English Party Activists*, 56 AMER. POL. SCI. REV. 360 (1962); Christoph, *Censensus and Cleavage in British Political Ideology*, 59 AMER. POL. SCI. REV. 629 (1965).
73. D. E. BUTLER and A. KING, THE BRITISH GENERAL ELECTION OF 1964 (1965); D. E. BUTLER and A. KING, THE BRITISH GENERAL ELECTION OF 1966 (1966); D. E. BUTLER and M. PINTO-DUSCHINSKY, THE BRITISH GENERAL ELECTION OF 1970 (1971); D. E. BUTLER and D. KAVANAGH, THE BRITISH GENERAL ELECTION OF 1974 (1975).
74. Christoph, 638.
75. Lucas v. Colorado General Assembly, 377 U.S. 713, 750 (1964) (dissenting opinion of Stewart, joined by Clark).
76. Ibid., 749–751.
77. Ibid., 751.
78. Ibid., 743 (dissenting opinion of Clark), and 745–750 (dissenting opinion of Stewart). Stewart joined Harlan's dissent in Kirkpatrick v. Preisler 394 U.S. 526

(1969) at 549 because both Justices believed the majority ignored the fact that representation was primarily designed to accommodate pluralistic interest groups.

79. Baker v. Carr, 369 U.S. 186, 259 (1962) (concurring opinion of Clark).
80. Lucas v. Colorado General Assembly, 377 U.S. 713, 753–754 (1964) (dissenting opinion of Stewart). See also Baker v. Carr, 369 U.S. 186, 251–262 (1962) (concurring opinion of Clark).
81. Lucas v. Colorado General Assembly, 377 U.S. 713, (1964) (dissenting opinion of Stewart, joined by Clark).
82. Ibid., 753.
83. Baker v. Carr, 369 U.S. 186, 259 (1962) (concurring opinion). The "practical opportunities" phrase comes from MacDougall v. Green, 335 U.S. 281, 284 (1948), and is also cited with approval in Justice Stewart's *Lucas* dissent, 377 U.S. 713, 753 (1964).
84. Lucas v. Colorado General Assembly, 377 U.S. 713, 742 (1964) (dissenting opinion of Clark); ibid., 758–759 (dissenting opinion of Stewart).
85. Baker v. Carr, 369 U.S. 186, 259 (1962) (concurring opinion of Clark).
86. Ibid.
87. Lucas v. Colorado General Assembly, 377 U.S. 713, 742–743 (1964) (dissenting opinion of Clark). See also his concurring opinion in Reynolds v. Sims, 377 U.S. 533, 588 (1964).
88. Lucas v. Colorado General Assembly, 377 U.S. 713, 754 (1964) (dissenting opinion of Stewart). See also his separate opinions in Reynolds v. Sims, 377 U.S. 533, 589 (1964); Maryland Committee v. Tawes, 377 U.S. 656, 676–677 (1964); Davis v. Mann, 377 U.S. 678, 693–694 (1964); and Roman v. Sincock, 377 U.S. 695, 712 (1964).
89. Baker v. Carr, 369 U.S. 186, 254 (1962) (concurring opinion).
90. Lucas v. Colorado General Assembly, 377 U.S. 713, 752 (1964) (dissenting opinion of Stewart).
91. See especially the right to counsel cases from Betts v. Brady, 316 U.S. 455 (1942), to Gideon v. Wainwright, 372 U.S. 335 (1963).
92. WMCA v. Lomenzo, 377 U.S. 633 (1964). Justice Stewart's dissent is at ibid., 763–764.
93. Ibid., 763–764.
94. Lucas v. Colorado General Assembly, 377 U.S. 713 (1964). Stewart's dissent (ibid., 744) for both the New York and Colorado cases is attached to the Colorado case. Justice Clark, who joined Stewart's opinion, wrote a separate dissent applicable only to the Colorado plan.
95. Ibid., 758 (dissenting opinion of Stewart).
96. Ibid., 759
97. Ibid.
98. Dixon, 385–436.
99. Professor Dixon has some acute observations on how a too stringent numerical standard might restrict use of devices for encouraging minority representation, ibid., 436–543.
100. 13 C. Q. Weekly Reports, 1574 (6 August 1965).

101. Dixon, 437.
102. M. Shapiro, Freedom of Speech: The Supreme Court and Judicial Review (1966), 47.
103. Ibid., 24.
104. Ibid., 32.
105. Ibid., 34–37.
106. Ibid., 37.
107. Choper, 817–848. See also, Fischer, *The Unwritten Rules of American Politics*, Harpers Magazine, 27 (Nov., 1948).
108. Shapiro, 38.
109. Ibid., 117–118.
110. Ibid., 47.
111. Ibid., 33.
112. The argument was most forcefully made by T. Hobbes, The Leviathan, first published in 1651. (M. Oakeshott, ed., 1957).
113. Ch. 1 above.
114. Dennis v. United States, 341 U.S. 494 (1951).
115. Although each Justice eventually changed his mind, this qualification on the scope of constitutionally protected speech was present in each of their 1951 opinions. ibid., 580 (Black); ibid., 581 (Douglas).
116. Ibid., 584 (dissenting opinion of Douglas). At ibid., 581, Justice Black refers to the "high preferred place" of First Amendment liberties.
117. Ibid., 590 (dissenting opinion). See also ibid., 580 (dissenting opinion of Black).
118. Ibid., 584–585 (dissenting opinion of Douglas); ibid., 580 (dissenting opinion of Black).
119. Ibid., 590 (dissenting opinion of Douglas).
120. Ibid., 589.
121. Communist Party v. Subversive Activities Control Board, 367 U.S. 1 (1961).
122. Ibid., 174 (dissenting opinion).
123. Ibid., 174–175.
124. Ibid., 175.
125. Ibid., 172.
126. Ibid., 175.
127. Albertson v. Subversive Activities Control Board, 382 U.S. 70 (1965).
128. United States v. Robel, 389 U.S. 258 (1967).
129. Ibid., 264.
130. Ibid., 265.
131. Ibid., 264.
132. Barenblatt v. United States, 360 U.S. 109 (1959). See ch. 6 above, notes 147–151.
133. United States v. Robel, 389 U.S. 258, 266–269 (1967). Warren indicated Congress could exclude active knowing members of the CPUSA who agreed with its unlawful aims.
134. Elfbrandt v. Russell, 384 U.S. 11, (1966)
135. Keyishian v. Board of Regents, 385 U.S. 589 (1967).

136. Elfbrandt v. Russell, 384 U.S. 11, 20 (1966) (dissenting opinion of White); Keyishian v. Board of Regents, 385 U.S. 589, 620 (1967) (dissenting opinion of Clark).

137. Keyishian v. Board of Regents, 385 U.S. 589, 602 (1967).

138. Watkins v. United States, 354 U.S. 178 (1967). See also the discussion in ch. 6 above, notes 222–223.

139. Ibid., 214–215.

140. Ibid., 198.

141. Ibid., 202.

142. Ibid., 206.

143. Wilkinson v. United States, 365 U.S. 399 (1961).

144. Braden v. United States, 365 U.S. 431 (1961).

145. Barenblatt v. United States, 360 U.S. 109 (1959).

146. Wilkinson v. United States, 365 U.S. 399, 423 (1961); Braden v. United States, 365 U.S. 431, 446 (1961).

147. Braden v. United States, 365 U.S. 431, 450 (1961). See Bendich, *First Amendment Standards for Congressional Investigations*, 51 CAL. L. REV. 311 (1963), for a systematic application of the preferred freedoms doctrine. Justice Douglas's dissenting opinions in *Wilkinson* and *Braden* were signed by Justice Black as well as by Chief Justice Warren and Justice Brennen. Black also wrote a dissenting opinion in each case emphasizing his absolutist interpretation of the First Amendment. Once again, Justice Douglas's opinions illustrate how the preferred freedoms doctrine was utilized as the lowest common denominator for Justices wishing to uphold certain individual rights.

148. Braden, *The Search for Objectivity in Constitutional Law*, 57 YALE L. J. 571 (1948).

149. See especially, Louisiana v. NAACP, 366 U.S. 293 (1961) and Gibson v. Florida Legislative Investigation Committee, 372 U.S. 539, 559 (1963) (concurring opinion).

150. Much the same could be said of Justice Marshall's reliance upon separation of powers arguments in order to uphold the newspapers' right to publish the Pentagon Papers. New York Times Co. v. United States, 403 U.S. 713, 740 (1971).

151. NAACP v. Alabama, 357 U.S. 449 (1958); Bates v. City of Little Rock, 361 U.S. 516 (1960). The opinions in these cases are discussed in ch. 6 above, *NAACP* at notes 171–181; *Bates* at 182–194.

152. Shelton v. Tucker, 364 U.S. 479 (1960).

153. Ibid., 499 (Frankfurter) and 496 (Harlan). For a discussion of these opinions, see ch. 6 above, notes 185-194.

154. Ibid., 485–486.

155. Ibid., 488.

156. Ibid., 490

157. NAACP v. Button, 371 U.S. 415 (1963).

158. Ibid., 429–431.

159. The other major reasons for so holding are discussed later in ch. 8, notes 137–140.
160. NAACP v. Button, 371 U.S. 415, 438 (1963). Emphasis added.
161. Ibid., 443
162. Ibid., 444.
163. Ibid., 455. Harlan's dissent is discussed in ch. 6 above, notes 195–202.
164. Gibson v. Florida Legislative Investigation Committee, 372 U.S. 539 (1963).
165. Ibid., 543–546.
166. Ibid., 547–549.
167. Ibid., 546. Emphasis added.
168. Ibid., 555–556.
169. Ibid., 576. For a discussion of Harlan's dissenting opinion, see ch. 6 above, notes 203–206.
170. Uphaus v. Wyman, 360 U.S. 72 (1959).
171. Gibson v. Florida Legislative Investigation Committee, 372 U.S. 539, 557 (1963). This quotation is from Justice Brennan's opinion in NAACP v. Button, 371 U.S. 415, 435 (1963).
172. Adler v. Board of Education, 342 U.S. 485 (1952); Beilan v. Board of Education, 357 U.S. 399 (1958).
173. Cohen v. Hurley, 366 U.S. 117 (1961); Konigsberg v. State Bar, 366 U.S. 36 (1961); In re Anastaplo, 366 U.S. 82 (1961).
174. Edwards v. South Carolina, 372 U.S. 229 (1963).
175. Ibid., 235.
176. Justice Stewart's opinion for the Court can surely be read as an application of the preferred freedoms doctrine, ibid., 235. It is also compatible with other interpretations of the First Amendment, ibid., 236–238.
177. Cox v. Louisiana, 379 U.S. 536 (1965).
178. Ibid., 544–552.
179. Ibid., 555.
180. Ibid., 558.
181. There was evidence to indicate that Baton Rouge officials had "exercised unbridled discretion." Although the statute provided an explicit exemption only for labor unions, Baton Rouge had not banned all nonlabor union parades and demonstrations, ibid., 556–557.
182. Cox v. Louisiana, 379 U.S. 559, 562 (1965).
183. Ibid., 562; ibid., 583 (separate opinion of Black).
184. Ibid., 562; 583–584 (separate opinion of Black).
185. Ibid., 564.
186. Ibid., 571.
187. Brown v. Louisiana, 383 U.S. 131 (1966). Fortas's opinion was joined by Chief Justice Warren and Justice Douglas. The two other members of the majority, Justices Brennan and White, each wrote a separate opinion.
188. Ibid., 142.
189. Ibid., 141–142.

190. Adderley v. Florida, 385 U.S. 39 (1966). Justice Black's opinion for the Court is discussed later in ch. 9, notes 158–161.

191. Ibid., 48 and 49, n.l.

192. Ibid., 51.

193. Ibid., 54.

194. Ibid., 49.

195. Ibid., 51.

196. The basic factual ambiguity centers around the question of whether the students were blocking the driveway to the jail after they had moved back from the door at the command of the deputy sheriff. Even though no vehicle attempted to use the driveway, the majority accepted as fact that it would have been impossible for automobiles to have access to the jail. To demonstrate this claim, they said a tradesman already inside the jail remained there because the protestors were preventing him from leaving; ibid., 45, especially n. 4. The minority argued the protesting students never located themselves so as to cause interference with traffic, that in fact both the sheriff and deputy sheriff were able to drive directly to the jailhouse door, that when asked to move back the students did so, and that the tradesman's behavior was just as consistent with his desire to satisfy his curiosity as with student obstruction of the driveway.

197. Ibid., 54–55.

198. Walker v. Birmingham, 388 U.S. 307 (1967).

199. Ibid., 315–316; ibid., 328 (dissenting opinion of Warren); ibid., 334–335 (dissenting opinion of Douglas); ibid., 343–344 (dissenting opinion of Brennan).

200. Ibid., 316–317; ibid., 328–330 (dissenting opinion of Warren); ibid., 338 (dissenting opinion of Douglas); ibid., 344–345 (dissenting opinion of Brennan). The majority contended the Alabama courts might have saved the statute by giving it a narrower interpretation; the minority Justices all insisted it was unconstitutional on its face.

201. Ibid., 317–318; ibid., 330–331 (dissenting opinion of Warren); ibid., 337–338 (dissenting opinion of Douglas); ibid., 346–347 (dissenting opinion of Brennan).

202. Ibid., 327 (dissenting opinion of Warren); ibid., 338 (dissenting opinion of Douglas); ibid., 346–348 (dissenting opinion of Brennan). Other aspects of the case are discussed in Edelman, *The Absurd Remnant: "Walker v. Birmingham" Two years Later*, 34 ALBANY L. REV. 523 (1970).

203. Walker v. Birmingham, 388 U.S. 307, 336 (1967) (dissenting opinion of Douglas): "For if a person must pursue his judicial remedy before he may speak, parade, or assemble, the occasion when protest is desired or needed will have become history and any later speech, parade, or assembly will be futile or pointless."

204. Walker v. Birmingham, 388 U.S. 308, 327 (1967).

205. A. FORTAS, CONCERNING DISSENT AND CIVIL DISOBEDIENCE (1968), 70–71.

206. Ibid., 70.

207. Adderley v. Florida, 385 U.S. 39, 54 (1966).

208. Douglas's *Adderley* dissent was joined by Warren, Brennan, and Fortas. The latter's prevailing opinion in *Brown* was joined by the Chief Justice and Justice Douglas.
209. FORTAS, 34.
210. Brown v. Louisana, 383 U.S. 131, 135–137 (1966) (opinion of Fortas); ibid., 152–154 (dissenting opinion of Black).
211. See FORTAS, especially pp. 122–127.
212. Ibid., 125–126. See also R. HECKART, JUSTICE FORTAS AND THE FIRST AMENDMENT (unpub. Ph.D. dissertation, 1973).
213. A. MALRAUX, ANTI-MEMOIRS (1968), 87.

8. LIBERAL NATURAL RIGHTS THEORY

1. In the area of our concern, see, for example, Powe, *Evolution to Absolutism: Justice Douglas and the First Amendment*, 74 COL. L. REV. 371 (1974).
2. Professor William Cohen, a former law clerk of Justice Douglas, puts this method in the most favorable light: *Introduction*, 16 UCLA L. REV. 701 (1969). See also, Glennon, *"Do Not Go Gentle": More Than an Epitaph*, 22 WAYNE L. REV. 1305 (1976).
3. See ch. 9, below.
4. W. O. DOUGLAS, THE RIGHT OF THE PEOPLE (1958), 161–171.
5. See ch. 9, 10, below.
6. W. O. Douglas, *The Bill of Rights is Not Enough*, in CAHN, ed., THE GREAT RIGHTS(1963), 117–158.
7. W. O. DOUGLAS, WE THE JUDGES (1956), 430–431.
8. W. O. DOUGLAS, THE ANATOMY OF LIBERTY (1963), 2.
9. W. O. DOUGLAS, DEMOCRACY'S MANIFESTO (1963); W. O. DOUGLAS, AN ALMANAC OF LIBERTY (1954), 5; ibid., THE ANATOMY, 2–3.
10. W. O. DOUGLAS, GO EAST YOUNG MAN (1974); W. O. DOUGLAS, THE COURT YEARS, 1939–1975 (1980). These 2 volumes comprise Douglas's autobiography.
11. DOUGLAS, THE RIGHT, 161.
12. DOUGLAS, AN ALMANAC, 5; ibid., THE ANATOMY, 2; ibid.,GO EAST, xv; ibid., DEMOCRACY AND FINANCE (1940), 292; ibid., THE RIGHT, 161; Douglas, *The Grand Design of the Constitution*, 7 GONZAGA L. REV. 239, 253 (1972).
13. Douglas, *Stare Decisis*, 4 RECORD 152–179, especially 176 (1949).
14. Sunshine Coal Co. v. Adkins, 310 U.S. 381 (1940); Oklahoma v. Guy F. Atkinson Co., 313 U.S. 508 (1941).
15. Helvering v. Griffiths, 318 U.S. 371, 404 (1943) (dissenting opinion).
16. Olsen v. Nebraska, 313 U.S. 236 (1941); Day-Brite Lighting, Inc. v. Missouri, 342 U.S. 421 (1952); Williamson v. Lee Optical Inc., 348 U.S. 483 (1955).
17. Williamson v. Lee Optical Inc., 348 U.S. 483 (1955); Village of Belle Terre v. Boraas, 416 U.S. 1 (1974).
18. Railway Express Agency v. New York, 336 U.S. 106 (1949); Village of Belle Terre v. Boraas, 416 U.S. 1 (1974).

19. Olsen v. Nebraska, 313 U.S. 236 (1941); Southern Pacific v. Arizona, 325 U.S. 761, 795 (1945) (dissenting opinion); Day-Brite Lighting, Inc. v. Missouri, 342 U.S. 421 (1952); New York v. United States, 326 U.S. 572, 590 (1946) (dissenting opinion); Williamson v. Lee Optical Inc., 348 U.S. 483 (1955); North Dakota State Board of Pharmacy v. Synder's Drug Stores, Inc., 414 U.S. 156 (1973).

20. Sunshine Coal Co. v. Adkins, 310 U.S. 381 (1940).

21. Berman v. Parker, 348 U.S. 26 (1954); Village of Belle Terre v. Boraas, 416 U.S. 1 (1974).

22. The leading cases are Railroad Commission of Texas v. Rowan & Nichols Oil Co., 310 U.S. 573 (1940), and 311 U.S. 570 (1941). Douglas joined Frankfurter's opinions for the Court in both cases. Scholars such as E. S. Corwin usually pointed to Douglas's opinion for the Court in FPC v. Hope Natural Gas Co., 320 U.S. 591 (1944) as also being applicable to state regulatory agencies. See CORWIN, ed., THE CONSTITUTION OF THE UNITED STATES OF AMERICA: ANALYSIS AND INTERPRETATION (1952) (1973 ed.), 1342, n. 5. See also the separate concurring opinion of Justices Black, Douglas, and Murphy in FPC v. Natural Gas Pipeline Co., 315 U.S. 575, 599 (1942).

23. International Association of Machinists v. NLRB, 311 U.S. 72 (1940); FPC v. Hope Natural Gas Co., 320 U.S. 591 (1944); FPC v. Idaho Power Co., 344 U.S. 17 (1952); PUC of California v. United States, 355 U.S. 534 (1958).

24. DOUGLAS, DEMOCRACY AND, 14–17.

25. DOUGLAS, GO EAST, 307.

26. DOUGLAS, WE THE JUDGES, 161–191. Right to hearing: Ashbacker Radio Corp. v. FCC, 326 U.S. 327 (1945); Joint Anti-Fascist Refugee Committee v. McGrath, 341 U.S. 123, 174 (1951) (concurring opinion). Right to cross-examine witnesses: Richardson v. Perales, 452 U.S. 389, 411 (1971) (dissenting opinion); United States v. Florida East Coast R. Co., 410 U.S. 224, 246 (1973) (dissenting opinion); Wolff v. McDonnell, 418 U.S. 539, 593 (1974) (dissenting opinion). See also United States v. Wunderlich, 342 U.S. 98 (1951); Public Affairs Associates v. Rickover, 369 U.S. 111, 114 (1962) (concurring opinion); Association of Data Processing Services v. Camp, 397 U.S. 150 (1970); Environmental Protection Agency v. Mink, 410 U.S. 73, 105 (1973) (dissenting opinion); Douglas, *The Human Welfare State*, 97 U. PA. L. REV. 597 (1949).

27. Doremus v. Board of Education, 342 U.S. 429, 435 (1952) (dissenting opinion). Flast v. Cohen, 392 U.S. 83, 107 (1968) (concurring opinion).

28. United States v. Richardson, 418 U.S. 166, 197 (1974) (dissenting opinion).

29. Sarnoff v. Schultz, 409 U.S. 929 (1972) (dissenting opinion); DeCosta v. Laird, 405 U.S. 979 (1972) (dissenting opinion); McArthur v. Clifford, 393 U.S. 1002 (1968) (dissenting opinion); Hart v. United States, 391 U.S. 956 (1968) (dissenting opinion); Holmes v. United States, 391 U.S. 936 (1968) (dissenting opinion); Mora v. McNamara, 389 U.S. 934, 935 (1967) (dissenting opinion); Mitchell v. United States, 386 U.S. 972 (1967) (dissenting opinion).

30. Village of Belle Terre v. Boraas, 416 U.S. 1 (1974).

31. DOUGLAS, THE COURT YEARS.

32. Douglas, *The Bill of Rights Is Not Enough*, 146–147.
33. Douglas, *Stare Decisis*, 157. See also, Douglas, *Federal Courts and the Democratic System*, 21 ALA. L. REV. 179 (1969).
34. Douglas, *The Bill of Rights Is Not Enough*, 145–146. See also Lombard v. Louisana, 373 U.S. 267, 274 (1963) (concurring opinion); Bell v. Maryland, 387 U.S. 226, 242 (1964) (separate opinion).
35. PUC v. Pollak, 343 U.S. 451, 469 (1952).
36. Griswold v. Connecticut, 381 U.S. 479 (1965) and Eisenstadt v. Baird, 405 U.S. 438 (1972)—right to contraceptive devices; Roe v. Wade, 410 U.S. 113 (1973) and Doe v. Bolton, 410 U.S. 179 (1973)—right to have an abortion.
37. Doe v. Bolton, 410 U.S. 179, 211 (1973) (concurring opinion). Emphasis in original.
38. Ibid. Emphasis in original.
39. Ibid. Emphasis in original.
40. Barsky v. Board of Regents, 347 U.S. 442, 472 (1954) (dissenting opinion); Peters v. Hobby, 349 U.S. 331, 351 (1955) (concurring opinion).
41. Kent v. Dulles, 357 U.S. 116, 126 (1958). Douglas is here quoting from Z. CHAFEE, THREE HUMAN RIGHTS IN THE CONSTITUTION OF 1787 (1956), 197.
42. W. O. DOUGLAS, BEING AN AMERICAN (1958), 123–133, 155–212; W. O. DOUGLAS, AMERICA CHALLENGED (1960), 40, 62–66, 70–71; DOUGLAS, DEMOCRACY'S MANIFESTO, ch. 3.
43. Knauer v. United States, 328 U.S. 654, 659 (1946).
44. Ibid.; Schneiderman v. United States, 320 U.S. 118, 161 (1943) (concurring opinion).
45. Perez v. Brownnell, 356 U.S. 44, 79 (1958) (dissenting opinion).
46. Nishikawa v. Dulles, 356 U.S. 129, 138 (1958) (concurring opinion of Black, joined by Douglas); Trop v. Dulles, 356 U.S. 86, 104 (1958) (concurring opinion of Black, joined by Douglas).
47. United States v. Richardson, 418 U.S. 166, 201 (1974) (dissenting opinion).
48. Perez v. Brownell, 356 U.S. 44, 84 (1958) (dissenting opinion). Douglas's position on the expatriation cases is all but indistinguishable from that of Justice Black, and Black wrote the leading opinion developing the theoretical underpinning of their interpretation. Afroyim v. Rusk, 387 U.S. 253 (1967). See the discussion in ch. 10 below, notes 26–30. In Perez v. Brownell, 356 U.S. 44 (1958), both Justices joined the dissent of Chief Justice Warren, and Black joined the separate dissent of Douglas. In Trop v. Dulles, 356 U.S. 86 (1958), both Justices joined Chief Justice Warren's opinion, and Douglas joined Black's separate concurrence. In Nishikawa v. Dulles, 356 U.S. 129 (1958), Douglas again joined Black's separate concurring opinion. They reaffirmed their position in a separate note in Kennedy v. Mendoza-Martinez, 372 U.S. 144, 186 (1963). Justice Black joined Justice Douglas's opinion for the Court in Schneider v. Rusk 377 U.S. 163 (1964). Justice Douglas joined Justice Black's dissent in Rogers v. Bellei, 401 U.S. 815, 836 (1971).
49. Schneider v. Rusk, 377 U.S. 163 (1964). See the discussions in ch. 7 above, notes 37–38, 58–59.

50. Ibid., 169–178.
51. Gunther, *Foreword: In Search of Evolving Doctrine on a Changing Court: A Model for a Newer Equal Protection*, 86 HARV. L. REV. 1 (1972).
52. Knauer v. United States, 328 U.S. 654, 659 (1946).
53. Perez v. Brownell, 356 U.S. 44, 79 (1958) (dissenting opinion of Douglas).
54. Harper v. Virginia State Board of Elections, 383 U.S. 663 (1966).
55. Douglas, *The Bill of Rights Is Not Enough*, 151; DOUGLAS, WE THE JUDGES, 56.
56. United States v. Classic, 313 U.S. 299, 329 (1941) (dissenting opinion). Douglas dissented in this landmark voting rights case because it involved the indictment of New Orlean's election commissioners. He did not challenge the Court's holding that primaries were an integral part of the state's election machinery and were therefore governed by the Constitution, nor did he question Congress's authority to control primary elections, especially for congressional offices. The only issue which separated Douglas from the majority was whether, in fact, Congress had legislated with sufficient specificity to sustain a criminal indictment. Douglas (along with Black and Murphy who joined his dissent) believed the reconstruction era statute was too vague and that, therefore, he was acting to protect civil liberties. Retrospectively, this position is difficult to maintain, and Douglas has never, to my knowledge, so argued.
57. South v. Peters, 339 U.S. 276, 279 (1950) (dissenting opinion).
58. MacDougall v. Green, 335 U.S. 281, 288 (1948) (dissenting opinion), emphasis added; ibid., 290.
59. Colegrove v. Green, 328 U.S. 549, 566 (1946) (dissenting opinion of Black, joined by Douglas); South v. Peters, 339 U.S. 276, 277 (1950) (dissenting opinion); Baker v. Carr, 369 U.S. 186, 241 (1962) (concurring opinion).
60. Douglas, *The Bill of Rights Is Not Enough*, 137; Baker v. Carr, 369 U.S. 186, 241, especially n. 1 (1962) (concurring opinion).
61. Wesberry v. Sanders, 376 U.S. 1 (1964) overturning Colegrove v. Green 328 U.S. 549 (1946). See the discussion in ch. 10 below, notes 56–65.
62. Gray v. Sanders, 372 U.S. 368 (1963). Justice Douglas's dissent in South v. Peters, 339 U.S. 276, 277 (1950) became the operative law.
63. Gray v.Sanders, 372 U.S. 368, 376–379, especially n. 8 (1963).
64. Ibid., 380.
65. Reynolds v. Sims, 377 U.S. 533 (1964).
66. Ibid., 565. Emphasis added. See also the language at ibid., 568.
67. Kirkpatrick v. Preisler, 394 U.S. 526 (1969). See the discussion in ch. 10 below, notes 76–82.
68. In Mahan v. Howell, 410 U.S. 325 (1973), and White v. Regester, 412 U.S. 755 (1973), he joined Brennan's opinions which called for a good faith effort at absolute equality among state legislative districts.
69. Avery v. Midland County, Texas, 390 U.S. 474 (1968); Hadley v. Junior College District, 397 U.S. 50 (1970).
70. Abate v. Mundt, 403 U.S. 182, 187 (1971) (dissenting opinion of Brennan, joined by Douglas).
71. Dusch v. Davis, 387 U.S. 112 (1967).

72. Sailors v. Board of Education, 387 U.S. 105 (1967).
73. In Wells v. Edwards, 409 U.S. 1095 (1973) he joined White's dissent when the majority failed to apply the principle to the election of local judges.
74. Fortson v. Morris, 385 U.S. 231 (1966). See the discussion in ch. 10 below, notes 97–99.
75. Ibid., 236 (dissenting opinion).
76. Carrington v. Rash, 380 U.S. 89 (1965).
77. Kramer v. Union Free School District, 395 U.S. 621 (1969).
78. Cipriano v. City of Houma, 395 U.S. 701 (1969).
79. Phoenix v. Kolodziejski, 399 U.S. 204 (1970).
80. It should be noted that the opinion for the Court did not apply this standard in *Carrington*. Douglas makes his own position on these cases clear in Oregon v. Mitchell, 400 U.S. 112, 135 (1970) (separate opinion).
81. Harper v. Virginia Board of Elections, 383 U.S. 663 (1966).
82. Ibid., 668.
83. Black's dissent is at ibid., 670, Harlan's dissenting opinion (joined by Stewart) is at ibid., 780. See also, Cox, *Foreword: Constitutional Adjudication and the Promotion of Human Rights*, 80 HARV. L. REV. 91, 95–96 (1966).
84. Breedlove v. Suttles, 302 U.S. 277 (1937); Butler v. Thompson, 341 U.S. 937 (1951). Douglas dissented from the Butler decision, ibid., 937.
85. Harper v. Virginia Board of Elections, 383 U.S. 663, 669 (1966). Emphasis in original.
86. *Brown* can be read as simply reversing *Plessy* on the basis of the intention of the framers of the Fourteenth Amendment to make race a "suspect" or "forbidden" category. *Reynolds* and its progeny can be read as dealing with individuals already entitled under state law to cast a ballot.
87. Harper v. Virginia Board of Elections, 383 U.S. 663, 670, particularly 675–677 (1966) (dissenting opinion).
88. The same conclusion can be derived from analyzing Douglas's opinions dealing with access of minority parties and individual candidates to a place on the ballot. MacDougall v. Green, 335 U.S. 281, 287 (1948) (dissenting opinion). Williams v. Rhodes, 393 U.S. 23, 35 (1968) (concurring opinion of Douglas). He wrote the opinion for the Court in Moore v. Ogilvie, 394 U.S. 814 (1969) which overruled *MacDougall*.
89. Oregon v. Mitchell, 400 U.S. 112 (1970). See the discussion in ch. 10 below, notes 112–116.
90. Ibid., 135 (separate opinion).
91. J. J. ROUSSEAU, THE SOCIAL CONTRACT, particularly book III, ch. 15.
92. Wright v. Rockefeller, 376 U.S. 52 (1964).
93. Ibid., 69. Douglas's dissenting opinion was joined by Goldberg; he also joined Goldberg's dissenting opinion, ibid., 67.
94. Whitcomb v. Chavis, 403 U.S. 124 (1971). Some black residents of Marion County (Gary) also claimed that their opportunity to vote for sixteen assemblymen placed them at a disadvantage to the black residents of Marion County (Indianapolis) who, although no greater in number, could vote for twenty three

assemblymen. The claim contended that the true test of voting power is the ability to cast a "critical," i.e. decisive, vote. Justice White found this contention lacking in political reality; ibid., 144–146. Justice Douglas passed over this aspect of the case in silence.

95. Ibid., 149–155.
96. Ibid., 171–181.
97. Wright v. Rockefeller, 376 U.S. 52, 67 (1964) (dissenting opinion).
98. 84 CONGRESSIONAL RECORD 3710–3715 (1939).
99. DOUGLAS, GO EAST, ch. 25.
100. Terminiello v. Chicago, 337 U.S. 1 (1949).
101. Beauharnais v. Illinois, 343 U.S. 250, 284–285 (1952) (dissenting opinion).
102. Dennis v. United States, 341 U.S. 494 (1951). See the discussion in ch. 6 above, notes 133–146.
103. Ibid., 581. For a fuller discussion of the "preferred freedoms" opinion, see ch. 7 above, notes 114–120
104. Brandenburg v. Ohio, 395 U.S. 444 (1969). The *per curiam* opinion for the Court reversed the Ku Klux Klan leader's conviction under the Ohio Criminal Syndicalism statute by using the distinction made in Yates v. United States, 354 U.S. 298, 318 (1957) between advocacy in the realm of action and advocacy in the realm of ideas. Since the Ohio statute did not distinguish between "mere advocacy and incitement to lawless action," it was unconstitutional. Whitney v. California, 274 U.S. 357 (1927) was overruled.
105. Brandenburg v. Ohio, 395 U.S. 444, 454 (1969) (concurring opinion). See also, W. O. DOUGLAS, THE SUPREME COURT AND THE BICENTENNIAL (1978), 17–23.
106. Brandenburg v. Ohio, 395 U.S. 444, 456 (1969). Emphasis added.
107. See ch. 10 below, notes 19–21.
108. Brandenburg v. Ohio, 395 U.S. 444, 454 (1969).
109. New York Times Co. v. United States, 403 U.S. 713, 720 (1971) (separate opinion); Gertz v. Robert Welch, Inc., 418 U.S. 323, 355 (1974) (dissenting opinion).
110. Byrne v. Karalexis, 396 U.S. 976, 980 (1969) (dissenting opinion).
111. Branzburg v. Hayes, 408 U.S. 665, 713 (1972) (dissenting opinion). This opinion also contains a major attack by Douglas on the "clear and present danger test" and the later "balancing" standard; ibid., 716.
112. Paris Adult Theatre I v. Slaton, 423 U.S. 49, 70 (1973) (dissenting opinion).
113. Branzburg v. Hayes, 408 U.S. 665, 714 (1972) (dissenting opinion).
114. Ibid., 715.
115. Ibid.
116. Broadrick v. Oklahoma, 413 U.S. 601, 620 (1973) (dissenting opinion).
117. Yates v. United States, 354 U.S. 298 (1957). See the discussion in ch. 6 above notes 167, 226–228; ch. 9 below, notes 84–86; and ch. 10 below, notes 131–133.
118. Ibid., 339 (dissenting opinion of Black).

119. Scales v. United States, 367 U.S. 203 (1961). See the discussion in ch. 6 above, note 157–159; ch. 9 below, notes 91–92; ch. 10 below, notes 142–143.
120. Ibid., 262 (dissenting opinion); Noto v. United States, 367 U.S. 290, 302 (1961) (concurring opinion).
121. Kent v. Dulles, 357 U.S. 116 (1958).
122. Aptheker v. Secretary of State, 378 U.S. 500 (1964).
123. Ibid., 519–521.
124. Konigsberg v. State Bar, 366 U.S. 36, 56 (1961) (dissenting opinion of Black, joined by Douglas); In re Anastaplo, 366 U.S. 82, 97 (1961) (dissenting opinion of Black, joined by Douglas).
125. Baird v. State Bar of Arizona, 401 U.S. 1 (1971); In re Stolar, 401 U.S. 23 (1971). Over the objection of the four-man plurality in these cases (which included Douglas), the Court still permitted inquiries into an applicant's views as to the soundness of the Constitution as part of the bar's assessment of character and fitness. Law Students' Research Council v. Wadmond, 401 U.S. 154 (1971).
126. Flemming v. Nestor, 363 U.S. 603, 628 (1960) (dissenting opinion).
127. Alder v. Board of Education, 342 U.S. 485, 508 (1952) (dissenting opinion); Beilan v. Board of Education, 357 U.S. 399, 412 (1958) (the dissenting opinion of Douglas also covers Lerner v. Cassey, 357 U.S. 468 [1958]); Speiser v. Randall, 357 U.S. 513, 532 (1958) (concurring opinion); Cramp v. Board of Public Instruction, 368 U.S. 278 (1961) (Douglas joined majority opinion); Baggett v. Bullitt, 377 U.S. 360 (1964) (Douglas joined majority opinion); Elfbrandt v. Russell, 384 U.S. 11 (1966); Keyishian v. Board of Regents, 385 U.S. 589 (1967) (Douglas joined the majority opinion).
128. Connell v. Higginbotham, 403 U.S. 227, 209 (1971) (concurring opinion).
129. Beilan v. Board of Education, 357 U.S. 399, 412 (1958) (dissenting opinion).
130. He joined, therefore, in Chief Justice Warren's opinion for the Court in United States v. Robel, 389 U.S. 258 (1967). See the discussion in ch. 7 above, notes 128–131.
131. Barenblatt v. United States, 360 U.S. 109, 134 (1959) (dissenting opinion of Black, joined by Douglas); Uphaus v. Wyman, 360 U.S. 72, 82 (1959) (dissenting opinion of Brennan joined by Douglas); Wilkinson v. United States, 365 U.S. 399, 423 (1961) (dissenting opinion). See the discussion in ch. 6 above, notes 160–162; ch. 9 below, note 98; and ch. 10 below, notes 150–159.
132. Communist Party v. SACB, 367 U.S. 1, 187 (1961) (dissenting opinion); Uphaus v. Wyman, 364 U.S. 388, 401 (1960) (dissenting opinion); Gibson v. Florida Legislative Investigation Committee, 372 U.S. 539, 559 (1963) (concurring opinion).
133. NAACP v. Alabama, 357 U.S. 449 (1958). See the discussion in ch. 6 above, notes 171–181.
134. See Justice Douglas's opinion for the Court in Louisana v. NAACP, 366 U.S. 293 (1961).
135. Bates v. Little Rock, 361 U.S. 516 (1960). See the discussion in ch. 6 above, notes 182–184.
136. Ibid., 528 (concurring opinion of Black and Douglas).

137. NAACP v. Button, 371 U.S. 415 (1963). See the discussion in ch. 6 above, notes 195–202; ch. 7 above, notes 157–163; and ch. 9 below, notes 109–112.

138. Ibid., 445 (concurring opinion). See also his dissents in Harrison v. NAACP, 360 U.S. 167, 182 (1959), and NAACP v. Overstreet, 384 U.S. 118 (1966).

139. Gibson v. Florida Legislative Investigation Committee, 372 U.S. 539 (1963). See the discussion in ch. 6 above, notes 203-206; and ch. 7, notes 164–169.

140. Ibid., 559–570 (concurring opinion).

141. Roth v. United States, 354 U.S. 476, 508 (1957) (dissenting opinion); Times Film Corp. v. Chicago, 365 U.S. 43, 78 (1961) (dissenting opinion); Memoirs v. Massachusetts, 383 U.S. 413, 424 (1966) (separate opinion); Miller v. California, 413 U.S. 15, 37 (1973) (dissenting opinion); Paris Adult Theatre I v. Slaton, 413 U.S. 49, 114 (1973) (dissenting opinion).

142. Ginsberg v. New York, 390 U.S. 629, 650 (1967) (dissenting opinion).

143. Young v. American Mini Theatres, Inc., 427 U.S. 50 (1976).

144. Above, note 30.

145. See for example M. DRUCKMAN, COMMUNITY AND POWER IN AMERICA (1971); McWILLIAMS.

146. See the discussion in chapters 9 and 10 below.

147. Public Utilities Commission v. Pollak, 343 U.S. 451 (1952).

148. Ibid., 467–468. Douglas claimed this was a case of first impression, without precedents to construe and without previously expounded principles to apply. In a technical sense he was correct, but others had expounded the principles he sought to apply. Justice Field, the great nineteenth-century proponent of the natural right of property once wrote:"By the term liberty as used in the provision, something more is meant than mere freedom from physical restraint or the bounds of prison," Munn v. Illinois 94 U.S. 113, 142 (1877) (dissenting opinion). For a discussion of Field's political theory see ch. 3 above, notes 5–7.

149. PUC v. Pollak, 343 U.S. 451, 469 (1952) (dissenting opinion).

150. Poe v. Ullman, 367 U.S. 497, 521 (1961) (dissenting opinion).

151. Griswold v. Connecticut, 381 U.S. 479 (1965). Because only one other member (Justice Clark) signed the Douglas opinion without expressing his own view, treating it as "the opinion of the Court" is problematical.

152. Ibid., 484. See also Beaney, The "Griswold" Case and the Expanding Right to Privacy," 1966 WIS. L. REV. 979.

153. DOUGLAS, THE RIGHT, 89–90.

154. In general, see Adler Toward a Constitutional Theory of Individuality: The Privacy Opinions of Justice Douglas, 87 YALE L. J. 1579 (1978).

155. See also Lehman v. City of Shaker Heights, 418 U.S. 298, 305 (1974) (concurring opinion).

156. New York Times Co. v. Sullivan, 376 U.S. 254 (1964). See the discussion in ch. 9 below, notes 32–38.

157. Ibid., 279.

158. Ibid.

159. Ibid., 293. See also Garrison v. Louisiana, 379 U.S. 64, 80 (1964) (concurring opinion).

160. Rosenblatt v. Baer, 383 U.S. 75 (1966) (supervisor of a county recreation area); St. Amant v. Thompson, 390 U.S. 727 (1968) (deputy sheriff); Time, Inc. v. Pape, 401 U.S. 279 (1971) (police captain).

161. Monitor Patriot Co. v. Roy, 401 U.S. 265 (1971); Ocala Star-Banner Co. v. Damron, 401 U.S. 295 (1971).

162. Rosenblatt v. Baer, 383 U.S. 75, 88 (1966) (concurring opinion).

163. This process was not easy or orderly. See Curtis Publishing Co. v. Butts and Associated Press v. Walker, 388 U.S. 130 (1967). Gertz v. Robert Welch, Inc., 418 U.S. 323, 339–348 (1974) indicates that it is now accepted doctrine.

164. The leading case is Gertz v. Robert Welch, Inc., 418 U.S. 323 (1974). See also Time, Inc., v. Firestone, 424 U.S. 448 (1976), decided after Douglas had retired.

165. Time, Inc. v. Hill, 385 U.S. 374, 401 (1967) (concurring opinion); Gertz v. Robert Welch, Inc., 418 U.S. 323, 355 (1974) (dissenting opinion). In his *Gertz* dissent, Justice Douglas seemed to argue that the First Amendment precluded any libel law, ibid., 356–357; but in a footnote he noted that since the case involved a discussion of public affairs, he need not decide the broader point, ibid., 357 n. 6.

166. Time, Inc. v. Hill, 385 U.S. 374 (1967). See the discussion in ch. 9 below, notes 134–138.

167. Ibid., 401 (concurring opinion).

168. Ibid.

169. Gertz v. Robert Welch, Inc., 418 U.S. 323, 357, n. 6 (1974) (dissenting opinion).

170. Ibid., 356.

171. T. EMERSON, TOWARD A GENERAL THEORY OF THE FIRST AMENDMENT (1967), 68–69, 74–75. See also the discussion in ch. 11 below, notes 182–184, for a suggestion different from Emerson's regarding reconciling individual privacy and the First Amendment rights of the media.

172. Hague v. C.I.O., 307 U.S. 496 (1936); Cox v. New Hampshire, 312 U.S. 569 (1941).

173. Edwards v. South Carolina, 372 U.S. 229 (1963). Douglas's decision to join the majority was no doubt made more enjoyable by Stewart's lengthy quotation from an earlier Douglas opinion, id., 237–238 (quoting from Terminiello v. Chicago, 337 U.S. 1 [1949]). Moreover, the lone dissenter, Clark, relied upon an opinion from which Douglas had dissented when it was first announced, ibid., 236. (The case was Feiner v. New York, 340 U.S. 315 [1951]).

174. Cox v. Louisana, 379 U.S. 536 (1965); Cox v. Lousiana, 379 U.S. 559 (1965). See the discussion in ch. 7 above, notes 177–186; ch. 9 below, notes 155–159; and ch. 10 below, notes 193–196.

175. Cox v. Louisana, 379 U.S. 536, 555 (1965). See also Cox v. Louisana, 379 U.S. 559, 563 (1965).

176. Brown v. Louisana, 383 U.S. 131 (1966). The plurality opinion by Justice Abe Fortas was signed by Warren and Douglas. Brennan, ibid., 143, and White, 150, wrote separate concurring opinions. Black's dissent, ibid., 151, was joined by Clark, Harlan, and Stewart. See the discussion in ch. 7 above, note 190–197; ch. 9 below, notes 163–167; and ch. 10 below, note 196.

177. Adderley v. Florida, 385 U.S. 39 (1966). See the discussion in ch. 7 above, notes 190–197; ch. 9 below, notes 158–161; and ch. 10 below, notes 198–200.
178. See the discussion in ch. 7 above, note 36.
179. Adderley v. Florida, 385 U.S. 39, 50–51 (1966) (dissenting opinion).
180. Ibid., 53.
181. Grayned v. City of Rockford, 408 U.S. 104 (1972).
182. Ibid., 116–117. Emphasis added, citation and footnotes omitted.
183. TRIBE, 690, n. 17.
184. Grayned v. City of Rockford, 408 U.S. 104, 121–124 (1972) (dissenting opinion).
185. See chapters 1–3 above.
186. Dennis v. United States, 341 U.S. 494, 521 (1951) (concurring opinion of Frankfurter).
187. DOUGLAS, THE RIGHT, 89.
188. A. COX, THE ROLE OF THE SUPREME COURT IN AMERICAN GOVERNMENT, (1976); Rostow, *The Democratic Character of Judicial Review*, 66 HARV. L. REV. 193 (1952).
189. Wright, *The Role of the Supreme Court in a Democratic Society—Judicial Activism or Restraint*, 54 CORN. L. REV. 1 (1968).
190. Douglas, *The Bill of Rights and the Free Society: An Individual View*, 13 BUFFALO L. REV. 1 (1963); ibid., *The Bill of Rights Is Not Enough*, 149.
191. Oppenheim, *The Natural Law Thesis*, 51 AMER. POL. SCI. REV. 41 (1957).
192. A. P. D'ENTREVES, NATURAL LAW (1951).
193. See, for example, T. EMERSON, THE SYSTEM OF FREE EXPRESSION (1970). Professor Emerson, who always appreciated Justice Douglas's defense of free speech, calls for the "full protection" of the freedom of expression but does not embrace a natural rights theory.
194. Ibid., TRIBE; ELY. See also J. RAWLS, A THEORY OF JUSTICE (1971); R. DWORKIN, TAKING RIGHTS SERIOUSLY (1977).

9. THE FUNCTIONAL CONTRACT

1. Reprinted as Part I of A. MEIKLEJOHN, POLITICAL FREEDOM (1965). All citations here are from POLITICAL FREEDOM.
2. Ibid., 12–13.
3. J. TUSSMAN, OBLIGATION AND THE BODY POLITIC (1960), 12–16.
4. MEIKLEJOHN, 162–163; TUSSMAN, OBLIGATION AND, 104–121.
5. MEIKLEJOHN, 88.
6. TUSSMAN, OBLIGATION AND, 7. See also MEIKLEJOHN, 17.
7. MEIKLEJOHN, 81.
8. Ibid., 18.
9. Ibid., 116.
10. Ibid., 99; TUSSMAN, OBLIGATION AND, 119–121.
11. MEIKLEJOHN, 99, 116; TUSSMAN, OBLIGATION AND, 119–121.
12. MEIKLEJOHN, 14; see also, TUSSMAN, OBLIGATION AND, 25–27.

13. Tussman, Obligation and, 9; See also, Meiklejohn, 15.
14. Tussman, Obligation and, 119; Meiklejohn, 15–16.
15. Tussman, Obligation and, 10; Meiklejohn, 20.
16. Meiklejohn, 108–109; id., *What Does the First Amendment Mean*, 20 U. Chi., L. Rev. 461 (1953).
17. Meiklejohn, *The First Amendment is an Absolute*, 1961 Sup. Ct. Rev. 245, 255.
18. Ibid., 255; Meiklejohn, 116–118.
19. Meiklejohn, 96–97.
20. Meiklejohn, *The First Amendment Is an Absolute*, 256; Meiklejohn, 34–35.
21. Meiklejohn, *What Does*, 463.
22. Meiklejohn, *The First Amendment Is an Absolute*, 256.
23. Meiklejohn, *What Does*, 473, quoting Justice Holmes in Frohwerk v. United States, 249 U.S. 204, 206 (1919).
24. Meiklejohn, *What Does*, 473.
25. Meiklejohn, 36–37.
26. Ibid., 57.
27. Ibid., 27.
28. Ibid., 24–28.
29. Meiklejohn, *Congressional Investigations*, 20 Law Guide Rev. 106 (1961).
30. Gordon Wood notes how the Federalists, in urging ratification of the Constitution, made a similar argument. *Democracy and the Constitution*, in R. Goldwin and W. Schambra, ed., How Democratic Is the Constitution? (1980), 15–17.
31. Brennan, *The Supreme Court and the Meiklejohn Interpretation of the First Amendment*, 79 Harv. L. Rev. 1 (1965).
32. New York Times Co. v. Sullivan, 376 U.S. 254 (1964).
33. Brennan, 14.
34. New York Times Co. v. Sullivan, 376 U.S. 254, 269 (1964).
35. Frankfurter's clearest statement of this point is his concurring opinion in Dennis v. United States, 341 U.S. 494, 524–525 (1951) when he relies heavily upon the majority opinion in Robertson v. Baldwin, 165 U.S. 275 (1897). See also L. Levy, Legacy of Suppression (1960).
36. Meiklejohn, *What Does*, 478. Meiklejohn quotes extensively from the first Justice Harlan's dissent in Robertson v. Baldwin, 165 U.S. 275, 288 (1897).
37. New York Times Co. v. Sullivan, 376 U.S. 254 (1964).
38. Ibid., 274–275.
39. Kalven, *The New York Times Case: A Note on "The Central Meaning of the First Amendment,"* 1964 Sup. Ct. Rev. 191, 208. Justice Brennan approvingly cites Kalven's comment in *The Meiklejohn Interpretation*, 16.
40. Barr v. Matteo, 360 U.S. 564 (1959).
41. Ibid., 571. Ironically, Justice Brennan was one of the dissenters in *Barr*.
42. New York Times Co. v. Sullivan, 376 U.S. 254, 282 (1964).
43. Kalven draws the same conclusion, *The New York Times*, 209. Brennan obviously agrees: *The Meiklejohn Interpretation*, 16–17.

44. Kalven, *The New York Times*, 221, n. 125. Also quoted approvingly by Brennan, *The Meiklejohn Interpretation*, 17.
45. Garrison v. Louisana, 379 U.S. 64 (1964).
46. Ibid., 75. The quotation comes from Chaplinsky v. New Hampshire, 315 U.S. 568, 572 (1942) which held that "fighting words" were not protected by the First Amendment. See also Justice Brennan's opinion for the Court in Rosenblatt v. Baer, 383 U.S. 75 (1965).
47. Brennan, 5–6, 18–19. See also, Henry v. Collins, 380 U.S. 356 (1965).
48. New York Times Co. v. Sullivan, 376 U.S. 254, 270 (1964).
49. TUSSMAN, OBLIGATION AND, 32–33.
50. MEIKLEJOHN, 3.
51. TUSSMAN, OBLIGATION AND, 34.
52. Ibid., 35–36.
53. Ibid.,35.
54. Ibid., 32.
55. Ibid., 39.
56. Ibid., 40. Thus, Tussman approves of the federal court decisions which held that the Americans of Japanese ancestry who renounced their American citizenship while interned in concentration camps during World War II had acted under the stress of events. Such acts could not be taken as proof of an individual's desire to withdraw permanently from our society. See Acheson v. Murakimi, 175 F. 2d 953 (1949); McGrath v. Abo, 186 F. 2d 766 (1951). These cases are discussed in J. tenBroek, E. Barnhart, F. Matson, Prejudice, War and the Constitution (1954), 311–321. The recent case, Vance v. Terrazas, 444 U.S. 252 (1980), involved both the issues of voluntariness and duress.
57. TUSSMAN, OBLIGATION AND, 40.
58. Ibid., 23–33.
59. TUSSMAN, OBLIGATION AND, 41. Meiklejohn also shares this view: POLITICAL FREEDOM, 21–23. This position does not foreclose a challenge on the ground (1) that an inappropriate (i.e. unauthorized) agency made the decision, or (2) that no agency was authorized to make that decision under the existing Constitution. Of course, this position does not preclude an attack upon the wisdom of the decision, even if it was made by the appropriate tribunal.
60. TUSSMAN, OBLIGATION AND, 118.
61. MEIKLEJOHN, 9–19.
62. TUSSMAN, OBLIGATION AND, 105. Emphasis added.
63. MEIKLEJOHN, 159–160.
64. Ibid., 24.
65. See ch. 2–5 above.
66. TUSSMAN, OBLIGATION AND, 107.
67. Ibid., 106.
68. Ibid., 56. Emphasis added.
69. Ibid., 52–59. This interpretation is very Hobbesian. Professor Tussman has impressive credentials as a Hobbes scholar. See his unpublished dissertation, THE POLITICAL THEORY OF THOMAS HOBBES (1947).

70. TUSSMAN, OBLIGATION AND, 99.
71. Ibid., 103.
72. Diamond. *Democracy and "The Federalist": A Reconsideration of the Framers' Intent*, 53 AMER. POL. SCI. REV. 52 (1959).
73. MEIKLEJOHN; TUSSMAN, OBLIGATION AND, 30.
74. Kirkpatrick v. Preisler, 394 U.S. 526 (1969), Wells v. Rockefeller, 394 U.S. 542 (1969); Mahn v. Howell, 410 U.S. 315, 333 (1972) (separate opinion); Gaffney v. Cummings 412 U.S. 735, 772 (1973) (dissenting opinion).
75. Ch. 8 above, notes 62–79; ch. 10 below, notes 56–90.
76. Gilligan v. Morgan, 413 U.S. 1, 11 (1973).
77. Meiklejohn, *The First Amendment and Evils That Congress Has a Right to Prevent*, 26 INDIANA L. J. 477, 484 (1951).
78. Ibid., 485.
79. Ibid., 487. Emphasis added.
80. Meiklejohn, *What Does*, 479.
81. Ibid.
82. MEIKLEJOHN, 122–123.
83. Ibid., 123.
84. Yates v. United States, 354 U.S. 298, 316–326 (1957).
85. Dennis v. United States, 341 U.S. 494 (1951). See the discussion in ch. 6 above, notes 133–146; and ch. 7 above, notes 114–120.
86. Yates v. United States, 354 U.S. 298 (1957). See the discussion in ch. 6 above, notes 226–228.
87. MEIKLEJOHN, *What Does*, 468.
88. Dennis v. United States, 341 U.S. 494, 545 (1951) (concurring opinion).
89. Communist Party v. Subversive Activities Control Board, 367 U.S. 1, 11–115 (1961). See the discussion in ch. 6 above, notes 152-156; and in ch. 7 above, notes 121-127, for Justice Douglas's handling of the same factor.
90. MEIKLEJOHN, 138.
91. Scales v. United States, 367 U.S. 203 (1961). See the discussion in ch. 6 above, note 163.
92. Noto v. United States, 367 U.S. 203 (1961). See the discussion in ch. 6 above, note 164.
93. Meiklejohn, *The Barenblatt Opinion*, 27 U. CHI. L. REV. 329, 331–337 (1960). His arguments on this point are essentially those employed by Chief Justice Warren is his Watkins v. United States, 354 U.S. 178 (1957) opinion.
94. Meiklejohn, *The Barenblatt Opinion*, 337–339.
95. Meiklejohn, *The Balancing of Self-Preservation against Political Freedom*, 49 CALIF. L. REV. 4, 6–7 including n. 12 (1961).
96. MEIKLEJOHN, 120.
97. Watkins v. United States, 354 U.S. 178 (1957). See the discussion in ch. 6 above notes 166, 222–223; and ch. 7 above, notes 138–142.
98. Barenblatt v. United States, 360 U.S. 109 (1959). See the discussion in ch. 6 above, notes 147–151.

99. Gibson v. Florida Legislative Investigation Committee, 372 U.S. 539 (1963). See the discussion in ch. 6 above, notes 203–206; and ch. 7 above, notes 164–169.

100. Cramp v. Board of Public Instruction, 368 U.S. 278 (1961). Justice Stewart's opinion for the Court held a Florida statute requiring an oath from each state employee that he had never lent aid, support, advice, counsel, or influence to the Communist party was void for vagueness.

101. Baggett v. Bullitt, 377 U.S. 360 (1964). Justices White's opinion for the Court held a Washington law which required teachers to swear by precept and example, to promote respect for the flag and institutions of the United States and the state of Washington, to promote reverence for law and order and to support undivided allegiance to the United States void because of vagueness. Another law which required all state employees to swear they were not subversive persons and did not aid, advise, teach, abet, or advocate the overthrow of the constitutional form of government by revolutionary force or violence, was also held void for vagueness.

102. Elfbrandt v. Russell, 384 U.S. 11 (1966). See the discussion in ch. 7 above, note 134.

103. Keyishian v. Board of Regents, 385 U.S 589 (1967). See the discussion in ch. 7 above, notes 135– 137.

104. MEIKLEJOHN, 120.

105. Ibid., Emphasis in original.

106. Ibid. See, P. STERN, SECURITY ON TRIAL (1969) for a discussion of the Oppenheimer case.

107. NAACP v. Alabama, 357 U.S. 449 (1958). See the discussion in ch. 6 above, notes 171– 181.

108. Bates v. Little Rock, 361 U.S. 516 (1960); Gibson v. Florida Legislative Investigation Committee, 372 U.S. 539 (1963). See the discussion in ch. 6 above, notes 182–194; and ch. 7 above, notes 164–169.

109. NAACP v. Button, 371 U.S. 415 (1963). See the discussion in ch. 6 above, notes 195–202; and ch. 7 above, notes 157–163.

110. Ibid., 429–30.

111. Ibid., 433. Emphasis added.

112. Ibid.

113. Ch. 7 above, notes 157–163.

114. Dombrowski v. Pfister, 380 U.S. 479 (1965).

115. Ibid., 486–487. Emphasis added.

116. Ibid., See above notes 45–46.

117. Kalven, *Metaphysics of the Law of Obscenity*, 1960 SUP. CT. REV. 1, 15–16.

118. Roth v. United States, 354 U.S. 476 (1957).

119. Ibid., 484.

120. Ibid., 484–485.

121. Manual Enterprises v. Day, 370 U.S. 478 (1962); Jacobellis v. Ohio, 378 U.S. 184 (1964); Memoirs v. Massachusetts, 383 U.S. 413 (1966); Ginzburg v. United States, 383 U.S. 463 (1966); Miskin v. New York, 383 U.S. 502 (1966);

Redrup v. New York, 386 U.S. 767 (1967); Ginsberg v. New York, 390 U.S. 629 (1968). McGrath, *The Obscenity Cases: Grapes of "Roth,"* 1966 SUP. CT. REV. 79.

122. The same point is masterfully made in Justice Harlan's opinion for the Court in Cohen v. California, 403 U.S. 15 (1971).

123. Meiklejohn, *The First Amendment is an Absolute,*, 262–263.

124. Paris Adult Theatre I v. Slaton, 413 U.S. 49, 73 (1973) (dissenting opinion).

125. Meiklejohn, *The First Amendment is an Absolute*, 259.

126. These cases are discussed above, notes 32–46.

127. Rosenblatt v. Baer, 383 U.S. 75 (1966).

128. Ibid., 85.

129. The New York Times actual malice requirement has been applied to policemen (Pape v. Time, Inc., 354 F. 2d 558 [1965]; Gilligan v. King, 264 N.Y. 2d 309 [1965]); to the chairman of the Democratic Party Primary Elections Board (McNabb v. Tennessean Newspapers, Inc., 400 S.W. 2d 871 [1965]); to a city assessor (Eadie v. Pole, 221 A. 2d 547 [1966]); and even to a student body president (Klahe v. Winterble, 418 P. 2d 404 [1970]).

130. Clark v. Pearson, 248 F. Supp. 188 (1965); Lorillard v. Field Enterprises, Inc., 213 N.E. 2d 1 (1965); Fignole v. Curtis Publishing Co., 247 F. Supp. 595 (1965).

131. Pauling v. National Review, 49 Misc. 2d 975 (1966); Pauling v. Globe-Democrat, 362 F. 2d 188 (1966); Walker v. Courier-Journal, 246 F. Supp. 231 (1965).

132. Pearson v. Fairbanks Publishing Co., 413 P. 2d 711 (1966).

133. Powell v. Monitor Publishing Co., 217 A. 2d 193 (1966); Afro-American Publishing Co. v. Jaffe, 366 F. 2d 649 (1966).

134. Time, Inc. v. Hill, 385 U.S. 374 (1967).

135. Ibid., 388.

136. Ibid.

137. Ibid., 389.

138. Ibid., 389. His attempt to distinguish this case under invasion of privacy statutes only increased the muddle. In a libel action, Brennan insisted, the additional state interest in protecting a private individual against damage to his reputation would still apply; yet, protecting private reputation was the paramount concern of the New York Right to Privacy Act.

139. See Johnson, *The Limits of Political Speech: "New York Times v. Sullivan" Revisited,* 14 UCLA L. REV. 631 (1967), for a discussion of this conception of the public arena.

140. Justice Fortas, in a dissent joined by Chief Justice Warren and Justice Clark, agreed that *New York Times* was the applicable standard, but did not believe that Hill's private life was still a matter of public concern, Time, Inc. v. Hill, 385 U.S. 374, 411 (1967). Justice Harlan, concurring in the result, thought the *New York Times* standard did not provide sufficient protection for the private interest involved and urged a different standard for cases not involving comment on public officials, ibid., 402. Justices Black and Douglas maintained that all restrictions on the press were unconstitutional, ibid., 398, 401.

141. Justices Harlan, Fortas, and Clark had indicated their disaffection with *New York Times* on this basis in Time, Inc. v. Hill, 385 U.S. 374, 404–411, 415 (1967). While Justice Stewart signed Justice Brennan's opinion in Hill, he indicated his reservation about extending *New York Times* in Rosenblatt v. Baer, 383 U.S. 75, 92–93 (1966) (concurring opinion).
142. See ch. 6 and 7 above.
143. Curtis Publishing Co. v. Butts, 388 U.S. 130 (1967); Associated Press v. Walker, 388 U.S. 130 (1967). The Court's current doctrine was enunciated in Gertz v. Robert Welch, Inc., 418 U.S. 323 (1974).
144. Gertz v. Robert Welch, Inc., 418 U.S. 323, 361 (1974) (dissenting opinion).
145. Meiklejohn, *The First Amendment is an Absolute*, 260–261.
146. Kalven, *The Concept of the Public Forum*, 1965 Sup. Ct. Rev. 1, 11–12.
147. Ibid., 12–15. In Hague v. C.I.O., 306 U.S. 572, 515 (1939) Justice Roberts wrote: "Wherever the title of streets and parks may rest, they have immemorially been held in trust for the use of the public and time out of mind, have been used for purposes of assembly, communicating thoughts between citizens, and discussing public questions. Such use of the streets and public places has from ancient times been part of the privileges, immunities, rights, and liberties of citizens."
148. Kalven, *The Concept*, 23. Justice Black's separate opinion in Cox v. Louisiana, 379 U.S. 537, 575 (1965) provided grounds for Kalven's concern.
149. Kalven, *The Concept*, 23.
150. Ibid., 25.
151. Ibid., 27.
152. Cox v. Louisiana, 379 U.S. 537 and 559 (1965).
153. Ibid., 553–558. See the discussion in ch. 7 above, notes 177–186.
154. Kalven, *The Concept*, 22–23.
155. Cox v. Louisiana, 379 U.S. 559, 562 (1965); ibid., 583 (dissenting opinion of Black); ibid., 589 (dissenting opinion of Clark); ibid., 591 (dissenting opinion of White joined by Harlan).
156. Kalven, *The Concept*, 31–32.
157. Ibid., 32.
158. Adderley v. Florida, 385 U.S. 39 (1966). See also the discussion in ch. 7 above, notes 207–212; ch. 8 above, notes 177–180; and ch. 10 below, notes 198–200.
159. Ibid., 51 (dissenting opinion of Douglas). Compare Kalven, *The Concept*, 32.
160. Ibid., 51 (dissenting opinion of Douglas). Compare Kalven, *The Concept*, 31–32.
161. Ibid., 54.
162. Walker v. Birmingham, 388 U.S. 307 (1967). See also the discussion in ch. 7 above, notes 198–204.
163. Brown v. Louisiana, 383 U.S. 131 (1966). See also the discussion in ch. 7 above, notes 187–189.
164. Ibid., 133 (plurality opinion).
165. Ibid., 142 (pluralilty opinion).

166. Kalven, *The Concept*, 12.
167. Brown v. Louisiana, 383 U.S. 131, 142 (1966) (plurality opinion). Compare, ibid., 267 (dissenting opinion of Black).
168. Kalven, *The Concept*, 28.
169. Ibid., 27–28.
170. Cameron v. Johnson, 390 U.S. 611 (1968).
171. Ibid., 615–617.
172. Cox v. Louisiana, 379 U.S. 559, 563 (1965) (separate opinion).
173. Ibid.
174. This account of the events is found both in Justice Brennan's majority opinion, Cameron v. Johnson, 390 U.S. 611, 614–615 (1968), and in Justice Fortas's dissenting opinion, ibid., 623–628.
175. Meiklejohn, *The First Amendment is an Absolute*, 261; Kalven, *The Concept*, 27. D. Meiklejohn, *Public Speech and the First Amendment*, 55 GEO. L. J. 234, 253–260 (1966).
176. This was the conclusion of a staff memo prepared for the President's National Advisory Commission on Civil Disorders. *The New York Times*, 6 March 1968, p. 24, col. 4.
177. See, for example, the case of William Epton, a leader of the Progressive Labor Party, convicted of conspiring to riot and criminal advocacy for his part in the 1964 Harlem riots, Epton v. New York, 27 A.D. 2d 645 (1966); ibid., 19 N.Y. 2d 1017 (1967); ibid., 390 U.S. 29 (1968).
178. Professor Donald Meiklejohn, a proponent of the functional contract theory, wrestled with the content of the message of a mass demonstration in his article, *Public Speech*. He was not too successful. Recently, Professor Ely has suggested a combination of a "specific threat" approach (where content of a particular message is irrelevant) and an "unprotected message" (where the danger is thought to be connected to the particular message); DEMOCRACY AND DISTRUST, 110–116. Ely's distinction is discussed in ch. 11 below.
179. Schenck v. United States, 249 U.S. 48, 52 (1919).
180. D. EASTON, THE POLITICAL SYSTEM (1953); ibid., A SYSTEMS ANALYSIS OF POLITICAL LIFE (1965); ibid., A FRAMEWORK FOR POLITICAL ANALYSIS (1965).
181. Ch. 5 above.

10. THE INDIVIDUALISTIC CONTRACT

1. Justice Black insisted his basic constitutional philosophy did not change throughout his judicial career. See BLACK, A CONSTITUTIONAL FAITH (1968). Unfortunately, that assertion cannot be squared with his own opinions. No doubt his basic concerns—especially with individual freedom—remained constant, but the theoretical framework within which these concerns were articulated changed markedly over the years. See Reich, *Mr. Justice Black and the Living Constitution*, 76 HARV. L. REV. 673 (1963).
2. "It is of paramount importance to me that our country has a written constitution." H. BLACK, 3.

3. In re Winship, 397 U.S. 358, 383 (1970) (dissenting opinion). See also Black, *The Bill of Rights*, 35 NYU L. Rev. 865, 867 (1960); and Cahn and Black, *Justice Black and First Amendment "Absolutes": A Public Interview*, 37 NYU L. Rev. 549, 559–563 (1962).

4. Ch. 1 above.

5. Black, *The Bill*, 869–871; H. BLACK, 3.

6. Reid v. Covert, 354 U.S. 1, 6–7 (1957).

7. Ibid., 40.

8. Chandler v. Judicial Council of Tenth Circuit of U.S., 398 U.S. 74, 141 (1970) (dissenting opinion of Black).

9. H. BLACK, 19. For a concise summary of the weakness of any historical argument for judicial review, see Levy, *Judicial Review, History and Democracy* in his JUDICIAL REVIEW AND THE SUPREME COURT, (1967).

10. Ibid., 19–20.

11. Ibid., 23–24.

12. Adamson v. California, 332 U.S. 46, 89 (1957) (dissenting opinion). See also Griswold v. Connecticut, 381 U.S. 479, 507 (1965) (dissenting opinion), and H. BLACK, ch. 2, for a further elaboration of this position.

13. J. FRANK, MR. JUSTICE BLACK (1949); C. WILLIAMS, HUGO L. BLACK (1950); G. DUNNE, HUGO BLACK AND THE JUDICIAL REVOLUTION (1977); Reich.

14. "Of course the Court's duty to strike down legislative enactments which violate the Constitution requires interpretation, and since words can have many meanings, interpretation obviously may sometimes result in contraction or extension of the original purpose of a constitutional provision, thereby affecting policy." H. BLACK, 35. Almost identical words are to be found in his Adamson dissent, 332 U.S. 46, 90–91 (1947).

15. Adamson v. California, 332 U.S. 46, 91–92 (1947) (dissenting opinion, footnotes and quotations in the original omitted). The same words are found in H. BLACK, 36.

16. Southern Pacific v. Arizona, 325 U.S. 761, 784 (1945) (dissenting opinion).

17. Harper v. Virginia State Board of Elections, 383 U.S. 663, 670 (1966) (dissenting opinion).

18. El Paso v. Simmons, 379 U.S. 497, 517 (1965) (dissenting opinion).

19. Cahn and Black, 553–554.

20. Black *The Bill*, 874–875. Emphasis added.

21. H. BLACK, 8.

22. Ibid., xvi.

23. Reid v. Covert, 354 U.S. 1, 5–6 (1957).

24. H. BLACK, 3.

25. In re Winship, 397 U.S. 358, 385 (1970).

26. Afroyim v. Rusk, 387 U.S. 253, 268 (1967).

27. Ibid., 257.

28. Ibid.

29. Ibid., 262.

30. Ibid., 257.

31. See the discussion in ch. 6 above, notes 67–72.
32. Niskikawa v. Dulles, 356 U.S. 129, 138 (1958) (concurring opinion).
33. Afroyim v. Rusk, 387 U.S. 253, 263 (1967).
34. Ibid., 263–267.
35. Ibid., 267. See the thorough attack made on Black's position in Justice Harlan's dissenting opinion, ibid., 282–293.
36. Ibid., 268.
37. Rogers v. Bellei, 401 U.S. 815, 837 (1971) (dissenting opinion).
38. Perez v. Brownell, 356 U.S. 44 (1958). See the discussion in ch. 6 above, notes 68-75.
39. Ibid., 62 (dissenting opinion of Warren) and, ibid., 79 (dissenting opinion of Douglas).
40. Afroyim v. Rusk, 387 U.S. 253 (1967).
41. Trop v. Dulles, 356 U.S. 86, 91–93 (1958). This was only Part I of the opinion for the Court, but it is the part to which Justice Black subscribed.
42. Kennedy v. Mendoza-Martinez, 372 U.S. 144, 186 (1963) (concurring opinion).
43. Schneider v. Rusk, 377 U.S. 163 (1964). See the discussions in ch. 7 above, notes 37–38, 58–59; ch. 8 above, notes 49–54
44. Rogers v. Bellei, 401 U.S. 815 (1971).
45. Afroyim v. Rusk, 387 U.S. 253, 268 (1967).
46. See, for example, Marsh v. Alabama, 326 U.S. 501 (1946).
47. H. BLACK, 62.
48. In re Winship, 397 U.S. 358, 385 (1970) (dissenting opinion).
49. Wesberry v. Sanders, 376 U.S. 1, 17 (1964).
50. Yick Wo v. Hopkins, 118 U.S. 356, 370 (1886).
51. See Part II, above.
52. Wesberry v. Sanders, 376 U.S. 1, 17 (1964); Williams v. Rhodes, 393 U.S. 23, 30–31.
53. Colegrove v. Green, 328 U.S. 549 (1946).
54. Ibid., 570–574 (dissenting opinion).
55. Ibid., 570. Justice Rutledge, in a separate concurring opinion, argued that the case be dismissed for want of equity. He thought no effective judicial remedy could be fashioned; ibid., 565–566. Justice Black disagreed. If the state could not develop a more equitable district system, the Congressmen could be elected at large; ibid., 574. Here again, in talking about a possible judicial remedy, clearly Justice Black was more concerned about vindicating the equal right of each voter than about devising a system to protect adequately all major interests in society.
56. Wesberry v. Sanders, 376 U.S. 1 (1964).
57. Ibid., 7–8 (footnotes omitted).
58. Ibid., 8.
59. Ibid., 8.
60. Ibid., 13. Justice Black knew that certain exceptions to this general rule were written into the Constitution—Indians were not counted, slaves were counted under the three-fifths rule, and every state, regardless of population, was to have at least one representative. But he viewed them as exceptions; ibid., 13, n. 30.

Justice Harlan thought those provisions were not exceptions; they show that no such general rule exists; ibid., 27–29.

61. Ibid., 31–32. Emphasis in original (footnote omitted).
62. See ch. 1 above, and FARRAND, vol. 1, 49 (Wilson); FARRAND, vol. 1, 50 (Madison).
63. See, for example, the statement by James Wilson attacking "Rotten Boroughs"; FARRAND, vol. 1, 457. The same point can be made by looking at the Justices' exchange on the relevance of Art. I, Sec. 4, to congressional reapportionment. Justice Harlan quotes Madison at great length to establish that "the Convention understood the State Legislatures to have plenary power over the conduct of elections for Representatives, including the power to district well or badly, subject only to the supervisory power of Congress"; Wesberry v. Sanders, 376 U.S. 1, 32–33 (1964). He is undoubtedly correct about the Convention's intention on this point; Congress, not the Court, was intended to oversee the states' conduct of federal elections. Justice Black and the Court majority simply chose to ignore this history because the "right to vote is too important in our free society to be stripped of judicial protection by such an interpretation of Article I"; ibid., 7. Yet this argument about justiciability—which federal institution was intended to protect federal elections from possible state encroachments—does not strengthen Justice Harlan's theoretical argument. Harlan's own materials show the Framers deliberately sought to prevent the states from undermining the legitimacy of the federal government by corrupting the election proces on which that government was based. FARRAND, vol. 2, 240–241 (Madison); FARRAND, vol. 3, 267–268 (Rufus King). For a more critical assessment of Black's use of history, see Kelley, *Clio and the Court*, 1965 SUP. CT. REV. 119.
64. Reynolds v. Sims, 377 U.S. 533 (1964). See the discussion in ch. 6 above, notes 103–106.
65. Ibid., 565.
66. Ibid.
67. Ibid., 576.
68. Ibid., 576.
69. Ibid., 579–581.
70. Ibid., 566. Emphasis added.
71. Lucas v. Colorado General Assembly, 377 U.S. 713 (1964). See the discussion in ch. 7 above, notes 75–97.
72. Ibid., 736.
73. Ibid., 736. Emphasis added.
74. Reynolds v. Sims, 377 U.S. 533, 579 (1964).
75. Ibid., 579–580. See Justice Harlan's objection to the majority's narrow definition of legitimate state interests for apportionment plans; ibid., 622–624 (dissenting opinion).
76. Kirkpatrick v. Preisler 394 U.S. 526 (1969). Justice Black joined the majority.
77. Ibid., 531.
78. Ibid.
79. Ibid., 533–535.

80. Ibid., 536 (concurring opinion).
81. Ibid., 553 (dissenting opinion).
82. " . . . opportunities for gerrymandering are greatest when there is freedom to construct unequally populated districts." Kirkpatrick v. Preisler, 394 U.S. 526, 533, n. 4 (1969).
83. Gaffney v. Cummings, 412 U.S. 735 (1973).
84. Wright v. Rockefeller, 376 U.S. 52 (1964); Whitcomb v. Chavis, 403 U.S. 124 (1971). Black signed White's opinion in Whitcomb where the inevitability of partisan factors is part of the argument.
85. Mahan v. Howell, 410 U.S. 315 (1973); Gaffney v. Cummings, 412 U.S. 735 (1973); White v. Regester, 412 U.S. 755 (1973).
86. Gaffney v. Cummings, 412 U.S. 735, 781 (1973).
87. White v. Weiser, 412 U.S. 783 (1973). In Karcher v. Daggett, 103 S. Ct. 2683 (1983), Justice Brennan's opinion for the majority continued to apply the *Kirkpatrick* standard to Congressional apportionments.
88. Avery v. Midland County, Texas, 390 U.S. 474 (1968).
89. Ibid., 482–486.
90. Ibid., 480.
91. Hadley v. Junior College District, 397 U.S. 50 (1970).
92. Ibid., 55.
93. Ibid., 55.
94. Avery v. Midland County, Texas, 390 U.S. 474, 484 (1968).
95. Dusch v. Davis, 387 U.S. 112 (1967). See the discussion in ch. 8 above, note 71.
96. Hadley v. Junior College District, 397 U.S. 50, 58 (1970). Sailors v. Board of Education, 387 U.S. 105 (1967) involved the method by which Kent County, Michigan chose its county school board. Biennially, delegates from local school boards elected the five member county board from candidates nominated by school electors. Justice Douglas's opinion held that since the choice of the county board did not involve a *popular* election, the principle of one person, one vote was not relevant.
97. Fortson v. Morris, 385 U.S. 231 (1966).
98. Ibid., 234.
99. Ibid.
100. Gray v. Sanders, 372 U.S. 368 (1963).
101. See the discussion in ch. 8 above, notes 74–75.
102. Justice Douglas's opinion for the Court in Sailors v. Board of Education, 387 U.S. 105, 110 (1967) tried to limit the Fortson opinion by limiting it to "non-legislative" positions. But as noted in the text, Justice Black's *Hadley* opinion rejects the "legislative," "administrative" distinction, relying instead only on the existence of popular elections.
103. Hadley v. Junior College District, 397 U.S. 50, 58–59 (1970); Wesberry v. Sanders, 376 U.S. 1, 14–18 (1964); Harper v. Virginia State Board of Elections, 383 U.S. 663, 670 (1966) (dissenting opinion); H. Black, 30–31.

104. Kramer v. Union Free School District, 395 U.S. 621, 626–627 (1969). Emphasis added.
105. Harper v. Virginia State Board of Elections, 383 U.S. 663 (1966) (dissenting opinion); H. BLACK, 30–31.
106. Harper v. Virginia State Board of Elections, 383 U.S. 663, 664–670 (1966).
107. Ibid., 674–675.
108. Carrington v. Rash, 380 U.S. 89 (1965); Cipriano v. City of Houma, 395 U.S. 701, 707 (1969) (concurring opinion of Black); Phoenix v. Kolodziejski, 399 U.S. 204, 215 (1970) (concurring opinion of Black). That Justice Black recognized that statutes defining the electorate impinged upon the fundamental right to vote and therefore required a slightly more stringent judicial scrutiny can be seen by contrasting the opinions in *Carrington* and *Cipriano* with those of Justice Harlan in the same cases.
109. Kramer v. Union Free School District, 395 U.S. 621 (1969). Justice Stewart's dissenting opinion, which Black joined, maintained that the proper equal protection standard was whether the voting classifications were rationally related to the law's objective. The Court had not denied that local taxpayers and parents had a direct and definable interest in school policy. The dissenters thought that was all that was needed to uphold the legislative classification as constitutional. Although Justice Stewart attempted to distinguish this school district election from general elections, he never challenged the Court's imputation of great significance to an individual's vote which the majority had carried over from the apportionment cases; ibid., 634–641. Justice Harlan also joined Stewart's dissent.
110. Harper v. Virginia State Board of Elections, 383 U.S. 663, 675, n. 4 (1966) (dissenting opinion of Black).
111. Colegrove v. Green, 328 U.S. 549, 574 (1946) (dissenting opinion).
112. Oregon v. Mitchell, 400 U.S. 112 (1970).
113. Ibid., 124. In addition to his own Wesberry opinion, Justice Black placed primary reliance upon Chief Justice Stone's opinion in United States v. Classic, 313 U.S. 299, 315 (1941) and Chief Justice Hughes's opinion in Smiley v. Holm, 284 U.S. 355, 366–367 (1932).
114. Oregon v. Mitchell, 400 U.S. 112, 134 (1970).
115. Ibid., 125.
116. Ibid., 237–130. See also South Carolina v. Katzenbach, 383 U.S. 301 (1966) (separate opinion of Black); and Harper v. Virginia State Board of Elections, 383 U.S. 663, 678–679 (1966) (dissenting opinion of Black).
117. See also Justice Black's handling of indigents' access to courts in civil matters in Boddie v. Connecticut, 401 U.S. 371, 792 (1971) (dissenting opinion).
118. Milk Wagon Drivers Union v. Meadowmoor Dairies, 312 U.S. 287, 301–302 (1941) (dissenting opinion of Black). See, also, Bridges v. California, 314 U.S. 252, 263 (1941). In general, see Reich, 680–681.
119. Dennis v. United States, 341 U.S. 494, 579–581 (1951) (dissenting opinion).
120. Wieman v. Updegraff, 344 U.S. 183, 193 (1952) (concurring opinion). See also Reich, 695–696.

121. Cahn and Black, 553.
122. Black, *The Bill*, 875.
123. Cahn and Black, 559–563.
124. Black, *The Bill*, 875: New York Times Co. v. United States, 403 U.S. 713, 714 (1971) (concurring opinion).
125. Black, *The Bill*, 874, quoting Madison's remarks in the first Congress, 1 ANNALS OF CONGRESS 738 (1789) (emphasis added by Black).
126. Black, *The Bill*, 880.
127. Ibid., 878. Black continues: "If 'balancing' is accepted as the test, it would be hard for any conscientious judge to hold otherwise in times of dire need." This statement may be a good indication of the lesson Black learned from his use of a balance weighted heavily in favor of individual rights to sustain the mass internment of loyal Japanese-Americans during World War II. Korematsu v. United States, 323 U.S. 214 (1944).
128. Black, *The Bill*, 879.
129. Ibid.
130. Dennis v. United States, 341 U.S. 494 (1951). See the discussion in ch. 6 above, notes 133–146; ch. 7 above, notes 114–120; ch. 8 above, notes 102–103; and ch. 9 notes 85–88.
131. Yates v. United States, 354 U.S. 298 (1957). See the discussion in ch. 6 above, notes 226–228; ch. 8 above, 117–118; and ch. 9, note 86.
132. Ibid., 479–581 (dissenting opinion).
133. Ibid., 344 (separate opinion).
134. Communist Party v. Subversive Activities Control Board, 367 U.S. 1 (1961). See the discussion in ch. 6 above, notes 152–156; and ch. 8 note 132.
135. Ibid., 143 (dissenting opinion). Justice Black also thought the act was a classic bill of attainder, ibid., 146. See his opinion for the Court in Lovett v. United States, 328 U.S. 303 (1946) for another example of Black's use of the bill of attainder clause.
136. Communist Party v. Subversive Activities Control Board, 367 U.S. 1, 149–158 (1961). The acts mentioned included a 1653 English law against Catholics, a 1799 English act against Jacobins, and the 1798 United States Sedition Act; he thought the 1950 act more repressive than "the almost universally condemned" Federalist Sedition Act.
137. Ibid., 167–168.
138. Ibid., 164–166.
139. Ibid., 147–148. Justice Black here quotes Justice Holmes's dissenting opinion in Gitlow v. New York, 268 U.S. 652, 673 (1925).
140. Scales v. United States, 367 U.S. 203, 259 (1961) (dissenting opinion). See the discussion in ch. 6 above, notes 157–159; and ch. 8 above, notes 119–121
141. Noto v. United States, 367 U.S. 290, 300 (1961) (concurring opinion). See the discussion in ch. 6 above, notes 164–165
142. Scales v. United States, 367 U.S. 203, 261–262 (1961). He also signed the dissenting opinions of Brennan, ibid., 278, and Douglas, ibid., 263.

143. Noto v. United States, 367 U.S. 290, 302 (1961) (concurring opinion). See also Aptheker v. Secretary of State, 378 U.S. 500, 517 (1964) (concurring opinion); Albertson v. Subversive Activities Control Board, 382 U.S. 70, 82 (1965) (concurring opinion).
144. Adler v. Board of Education, 342 U.S. 485, 496 (1952) (dissenting opinion); Wieman v. Updegraff, 344 U.S. 183, 193 (1952) (concurring opinion).
145. Speiser v. Randall, 357 U.S. 523, 529 (1958) (concurring opinion).
146. Flemming v. Nestor, 363 U.S. 603, 621 (1960) (dissenting opinion).
147. Carlson v. Landon, 342 U.S. 524, 547 (1952) (dissenting opinion).
148. Konigsberg v. State Bar, 366 U.S. 36, 56 (1961) (dissenting opinion); In re Anastaplo, 366 U.S. 82, 97 (1961) (dissenting opinion); Baird v. State Bar, 401 U.S. 1 (1971) (plurality opinion); In re Stolar, 401 U.S. 23 (1971) (plurality opinion); Law Students' Civil Rights Research Council v. Wadmond, 401 U.S. 154, 174 (1971) (dissenting opinion).
149. Baird v. State Bar, 401 U.S. 1, 6 (1971).
150. Barenblatt v. United States, 360 U.S. 109, 134 (1959) (dissenting opinion); Wilkinson v. United States, 365 U.S. 399, 415 (1961) (dissenting opinion); Braden v. United States, 365 U.S. 431, 438 (1961) (dissenting opinion). See the discussion of these cases in ch. 6 above, notes 147–151; and ch. 8 above, note 131.
151. Snowiss, *The Legacy of Justice Black*, 1973 SUP. CT. REV. 187.
152. NAACP v. Alabama, 357 U.S. 449 (1958). See the discussion in ch. 6 above, notes 171–277. Justice Black also joined Justice Brennan's opinion for the Court in NAACP v. Button, 371 U.S. 415 (1963), which treated access to the courts as a political right protected by the First Amendment. See the discussion in ch. 6 above, notes 195–202; ch. 7 above, notes 152–159; and ch. 8 above, note 137.
153. Bates v. Little Rock, 361 U.S. 516 (1960). See the discussion in ch. 6 above, notes 182–183.
154. Ibid., 528. Justice Black also joined Justice Stewart's opinion for the Court in Shelton v. Tucker, 364 U.S. 479 (1960) which declared unconstitutional Arkansas's attempt to compel its teachers to disclose all their associational ties. See the discussion in ch. 6 above, notes 184–194; and ch. 7 above, notes 152–159.
155. Gibson v. Florida Legislative Investigation Committee, 372 U.S. 539, 559 (1963). See the discussion in ch. 6 above, notes 203–206; and ch. 7 above, notes 164–169.
156. Uphaus v. Wyman (I), 360 U.S. 72, 83 (1959) (the dissenting opinion of Brennan was joined by Black); Uphaus v. Wyman (II), 364 U.S. 388, 389 (1960) (the dissenting opinion of Douglas was joined by Black).
157. Barenblatt v. United States, 360 U.S. 109, 134 (1959) (dissenting opinion).
158. Above, note 248.
159. Barenblatt v. United States, 360 U.S. 109, 144 (1959) (dissenting opinion). Emphasis added.
160. New York Times Co. v. United States, 403 U.S. 713 (1971).

161. Ibid., 748–763 (dissenting opinions of Burger, Harlan, and Blackmun).
162. Ibid., 727–741 (opinions of White and Stewart).
163. Ibid., 741–748 (opinion of Marshall).
164. Ibid., 714–727 (opinions of Black, Douglas, and Brennan). Justice Brennan's opinion is discussed in ch. 11 below, notes 57–58.
165. Ibid., 717 (opinion of Black).
166. Ibid., 719.
167. Ibid., Justice Black was quoting from Chief Justice Hughes's opinion for the Court in DeJonge v. Oregon, 299 U.S. 353, 365 (1937).
168. H. BLACK, 46–47. The discussion of obscenity under the functional contract theory is found in ch. 8 above, notes 117–124.
169. D. CAUTE, THE GREAT FEAR (1978).
170. Franz, The First Amendment.
171. C. Black, Mr. Justice Black, the Supreme Court and the Bill of Rights, HARPER'S MAGAZINE (Feb., 1961).
172. Cahn and Black, 558. See also, H. BLACK.
173. New York Times Co. v. Sullivan, 376 U.S. 254 (1964). See the discussion in ch. 9 above, notes 32–42.
174. Ibid., 293–297 (concurring opinion). See also Rosenblatt v. Baer, 383 U.S. 75, 94 (1966) (separate opinion).
175. The leading cases involving public figures are Associated Press v. Walker; Curtis Publishing Co. v. Butts, 388 U.S. 130 (1967) (Butts was a well-known football coach). The leading cases involving public issues or events are Time, Inc. v. Hill, 385 U.S. 374 (1967) and Rosenbloom v. Metromedia, 403 U.S. 29 (1971).
176. Time, Inc. v. Hill, 385 U.S. 374, 398–401, 547–549 (1967) (concurring opinion).
177. Leflar, The Social Utility of Criminal Law, 34 TEX. L. REV. 984, 1032 (1956); Anderson, Libel and Press Self-Censorship, 53 TEX. L. REV. 422 (1975). See also Herbert v. Lando, 441 U.S. 153 (1979) for further evidence that Black may have been correct in his claim that the "actual malice" test provides insufficient protection to the media.
178. West Virginia Board of Education v. Barnette, 319 U.S. 624, 638 (1943).
179. Brandeis and Warren.
180. Rosenbloom v. Metromedia, Inc., 403 U.S. 29, 79 (1971) (dissenting opinion of Marshall). See Gertz v. Robert Welch, Inc., 418 U.S. 323, 346 (1974), expressly rejecting the Rosenbloom decision and approving Marshall's dissent.
181. Olmstead v. United States, 277 U.S. 438, 478 (1928) (dissenting opinion).
182. Griswold v. Connecticut, 381 U.S. 479, 507–510 (1965) (dissenting opinion).
183. In 1967, at least 35 states had created a distinct right to privacy by legislation of common law. Time, Inc. v. Hill, 385 U.S. 374, 413 (1967) (dissenting opinion of Fortas).
184. Ibid. See also the discussion in ch. 8 above, note 171.
185. Kalven, Upon Rereading Mr. Justice Black on the First Amendment, 14 UCLA L. REV. 428 (1967).

186. In later years, Black insisted this distinction was part of his thought as early as Giboney v. Empire Storage & Ice Co., 336 U.S. 490 (1949). In that case, Justice Black did not say, as he was to contend later in his career, that picketing and patrolling were not forms of expression. Rather, he held that such expression, when it was an integral part of conduct in violation of a valid criminal statute, had no constitutional immunity, ibid., 498.

187. Barenblatt v. United States, 360 U.S. 109, 140–142 (1959).

188. Bell v. Maryland, 378 U.S. 226 (1964). See also, Amalgamated Food Employees v. Logan Valley Plaza, 391 U.S. 308, 337 (1968) (dissenting opinion).

189. Bell v. Maryland, 378 U.S. 226, 325 (1964) (dissenting opinion).

190. Garner v. Louisiana, 368 U.S. 157, 196–204 (1961) (concurring opinion). See Nimmer, *The Meaning of Symbolic Speech under the First Amendment*, 21 UCLA L. Rev. 29 (1973).

191. Cox v. Louisiana, 379 U.S. 559 (1965). See also the discussion in ch. 7 above, notes 177–186; ch. 8 above, notes 174–176.

192. Ibid., 577–578. See also, H. BLACK, 53–63.

193. Cox v. Louisiana, 379 U.S. 559, 576–580 (1965). For a further elaboration of Justice Black's reasons for declaring all vague regulations of conduct affecting speech unconstitutional, see his concurring opinion in Gregory v. Chicago, 394 U.S. 111, 113 (1969).

194. Cox v. Louisiana, 379 U.S. 559, 580–581 (1965). See also Schact v. United States, 398 U.S. 58 (1970).

195. Cox v. Louisiana, 379 U.S. 559, 583 (1965).

196. Ibid., 583. Black also rejected the entrapment argument utilized in Justice Goldberg's opinion for the Court, ibid., 582–583.

197. Brown v. Louisiana, 383 U.S. 131 (1966). See also the discussion in ch. 7 above, notes 187–189.

198. Adderley v. Florida, 385 U.S. 39 (1966). See also the discussion in ch. 7 above, note 190–197; ch. 9 above, notes 158–161.

199. Ibid., 47.

200. See Justice Douglas's dissent, ibid., 51, discussed in ch. 7 above, notes 177–179; and the discussion in ch. 9 above, notes 158–161.

201. H. BLACK, 58.

202. At an earlier point in his judicial career, Black was well aware of this point. In Marsh v. Alabama, 326 U.S. 501 (1946), for example, he held that the streets of a private company town should be treated, in part, as a public forum, precisely to promote public discussions.

203. Bridges v. California, 314 U.S. 252–253 (1941). Obviously, the facts differ considerably. Bridges involved a contempt conviction for newspaper editorials, an editorial cartoon, and a telegram sent by a labor leader to the secretary of labor critical of court proceedings. But *if* Justice Black *had* seen demonstrations as a form of expression, it is difficult to see how he could have avoided the kind of analysis suggested in the text. Certainly his general First Amendment stance would then have precluded him from stopping with the assumption that the concept of dedication eliminates the need for a sensitivity to First Amendment

values. So the focal point remains Justice Black's constricted reading of the First Amendment rights of petition and assembly.

204. Compare Adderley v. Florida, 385 U.S. 39, 45, especially note 4 (1966) (Black's opinion for the Court), with ibid., 51–52 (dissenting opinion of Douglas).

205. See Justice Brennan's dissent in Greer v. Spock, 424 U.S. 828, 849 (1976) in which he argues that the parade grounds at the Fort Dix military installation were not automatically unavailable for political rallies.

206. Adderley v. Florida, 385 U.S. 39, 54 (1966).

207. Tribe, 598–600. An analysis of another line of cases where Justice Black utilized the distinction between speech and conduct leads to the same assessment. See the draft card burning case—United States v. O'Brien, 391 U.S. 367, especially at 367 (1968) (Black signed Warren's majority opinion)—and the school armband case—Tinker v. Des Moines School District, 393 U.S. 503, 515 (1969) (dissenting opinion of Black).

208. Bell v. Maryland, 378 U.S. 226, 346 (1964) (dissenting opinion).

209. Cox v. Louisiana, 379 U.S. 559, 584 (1965) (separate opinion).

210. Brown v. Louisiana, 383 U.S. 131, 165–168 (1966) (dissenting opinion); Gregory v. Chicago, 394 U.S. 111, 124–126 (1969) (concurring opinion). In Walker v. Birmingham, 388 U.S. 307 (1967), Black signed Stewart's majority opinion which stressed that "respect for the judicial process is a small price to pay for the civilizing hand of law," ibid., 321. See the discussion in ch. 7 above, notes 198–204.

211. H. Black, 62–63.

212. See above, notes 181–184.

213. Saia v. New York, 334 U.S. 558 (1948) (Black joined Douglas's opinion for the Court); Kovacs v. Cooper, 336 U.S. 77, 98 (1949) (dissenting opinion).

214. Martin v. Struthers, 319 U.S. 141 (1943); Breard v. City of Alexandria, 341 U.S. 622, 649 (1951) (dissenting opinion of Black).

215. Gregory v. Chicago, 394 U.S. 111, 124–126 (1969) (concurring opinion of Black). The tension between Black's belief in the importance of communicating ideas and his concern for the privacy of a person's home is discussed, briefly, by Murphy, 69–72.

216. H. Black, 63.

217. Ch. 1 above.

218. For the individualistic cast in Populist thought see, Ch. 3 above, notes 26–28. For biographical accounts of Black's career, see the volumes cited at note 13 above.

11. THE UTILITY OF REASON

1. Ch. 1 above.

2. Ch. 2–4 above.

3. Supreme Court decisions helped to minimize the changes portended by the Thirteenth, Fourteenth, and Fifteenth Amendments. R. Kluger, Simple Justice (1975) 64–85.

4. Ch. 2–4 above.

5. Frankfurter, *Supreme Court, United States*, 14 ENCY. SOC. SCI. 480 (1930 ed.). See also, CARDOZO, THE NATURE OF THE JUDICIAL PROCESS, (1921), 12.

6. DAHL, A PREFACE, 137.

7. N. POLSBY, CONGRESS AND THE PRESIDENCY, (1964), 4.

8. H. McILWAIN, CONSTITUTIONALISM: ANCIENT AND MODERN (1940).

9. ELY, 2; Gray, *Do We Have an Unwritten Constitution?* 27 STAN. L. REV. 703 (1975).

10. The problem of mass political participation in postindustrial societies is most explicitly confronted by neo-Marxist democratic theorists. See, for example, J. HABERMAS, TOWARD A RATIONAL SOCIETY (1971); ibid., LEGITIMATION CRISIS (1975). The actual forms and rates of political participation are examined in VERBA and NIE.

11. T. LOWI, THE END OF LIBERALISM (1969); VERBA and NIE, 342.

12. This precise argument is in two thoughtful examinations of American constitutionalism: Thompson, *Constitutional Theory and Political Action*, 31 J. OF POLITICS 655 (1969); Gunnell, *The Theory of Technocracy*, 2 OCCASIONAL PAPER SERIES (GSPA, SUNY-Albany) 41–47 (1979).

13. Hofstadter, THE AMERICAN POLITICAL TRADITION , (1948), ch. 1; Diamond; Jacobson, *Political Science and Political Education*, 57 AMER. POL. SCI. REV., 561 (1963).

14. HAMILTON, JAY, MADISON, no. 51 (Madison), 337.

15. Ibid., no. 10 (Madison), 57.

16. Ch. 1 above; Berns, *Does the Constitution "Secure These Rights?"* in R. GOLDWIN and W. SCHAMBRA, ed., HOW DEMOCRATIC IS THE CONSTITUTION? (1980), 59.

17. A notable exception is Bessette, *Deliberative Democracy: The Majority Principle in Republican Government*, in GOLDWIN and SCHAMBRA, HOW DEMOCRATIC IS THE CONSTITUTION? (1980), 102.

18. C. BECKER, THE HEAVENLY CITY OF THE EIGHTEENTH CENTURY PHILOSOPHERS (1932); C. BECKER, THE DECLARATION OF INDEPENDENCE (1922); B. WRIGHT, AMERICAN INTERPRETATIONS OF NATURAL LAW (1931); R. ADAMS, POLITICAL IDEAS OF THE AMERICAN REVOLUTION (1922).

19. Bainton, *The Appeal to Reason and the American Constitution*, in C. READ, ed., THE CONSTITUTION RECONSIDERED, (1968 rev. ed.) 121.

20. The genesis and content of this meaning of reason are fully explored in works cited in notes 18 and 19, above.

21. D'ENTREVES, 52.

22. HAMILTON, JAY, and MADISON, no. 31 (Hamilton), 188.

23. Ibid., no. 9 (Hamilton), 48.

24. Ibid., no. 31 (Hamilton), 189. See also, ibid., no. 37 (Madison), 225. The similarity between Hamilton's language and use of geometry as the model science and Hobbes's thought is striking. HOBBES, ch. 11. Hobbes explicitly connected science with the human power to control events.

25. HAMILTON, JAY, and MADISON, no. 63, 409–410. See also, ibid., no. 71 (Hamilton), 464–465.
26. Ibid., no. 37 (Madison), 228–230.
27. Ibid., no. 50 (Madison), 334.
28. Bainton, 128–129.
29. HAMILTON, JAY, and MADISON, no. 49 (Madison), 329.
30. Ibid., no. 27.
31. Ibid., no. 42, 274. See also ibid., no. 6 (Hamilton), 30.
32. Ibid., no. 55 (Madison), 365.
33. Ibid., no. 49, 331.
34. Ibid., no. 51 (Madison), 337; Bessette.
35. Kenyon, *Constitutionalism in Revolutionary America*, in J. PENNOCK and J. CHAPMAN, eds., CONSTITUTIONALISM (1979), 88.
36. Young, *Conservatives, the Constitution, and the Spirit of Accommodation*, in GOLDWIN and SCHAMBRA, eds., HOW DEMOCRATIC IS THE CONSTITUTION?, 117, documents Jefferson's reactions, at 141–145.
37. Quoted in Bainton, at 128.
38. HAMILTON, JAY, and MADISON, no. 37 (Madison), 232.
39. See. for example, the articles above, note 10; MCWILLIAMS; DRUCKMAN.
40. There is a discussion of the importance of this "myth" in V. O. KEY, JR., PUBLIC OPINION, 547; in ALMOND and VERBA, THE CIVIC CULTURE (1965), ch. 13; and a critique in ch. 6 above.
41. Ch. 1 above; Berns.
42. HAMILTON, JAY, and Madison, no. 51, 340.
43. Ibid., no. 62, 404.
44. TUSSMAN, GOVERNMENT AND THE MIND (1977), 143.
45. Ibid., 95, 169–170.
46. Ibid., 95.
47. MEIKLEJOHN, 19–20.
48. This is similar to the relationships of the two principles of justice in RAWLS, 60–65. The matters covered by Rawls's first principle of justice cannot be sacrificed for the concerns embraced by the second.
49. In applying this standard, the Supreme Court has held invalid statutes that prevented aliens from obtaining state welfare benefits, Graham v. Richardson, 403 U.S. 365 (1971); from entering a state's classified civil service, Sugarman v. Dougall, 413 U.S. 634 (1973); from practicing law, In re Griffiths, 413 U.S. 717 (1973); from working as an engineer, Examining Board v. Flores de Otero, 426 U.S. 572 (1976); and from receiving state educational benefits, Nyquist v. Mauclet, 432 U.S. 1 (1977).
50. This language tracks Sugarman v. Dougall, 413 U.S. 634, 647 (1973). The Court has applied this distinction to sustain statutes which exclude aliens from a police force, Foley v. Connelie, 435 U.S. 291 (1978); and from teaching in the public schools, Ambach v. Norwick, 441 U.S. 68 (1979). In both cases I think the correct distinction was erroneously applied. Neither a policeman nor a teacher

makes basic public policy; an alien as well as a citizen in either position would
be responsible to superiors for the proper public policy.

51. In Perez v. Brownell, 356 U.S. 44 (1958), voting in a foreign election would
not be automatic grounds for expatriation. A transfer of loyalty cannot be so
easily assumed, and the danger to this country of voting, as permitted, in a
Mexican election, was minimal. In Trop v. Dulles, 356 U.S. 86 (1958), conviction
for desertion from the armed forces in time of war would not lead to expatriation.
Desertion may be prompted by a variety of factors, and the actual damage to
this country was, in that case, negligible. Similarly, draft evasion, as in Kennedy
v. Mendoza-Martinez, 372 U.S. 144 (1963), could be subject to criminal sanctions;
it would not warrant denationalization. Afroyim v. Rusk, 387 U.S. 253 (1967)
would still be resolved in favor of the individual who voted in a foreign election,
but the language would not be so absolutist. It would emphasize that the complete
abnegation of Afroyim's commitment to this democracy had not been sufficiently
demonstrated.

52. TUSSMAN, GOVERNMENT AND, ch. 4.

53. Compare Red Lion Broadcasting Co. v. FCC, 395 U.S. 367 (1969), upholding
two aspects fo the fairness doctrine, with Columbia Broadcasting System, Inc.
v. Democratic National Committee, 412 U.S. 94 (1973), refusing to compel the
network to sell the committee air time.

54. Kirkpatrick v. Preisler, 394 U.S. 526 (1969).

55. See, for example, plans B and C in White v. Weiser, 412 U.S. 783 (1973). Justice
White, for the Court, and Justice Marshall, concurring, disagreed about the extent
of each plan's deviation from the ideal. Both were extremely minor.

56. Using the functional contract theory, I would recommend a 1 to 2 percent range
in Congressional district, and about 5 percent in the very much smaller state and
local districts.

57. New York Times Co. v. United States, 403 U.S. 713 (1971).

58. Ibid., 726–727.

59. Nebraska Press Association v. Stuart, 427 U.S. 539, 612 (1976) (concurring
opinion). Justice Brennan's whole opinion illustrates the point made in the text,
ibid., 572–617.

60. Time, Inc., v. Hill, 385 U.S. 374 (1967).

61. New York Times Co. v. Sullivan, 376 U.S. 254, 279, 280.

62. Gertz v. Robert Welch, Inc. 418 U.S. 323 (1974), and Time, Inc. v. Firestone,
424 U.S. 448 (1976), do not give sufficient weight to the importance of
communication. Paul v. Davis, 424 U.S. 693 (1976) argues there is no
constitutional cognizable right of reputation.

63. Ch. 10 above, note 197.

64. Roth v. United States, 354 U.S. 476 (1957); ch. 8 above, note 141.

65. Miller v. California, 413 U.S. 15, 47 (1973) (dissenting opinion of Brennan);
Paris Adult Theatre I v. Slaton, 413 U.S. 49, 73 (1973) (dissenting opinion of
Brennan).

66. Young v. American Mini Theatres, Inc., 427 U.S. 50 (1976) " . . . even though
we recognize that the First Amendment will not tolerate the total suppression of

erotic materials that have some arguably artistic value, it is manifest that society's interest is protecting this type of expression is of a wholly different, and lesser, magnitude than the interest in untrammeled political debate." ibid., 70 (plurality opinion of Stevens). Justice Brennan does not agree; he joined Stewart's dissent, ibid., 84 and Blackman's dissent, ibid., 88.

67. TUSSMAN, GOVERNMENT AND, 99–110.
68. See, for example, the case of William Epton, a leader of the Progressive Labor Party, convicted of conspiring to riot and criminal advocacy for his part in the 1964 Harlem riots. Epton v. New York, 27 A.D. 2d 645 (1966), 19 N.Y. 2d 1017 (1967); 390 U.S. 29 (1968).
69. See the discussion of Brown v. Louisiana, in ch. 7 above, notes 187–189; ch. 9 above, notes 163-167; and ch. 10 above, note 197.
70. ELY, 111–116.
71. Ibid., 115–116.
72. FARRAND, vol. 3, 85.

BIBLIOGRAPHY

BOOKS

ADAMS, R., POLITICAL IDEAS OF THE AMERICAN REVOLUTION (1922).
ADRIAN, C. and C. PRESS, THE AMERICAN POLITICAL PROCESS (1965).
ALMOND, G. and S. VERBA, THE CIVIC CULTURE (1965).
ANDREWS, J. ed., THE WORKS of JAMES WILSON (1896).
ARENDT, H., ORIGINS OF TOTALITARIANISM (1951).
ARENDT, H., THE HUMAN CONDITION (1958).
ARON, R., GERMAN SOCIOLOGY, trans. by M. and T. BOTTOMORE, (1957).
BAILYN, B., THE IDEOLOGICAL ORIGINS OF THE AMERICAN REVOLUTION (1967).
BASLER, R., ed., THE COLLECTED WORKS OF ABRAHAM LINCOLN (1953).
BLAU, J., ed., SOCIAL THEORIES OF JACKSONIAN DEMOCRACY (1954).
BECKER, C., THE DECLARATION of INDEPENDENCE (1922).
BECKER, C., THE HEAVENLY CITY OF THE EIGHTEENTH CENTURY PHILOSOPHERS
    (1932).
BICKEL, A., THE LEAST DANGEROUS BRANCH (1962).
BICKEL, A., THE MORALITY OF CONSENT (1975).
BLACK, C., JR., THE PEOPLE AND THE COURT (1960).
BLACK, H., A CONSTITUTIONAL FAITH (1968).
BUCHLER, J., ed., PHILOSOPHICAL WRITINGS OF PEIRCE (1940).
BURDICK, E. and A. BRODBECK, ed., AMERICAN VOTING BEHAVIOR (1959).
BURNHAM, W. D., CRITICAL ELECTIONS AND THE MAINSPRINGS OF AMERICAN
    POLITICS (1970).

Burns, J. M., Congress on Trial (1949).

Burns, J. M., The Deadlock of Democracy (rev. ed., 1963).

Burns, J. M. and J. W. Peltason, Government by the People (6th ed., 1966).

Butler, D. E., and D. Kavanagh, The British General Election of 1974 (1975).

Butler, D.E., and A. King, The British General Election of 1964 (1965).

Butler, D. E., and A. King, The British General Election of 1966 (1966).

Butler, D.E., and M. Pinto-Duschinsky, The British General Election of 1970 (1971).

Cahn, F., ed., The Great Rights (1963).

Campbell, A., P. Converse, W. Miller, and D. Stokes, The American Voter (1960).

Cardozo, B., The Nature of the Judicial Process (1921).

Caute, D., The Great Fear (1978).

Chafee, Z., Three Human Rights in the Constitution of 1787 (1956).

Cooley, T., Constitutional Limitations (6th ed., 1890).

Corwin, E. S., ed., The Constitution of the United States of America: Analysis and Interpretation, 1952 (1973 ed.)

Corwin, E. S., The "Higher Law" Background of American Constitutional Law (1955).

Cox, A., The Role of the Supreme Court in American Government (1976).

Craille, R., ed., Works of John C. Calhoun (1883).

Current, R., Daniel Webster and the Rise of National Conservatism (1955).

Dahl, R., Who Governs? (1961).

Dahl, R., A Preface to Democratic Theory (1956).

Dahl, R., Modern Political Analysis (1963).

Dahl, R., Political Oppositions in Western Democracies (1966).

Dahl, R., Pluralistic Democracy in the United States (1967).

DeGrazia, A., Essay on Apportionment and Representative Government (1963).

D'Entreves, A. P., Natural Law (2nd ed., 1972).

Dewey, J., The Influence of Darwin on Philosophy and Other Essays (1910).

Dewey, J., The Public and Its Problems (1927).

Dewey, J., The Quest for Certainty (1960 ed.).

Dewey, J., and J. Tufts, Ethics (1908).

Dixon, R., Democratic Representation (1968).

Douglas, W. O., Democracy and Finance (1940).

Douglas, W. O., An Almanac of Liberty (1954).

Douglas, W. O., We the Judges (1956).

Douglas, W. O., The Right of the People (1958).

Douglas, W. O., Being an American (1958).

Douglas, W. O., America Challenged (1960).

Douglas, W. O., The Anatomy of Liberty (1963).

DOUGLAS, W. O., DEMOCRACY'S MANIFESTO (1963).
DOUGLAS, W. O., GO EAST YOUNG MAN (1974).
DOUGLAS, W. O., THE SUPREME COURT AND THE BICENTENNIAL (1978).
DOUGLAS, W. O., THE COURT YEARS 1939–1975 (1980).
DOWNS, A., AN ECONOMIC THEORY OF DEMOCRACY (1957).
DRUCKMAN, M., COMMUNITY AND POWER IN AMERICA (1971).
DUNNE, G., HUGO BLACK AND THE JUDICIAL REVOLUTION (1977).
DWORKIN, R., TAKING RIGHTS SERIOUSLY (1977).
EASTON, D., THE POLITICAL SYSTEM (1953).
EASTON, D., A FRAMEWORK FOR POLITICAL ANALYSIS (1965).
EASTON, D., A SYSTEMS ANALYSIS OF POLITICAL LIFE (1965).
ELDERSVELD, S., POLITICAL PARTIES: A BEHAVIORAL ANALYSIS (1964).
ELLIOT, J., ed., THE DEBATES IN THE SEVERAL STATE CONVENTIONS ON THE FEDERAL
    CONSTITUTION (1941 reprint).
ELY, J., DEMOCRACY AND DISTRUST (1980).
EMERSON, T., TOWARD A GENERAL THEORY OF THE FIRST AMENDMENT (1967).
EMERSON, T., THE SYSTEM OF FREE EXPRESSION (1970).
EVERETT, E., ed., THE WORKS OF DANIEL WEBSTER (10th ed., 1857).
FARRAND, M., ed., THE RECORDS OF THE FEDERAL CONVENTION OF 1787 (1937
    ed.).
FIELD, S., OPINIONS AND PAPERS OF JUSTICE FIELD (n. d.).
FINER, S. E., H. BERRINGTON, and D. BARTHOLOMEW, BACKBENCH OPINION IN
    THE HOUSE OF COMMONS, 1955–1959 (1961).
FORD, P., ed., PAMPHLETS ON THE CONSTITUTION OF THE UNITED STATES, 1787–
    1788 (1888).
FORD, P., ed., THE WRITINGS OF THOMAS JEFFERSON (1899).
FORTAS, A., CONCERNING DISSENT AND CIVIL DISOBEDIENCE (1968).
FRANK, J., MR. JUSTICE BLACK (1949).
FRANKFURTER, F., THE PUBLIC AND ITS GOVERNMENT (1930).
FRIEDMAN, L., and F. ISRAEL, THE JUSTICES OF THE UNITED STATES SUPREME
    COURT, 1789–1969 (1970).
GILMORE, G., THE AGES OF AMERICAN LAW (1977).
GOLDMAN, E., RENDEZVOUS WITH DESTINY (1956).
GOLDWIN, R., and W. SCHAMBRA, ed., HOW DEMOCRATIC IS THE CONSTITUTION?
    (1980).
HABERMAS, J., TOWARD A RATIONAL SOCIETY (1971).
HABERMAS, J., LEGITIMATION CRISIS (1975).
HAMILTON, A., J. JAY, and J. MADISON, THE FEDERALIST (E. M. Earle, ed., n.d.).
HAMMOND, B., BANKS AND POLITICS IN AMERICA: FROM THE REVOLUTION TO
    THE CIVIL WAR (1957).
HAND, L., THE BILL OF RIGHTS (1958).
HANSON, R., THE POLITICAL THICKET: REAPPORTIONMENT AND CONSTITUTIONAL
    DEMOCRACY (1966).
HARRINGTON, M., THE OTHER AMERICA (1962).

HARTZ, L., ECONOMIC POLICY AND DEMOCRATIC THOUGHT: PENNSYLVANIA 1776–1860 (1948).

HARTZ, L., THE LIBERAL TRADITION IN AMERICA (1955).

HECKART, R., JUSTICE FORTAS AND THE FIRST AMENDMENT (unpub. Ph.D. dissertation, 1973).

HICKS, G., THE POPULIST REVOLT (1931).

HOBBES, T., THE LEVIATHAN, 1651 (M. Oakeshott, ed., 1957).

HOFSTADTER, R., THE AMERICAN POLITICAL TRADITION AND THE MEN WHO MADE IT (1955).

HOFSTADTER, R., SOCIAL DARWINISM IN AMERICAN THOUGHT (1955).

HOFSTADTER, R., THE AGE OF REFORM (1960).

HOLMES, O. W., THE COMMON LAW (1881).

HOLMES, O. W., COLLECTED LEGAL PAPERS (1921).

HOLMES, O. W., SPEECHES BY OLIVER WENDELL HOLMES (1913).

HOOK, S., REASON, SOCIAL MYTHS AND DEMOCRACY (1940).

HOOK, S., HERESY, YES—CONSPIRACY, NO! (1953).

HOOK, S., POLITICAL POWER AND PERSONAL FREEDOM (1962).

HOOK, S., THE PARADOXES OF FREEDOM (1964).

HORWITZ, M., THE TRANSFORMATION OF AMERICAN LAW, 1780–1860 (1977).

HOWE, M., ed., HOLMES-POLLACK LETTERS (1941).

HOWE, M., ed., HOLMES-LASKI LETTERS (1953).

HUNT, G., ed., THE WRITINGS OF JAMES MADISON (1900–1910).

IRISH, M., and J. PROTHRO, THE POLITICS OF AMERICAN DEMOCRACY (3d ed., 1965).

JACOBS, C., JUSTICE FRANKFURTER AND CIVIL LIBERTIES (1961).

KARIEL, H., THE DECLINE OF AMERICAN PLURALISM (1961).

KENT, J., COMMENTARIES ON AMERICAN LAW (6th ed., 1848).

KEY, V. O., PUBLIC OPINION AND AMERICAN DEMOCRACY (1961).

KEY, V. O., THE RESPONSIBLE ELECTORATE (1966).

KLUGER, R., SIMPLE JUSTICE (1975).

KONEFSKY, S., THE LEGACY OF HOLMES AND BRANDEIS (1961).

KOCH, A., JEFFERSON AND MADISON (1950).

KOCH, A., and W. PEDEN, ed., LIFE AND WRITINGS OF THOMAS JEFFERSON (1944).

KUHN, T., THE STRUCTURE OF SCIENTIFIC REVOLUTIONS (1962).

LANE, R., POLITICAL LIFE (1959).

LEVY, L., LEGACY OF SUPPRESSION (1960).

LEVY, L., JUDICIAL REVIEW AND THE SUPREME COURT (1967).

LIEF, A., ed., THE SOCIAL AND ECONOMIC VIEWS OF MR. JUSTICE BRANDEIS (1930).

LIPSET, S. M., POLITICAL MAN (1959).

LOWI, T., THE END OF LIBERALISM (1969).

MALRAUX, A., ANTI-MEMOIRS (1968).

MACIVER, R., THE WEB OF GOVERNMENT (1947).

MACIVER, R., THE RAMPARTS WE GUARD (1950).

MASON, A. T., BRANDEIS: A FREE MAN'S LIFE (1946).

MASON, A. T., HARLAN FISKE STONE (1956).
MAYO, H., An INTRODUCTION TO DEMOCRATIC THEORY (1960).
McCLOSKEY, R., THE AMERICAN SUPREME COURT (1960).
McILWAIN, H., CONSTITUTIONALISM: ANCIENT AND MODERN (1940).
McKAY, R., REAPPORTIONMENT: THE LAW AND POLITICS OF EQUAL
    REPRESENTATION (1965).
McKENZIE, R., BRITISH POLITICAL PARTIES (2nd ed., 1964).
McWILLIAMS, W., THE IDEA OF FRATERNITY IN AMERICA (1973).
MEIKLEJOHN, A., POLITICAL FREEDOM (1965).
MISES, L. VON, BUREAUCRACY (1944).
MURPHY, W., CONGRESS AND THE COURT (1962).
MURPHY, W., THE ELEMENTS OF JUDICIAL STRATEGY (1964).
PAINE, T., THE RIGHTS OF MAN (Dolphin ed., 1961).
PENNOCK, J., DEMOCRATIC POLITICAL THEORY (1979).
PENNOCK, J., and J. CHAPMAN, ed., CONSTITUTIONALISM (1979).
PITKIN, H., THE CONCEPT OF REPRESENTATION (1967).
POLLACK , E., ed., THE BRANDEIS READER (1956).
POLSBY, N., CONGRESS AND THE PRESIDENCY (1964).
PRITCHETT, C. H., CONGRESS VERSUS THE SUPREME COURT, 1957–1960 (1961).
PRITCHETT, C. H., THE ROOSEVELT COURT (1963).
RANNEY, A., THE DOCTRINE OF RESPONSIBLE PARTY GOVERNMENT (1962).
RAWLS, J., A THEORY OF JUSTICE (1971).
READ, C., ed., THE CONSTITUTION RECONSIDERED (1968 ed.).
RICHARDSON, J. D., A COMPILATION OF THE MESSAGES AND PAPERS OF THE
    PRESIDENTS, 1789–1897 (1897).
ROOSEVELT, T., THE NEW NATIONALISM (1910).
ROSSITER, C., SEEDTIME OF THE REPUBLIC (1953).
ROUSSEAU, J. J., THE SOCIAL CONTRACT, 1762 (E. Banken, ed., 1962).
SARTORI, G., DEMOCRATIC THEORY (1962)
SCHATTSCHNEIDER, E. E., PARTY GOVERNMENT (1942).
SCHATTSCHNEIDER, E. E., TOWARD A MORE RESPONSIBLE TWO-PARTY SYSTEM
    (1950).
SCHATTSCHNEIDER, E. E., THE SEMISOVEREIGN PEOPLE (1960).
SCHLESINGER, A. M., JR., THE AGE OF JACKSON (1950).
SCHLESINGER, A. M., JR., THE IMPERIAL PRESIDENCY (1973).
SCHUMPETER, J., CAPITALISM, SOCIALISM, AND DEMOCRACY (3d ed., 1950).
SHAPIRO, M., FREEDOM OF SPEECH: THE SUPREME COURT AND JUDICIAL REVIEW
    (1966).
STERN, P., SECURITY ON TRIAL (1969).
STORY, J., MISCELLANEOUS WRITINGS (1852).
STORY, J., COMMENTARIES ON THE CONSTITUTION (5th ed., 1891).
STOUFFER, S., COMMUNISM, CONFORMITY AND CIVIL LIBERTIES (1955).
TENBROEK, J., E. BARNHART, and F. MATSON, PREJUDICE, WAR AND THE
    CONSTITUTION (1954).
THORSON, T. L., THE LOGIC OF DEMOCRACY (1962).

TOCQUEVILLE, A. de, DEMOCRACY IN AMERICA (1954).
TRIBE, L., AMERICAN CONSTITUTIONAL LAW (1978).
TRUMAN, D., THE GOVERNMENTAL PROCESS (1951).
TUSSMAN, J., THE POLITICAL THEORY OF THOMAS HOBBES (unpub. Ph.D. dissertation, 1947).
TUSSMAN, J., OBLIGATION AND THE BODY POLITIC (1960).
TUSSMAN, J., GOVERNMENT AND THE MIND (1977).
TWISS, B., LAWYERS AND THE CONSTITUTION (1942).
VERBA, S., and N. NIE, PARTICIPATION IN AMERICA (1972).
WALDO, D., THE ADMINISTRATIVE STATE (1948).
WALZER, M., OBLIGATIONS (1970).
WEBER, M., LAW IN ECONOMY AND SOCIETY (M. Rheinstein, ed., trans. by M. Rheinstein and E. Shils, 1954).
WESTIN, A., ed., AN AUTOBIOGRAPHY OF THE SUPREME COURT (1963).
WHITE, M., THE ORIGIN OF DEWEY'S INSTRUMENTALISM (1943).
WHITE, M., SOCIAL THOUGHT IN AMERICA (1957).
WILLIAMS, C., HUGO L. BLACK (1950).
WILLIAMSON, C., AMERICAN SUFFRAGE: FROM PROPERTY TO DEMOCRACY (1960).
WILSON, E., PATRIOTIC GORE (1962).
WILSON, W., THE NEW FREEDOM (1913).
WOLIN, S., POLITICS AND VISION (1960).
WOOD, G., THE CREATION OF THE AMERICAN REPUBLIC, 1776–1787 (Norton, ed., 1972).
WRIGHT, B., AMERICAN INTERPRETATIONS OF NATURAL LAW (1931).

ARTICLES

13 C. Q. WEEKLY REPORTS, 1574 (6 August 1965).
Adler, Toward a Constitutional Theory of Individuality: The Privacy Opinions of Justice Douglas, 87 YALE L. J. 1579 (1978).
Anderson, Libel and Press Self-Censorship, 53 TEX. L. REV. 422 (1975).
Auerbach, The Communist Control Act of 1954: A Proposed Legal-Political Theory of Free Speech, 23 CHI. L. REV. 173 (1956).
Bainton, The Appeal to Reason and the American Constitution, in C. READ, ed., THE CONSTITUTION RECONSIDERED (1938; rev. ed., 1968), 121.
Beaney, The "Griswold" Case and the Expanding Right to Privacy, 1966 WIS. L. REV. 979 (1966).
Bendich, First Amendment Standards for Congressional Investigations, 51 CAL. L. REV. 311 (1963).
Berns, Does the Constitution "Secure These Rights"? in R. GOLDWIN and W. SCHAMBRA, ed., HOW DEMOCRATIC IS the CONSTITUTION? (1980), 59.
Bessette, Deliberative Democracy: The Majority Principle in Republican Government, in R. GOLDWIN and W. SCHAMBRA, ed., HOW DEMOCRATIC IS the CONSTITUTION? (1980), 102.
Black, The Bill of Rights, 35 NYU L. REV. 865 (1960).

Black, *Mr. Justice Black, the Supreme Court and the Bill of Rights*, HARPER'S MAGAZINE (Feb., 1961).

Braden, *The Search for Objectivity in Constitutional Law*, 57 YALE L. J. 571 (1948).

Brandeis, *The Living Law*, 10 ILL. L. REV. 461 (1916).

Brandeis and Warren, *The Right to Privacy*, 4 HAR. L. REV. 193 (1890).

Brennan, *The Supreme Court and the Meiklejohn Interpretation of the First Amendment*, 79 HARV. L. REV. 1 (1965).

Brinkman, *Citizenship*, 3 ENCYCLOPAEDIA OF THE SOCIAL SCIENCES 471 (1930 ed.).

Burnham, *The Changing Shape of the American Political Universe*, 59 AMER. POL. SCI. REV. 7 (1965).

Cahn and Black, *Justice Black and First Amendment "Absolutes": A Public Interview*, 37 NYU L. REV. 549 (1962).

Choper, *The Supreme Court and the Political Branches: Democratic Theory and Practice*, 122 U. PA. L. REV. 810 (1974).

Christoph, *Censensus and Cleavage in British Political Ideology*, 59 AMER. POL. SCI. REV. 629 (1965).

Cohen, *Introduction*, 16 UCLA L. REV. 701 (1969).

Cox, *Forward: Constitutional Adjudication and the Promotion of Human Rights*, 80 HARV. L. REV. 91, 95–96 (1966).

Dahl, *The City in the Future of Democracy*, 61 AMER. POL. SCI. REV. 953 (1967).

Dewey, *Evolution and Ethics*, 8 MONIST (1898).

Diamond, *Democracy and "The Federalist": A Reconsideration of the Framers' Intent*, 53 AMER. POL. SCI. REV. 52 (1959).

Douglas, *The Human Welfare State*, 97 U. PA. L. REV. 597 (1949).

Douglas, *Stare Decisis*, 4 RECORD 152 (1949).

Douglas, *The Bill of Rights and the Free Society: An Individual View*, 13 BUFFALO L. REV. 1 (1963).

Douglas, *The Bill of Rights is Not Enough*, in CAHN, ed., THE GREAT RIGHTS (1963), 115.

Douglas, *Federal Courts and the Democratic System*, ALA. L. REV. 179 (1969).

Douglas, *The Grand Design of the Constitution*, 7 GONZAGA L. REV. 239 (1972).

Edelman, *The Absurd Remnant: "Walker v. Birmingham" Two Years Later*, 34 ALBANY L. REV. 523 (1970).

Fischer, *The Unwritten Rules of American Politics*, HARPER'S MAGAZINE 27 (Nov., 1948).

Frankfurter, *Supreme Court, United States*, 14 ENCYCLOPAEDIA OF THE SOCIAL SCIENCES 480 (1930 ed.).

Frantz, *The First Amendment in the Balance—A Reply to Professor Mendelson*, 71 YALE L. J. 1424 (1962).

Frantz, *Is the First Amendment Law?*, 51 CAL. L. REV. 729 (1963).

Glennon, *"Do Not Go Gentle": More Than an Epitaph*, 22 WAYNE L. REV. 1305 (1976).

Gordon, *The Citizen and the State: Power of Congress to Expatriate American Citizens*, 53 GEO. L. J. 315 (1965).

Gray, *Do We Have an Unwritten Constitution?* 27 STAN. L. REV. 703 (1975).

Gunnell, *The Theory of Technocracy*, 2 OCCASIONAL PAPER SERIES (GSPA, SUNY-Albany) (1979).

Gunther, *Foreward: In Search of Evolving Doctrine on a Changing Court: A Model for a Newer Equal Protection*, 86 HARV. L. REV. 1 (1972).

Hamilton, *Constitutionalism*, 4 ENCYCLOPAEDIA OF SOCIAL SCIENCES 255 (1930 ed.).

Hofstadter, *The Founding Fathers*, in THE AMERICAN POLITICAL TRADITION (1948), 3.

Jacobson, *Political Science and Political Education*, 57 AMER. POL. SCI. REV. 561 (1963).

Johnson, *The Limits of Political Speech: "New York Times v. Sullivan" Revisited*, 14 UCLA L. REV. 631 (1967).

Kalven, *The Concept of the Political Forum*, 1965 SUP. CT. REV. 1.

Kalven, *Metaphysics of the Law of Obscenity*, 1960 SUP. CT. REV. 1.

Kalven, *The New York Times Case: A Note on "The Central Meaning of the First Amendment"*, 1964 SUP. CT. REV. 191.

Kalven, *Upon Rereading Mr. Justice Black on the First Amendment*, 14 UCLA L. REV. 428 (1967).

Karst, *Foreward: Equal Citizenship under the Fourteenth Amendment*, 91 HARV. L. REV. 1 (1977).

Kelley, *Clio and the Court*, 1965 SUP. CT. REV. 119.

Kenyon, *Men of Little Faith: The Anti-Federalists on the Nature of Representative Government*, 12 WILLIAM AND MARY Q. (3rd ser.) 3 (1955).

Kenyon, *Constitutionalism in Revolutionary America*, in J. PENNOCK and J. CHAPMAN, ed., CONSTITUTIONALISM (1979), 88.

Leflar, *The Social Utility if the Criminal Law of Defamation*, 34 TEX. L. REV. 984 (1956).

Lerner, *The Supreme Court and American Capitalism*, 42 YALE L. J. 668 (1933).

Levy, *Judicial Review, History and Democracy*, in JUDICIAL REVIEW AND THE SUPREME COURT 1 (1967).

Lokken, *The Concept of Democracy in Colonial Political Thought*, 16 WILLIAM AND MARY Q. (3rd ser.) 570 (1959).

Mason, *The Core of Free Government, 1938–40: Mr. Justice Stone and Preferred Freedoms*, 65 YALE L. J. 598 (1956).

McClosky, *Consensus and Ideology in American Politics*, 58 AMER. POL. SCI. REV. 361 (1964).

McClosky, Hoffmann, O'Hara, *Issue Conflict and Consensus among Party Leaders and Followers*, 54 AMER. POL. SCI. REV. 406 (1960).

McGrath, *The Obscenity Cases: Grapes of "Roth"*, 1966 SUP. CT. REV. 79.

McKay, *The Preference for Freedom*, 34 NYU L. REV. 1182 (1959).

Meiklejohn, *The First Amendment and Evils That Congress Has a Right to Prevent*, 26 INDIANA L. J. 477 (1951).

Meiklejohn, *What Does the First Amendment Mean*, 20 U. CHI. L. REV. 461 (1953).

Meiklejohn, *The Barenblatt Opinion*, 27 U. CHI. L. REV. 329 (1960).

Meiklejohn, *The First Amendment Is an Absolute*, 1961 SUP. CT. REV. 245.

Meiklejohn, *The Balancing of Self-Preservation against Political Freedom*, 49 CALIF. L. REV. 4 (1961).
Meiklejohn, *Congressional Investigations*, 20 LAW GUIDE REV. 106 (1961).
Meiklejohn, D., *Public Speech and the First Amendment*, 55 GEO. L. J. 234 (1966).
Mendelson, *On the Meaning of the First Amendment: Absolutes in the Balance*, 50 CAL. L. REV. 821 (1962).
Murphy, *Deeds Under a Doctrine: Civil Liberties in the 1963 Term*, 59 AMER. POL. SCI. REV. 64 (1965).
Nimmer, *The Meaning of Symbolic Speech under the First Amendment*, 21 UCLA L. REV. 29 (1973).
Oppenheim, *The Natural Law Thesis*, 51 AMER. POL. SCI. REV. 41 (1957).
Palmer, *Notes on the Use of the Word "Democracy", 1789–1799*, 68 POL. SCI. Q. 203 (1953).
Pound, *Liberty of Contract*, 18 YALE L. J. 454 (1909).
Powe, *Evolution to Absolutism: Justice Douglas and the First Amendment*, 74 COL. L. REV. 371 (1974).
Prothro and Griggs, *Fundamental Principles of Democracy: Bases of Agreement and Disagreement*, 22 J. OF POLITICS 276 (1960).
Ranney and Kendall, *Democracy: Confusion and Agreement*, 4 WEST. POL. Q. 430 (1951).
Reich, *Mr. Justice Black and the Living Constitution*, 76 HARV. L. REV. 673 (1963).
Roche, *The Expatriation Cases*, 1963 SUP. CT. REV. 325.
Rogat, *Mr. Justice Holmes: The Judge as Spectator*, 31 CHI. L. REV. 213 (1964).
Rose, *The Political Ideas of English Party Activists*, 56 AMER. POL. SCI. REV. 360 (1962).
Rossi, *Four Landmarks in Voting Research*, in E. BURDICK and A. BRODBECK, eds., AMERICAN VOTING BEHAVIOR (1959), 15.
Rostow, *The Democratic Character of Judicial Review*, 66 HARV. L. REV. 193 (1952).
Shoemaker, *"Democracy" and "Republic" as Understood in Late Eighteenth Century America*, 41 AMER. SPEECH 83 (1966).
Snowiss, *The Legacy of Justice Black*, 1973 SUP. CT. REV. 187.
Stokes and Miller, *Party Government and the Saliency of Congress*, 26 PUBLIC OPINION Q. 531 (1962).
Thompson, *Constitutional Theory and Political Action*, 31 J. OF POLITICS 655 (1969).
Truman, *The American System in Crisis*, 74 POL. SCI. Q. 418 (1959).
Wechsler, *Toward Neutral Principles of Constitutional Law*, 73 HARV. L. REV. 1 (1959).
Wood, *Democracy and the Constitution*, in R. GOLDWIN and W. SCHAMBRA, ed., HOW DEMOCRATIC IS THE CONSTITUTION? (1980), 1.
Wright, *The Role of the Supreme Court in a Democratic Society—Judicial Activism or Restraint*, 54 CORNELL L. REV. 1 (1968).
Young, *Conservatives, the Constitution, and the Spirit of Accommodation*, in R. GOLDWIN and W. SCHAMBRA, ed., HOW DEMOCRATIC IS THE CONSTITUTION? (1980), 117.

TABLE OF CASES _____

INDEX